MADISON CAMPUS

Vinny

Victory Over Drugs, Death and Degradation

by Vincent C. Marino

Edited by Jay Stewart

VVM, Inc.
Kaneohe, Hawaii

Published by VVM, Inc.
P.O. Box 801, Kaneohe, Hawaii, 96744

Printed and bound in the United States of America.

ISBN 0-961-0318-08

Library of Congress Cataloging in Publication Data

Marino, Vincent C. (Vincent Carmine) 1938–
Vinny: victory over drugs, death, and degradation.

1. Marino, Vincent C. (Vincent Carmine) 1938–
2. Narcotic addicts – United States – Bibliography.
3. Narcotic addicts – Rehabilitation – Hawaii – Case studies.
I. Stewart, Jay. II. Title.
HV5805.M367A38 1983 362.2'93'0924 [B] 82-24740.

ISBN 0-961-0318-08

Design and production coordination by Marilyn Langfeld.
Typography by Barlow Printing, Inc.

To my darling mother, Gemma, with love.
I told you I'd be back.

Special thanks to Vickie and my daughters Lila and Victoria, for all the love, understanding and patience which allowed me to continue my work.

Many thanks to my brothers Frank and Joey, without whom I wouldn't be alive to write this book.

And to my father Joe, who has really changed a lot.

Finally, to Pat Rohloff, without whose perseverance this book would never have been completed.

Table of Contents

1 // Little Italy 1
2 // By Hook or Crookedness 14
3 // A Junkie with No Relief 25
4 // Making Doctors and Cracking Churches 44
5 // Crazed Addict 55
6 // If You Can't Do the Time 69
7 // My Summer Job in the Country 86
8 // Scams, Heists, and Legitimate Business 107
9 // Synanon for Life? 130
10 // Reno Clean 151
11 // Smart Money on the Move 173
12 // Back in the Tracks 192
13 // Setup and Knocked Down 211
14 // A New Twist on Rehab 230
15 // Peddling Softcore and Swag 252
16 // A Handshake Back to Hell 267
17 // Phoenix House Restoration 280
18 // Even When I'm Innocent 301
19 // On Trial for Life 315
20 // What Goes Around, Comes Around 340
// Epilogue 356

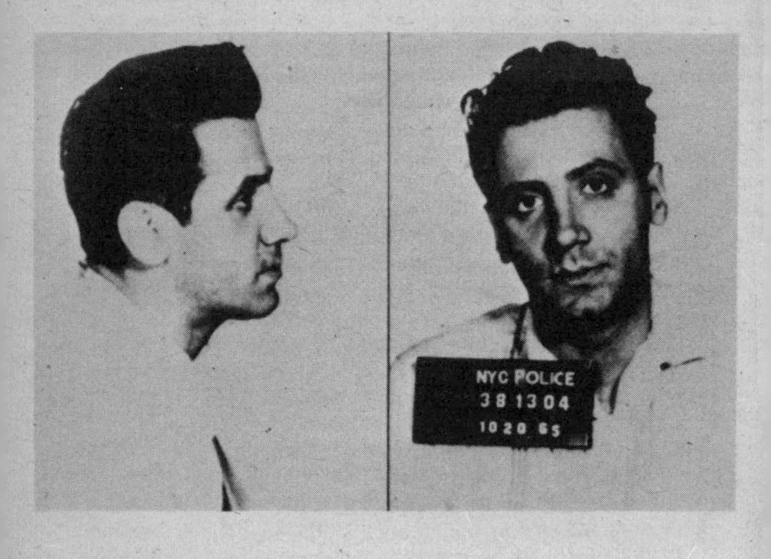
NYC POLICE
38 13 04
10 20 65

MARTINO [sic] VINCENT L65904C

12/22/38

1017-44th St. Bklyn. 602710X

M 5 11

180 9U 000 16
L18 R 001 #B 3 8 1 3 0 4
9/20/56

Assauth [sic] & Robbery

Carmine V. Marino

9/20/56	Carmine Marino	Bklyn.	asslt. Robbery	Gillen 66 Sqd.	3/5/57 1 yr. NYC Pent' Sent. susp. Judg. Joyce, Co. Ct.
X9/10/57	Vincent C. Marino	Miami Bch, Fla.	B&E Larc. & DC		Nolle Prosse on all chgs. D of J 5/26/58.
5/18/58	Vincent C. Marino	Bklyn.	Assault & Robbery	Perderson 66 pct.	6/6/68 Adjudged a Wayward Minor, Judge Levy, Adol. Ct.
7/18/58	Vincent C. Marino	Bklyn.	889-b PL Final Att. Forgery 3rd.	Mittledorf 68 pct.	1/16/59 NYC Ref'ty Judge Leibowitz, Co. Ct.
11/17/60	Vincent C. Marino	Manh.	Att. Grand Larc. Final Plea Pet. Larc.	Walsh 19 Sqd.	1/23/61 Time Served, Judg. Postel, Gen. Sess. Ct.
9/13/62	Vincent C. Marino	Bklyn.	3305 PL	Ponzi 68 Pct.	1/16/63 Dismissed Jdg. Malloy.
10/6/62	Vincent C. Marino	Manh.	3305 PL 1747d PL	McHugh TPF	11/27/62 Dismissed Jdg., Grey, Crim. ct.
4/10/63	Vincent C. Marino	Bklyn.	Assault & Rob.	Samuelson 66 sqd.	4/16/63-Dismissed judg Damiani, crim. Ct. Pt. IA

Partial police record

5/25/63	Vincent C. Marino	Bklyn.	Dis con	Becker 66 pct.	7/29/63 Crim. Ct. Pt 2A Doc. #7864 S/S judg. Sche
1/27/64	Vincent Marino	Bklyn.	GL Auto	Calltagerone 68 Sqd.	2/4/64-Dismissed Jdg. Gullen Criminal Court
3/3/64	Vincent Marino	Bklyn.	3305 PL	McClean N.B.	8/6/64-Crim. Crt. Dismissed Jdg. Gagliano
6/11/65	Vincent Marino	Manh. 2640-16	1747d PL 3305 PL 722-2 PL	Lucarelli 16 pct.	
10/19/65	Vincent Marino	Manh.	GL	Hopper 5th pct.	12/14/65-Cr. Ct. Pt. 28 Doc. #A 13270 Final Charge Att. Pet. Larc. 1-4-66
8/30/65	Vincent Marino	Manh.	Pet. Larc.	Moynihan 24 Sqd.	11/10/65-Cr. Ct. Pt. 2A Doc. #C-16359 11/30/65 Reprint 1/4/66 1/18/66 3 mos. SS prob. Concurrent 13270 Jdg. Gomes
5/5/69	Vincent C. Marino	Manh. 839-6	160.15 PL Robbery 1st.	Walsh 6 Sqd.	

Partial police record.

UNDESIRABLE DISCHARGE

FROM THE ARMED FORCES OF THE
UNITED STATES OF AMERICA

THIS IS TO CERTIFY THAT

CARMINE V MARINO RA12 493 105 Private (E-1) Regular Army

WAS DISCHARGED FROM THE

ARMY OF THE UNITED STATES

ON THE 15th DAY OF August 1956

AS UNDESIRABLE

LESTER B WILLIAMS
Major, Adjutant General's Corps

DA AGO FORM 1 JAN 50 59

With This Needle, I Thee Wed

So now little man, you're tied of grass
LSD, acid, cocaine, and hash
When someone pretending to be a true friend
Said "I'll introduce you to Miss Heroin."

Well, honey, before you start fooling with me
Let me inform you of just how it'll be.
For I will seduce you and make you my slave.
I've sent stronger men than you straight to their graves.

You'll think you could never be such a disgrace
Then you'll end up addicted to poppy seed waste.
You'll start by inhaling me, one afternoon
Then you'll take me into your arms very soon.

And once I have entered deep down in your vein
The craving will really drive you insane.
You'll need lots of money (Have you already been told?)
For darling, I am much more expensive than gold.

You'll swindle your mother for less than a buck,
You'll end up an animal, vile and corrupt,
You'll mug and you'll steal for a narcotic charm,
And only feel content when I'm deep in your arm.

One day you'll realize the monster you've grown
Then solemnly promise to leave me alone.
If you think that you'll have the mystical knack
Just come on and try getting me off your back.

The vomit, the cramps, your guts in a knot
The jangling nerves screaming for just one more shot,
The hot chills, the cold sweat, the withdrawal pains
Can only be eased by my little white grains.

There is no other way, no need to look
For deep down inside you'll know that you're hooked.
You'll desperately run to the pusher and then
You'll welcome me back to your vein once again.

And when you return, as I have foretold,
You'll ultimately give me your body and soul.
You'll give up your morals, your conscience, your heart,
And then you'll be mine, 'til death do us part.

Author Unknown

Vinny

1 / Little Italy

It only stands to reason that some people are what they are strictly because of environment and conditioning. I am one of them without question. I grew up on the streets of New York, and my friends called me Vinny, although my given name is Carmine Vincent Marino. When I entered this world on December 22, 1938, everybody was still stuck in the post-depression-prewar blues, and the economy was damn near flat on its ass, at least as far as we were concerned. My old man never had any money to speak of, so what does "the economy" really mean beyond that?

My father, whose name is Poppa Joe "Rocks" Marino, was some character. He was born in an Italian ghetto called Little Italy on the lower east side of Manhattan in 1912. His dad died a miserable death of cancer a year later, so pop never had the benefit of male guidance as he came up the hard way, on the streets. His mother Rosa was only twenty-four when her husband died, and she took work as a seamstress in a garment district sweatshop to support my pop and her three other kids.

Right after the depression, in 1935, when pop was twenty-three, he had the good fortune to meet the woman who was to become my mother, Miss Gemma D'Onofrio. Pop must have been some special Romeo because momma went for his pitch and married him in less than sixty days. She was only seventeen at the time and got pregnant a couple of months after that. The baby turned out to be my older brother, Frank.

To earn us a living, my pop had his own fish pushcart on the streets of Little Italy and would have done all right if it weren't for an insatiable gambling streak pop had running right down the middle of his spine. That streak controlled (most of) his actions because he risked a hell of a lot on the turn of events, which usually turned out against him. My mom had to beg him for money to buy the bare necessities, and when he had cash he never gave her more than half what she asked for.

Things were so bad when I was born that pop was forced to move us six times in the first eleven months of my life. We shifted from one cold-water tenement flat to the next because the old man couldn't make the ten to twelve dollars rent for the month. He would storm in and order my mom to "Pack everything up!" so we could sneak off like thieves to go settle for a while in another broken-down building.

When times got tight in the city, lots of people transformed themselves into lower animals. They would blindly gouge for a buck or eat garbage from the trash cans lined up on the street for collections. Some would literally kill for less than a fifty-dollar bill. I don't remember any of this from when I was first born, but it sure became vivid as time went along, and I picked up words to go with the pictures in my head so that everything made sense.

Brief flashes of those two-room, cold-water flats we used to call "home" still come up in my memory now and then. They were pure hell to live in because all they had was one gas stove for the cooking and to heat water for washing the dishes, doing the laundry, and bathing. One bathroom, usually located in the middle of the hallway, was common to eight or ten families. The halls were always filthy with trash and cigarette butts, and the lead-based paint was peeling off the walls, adding to the dangerous mess. How many kids died in those days from eating poisonous paint chips is known only to God and the slumlords, but there was no conscience in the picture at the time. You survived if you survived, and if you didn't, well, that was too bad because life went right on and never skipped a beat.

Little Italy is a ghetto made up almost entirely of Italians on one side of Canal Street and Chinese on the other. You are obviously free to speculate about how these two diverse groups of people ended up in the same neighborhood, but it was probably because most other people thought the "guineas" and the "chinks" were the lowest forms of human life.

Let me give you the basic ethnic structure my pop was facing as the breadwinner for our family. The Jewish people owned most of the tenement buildings and were referred to as "the man." They also controlled most of the judgeships and DA-type positions in the city. Then in my neighborhood, all the firemen and cops were Irish, and they looked down on Italians with a vengeance, calling us "greaseballs" or "wops" as they arrogantly walked their beats, lifting apples from the street vendors. Of course, the pushcart vendors didn't pay any rent, so the cops kept tabs on them and "assigned" their locations. In return, the cops took whatever they wanted, and if you didn't play their game, you'd get a citation and be forced to spend a whole day in court fighting the issue instead of earning a living.

Little Italy came together as a defensive move against all the outside forces that were hell-bent on wiping out any group that failed to maintain a constant vigil. The neighborhood had definite boundaries—Canal, Houston, Baxter, and Elizabeth Streets—and on the inside everybody knew everybody else, which imparted an incredible sense of security. My grandma Rosa, for example, took walks any time she wanted, night or day, and she never had any worries about being attacked.

What was commonly called "the mob" was also born under those conditions—survival. As the Italians saw the way things were, they got so tired of being abused they had no choice but to organize or be destroyed. For this reason you would never see anyone acknowledge the mob's existence for the "official" record.

My pop went away just after I celebrated my first birthday, and my momma always told me, "Your daddy is away in the Navy, fighting a war." My older brother heard the same line, and he didn't balk at it, so I figured what mom said was true. Because pop was away, mom had either to put us on welfare or find some other way to make ends meet. She had too much pride and integrity to accept a handout, so she started taking in laundry and doing outside work for people who had enough cash to spend on frivolous extras. I saw fine lace, linens, and expensive dress shirts all come and go. My momma had none of these luxuries. For her appearances in church she wore the mandatory minimum—a plain black dress and a kerchief bobby-pinned to her hair.

In those days Little Italy was a mixture of smells from fresh baking bread, pasta, fruits and vegetables, garlic, oregano, anise, provolone cheese, sweet pastries, and various salamis—all hitting your nose at once. That, put together with the blare of Italian music being piped out of the stores made it hard to feel depressed when you woke up. My mom took Frank and me out on those streets every morning while she shopped for the vegetables. With our tight budget, we usually had some kind of starch at every meal—potatoes and eggs, spaghetti with oil and garlic, macaroni with onions, macaroni with beans, macaroni with peas, and lots and lots of bread. On rare occasions we got some meat, cooked up in a stew so a little went a long way.

The next thing I remember was my introduction to the Roman Catholic Church. I was overwhelmed by the size of that cathedral over on Baxter Street. The ceiling must have been two hundred feet high, and the stained-glass windows broke up the morning light into all sorts of radiant colors. We saw the place more and more often right after pop joined the Navy because mom found emotional relief in the ideas the church had to offer.

She got up every morning around 5:30, then she woke Frankie and me to feed us before we went to 6:30 Mass. The cathedral was always jam-packed in the mornings because a lot of neighborhood people wouldn't go to work before they went to church. Frank and I were always dressed up and trooped around in our Sunday best outfits to all the ceremonies the priests put on in that mighty canyon, too—benediction on Monday nights; Stations of the Cross on Fridays; a confessional parade in the pews on Saturdays; then the whole neighborhood attended Mass served with Holy Communion on Sunday mornings between 6:30 A.M. and noon.

One hot sunny day in July, momma put me down by her feet outside my carriage for the first time and turned to talk with a neighbor lady. I crawled a little distance when without warning a huge dog jumped out of nowhere and pawed my head down to the concrete. He growled angrily with that rotten stench of dog breath and started ripping at my face with his teeth. I tried to scream, but he locked onto my upper lip, biting and tearing the skin wide open all the way to the nose. Finally I screamed and managed to roll over on my stomach before he could bite me again. Blood was all over me.

When my mom saw what that mongrel bulldog had done, she fainted on the spot. The neighbor, Mrs. Anniballi, ran to call an ambulance. It was her goddamn dog that had just permanently altered my face.

I blacked out on the street and woke up in the charity ward of the neighborhood hospital with twenty-eight stitches in my stiff upper lip and a vivid picture of that monster burned in my mind.

Since my case was taken by charity, two doctors dealt with it quickly and left me with a permanent disfiguring scar. As a result I was tagged with the nickname "Scarface" which I've carried around with me ever since.

In the war years between 1941 and 1944, my mom started taking Frank and me over to grandma's place regularly so that she could babysit for us, or sometimes Rosa would come to our flat. Once the ritual got going, every Saturday morning right after Mass grandma would ring our doorbell, then come storming in with a big smile and two or three shopping bags bulging with fresh food. She would take over our kitchen, singing in Sicilian while frying up delicious Italian meatballs on the stove. There was no better way to start off a Saturday than with Rosa Marino's meatballs smothered in some dynamite sauce with a side dish of hot Italian bread straight from the oven.

Grandma Rosa was one of the most widely admired "stand-up" women in the neighborhood. All sorts of men would nod and tip their hats to pay their respects or offer to do things like help her across the street. Even though grandma was in her forties, she was still a beautiful woman, and quite a few connected guys made proposals to marry her, but she said she could never love another man. She put all her energy into her grandchildren instead. In all of her ninety-four years with us, grandma never bothered much with the English language. It seemed that all she knew was "thatsa nice," "hello," and "goodbye." One subject that Rosa always made a special point of was her native Sicily with all of its natural beauty. Then in the same breath, she would relate the not-so-good parts and finish up with how proud she was to be an American citizen, with the freedom in this country. Those words never left me.

My mother was like Rosa in character: strong, proud, and self-determined, but at the time mom was very young, and naive about some of the realities to be faced in life. She had been raised in a family with nine children where she was the youngest, so her father Carmine kept a special protective eye out for "his" Gemma.

It was somewhere during that period when I first learned about my name and how it broke with Italian tradition. In Italian families the male children were named after the males on the father's side, so that the family name would be perpetuated. Thus, my brother Frank was named after grandpa Frank Marino, and by all rights I should have been James Vincent, after my dad's oldest brother. But some unusual pressure came down from my mother's side, and I ended up being named after mom's dad, Carmine. I always hated the name and early on in life I changed it to Vinny, while most of my peers had already tagged me with Scarface.

For some reason it still remains a mystery to me, my brother Frank turned out to be the favorite of both my mom and grandma Rosa. He was eighteen months older than me, a bright and outgoing kid, so he gots lots of attention to start with. Once Frank lied to my mother about where he had been, and she slapped him hard across the face for it. At that point, grandma Rosa came out of her chair and for no apparent reason she laid an even harder backhand on me. It reinforced the notion that Frankie got better treatment than me everywhere we went.

As soon as I learned about mirrors, I started to notice the disfiguring scar on my upper lip and began to wonder if I wasn't getting second-rate treatment because of my physical appearance. The older I got, the worse my mouth began to look, to the point where I felt like crying about it, but I never showed those feelings. Sure, I felt the tears well up in my eyes, but then I swallowed hard and held everything inside. That was the beginning of a long and difficult trip into my guts. I had some kind of terrible fear that I couldn't locate exactly, and yet it seemed to be everywhere. I saw ugliness when I looked in a mirror, plus the mocking way other people looked at me. I felt loneliness of the worst kind where no one really cared, and even if they did, nothing could be done about our condition. Then I had a feeling of total emptiness stemming from the lack of love for life itself, family, and friends.

When I think back to the fall of 1944 when I was six years old, I remember feeling confused and depressed. My mom enrolled me in the nearby Catholic elementary school at that time. The nuns who taught there were from some French order, and they insisted we address them as "Madam," while the grand dame reigning over the whole school was the "Reverend Mother." The nuns lived in a gloomy old gray building behind the rectory. Just observing the nuns' habits was funny to me, I mean the uniforms they wore, not the way they ate or spoke. The dresses were more like full-on robes that covered them from head to toe in solid black. You couldn't see their faces much because a white circle of cloth sat on the ridge above the eyebrows, covered both ears and fastened underneath the chin. As breast-plates they wore a two-foot, moon-shaped piece of stiff white linen, and to top everything off they had a six-foot long string of wooden beads with Christ the Savior on a cross hanging at the end, a rosary. As a nun walked, her beads banged loud enough to warn those of us raising hell that higher authority was approaching.

The nuns were primary dealers in absolute fear, a dimension I could have done without at the time. I remember being shaken by the shoulders once as a nun screamed in my face, "A young boy like you committed a mortal sin, and God struck him dead with lightning right on the spot!" When I heard that stuff, I wondered, "What kind of God would allow that to happen to innocent kids?" I didn't know quite what to think, but they went on and on with some incredibly illogical sermons. There was one on limbo, a story about how young unbaptized children who died suddenly were doomed to spend all eternity in some never-never land without seeing God.

Most of what they said about religion didn't make any sense to me, and as time went on I discovered that a lot of things related to the church didn't add up in my head. Many times a celibate priest would give my mom instructions about her marital situation, saying things like, "It must be God's will, my child, for you to suffer," or "God hurts those he loves." I asked myself, "Who is this God and if he's so good, why are we living like this?"

Frankie was a year ahead of me in school, and the nuns favored him because he was quiet and very obedient. He became the natural star of the books, and I saw no point in trying to score in that arena, so I paid attention to mischief instead of mastering academic subjects. But Frank was also getting upset about my dad's long absence. We shared a single bed. Frank would be half asleep, and he would shudder and grab onto me crying, "Dad! Where are you? Come home. We need you!" A variety of feelings would build up behind my eyes, but I just gritted my teeth and kept them in until they went away.

By the time I entered second grade, my reputation for acting out was firmly established, so the nuns had me become an altar boy. I started to serve every day at 6:30 A.M. Mass for nothing but thanks and, "God's blessings, my son." The only exception was an occasional Saturday when I got to serve at a wedding, which meant a tip from the groom, but my mom and grandma

Rosa watched me with pride up on the altar at Mass every morning.

One night the tinny doorbell sounded in our tenement flat. I was about to get up and answer it, but mom got there before me. When she opened it, she screamed and cried out, "Joe! Joe! You're home!" I looked up from my chair and saw a man standing in our dimly lit hallway, hugging and kissing my momma. He was rather nattily dressed in a Navy uniform. He had been gone five years, and I didn't recognize him, so I just stayed glued to my seat.

Now that he was back from the war, I hoped pop would help mom out so she could do a little less work and take better care of her health. She was burning the candle at both ends and then some, what with us and the household and paying strict attention to the Italian family scene with phone calls and visits, then doing a heavy load of outside housework and inside ironing. Plus the parish priest would regularly tap her time for church activities to raise money.

Everyone in the neighborhood came by to welcome pop home from the high seas. A couple of Sicilian friends even threw a big block party for him a few weeks later when the last peace treaty was signed. There was a ticker-tape parade on Wall Street the same day my old man was the war hero of an entire city block downtown.

Pop was always willing to work hard so he soon got himself another pushcart on the streets and peddled fish everyday. In a short time he was making fairly good money, but we didn't see much because he gambled it away, just like before. On the rare occasions he won, things were good, with everyone laughing and the table full of food. But when he lost, he started to get mean and abused mom, first verbally, then it got physical. Frank and I couldn't stand to listen from the other room where we were cuddled together. "Gemma, get off my goddamn back!" followed by another loud crack. Frank and I whispered a vow in the dark to give mom everything that the old man was depriving her of, someday.

It wasn't long before I couldn't see any purpose in life so I took up creative hell-raising to find out where it might lead. I first met my partner then. His name was "Hooks." It all started at school when a nun assigned us to serve together at 6:30 Mass. After the service and before school got started, we used to pull off a prank that we called "wiring the girls' johns for sound."

We tied a piece of plastic wrap tightly over the toilet bowls in the girls' room. When the little girls peed, it ran onto their knees, and if they shit, well, that was it. It only took a second for them to realize what had happened and start screaming their lungs out.

We made the classroom scene every bit as much fun. One of our standard numbers would start with Hooks banging his feet on the floor, while the nun was busy writing on the blackboard. She would whirl around and demand to know who was disturbing the order of the day. Naturally, no one would say anything as we tried to hold back the giggles. The nun would return to her work, and old Hooks would start banging again. I guess I had the mark of a guilty face because I'd usually get a whack across the knuckles with a thin hickory stick. It hurt like hell but only served to make me more devious about our tricks.

Another act was to wait until the nun was writing on the board, then lob a chalk-filled eraser, hitting the slate as close to her as possible. The cloud of white dust would break everybody up since it came down snow-white all over her solemn black outfit. Then the nun would do one of those wet-dog shakes just trying to breathe and dust off. Nobody knew it then, but another kind of white dust had a place in my future, and when it happened, Hooks would be right alongside for the ride.

By the time 1947 rolled around, events were fairly well fixed from my point of view. The old man was out more than he was home, and when he did show it was with heavy words and empty pockets; the nuns were totally dictatorial, citing God Almighty as the source of their authority; Frank found that he was gifted with a voice in the same crooning style as Sinatra—so the whole family got behind his act, and that left me standing alone out in the cold wearing hand-me-downs.

Next I noticed mom was beginning to gain weight, especially around her midsection. It turned out she was pregnant with my younger brother Joe. This was her last-ditch attempt to get my old man away from a gin rummy table and back into family life, but of course it didn't work, and the baby's birth turned out to top it for me, now the scar-marked middle kid. Any money we had was lavished on Frank, hoping his voice might ring the cash register in the sky that would lift us from our abject poverty. And baby Joey picked up all the love and attention since he was a cute kid, even I had to admit. Right around that time I walked out to the front stoop of our building and looked down hard at the concrete, wondering what to do.

Mulberry Street in Little Italy had a special cheese flavor, most notably provolone and mozzarella being cooked up in pizzas. I got some immediate relief from the pressures at home every time I took a walk around the neighborhood. After a while, I took to a certain route, picking up a feel for things while I carefully watched the action unfold. I would walk down Mulberry Street to Grand, then around the corner to old man Quatrini's shoemaking shop. He was a friendly codger in his seventies who didn't mind me hanging around watching him put the finishing touches on the shoes. I used to query him on just about everything he did, and one day I asked him to teach me how to duplicate his spit shine. He agreed, and after that I started to give him a hand.

At supper one night, I asked mom if I could get a shoeshine box and earn money to help put food on the table. She didn't have any objections, and pop wasn't home, so I was in business for the first time. Those days on the streets shining shoes were far more pragmatic an education than anything the nuns taught me at school. I quickly found a new purpose in life to shoot for, since most of the neighborhood clubs were populated with "men of respect" who were connected and had money to burn. One day I glanced down to see an expensive pair of Florsheims on a guy like that. When I approached, the owner was easy because I said nothing more than, "Shine, Mister?" and he said, "Sure, kid, go ahead."

As I bent down to begin, his tiptoe reflection revealed the sharp crease in a pair of fine mohair dress pants. Then, from glances as I worked, I noticed his white-on-white silk shirt, the Countess Mara tie with a diamond stickpin, and a flashy diamond ring on his little finger. I put one hell of a finish on that pair of shoes, and he tipped me a dollar. No kidding, I wanted to holler, but I kept my trap shut and started plotting how one day I was going to emulate that style in fancy dress and money. I swore to myself that no way was I ever going to get into ordinary labor like my old man with his smelly fish cart or the hard hats who riveted all the high rises together.

Within a few months I had developed a profitable shine route. It included all the wise-guy bars where gamblers plied their endless lines of bullshit between various games of chance and the three-digit daily bet on the numbers game, the local clubs I already mentioned, and then offices, places like that. Every day after school I hit my beat and got back home by 8:30 with three or four dollars. That may not sound like much, but it was enough to buy some basics and really help my mom out, while Old Joe "Rocks" was probably sitting in a poker game somewhere, hoping for a one-card draw to an inside straight.

That shoeshine box was my ticket to a whole new world, and I soon had customers who would wait for me because I hustled hard and gave a damn good shine. The weekends really paid off because I had all day both days, except for church on Sunday morning, straight through until five or six in the afternoon. I took in twenty, sometimes twenty-five dollars for just those two days' work. I just kept up the pace and told nobody about my route or my secret to success in the business.

By the time I had been waxing brogans for six months, I started to pick up chances to deliver packages as I went along. I learned fast never to ask what was inside, just tell the recipient who had sent it, take whatever tip offered, bow out, and whistle all the way to the next stop. I began collecting two to five dollars extra per day in deliveries. Then when winter and snow hit the city, I would grab a shovel and pick up a few extra dollars there.

Back home, the situation brightened at our dinner table with what I added, but there wasn't much relief in sight. Mom got more frequent beatings from the old man and threatened to leave him for good. Frank kept his following by winning two consecutive firsts on the "Ted Mack Original Amateur Hour," while little Joe held onto his celebrity position as the baby. Me? I just bit my lower lip until it almost bled and kept on moving.

Looking back at myself in 1950, I realize now that only some incredible challenge could have turned my life around in a meaningful way. I mean an event or person of importance, some overriding reason to go straight and never vary. From my situation in New York City, nothing came up that made that difference.

Sheer survival was what we dealt with, and that had been the name of the game for several generations in our clan. When my people faced the reality of Manhattan, they knew damn well that if they were going to make it, the key would be family ties and a total willingness to act immediately upon each situation as it dictated. The slogan for this in Sicilian is *Fata di, fata doi!*, roughly translated as, "Mind your own business and nothing else." My business was surviving with a shoeshine kit, avoiding the hassles of home life, turning as many devious tricks on the nuns as possible, and learning as much as I could about the methods and connections necessary to become a "made-man" one day.

For relief from the oppressive summer heat and drudgery, we played stickball in the streets. The best games were staged around the time of the Feast of San Genaro, a week-long celebration in September. The festivities began with a procession, when the statue of the legendary saint, covered with paper American money, was paraded through the thoroughfares on the backs of various made-men. Outside teams appeared in Little Italy for some heavy competition, guys from Brooklyn, East Harlem, the Bronx, Staten Island, all over. The action was hot enough to attract the attention of bookies, too.

Whole families came loaded down with folding chairs, potato salad, hero sandwiches, ice chests, and beer. A massive horde of people squeezed themselves into a city street twenty feet wide. Then there were tenement steps to contend with. Inevitably somebody from outside always parked his car right where we intended to play so before the kickoff we would ask the driver in nicely-New-York to "move it" and not-so-nicely if he refused. Some guys who refused hardly recognized stripped metal hulks we left behind, propped up on milk boxes.

We played by strict rules, since the stakes were high. Someone would stand up and yell, "A hit on the wall in front of Piracci's fire escape, that's a fair ball. Hits on the back wall and she's foul. Automatic double for scoring the Widow Talmotese's clothesline. Home run is a fly ball over the line from the Berlotti Bakery sign to that fire hydrant across the street. You guys ready?"

Were we ever. Those games were so highly charged you could almost see the sparks. After the games, towards evening, the men retired leisurely to the local neighborhood clubs where all sorts of action would begin—horse races on the radio, card games at the round tables. The numbers game also siphoned off a significant piece of the action. As gamblers won a bet on anything, they would throw a portion onto a three-digit pick for the next day. One could choose from the Italian numbers, the Brooklyn numbers, or the New York numbers. I just cruised around the action, taking in everything, figuring it might do me some good later on.

When night fell, the crap tables opened up and the real action started. Sometimes the clubs called a three-hundred dollar limit, other times it was five hundred. It was hard to believe the amount of money that changed hands. The house protected the games since the whole operation was under the control of a made-guy, someone known and trusted by several family circles. He insured there would be no back door entries or exits and "no stinkin'' stick-ups!'' The guys who shuffled the daily numbers records and payoffs all over town were known as ''connected,'' which meant that they were something to somebody but only within a particular family. It was one complex world inside another. Certainly there were rules and there were regulations, but most of them were not written down anywhere and were rarely spoken. They were universally understood on the streets, however, where many of us, by hook or crookedness, ended up operating.

One street character named Bones was a fixture on corners. He was tall and paunchy with cropped hair and a nose that looked as if it had been broken once a week for most of his life. He also carried several scars, all clean, as if they had been cut in, not knocked. For a fee, Bones handled the neighborhood problems. If you needed somebody ''dealt with,'' you would go find Bones. He would ask what the difficulty was and how you wanted it taken care of. Then he would pull a typed-up list in a plastic window out of his pocket: ''Slap on the face, $10. A broken arm, $50. Broken jaw, $200.'' Bones would eagerly whisper the final treatment, ''For $400, I'll take off the guy's ear, wrap it in newspaper, and mail it to you.'' When Bones spoke, it was all I could do to hold back the laughter, but he was dead serious. The local characters only illustrate my main point: Most people from my New York neighborhood were born with a black belt in abuse, verbal or otherwise. And, of course, they never hesitated to use it.

2 / By Hook or Crookedness

A week after I turned thirteen, we were forced to move for economic reasons. Again I felt disjointed, out of place, like everything was coming apart at the seams. My old shoe-shine route was too far from out new apartment. We were now in Brooklyn, the Borough Park section, primarily a Jewish and Italian neighborhood, and there weren't many Florsheims in sight, as our dilapidated building had forty odd families stacked up inside. The old man was the same or a little worse, and momma was treading desperately trying to hold everyone's head above the high water mark.

The only relief was when the building superintendent agreed to let some of us guys use part of the basement as a clubhouse in return for cleaning up the other side. None of us had much money, so the club activities consisted of teenage bullshit and stickball, but we weren't complaining. Anything was better than being upstairs in an apartment crammed full of your average destitute family-in-fight.

One night at the end of round four of another family fight, I drifted out the back door headed toward the basement to check what was happening. Just as I hit the pavement, a sweet little treat named Mary Jane came out of her house across the way. I knew her from high school where she was always teasing me about my face. She leaned against the fence in front of her place and waved with her right hand that I should come over.

As I approached, she gently arched her back to emphasize the sunny-side-up egg size of her budding breasts. The sight struck a responsive chord, and I slipped into a new dimension, though I couldn't name it yet. "You look pretty cool tonight," I said and stood next to her with my back to the fence. Mary Jane smiled. "Say, Vinny," she pleaded lightly, touching each button on my shirt, "can you help me out?"

"Sure, Mary Jane. What do you need?" She grinned and turned toward her building. "Help me find my kitty. I lost him in the basement."

"Sure, Mary Jane. Where's the basement?" She strutted to the front of the building and took my hand. Once inside, the first thing visible in the dark was a red and yellow glow from a huge coal furnace. Mary Jane led me around to the back of the boiler and then down between some rows of cardboard boxes in storage. She whispered so low that I thought only a cat could hear the call, "Here, kitty. Here, kitty, kitty." I asked her what the kitty's name was, and that was all she needed. She turned around and pressed her body full-on against mine as she murmured, "Dick." I said, "Oh," and before another thought could pattern into words, we fell down together on a cardboard box, and in less than two minutes my first sexual experience was over.

When Mary Jane stopped moving, I felt a streak of embarrassment. It was easy enough to get into this, but how do you withdraw? What should I say? I put my hands on her shoulders, urging her to stand up. She did, and we kissed again as I reached down to put "Dick" away, and Mary Jane said, "Vinny, anytime you lose your kitty, I can help you find it. I'm good at it."

"You don't have to tell me," I said as I backed off to the exit. "I'll see you soon, Mary Jane. Keep a close eye on your little kitty."

Ten minutes later, across the street in the basement, the guys and I decided to get more into sports. We sauntered into Davega's Sporting Goods Store on Thirteenth Avenue, where we all split up, each checking out a different section. My buddy Willy dribbled a basketball right out the front door, with no register ringing up anything as he shuffled on by. Later on, near dusk, we watched the end of a ball game in Prospect Park and left with all the bases, balls, bats, and gloves after the team went to the showers. When we got safely back to the basement, I hung my shoeshine kit up on a nail and retired from the "straight" business world.

The morning after that first experience with stealing, I felt a twinge of conscience. I guess it was from my strict Catholic training, but I quickly substituted two new notions to replace the guilt that was causing short circuits in my brain. First, I envisioned the whole enterprise as a game with the object being to steal right and not arouse suspicion, just like perfecting a hobby or a skill. Then I worked up a feeling of anger if I didn't steal enough. Meanwhile, we were amassing a small warehouse of sporting goods. For guys who couldn't afford the iron-on letters for T-shirts, we ended up the best equipped sandlot team in all of Brooklyn.

One afternoon in June 1951, while we were sitting around rapping, a guy named Jocko brought out this brown paper bag of stuff he called "weed." He claimed it would "get us all high." With that, he threw this Mexican-grown leafy stuff onto the table, along with some rolling papers. Like everybody else under the peer gun, I went for it. Taking my first deep drag as instructed, I first felt lightheaded and after that everything seemed humorous as hell, as if some kind of bell had gone off, putting a light touch on all the stinking bullshit in the world. Then I got a gargantuan ape of an appetite and downed nine Creamsicles. On the way down from the high, I felt streaks of paranoia and envisioned cops on my tail about to yank me over for a frisk and directly off to the joint.

What eventually got me down on marijuana was that I felt so tired when the effects wore off. A guy named Zip provided something more like what I was looking for when he came up with a prescription for benzedrine pills, which made me stay awake for almost countless hours, and seconal, which made me feel real mellow.

Then during lunch break from classes one day, Hooks and I were hopping on and off various trolley cars, high as two kites. The particular trolley we were on usually stopped at the light just before the street the school was on and we had to abandon ship there or be late for the afternoon session. Trouble was, no one was getting off or on, and I couldn't reach the buzzer, so I figured to jump. Hooks tried to stop me, but as I jumped I shouted, "I gotta 'cause if I'm late, they'll call my mother and then the old man's gonna crack my head."

I did it for him. Instead of landing front and running with the forward momentum, I landed flat on my heels, bounced in the air, and came down on my head hard, rolling under a parked car. An ambulance screamed me off to the nearest hospital where I lay in a coma for five days. They called it a concussion and sent me home. Within two weeks I popped a half dozen seconals at once and got so loaded I couldn't see two feet ahead of me. On a lark, I climbed up a tree, which seemed higher than hell at the twenty-five foot level. When a fragile branch broke, I went sailing back down. Luckily, a friend's shoulder broke my fall, but I was out of it again, deep in a two-day coma.

Because of the head-bangings and my unusual behavior, my parents began to think I had some kind of brain damage or that I was a "mental case." No one suspected I was into drugs. Momma finally arranged for me to see a psychiatrist. At the first appointment, I saw that this guy had a lot of impressive credentials on his walls, but he clearly had no idea about what was really going on. In fact, the man had the most amazing willingness to believe and write down whatever line I handed him.

He was always pushing the conversation deeper for some sexual reason to link with my weird behavior. Since I didn't have anything to give him except my experiences with Mary Jane, I wasn't about to share my sweet tale with that wimp. Late on Wednesday near the end of a session when I was bored and not answering half of his questions, he came on soothing, "What's wrong with you?" He was out to convince me that he was one of the guys, and we'd soon have "all these nasty problems out of the way."

I said, "I hate my mother."

He leaned forward slightly, as if a particular chord had been strummed, asking, "Why do you hate her?" To me it was a telltale giveaway. Here was another gullible bastard totally out of touch with reality, pressing to get hit in the face with it. "Well, why, Vinny?" he persisted. "You can tell me." I faked a look of fear and put my hand on my chin. "Because she makes me eat *oatmeal*. Man, I say 'Mother, *please* give me some farina, wheatina, cornflakes, shredded wheat, puffed rice, *anything* but oatmeal!' " And this joker bought it. I looked at him directly, and said to myself so loud I thought he'd hear, "What a balloon!"

When the session was over, I got up and walked out, then lit a joint before hitting the stairwell down to the street. Home, sweet home. When I got there, the old man was all over the couch, watching Cleveland play the Yankees. "What's the score?" He grunted up from his beer, "Five-to-one Yanks, bottom of the eighth." I let out a hoot and yelled, "Alright!" with my fist in the air. Pop got up off the couch and gave me a kick in the ass because he had his last fifty bet on Cleveland. Fuck it, I figured, and took off thumbing for Florida.

While I was in Miami, floating around on the waves and reaching for new highs with cocaine, speed, and downers, some idiot in our building sent a two-pound rocket shooting off the roof. It blasted through a neighbor's front window, and later the lady of the house started sweeping up the glass and saying she was certain one of "those young farts" was me. I had only the day before sent momma a regular telegram so she wouldn't worry. It was in her hands when she got the drift of the neighbor's words, so she went up there in a flash saying, "My son didn't do it! Look at this date!" And then she read the message: "In Miami Beach having fun. Don't worry."

Hitching home through Virginia, my mind began to wander right after the drug company salesman who was driving finally shut up. Where the hell was I going and why? Was this all there was? In Florida I had boosted some balmy girl's wallet with over two hundred dollars in it. Being a nice guy, I mailed the ID cards to her home in Alabama and got high with the balance. I wondered about the cost of this lifestyle in the end, and then I was back home, and everything was almost exactly the same, emphasis on almost. The old man had one of his perennial slumps and was hanging his IOU's on the other side of town, trying to hide from the guys he owed on our side. My mother was split between reconciliation and hate when she saw me at the gate beneath our kitchen window. I had just eaten three bennies to recover from the ride and insure that my eyes were wide open.

Following the normal stroking motions and a bite to eat, momma broke down and told me that the day before—a Sunday—she had been helping the church with the booths at the annual bazaar. She went to throw pennies at another booth, stashing her purse under one of the counters for safekeeping. Her last sixty dollars was in that bag, and someone stole it. "Now what can I do, Vinny? Your dad has been gone for two weeks?"

I was broke and not really clearheaded enough to think about the answer, but I figured the priests certainly owed momma if they owed anybody. After all, she was the one who was there at 6:30 Mass everyday; her two older sons had been altar boys, and she had always given every dime she could to fulfill the commandment about supporting the church all the time. She also had worked long and often on many fund-raising events to help build a new parochial school.

I thought of that, plus the fact that I used to deeply resent the priests' regular habits of cruising around in fancy cars, getting shit-faced on booze, and smoking eighty-five-cent cigars when there was such poverty surrounding their fancy rectories. They were always installing more elaborate stained-glass windows from "special" collections when the parishioners were in need of nothing more than some simple food on the table.

Anyway, I suggested to mom that she might approach Father Keogh, explain what had happened, and ask him for some temporary relief from our plight. After all, they had made money on the bazaar. That afternoon she went, and the priest turned her down cold. This presented a disillusionment with life so sharp, so final, that I backed off and looked for some ultimate escape from reality.

All the hip guys on the street knew that heroin was around, and we also knew it was "bad stuff." One skinny slum character named Tommy the Turk would come down to our club from time to time, stoned out of his mind, nodding all over the place. He had what was reputed to be the expensive habit of mainlining the junk, straight into his veins.

The day I made the turn to fourteen, nobody threw a party so I figured to throw one of my own. I was so fed up with all the crap in the world around me, I was bound and determined to check heroin out. That day I wouldn't let the Turk get away until he turned me on and I gained my "wings," street jargon for a first flight under the influence of the crystal white lady from China. The Turk hemmed and hawed, then agreed to let me "skin-pop" a two-dollar cap of his dope. With the deal consummated, we retired to the bathroom at a Burgerama joint where my thoughts were onto the new feeling of spirits about to be lifted off of this and up to another place. Turk filled the eyedropper after cooking the junk in a bottle cap behind the closed door. He hit me with the needle on the upper left arm near my vaccination scar.

Nothing happened. My high anticipation turned straight to anxiety as we sauntered out the door, with me full of questions. Turk told me to hold on. "You'll feel it." We drifted into the corner store where I bought a cold Coke. As I handed the money to the clerk, I felt my stomach turn, halfway between nausea and a hot glowing ball, and then it started to rise toward my gullet, on its way to my heart and my head. Before the clerk could hand me my change, a flash feeling of incredible peace, love, joy, and no pain drained everything else from my mind.

I was away, out on a seacoast somewhere in space where every rush of the tide brought a new wave of happiness. God only knows how I got out of that store or whatever happened to the Coke and my coins. Suddenly I had no past and no future, only the present on a plane where all things were possible. Vinny the Scarface was finally the master of all time and space, the land and the sea. I saw myself walking across an ocean of joy where all hands welcomed my presence. I stepped into another age in search of even vaster oceans. I transcended everything and everyone I had ever known, and nothing mattered. I was reaching out to destiny—a sweet sense of overwhelming personal power and the sure gut feeling that Vinny Marino had found *truth*.

And the truth would set me free! I took to it like a duck takes to water.

Within a month of that initial expeience with junk, Hooks heard about it, and to stay even with his partner, he earned his own set of wings. We discussed the dynamics of teaming up tightly and scoring the maximum that bravado would allow. Late one night, Hooks and I each skin-popped a two-dollar cap and decided as we tripped along that the New Utrecht train station would supply our needs for at least another month if only we could pull it off.

This was to be our first real heist. Hooks and I talked about how we would do it. We decided to ask a third party to accompany us, a guy named Tony who owned a big car we figured we'd need for a fast getaway. Well, at least that part was right. Tony came on like he was the key man in the deal since he had the wheels. Hooks and I didn't particularly care what he thought of himself, as long as he could drive.

As the picture rolled on, we all came to the rendezvous on time at 8:45 in Brooklyn, with Tony upright and chewing gum like it was going out of style. We knew that the last train pulled out of the station at 9:02, and the office usually stayed open another ten minutes or so while the agent counted out the cash. The plan was to scoot up to the platform and bully the agent into turning over the money, and there would be "no trouble."

Tony pulled the Buick up under the steps leading to the platform, dimmed the lights, and let the engine purr. Hooks and I signaled go and stalked the stairs to get in the door before the man locked it. The last train was just leaving the station up above, and everything was coming off smooth. When we entered the cage, I waved a knifeblade at the uniform sitting in the corner and yelled, "Give us the money and there won't be any trouble!"

As he stood up, that ride collector turned out to be one big Irish character with a pudgy pot belly in his mid-forties, a ten-cent cigar in the crunch of his jaw. He looked as if he could do a bunch more than just handle himself as he clenched his fist and barked, "Don't kid around with me! You guys get the hell outa here!"

At this point, I noticed the barrel of a high-powered rifle on my right held by Tony and pointed in the general direction of the uniform. Then the goddam cannon went off with a shattering boom. "Jeezes!" I thought, as the shell whizzed past the conductor's ear and tore shit out of a wooden pillar about six inches behind him. We all stood transfixed.

I was the first in the room to come unglued, and I hit the steps out of there on a dead run. Hooks followed my act, and I didn't see Tony, but I could hear the rifle butt banging the steel rungs of the staircase. We crammed into separate doors of the Buick and were off. After a mile or so, safe from the scene, I took a deep breath and jerked the wheel over to the curb, telling this asshole Tony to stop dead. When he did, I hit him with every foul name in the book and then spent time making up new descriptions to fit the chump. We had no score, and worse a charge of attempted murder would be on the books. Hooks and I slammed our way out of the car.

My head was banging so hard that I had to push on my eyeballs for relief, and my gut was tied in a knot, and pulling tighter. Adrenalin and sweat kept me cold and hot at the same time, and the misery was compounded by the long walk home, nearly three miles in the dark.

After we blew the train station heist with Tony's high-powered assistance, we sat down and thoroughly discussed the what-ifs. We were scared absolutely shitless. For instance, what if that idiot had killed the agent? Christ, we could have been arrested for murder. What if we had been caught? The minimum would have been armed robbery. And the ironic thing was that we didn't have a dime.

It wasn't more than ten minutes before Hooks and I decided to work together on our own. Then we talked about the smack and whether it could have had a negative effect on our performance. We concluded that it certainly didn't help any, and we made another pact: *never* to get hooked on the stuff. We reasoned that we were "too intelligent" to allow ourselves to become slaves to a drug or anything else. We were "smart money," and our intention was to become made-men. Right then we flatly declared to restrict our junk highs to weekends, for recreational use, and nothing was really wrong with that. After all, everybody relaxed on weekends. The final pact we made was never to give the other guy up. No matter what a cop said, we would know that the other guy had said nothing.

During the week, Hooks and I became involved in the excitement of small, petty thievery. We could have bought our dope with soda bottle and milk bottle refund money because China white was cheap in 1953, but the thrill of stealing really turned us on, plus the fact that we could get something for nothing just made sense to us. Not only that, the stuff we boosted was relatively easy to sell because a lot of people out there also wanted to get something for next to nothing.

We started with boosting cigarettes from the A&P stores. Most of the time our method was very direct: I just put on a working cap, a pencil behind my ear, walked in, loaded up, and walked out again. If anyone asked a question, I'd just mutter something like: "These are going to the Eighty-fifth Street store," and keep on going. Over the years, my record in stealing cigarettes would warrant an entry in the Guinness book. A&P stock must have dropped twenty points from our cigarette operations alone.

The fact that Hooks and I had been together since we were six years old probably made us think and act somewhat alike. Our instincts were totally together, and we usually saw the same opportunities and problems at the same time. From cigarettes we invented a game that eventually became known in criminal circles as "cattle rustling." First we would have a false pocket sewn into a massive black overcoat. Then we'd go into a supermarket and stuff frozen steaks, chops, pork ribs, roast beef, and other premium cuts into the special lining and simply walk out the door. Like modern-day Robin Hoods, we stole from the rich companies and sold cheap to the poor. We became proud of ourselves and our new role in society. It was a real challenge, plus we figured, "What the hell can anybody do, even if we get caught?" After all, we were just kids according to the law—minors. We'd go to juvenile court and get probation or a suspended sentence. Nothing to worry about.

As we started to pull in "regular" money, we also started to use more drugs. We told ourselves it was a bonus for work well done. Before we knew it, the weekends seemed too far apart, so we figured, "Why not get loaded on Wednesday evenings, just to break up the long stretch." One thing led to another, and in a few months we realized we were pretty heavy into drugs. One Friday night we agreed "to keep up with the stealing, but stop using smack for a while." Of course, this conversation took place right after we had both stuck a needle in our arms.

The following day just after noon I was busy doing nothing when I started to feel that something was missing from my body. I thought maybe I was coming down with some kind of cold or flu virus. I laid down on my bed but could not sleep. Involuntary twitching spasms prevented that, so I got up and drank some water, brushed my teeth, and took a shower, but nothing helped. I was still uneasy and on the brink of some sickness.

That night I climbed into bed early, weary as hell, but I couldn't sleep a wink. I yawned a thousand times, twitched nervously, felt alternate chills and hot flashes, and my stomach was knotted into a ball. Right after dawn the next morning, I got out of bed before six, dressed, said "to hell with eating," and went to see Hooks. On the way, I got deep, double-over cramps in my belly and icy chills throughout my body, yet I was sweating at the same time. When I saw Hooks outside his place, his face looked really bad. Before I could say anything, he asked me if I had any trouble sleeping last night. I nodded, and we started comparing notes.

Suddenly it dawned on us. We were totally hooked on heroin. A shock of terroristic fear went straight through my heart. How the hell did we get into this position when we so adamantly agreed we wouldn't? It couldn't happen to us—we knew better. But there was no time to waste sitting around sharing philosophies about the past. My gut was killing me, and sweat was runnng off Hooks' face. We hailed a cab and went downtown for a visit with our pusher.

After we scored and got loaded, I was immediately and almost magically relieved. The cramps died down, the chills left, and I stopped sweating. Once again the extremes of feeling warm and mellow swept through my body and took all my troubles away. During the entire twenty-minute cab ride back, Hooks and I didn't say a word. It wasn't necessary. When we got back, the nearest stoop seemed like the place to sit down and relax. It was then that I looked at Hooks in a stupor, and he looked at me. I sensed the fear jolt through both of us. Without talking, we understood the no-win swindle we were up to our necks in. That's how the vicious circle began. Every day stealing, and every day using drugs.

My old man was wrapped up in his gambling losses and didn't bother to notice my stretches of absence from home. My mother thought I was working long hours, and to keep up that front, I gave her some money each week, saying it was "part of my pay." I was having a lot of problems in school when I bothered to go. It was amazing that the school didn't know, my parents didn't know, my brother Frank didn't know, Mary Jane across the street didn't know, and I wasn't about to tell them. I knew it, however, at the base of my soul. Vinny Marino, age fifteen, was a full-on, vein-shooting, heroin-hooked junkie. And I was beginning to wonder how long I would be able to cover my tracks.

3 / A Junkie with No Relief

By this time the Scarface alias was stuck to my countenance in the neighborhood, and people pointed and laughed behind my back. This made me angry and extremely self-conscious, but more and better drugs seemed to temporarily alleviate the problem. Outwardly, my attitude ran from distinctly aloof to downright contemptuous to the point that my behavior had gotten me thrown out of five different high schools before I was sixteen. Since you had to be sixteen to quit school, the New York State Board of Education simply suspended me for the last year and let me wait it out on the streets.

Being accountable to no one, I hung out with people who would at least give me some recognition for what I was good at—stealing. We sat around and plotted crime scenes, high as a kite on a horrendous combination of drugs. Shooting "speedballs"—a mixture of cocaine and heroin—became a favorite pastime. I started to do some ballsy, way-out things, which increased my recognition, and I became a leader of sorts.

One night in the clubhouse I suggested we go out and rob someone in the park. The other three guys were all sons of a prominent lieutenant in the police department, and they were missing some of the same things at home that I was it seems. At any rate, they were totally willing to play along, so the four of us—me, Leech, Bubba, and Butchie—headed past the iron gates into Prospect Park on a Tuesday evening. Leech had lifted his old man's .38 service revolver, thinking that we might run into more trouble than we could handle with our bare hands. Inside the wooded area, we passed several people who looked as if they had nothing worth taking, but then we came up behind a couple holding hands on a grass path, very much in love, I figured, looking at the size of the engagement ring on her left hand. I motioned that these were the marks, and Leech handed me the gun. I felt an abdominal surge of adrenalin enter my bloodstream, and sweat broke out on my forehead.

I reached for the victim's shoulder and spun him around. He was startled and scared all at once, and he jumped at the sight of the gun barrel pointing directly at his midsection. The girl screamed, "Oh, God!" with an inhale and moved behind him to protect herself. I told him to freeze and lifted the wallet from his back pocket. Leech grabbed her hand, and Bubba relieved her of the diamond ring. We told them to stay quiet under a tree for at last fifteen minutes or risk getting shot.

Slipping off into the darkness, we found ourselves in big trouble almost immediately. The victims ran into a beat cop only half a block from where we had hit them, and he radioed for assistance, calling in four squad cars that surrounded the park in no time. Near panic, the four of us split up, after I shoved the gun back into Leech's hand. I learned later he threw it in the duck pond. Sirens were wailing as if calling for "Vinny!" all over in my head, and I broke into a fast run toward the park perimeter to see if there was any way out of this jam. Luckily, I saw an opportunity to make an alleyway across Thirty-eighth Street. In one dash I got to a series of trash cans and huddled down out of sight, breathing hard. I eased out of the alley and ran the better part of two miles home.

When I got there—damn!—the old man was home watching TV and drinking beer. I looked like I had just done a marathon, with my shirt hanging out and sweat all over my body. The old man asked where I had been and how come I was out of breath. I gave him some line about a game of kick-the-can, but before he could call me anything in rebuttal someone knocked at the door. Behind it were two cops, detectives from the local precinct. They told the old man I was wanted for suspicion in the park robbery, and pop whirled to whisper to me in Sicilian, "Don't say anything! Don't say a word!"

The bulls took me downtown to the lockup. When we got there I saw Bubba, and he started babbling about me being the guy who had done it all, and he was just along for the cheap thrills of observation. I called him a punk liar, and the cops booked us both.

Within two hours I was out—pop had come down to the station and signed the papers necessary to get this "juvenile delinquent" released into his custody, a standard procedure under the law at that time. On the way home, pop shocked me as he started talking, "I don't believe you would get involved in this nickel and dime shit. Maybe you didn't know, but I spent seven years behind bars, but not for loose change! If you're gonna do something, go out and take over a payroll or somethin' worth your while. And do it with people you can trust, not these stool pigeons you're hanging out with!"

In one sense, the old man struck a responsive chord in my head. He had opened up with me for the first time in his life, and I felt closer to him for that split second than I had ever before. But why hadn't he told me earlier? Why the whole bit with the Navy uniform and the war stories, being the hero of the block party and preaching when he was really nothing more than an ex-con?

Whether an earlier revelation would have made any difference to my crazy life is debatable. As it was, I drew a suspended sentence and probation for the mugging, since they failed to turn up any evidence. I had stashed the ring and the wallet in a trash can in the alley so the haul went to the garbage dump. For me it was straight back to the streets almost without interruption for more scheming, stealing, robbing, lying, manipulating, and cheating—all done to get more drugs.

One day I wandered into the local library and for kicks looked up the day I was born in the archives of *The New York Times*. I figured the paper might give me some perspective on life or perhaps shed some light on future directions. Judging from the headlines, December 22, 1938, was a bad time for nearly everyone:

Tokyo Press Calls United States
'Tool of Britain'

Britain to Expend £20 Million
To Reinforce Homes Against Air Raids

German Jewish Leader Menachim Begin
Warns World of Nazi Threat

We had all heard about what happened to the Jews in World War II. I wasn't particularly for or against them, but I figured they were a people somehow accustomed to doing what they were told. I just couldn't envision a bunch of Sicilians going quietly off to a gas chamber—there had to be something different about the Jews. If nothing else, they seemed to be easy marks, so I decided to open some hunting grounds at the school a lot of them went to.

After that, three times a week on a regular basis, I would show up and terrorize the Jewish kids, demanding their allowances in return for "protection." Using the tactics of the best Sicilian mobster I could imagine, I painted a verbal picture of the strange and brutal actions they faced if they failed to come across with the cash. They were obviously convinced, because I was raking in a lot of money for those days—about fifty dollars a week—within a month after I put the pressure on. The scam was so easy and went on for so long that I came to believe the Jews had some sort of guilt to redeem since they seemed to lay down at the slightest threat.

How wrong I was. They finally had it up to the eyeballs, with my presence and demands for money. One of the kids told his parents, and from there it went to the cops. I was sitting on a stoop across from my building one afternoon after collecting when two detectives pulled up in an unmarked car and approached me. One of them slapped me hard across the face twice before bothering to tell me anything. Then he said, "So, you want to be a tough guy, Marino? You want to shake down kids in my precinct? You're under arrest. Stand up and put your hands on the car!" The other guy handcuffed me, then shoved me in the back seat of their car. They drove me to the precinct.

I was getting scared. That was the first time in my life for booking, fingerprinting, and a mug shot. Not only that—this could mean a jail sentence, especially heavy because the police could line up over twenty personal victims. I had to spend the night in a tank and what a night it was. My drug habit was coming straight down, all around me, and this was also the first time I had experienced a cell. I was terrified at being locked up in a six-by-nine-foot space to ride it out.

An hour inside that closed cell, and my body began to do its number, like, "Get up off your ass and get me some heroin, now!" This time I knew it wasn't the flu—it was going to be cold turkey in a jail cell. Crashing bells started going off in my head, and sharp abdominal pains shot through my midsection. I couldn't stand to put my head down because of spasms and chills. Then I vomited uncontrollably until nothing came up. No one noticed. As soon as I finished the vomiting session in the toilet, I turned around and had diarrhea. I hugged myself hard, but there was no comfort coming, only sharper pains everywhere. I swore silently, "If I get out of this, no more drugs!"

After a night on the steel rack, I saw the first light of Saturday morning. Just after six a hack brought in a cup of black coffee and a roll with butter. Three sips of coffee, and I vomited for the next half hour. My head was swimming with pain, and my gut was wrenched so tight it was hard to breathe. Next thing I saw through my blurred vision was another hack. As he approached the cell, he yelled, "Let's go, Marino!"

You wouldn't believe how happy I was. I imagined it was all a mistake, they were going to cut me loose, and then I'd be able to shoot straight downtown and cop a fix to get my body back in shape. Instead, the guard had me put my hands behind my back and handcuffed me. I said in dismay, "What the fuck is going on?" Everything went foggy until a fast backhand slammed into my left ear by a detective, who then had me by the throat. "So you want to play tough, huh, mister? So, what we're gonna do is help you. We're going to send you to a nice tough place called Raymond Street. Stand up."

Raymond Street was in downtown Brooklyn, just a couple of blocks from where Hooks and I used to connect. The building was an old fortress, with stones four feet thick. It was the kind of place George Washington must have invaded at some point in his career. They signaled a hack to open up the huge iron gate to let us in, and I could tell immediately that clubs were trump in that joint. All the bulls carried big sticks, weighted with lead, I was sure. I was taken into a big room with a board that said Receiving.

Twenty-five other guys were in the room when they began the processing. First they took my thumbprint and told me to empty everything from all pockets. Next was a twenty-minute wait to fill out a 3×5 card with my name, address, age, and the charge—robbery. Then they had us all line up and undress. "Okay, put your hands high in the air and stretch. Alright, now run your hands through your hair. Now lift up your balls. Turn around, bend over and spread 'em." I flashed for a split-second on how I'd hate to be the bull assigned to check all the spread-eagled cons, when a gut pain shot me back to reality.

We were escorted into a tiled room full of showers, all with only one tap—cold. My body was so racked with pain I would have given anything to leave it there. Again I swore to the gods, "If I ever get out of this mess, no more drugs!" The bulls handed our clothes back after searching through them, and we were told to get dressed. I wanted to sit down, but instead we were led into another room, bright as hell, and it added to the pain in my eyes. The room was labeled Examination. When I saw the first white gown, I thought, "Goddam! These guys are gonna know I'm an addict!"

I panicked, but there was nowhere to run. When my name came up, the white gown had me sit down opposite him at the desk and rull up my sleeves. I saw the end coming as he checked out my arms, but he must have been some kind of idiot because he didn't even look at my left hand, which was where I got off. Then he asked directly, "Do you use drugs?"

"No."

"Okay. Next."

We went up a flight of stairs with me huddled over and entered the Annex, their place for keeping adolescents. The hack found my cell on his official lockup list, number C-7, and led me to it. With no visible alternative, I walked the three steps in, and as the key clicked the lock latch behind me, I was gripped with certain fear that I was going to lose my mind.

It was the worst weekend I could remember in my life. There was constant, unbearable pain over every inch of my body. Thoughts had trouble getting in, and no way could I concentrate, only think in flashes. "Can Hooks get in here with a fix?" The gut-wrenching pain doubled me over with the question. "Did my parents even know I was in here?" I vomited until the dry heaves left me hanging on the edge of the cold porcelain. "What happened to 'probations' and 'suspended sentences' for juveniles? Shit, these guys were *serious*." I twitched all over with the absence of junk calling out to my body, screaming in the back of my mind, "Get me some heroin!"

After a while I started to feel my way around the cell with my hands, just to take my mind off the pain—stone walls cold as me or colder. I felt chills as I ran my fingers over the round steel bars. There I was, a groveling caged monster junkie with no relief in sight.

The sink basin had the standard one tap. It seemed that "hot water" was what we were all doing in the joint in the first place so they only ran the cold for us. We each got three wool blankets to use on the steel bunk—no pillows, no mattress. I guessed as I grabbed one that these coarse blankets were straight off the horses' back the bulls rode in the parks. As I shivered all over, I rolled up in the blankets on the floor. Then I started to sweat.

I thought to get up—that might help. It didn't. I hung over the commode and retched again a dry heave. I felt like climbing into the damn bowl and flushing myself down. Maybe the ride would be a high, circling around in water. Anything but the misery. "Why won't someone come down and bail me out? I won't do it again! I didn't even meant it! I'll give it all back! Just let me out!" Then I started to yawn. By an hour later, I must have yawned a hundred times. With the second hour it tripled to three hundred, and before the ordeal ended, I must have done a thousand or more. No sleep, just yawning to the point where my jaw felt like it was going to fall off from the agony, and then a charlie horse locked itself into my jaw muscle.

Back to the toilet to retch more deeply than before, after drinking some cold tap water. I felt like a crazed Indian out on a prairie somewhere, huddled alone in a gray horse shawl, cold as hell, no matches to build a fire, no tepee to sleep in, no junk to stick in a vein. I complained loud as hell and rattled the bars of my cage. Nothing came back but the hollow bitching of the other customers, bouncing without meaning or effect off the bare stone walls.

"What in hell am I gonna do and what day is it?" Those words went over and over in my mind, the whole time I was cramped over in that cell. At about noon we were brought out into what they called the day room for lunch. Everyone sat down to eat after passing along the stainless steel cafeteria line. All you could draw for utensils was one spoon, which you also had to hand in before leaving since they figured somebody could easily make a knife and after that a getaway.

What I managed to get down on Saturday was two sips of cocoa. On Sunday I got a whole cup of tea down. Other than that, just the thought of food made me nauseous, usually followed by awful retching. The confined space of the cell threatened to drive me absolutely crazy, and everything was hell. I held out my hand once to see if it was steady at all, and it jerked so far to the left that I thought it was leaving without me.

Saturday night after supper slid under the door, they announced Catholic confession followed by Jewish services. Figuring anything to get out of the cell, I went to both services, and no one caught on. The next day I got out for Catholic Mass and the Protestant service. No one seemed to mind that Marino had found religion. I just wanted to move around, anything to get my mind off the incredible body pain.

Back in the cell it was dark, and I folded my arms over my gut, trying to ride the hellish pain and not cry or show what was inside. I thought I would either go insane or get some sleep and forget about the misery for a while. I laid down on the steel bed-slab and closed my eyes. Just when I was about to fall asleep, a shooting pain would hammer home, raising my eyelids, and jerking my body to any other position but the one it was in. I went through several hellish hours of cat-naps, brief flashes of shut-eye before another blinding pain jolted me. I would get sane to the point of standing up to circle the cell, all doubled over like a hunchback, hugging myself and searching the ceiling for some relief from the drug withdrawal.

The next thing was the smell of freshly brewed coffee drifting into my cell on what turned out to be a Monday morning. Arraignment day, and the damp and cold were seeping into my bones when I woke up. I thought of a tooth-brushing but didn't have any gear; no razor either, so I splashed some cold water on my face to revive. Then I went back to the bunk and sat with my head in my hands, totally drained and still in pain.

Soon a black hack let me out and led me back to the bull pen, where they called out my name and another guy's, then handcuffed us together. When about fifteen pairs of cons were ready, a bell rang and a whole fleet of hacks came out to transport us to court. By that time I was feeling a little better since some fresh air came in as we moved. When we arrived at the adolescent court, I was overwhelmed to see my mom and dad standing there. I was handcuffed, with a three-day growth of stubble and my clothes all crumpled to hell, but I was so relieved to see someone I knew that I managed a big, shit-eating grin. My momma was ashamed and holding back tears; pop's stare said he didn't like the action at all. I could tell that immediately.

We were escorted into the courtroom, about thirty guys total, cuffed in pairs until all were seated. As soon as they freed my hands, I used them to double up over my stomach in an attempt to hide the pain that kept coming back for more. I wanted to sit up straight, but the knot refused to cooperate. Finally I heard my name called and stood up in front of the judge. They read the charges and asked, "How do you plead?"

"Not guilty, your Honor," I said. The judge banged his

gavel, set a trial date for three months in the future, and set my bail at twenty-five hundred big ones. I was in a fog the while time the judge was talking and banging until he came to the bail part. "Damn," I said to myself, "who has that kind of money?" They took me back to the courthouse bull pen, and a shyster lawyer my pop had hired came in to see me. He said some reassuring words, but somehow I didn't trust him. "Don't worry, Vinny. We'll have you out of here in ten minutes."

Even with my body so full of pain, I felt a surge of excitement. I stood up and told the man representing me, "Please hurry! I have a terrible flu and couldn't get any medicine inside. I gotta go see a doctor!" The actual thought running through my addict-consciousness was, "How the hell am I gonna get away from my mother and father and get straight again?"

An hour and a half more I sat there with no way of covering the pain and nothing to do before I heard my name called by the bailiff. They brought me up to the receiving area and gave me back my personal stuff, took off the handcuffs, and opened the door to freedom. Mom and pop were waiting outside in the cold. Mom rushed over and hugged me, mainly out of concern for my disheveled condition, not out of love for the criminal element in her son. Pop stood still, a frozen look deep in his eyes. I thanked momma for coming and told her it wasn't the way they said it in the courtroom. I told her that I would tell her all about it and then asked my pop if he had a dollar and a cigarette. "Yeah," he said as he gave me one of each.

"I gotta go see somebody first," I told them, "but then I'll come straight home in less than an hour and we'll talk about everything, and I promise this kinda thing won't ever happen again." While they were hemming and hawing about what they wanted me to do, I excused myself and skipped away backwards, then jumped on the next bus going in any direction. It was a Number 51 bus that routed right past Hooks' place. At the nearest stop, I was out in a flash, dashing over the street to leap on the stoop and bang loud as hell on the door. More good luck—Hooks was home. As he opened the door, he looked at me and grinned, "Where the fuck have you been?"

I would have throttled him—if only he knew where I'd been. Instead, I just pleaded for mercy, "Hooks, I gotta have dope. You got any?" He nodded in the affirmative. He had just bought a bundle the day before and was moving it to friends since it was excellent quality dope. I was in such a bad shape with the shakes and chills that Hooks had to do the cooking and loading, and fire the needle into my vein. It was like a flash from heaven when it landed. My stomach turned in that halfway twist, and the ball of warm glow shot straight toward my head. The cramps went out the window, and the weekend was erased from memory. I was alive again, junk running freely in my veins.

After a twenty or thirty minute nod, consisting of pure ecstasy, I thought about mom and pop. So I shuffled back home within the hour as promised, then begged off to the bathroom to "clean up, and then I'll explain." Once inside the door, I locked it and nodded pleasantly in the never-never land for over an hour, then shaved and showered. It was time to emerge and face the music.

"What the hell did you do?" pop asked. "It wasn't like they made it sound, pop." He pressed further. "Well, what the hell *did* you do?" I told him some Jewish guys were getting pressure from another neighborhood, so they were looking for help. I was just trying to help for a fee. I promised pop to get out of doing that kind of stuff and stay out. I promised to behave totally. I would have promised them anything. Pop seemed to at least halfway buy my story, while momma didn't do much but wring her hands and circle the room, sobbing, "Why, Vinny, why?"

"Alright," pop said, "but you still got a robbery rap to beat. You'll have to go see some guys I know tomorrow. And don't go pulling any shit tonight. Got that?"

Once again I was out of it. The next day pop's connected friends recommended a lawyer, and one of them made an introductory call for an appointment. It was at this point that I got a special perspective on the American judicial system. I located the tattered box-shaped building covered with ragged posters from old rock events. Inside, dustballs the size of medium rats drifted down the halls. When I saw my lawyers' name on a brass plate, I knocked and he said to enter. Behind the desk was this character about fifty, with an egg-stained tie loose at the neck and a yellowing shirt that was once white. He was chain-smoking cigarettes and losing the ashes in a massive pile of papers strewn over the desk top.

He couldn't locate my case file, so he asked me to tell him what had gone down. After I gave him my story, he lost no valuable time telling me exactly where he stood, which was in a position to know every dirty angle about the law—every corrupt judge and the proper approach, and then how I had no choice but to pay for his services, assuming I wanted to remain a free man.

With a twinge of fright, I recalled the weekend at Raymond Street and asked, "How much?" He weighed the situation for a good twenty seconds before informing me coldly that the fee would be two thousand dollars cash for "taking care of things," all at once and with no strings. So within ten days I sold everything of value I could find or steal. I even borrowed three hundred to cover this legal beagle who was going to bark up the right judge's tree, loaded with money, begging for a favor.

It worked like a charm. The next thing I knew, the courtroom alarm went off, the judge came in, and with no trial or anything, I ended up convicted up a misdemeanor. The judge sentenced me to "one year on Riker's Island, suspended." The Jewish kids screamed and stomped around in circles at the total injustice of the penalty. I just vowed to stay the hell away from actions that might lead me back to Raymond Street.

The thing about feeling really good and being high on the times was that someone or something always seemed to come along and screw it up. With Hooks and me, it was a local precinct cop named Brannigan. He was Irish, and he haunted us day and night after we became notorious neighborhood characters. Ultimately he failed to get anything out of us but not because he didn't try. When he asked questions, Hooks would flip him a dime and tell him to call information. One time Brannigan rolled up in his blue-and-white and told us to get up against the car. After the frisk, he asked, "Where were you two at 10:15 last night?"

"Fuckin' your sister," was the comeback that got Hooks a righteous slap on the side of the head. Next thing we were on our way down to the station again. Brannigan would routinely hold us in detention without charges for ten or twelve hours, to the point where he had to let us go or get in trouble himself. He would pull us in on trumped-up charges just to make it look like he was working hard. Meanwhile we were pulling jobs and heists he knew nothing about.

Once Hooks and I were loaded to the gills, drinking ice-cold sodas at the counter of a greasy spoon. The wind outside was gusty, blowing old newspapers in the air, and one minute it was sunny, the next cloudy. A definite do-nothing kind of day. The rickety diner door opened to admit a decrepit junkie from Queens named Digger in dire need of a fix. We knew him vaguely but avoided him like the plague because he didn't have any part of his act together. Digger weasled up and slid his rear over a counter stool next to me. His breath was worse than a Russian trooper's damp socks after a week in the trenches, and I felt like leaving before a word was said. ''Listen,'' Digger came on. ''I gotta talk to you two.'' Digger leaned closer and started licking his lips, getting more excited as he shifted around. The waitress came over and I ordered him some coffee to cover the foul air that came out with his conniving words.

He edged the smell a little closer and whispered, ''Listen, this little old lady, she lives at my place, see. One day last week I'm passin' her door, and it's open a crack, held by the chain. I see she's got her back to me, so I slow down and peek in, you know. Well, she's countin' a lotta money outa this sack, see? Hell, there ain't nothin' but hunnerd-dollar bills for as long as I'm standin' there!''

Hooks shot back, ''So what, you asshole. You wanna hit the old lady right in your building?'' Digger shrank back a little, as if to avoid the charge. His eyes still rotating. ''No, no. You do it. The two of you.''

''What's in it for you?'' I demanded, knowing the answer. ''I finger her apartment, and we split. Fifty-fifty.''

I laughed out loud and pushed him back to an upright position. Looking back at Hooks, I said quietly, ''Listen to this man. We take all the risks and he wants fifty percent.'' Hooks got up and walked past me, then landed on the stool next to Digger. He yanked the jerk's collar up a bit tighter towards the throat and dictated to Digger, ''Get the fuck outa here! You're nuts!'' Digger was literally bouncing up and down off the stool at this point, begging, ''Please you guys. It's a helluva lotta money. Thousands! I saw it!''

Hooks looked over at me, signaling his dislike for Digger but said nothing. I told Digger the conditions, flatly. ''We get seventy, you get thirty. And it better be smooth.''

''Okay, okay,'' Digger breathed in relief. ''When do we do it?''

''Tonight, after dark,'' I told him. We agreed to meet him at 8:30 outside the diner. Hooks and I drifted off to shoot some pool, where we talked over Digger and the upcoming move. Something didn't smell right, but neither of us could nail anything down to an explanation. Back in my basement we got loaded again and slipped into outfits for our evening's work. I wore black shoes, black pants, and a black leather jacket. Hooks got into some gear that looked straight out of a Dracula flick. It nearly cracked me up.

Digger was twenty minutes late and came in totally loaded. Once again we nearly walked away, but instead took a cab to within a block of his building in Queens, got out, and scouted the area. There were several good getaway alleys nearby. Then we all went over the plan again. The three of us would go to the third floor by the stairwell, and Digger would point out the apartment, then get the hell out of sight. Hooks and I would knock and break in if necessary, wearing stocking masks to avoid being made by the lady. We agreed to meet an hour after the heist outside the diner and split the take. As operations went, this caper didn't compare with the Normandy landing in terms of preparations and details, but it should have worked.

We got into the building unnoticed and went craftily up three flights of stairs. Then we shuffled down the hall, which was much too bright and narrow for my liking. Digger stopped suddenly and pointed at a door in silence. I shoved Digger out of the way and he took off—presumably out of the action. We slipped on the stocking masks and rapped on the door.

"Who is it?" came from inside.

I said "Western Union. Telegram!" then pulled out the .38 special message I had for the occasion, while Hooks stood back flat to the wall with a .22 pistol aimed up in the air. The old lady unlatched the door except for the feeble chain, which was fairly useless, especially when it was mounted on old wood, like hers was. I took a deep breath but couldn't have muttered a word because my mouth was too dry. When we went bursting in the door, my heart was pounding over every inch of me as we tipped the old woman backwards just enough so she fell over the coffee table and crashed all the knicknacks. Then she slid off onto the floor and looked up at us.

We waved our guns like a couple of regular banditos, but she was already scared out of her wits, you could see it in her eyes. We had no intention of hurting the lady, but I wanted to be sure she kept her mouth shut. I should have done the same. When I warned her about screaming, she went into a tantrum that could have brought the neighborhood for two blocks around. I went straight for the vanity drawer while Hooks tried in vain to calm her down. Madly stuffing the bag I found there inside my belt, I heard a noise. I spun around toward the door, and my heart sank to my knees.

There came Digger bounding into the room, holding an overcoat halfway across his face like Zorro with a cape and wilding waving his right index finger at a china closet behind me. "Wait! There's more!" he yelled, "In that bureau!" For some stupid reason he had never told us about that second stash. Maybe he felt guilty about it and had come back to redeem himself, or maybe he just forgot since he was so excitable. The lady got her first serious look at Digger, and she tripled her decibel output. I heard the clack of a deadbolt door latch opening somewhere nearby.

"Let's go!" I motioned to Hooks, and we broke into a quick sprint for the open door. Running down the hall full tilt, we passed a tenant who had just stepped out to see what he was hearing, and trailing far behind us like a pure fool was Digger. The tenant was thunderstruck at first sight, and I knew right away that Digger was made. We jumped out a hall window and over a roof with the tenant yelling, "Hey! Hey! Don't let 'em get away!" but I was adrenalin ready to run into the next day, what with visions of Raymond Street in my head. We took a fire escape to a dark alley below. Meanwhile, Digger had disappeared in some other direction, and I wasn't stopping for any investigations.

We carried on in the rush to get the hell out of there, only slowing down to dump the masks along the way. Sliding into a cab about four blocks from the scene, we finally caught the first available breath of relief. "Fuckin' Digger!" Hooks shook from the visible fear gripping his insides. "That guy made him!" In the light provided in moving slices by the street arcs above the cab I counted out the haul, putting it at just over seven thousand dollars. That presented partial relief from the question of what to do next. I gave the cabbie a fifty and told him to have a nice evening. Hooks and I each stuffed half in our pockets and took off in opposite directions.

It came out in the morning newspapers that Digger, a parolee junkie, was made clear and clean by both the victim and the tenant. They sang a real sweet song and in no time flat Digger was in a cell. That was as far as the printed words went, but the street vine had it that Digger was spilling his guts. Within a day or two Hooks and I got together once again, quietly, in a bus station out on Staten Island. We stood there, shivering like hell, partly from fear and partly from loathing for Digger. Hooks and I had no choice but to go on the lam. We just drifted out of sight, cruising in various parts of the city, but nowhere near Brooklyn. Finally I had my fill of the haunts and the cold hallways. Four months had passed since Digger went down, so I figured to go back home. I never got any closer than the sidewalk out front.

Two cops jumped out of an unmarked car and ran up to me, pulling at their holsters. One of them was Brannigan, who loved to point guns at people, never mind the reason. "Get 'em up in the air!" he ordered, straining his mental faculties to put that much out in one phrase. Brannigan went on to mutter, "We gottcha you this time, Marino!" I refused to say anything after they read me my rights, so we rode to the station. They dumped me in an old waiting room while they scribbled out the standard mountain of police paperwork. As I sat there I could feel the ghosts and emotions of all the bastards who must have been dragged through the room. I could almost taste the hopelessness associated with those earlier transients straight on their way to long sentences, but I swore they weren't going to break me.

I hung up the receiver from one standard phone call somewhere between hope and despair and turned around to see Brannigan and another bull bringing in Hooks wearing handcuffs. Brannigan didn't hesitate to get us both separately into the "Your pal's a fink" routine. But I knew Hooks was a stand-up guy, my partner, and that he wouldn't admit it was dark outside at midnight. He knew me to be the same, and that ultimately wore them down.

It turned out that the tenant refused to come down and identify us, and the old lady "wasn't sure." Digger was made, though, and he ended up drawing ten years for rushing the china closet, plus he already owed them seven on a previous parole. Down went Digger.

The day Hooks and I were released, Brannigan was standing forlorn on the steps of the courthouse near the lion statue with white pigeon shit all over its cement name. The only thing I could think about was getting loaded to wipe that out of my system and Brannigan out of my mind.

* * *

Some days came together like a charm, especially when my junkie mind was hot to score. I got up out of bed one day and all I could think of was a fix to straighten my head. Problem was I had no money—time to hit the streets. Five minutes and three blocks away, I ran across a delivery boy on a bicycle loaded with three sacks of meat from Al's Butcher Shop. I stopped the kid to bullshit for a while and appealed to his greedy side by offering him three bucks to turn his back while I went south with the goods. I told him he could always claim a thief must have hit the bike when he was away urinating in a building or something. He reluctantly agreed and held out his hand for the money. Naturally, I didn't have any, so I just grabbed two of the bags and told him I'd be right back.

When I got to the apartment indicated on the delivery sheet, I knocked and stood back from the entrance politely. A maid came to the door in a black dress and white apron. She relieved me of the delivery, saying she would be right back with the money. I stood there idly, waiting for the servant to come back with the $23.50 they owed me. My eyes lit up when I saw the $50 bill in her hand. I accepted it graciously and told her I didn't have the right change but would run straight down to a store for it and hurry back. She smiled in trustad closed the door.

Back on the street I stalled the boy and took the last bag in my arms, heading for delivery. The lady of the second house handed me a twenty and a ten to pay for her $29-order. Again I had no small bills, and I couldn't believe it when she told me to keep the change. I smiled warmly with a salute to her and said, "Why, thank you, ma'am."

Back on the street again, I told the delivery boy to wait just a second longer while I went to a Western Union Office get some change and pay him off. As I entered the double doors with the twenty in my hand, I motioned it to the clerk behind the cage indicating I was interested only in making change. She nodded in the affirmative as I came up to the window.

Standing off slightly to the right I noticed a lady writing an official telegram paper, and I also noticed a twenty she had laid out to pay for the wire service. She never saw me lift it from right under her nose. I stashed my bill and inserted hers under the cage for the change. Five seconds later when she noticed the missing money and started complaining, I said, "Hey, don't look at me, lady. I came in here with this,'' and held up my hands in innocence as if she were pointing a gun. The clerk defended my position by waving the note like a flag. ''You must be mistaken, ma'am, I saw him come in here with this twenty, too.''

I went out and gave the delivery boy five bucks for his trouble and headed for the train to Harlem. I added up the triple windfall, which had taken all of twenty minutes to rake in. Fifty from the first stop, thirty at the second, and a bonus twenty from the Western Union stop, less five to the bike pedaler, and I ended up with a net ninety-five to buy heroin. I had to laugh all the way to the Spanish section, where my connection was located.

Dope fiends are typically notorious losers in life. Not only are they usually weak and mentally deficient, but within a very short time after the first fix they tend to go down physically as well. Under the influence of junk, nothing seems to matter, and sweets are mostly what you think of in terms of eating. Cold liquids and sweets, like cola or some other soft drink, never alcohol.

Addicts also live from one fix to the next and never think to ask about the quality of what they buy. The junk always varies from buy to buy, from day to day, and from pusher to pusher. Sometimes it would be dynamite; other times it was not, and there was no way to tell beforehand in an alley. The only way to find out is to load up and stick the needle in your vein. Given this rather random condition, most users would ''boot'' the junk, meaning shoot a little and see what the effect was, then a little more and so forth. I didn't see any point in wasting time. My way was to fill the eye dropper, put on the spike, and shoot it all in. Come hell or high water, let's go for broke.

That day I got off the train in Harlem and started looking for a Puerto Rican named Diego—everybody called him Dago for short. He lived on the sixth floor of this broken building where everything was coming apart. I would whistle under his kitchen window three times. When Dago heard me and signaled back with a ''Yo,'' I'd tell him many caps I wanted and then he'd lower a tin can on a string to collect the money, up front. He'd send your order back down the same way. Dago had the situation wired because he couldn't get busted from that distance, and even more important, he couldn't be taken off since all his customers paid cash through the tin can before they saw the goods.

I bought a bundle from Dago, twenty-five two-dollar capsules, and headed for a quiet place to get off and taste the stuff. Then I remembered that I didn't bring any "works" with me so I looked for another guy I knew, named Haysoos. I soon caught sight of him, and he agreed to lend me his works in return for a free cap. With that we slipped into his building and went up to the stairwell above all the residential floors, right next to the roof. I tied off my arm with his black leather strap and loaded the eye dropper. As soon as I found the vein and the heroin hit my stomach, I knew it was dynamite to the point of too much. I also knew I was going out. In that dense fog just before blackness, I begged Haysoos not to leave me. Then there was pitch black up ahead, and it was coming down fast. I knew there was no way out. I figured I was dying.

When I opened my eyes again, it was only slightly. I had no idea how much time had passed, but I made out a huge lamp overhead that flooded the table where I was laid out, drenched in my own sweat. A white sheet covered me and a green tag attached to my big toe, left foot. Off to my right and standing against the wall was a Roman Catholic priest I didn't recognize, holding his holy missal and wearing a sash around his neck, the same one they used for the sacramental administration of extreme unction. I remembered that much but not much else. Turning my head slightly to the left, a wave of incredible nausea swept over me, and I thought I was going to lose it completely when I saw mom and pop at the other end of the stark white room. It was the first time I had ever seen my father cry. Pop came over and took my hand saying, "Thank God, thank God."

"Where am I, pop?" was the only question I could think of. "In the emergency room of St. Luke's Hospital, and damn lucky to be alive." I could tell pop was really upset, although I couldn't see anything clearly. "How'd I get here?" Pop came up and loomed over me, visibly pissed off with what had happened and now with all the questions. He strained to hold back his fury, and his face went white as he spoke. "Vinny, you idiot, somebody called an ambulance, and then the hospital called and told us you were in trouble. When we got here, they had you covered up. Dead. The priest saw you move while he gave you the Last Rites."

"Jesus Christ," I murmured, and the priest's ears perked up as if someone had called him for another resurrection. My momma burst into tears. She couldn't bear to face all the naked grief—her son a heroin addict, taking too much and ending up in a hospital with a DOA tag on his big toe. I pulled the sheet back over my head and played dead, wondering about what had happened to the rest of my bundle of dope.

4 / Making Doctors and Cracking Churches

Nobody bothered to tell me how lucky I was. The building I had overdosed in was only a short block and a half from St. Luke's emergency room, where they had worked hard to save my life in a hurry. I learned later Haysoos had lifted my bundle but called an ambulance for me.

When the light of the next day came streaming into the hospital ward, I was still in a semicoma, but I was alive enough to realize my body wasn't racked with the blinding pain that came from the absence of junk. I discovered an intravenous needle in my left arm and thought maybe they were taking care of my habit. The bottle turned out to be glucose, but I learned about the doses of methadone, a drug permitting withdrawal from heroin but no pain.

This pretty nurse came in with a broad smile and a tray full of medicinal dishes, something for everyone in the room. She was a strawberry blonde with her hair tied up in a bun at the back, plus she had two very interesting breasts that perked up the front of her uniform and made my day a little brighter. Her name was Wanda, I saw by the tag, and I gave her a weak wolf whistle, just so she'd know I was alive. After dropping some pills into an old guy who must have been dying because he wheezed instead of breathed, Wanda walked over to my bed, examined my chart, and said, "Well, Mr. Marino, you sure are a lucky guy."

I told her I'd give up everything if only she would agree to spend a day with me, drifting around in a park somewhere, perhaps on a picnic. Her cheeks flushed and she let a smile get past her official position. "We might just do that, as soon as you're on your feet.'' She poured me some ice water from the chrome pitcher on the bed stand, trying hard to avoid commenting any more on the invitation. Extending the glass, she said, ''Take this with your pills, and you stay right in that bed.'' I smiled and asked if she wouldn't climb in with me to chat for a while. Wanda couldn't take any more, so she walked away, looking back with a sheepish grin, as close as I got to a guarantee that we would see each other again.

My thoughts moved to the subject of junk and how much I had been using. I thought about how lucky I was to have made it off the rooftop alive and how easily it might have gone the other way to a real DOA. I thought about my mom and pop and how they would react now that my drug use was out in the open and about reducing my habit to get it under control. I thought about the methadone they were already giving me, and about Wanda again, wondering when we would get together for the picnic in the park.

The next morning I woke up to sounds of construction coming from outside the window of the ward. Then Wanda whirled in and her presence immediately took my attention. I decided to play it more reserved, like a nice guy. Before long, it was obvious that she cared about me and was concerned about my habit and what it would do to my health. ''Vinny, you do know that drug can kill you.'' She looked at me directly in the eye. I tried to let it slide, saying, ''Well, lots of stuff can kill you. They say the air in New York is like smoking two packs of cigarettes a day.''

She didn't go for it. ''Vinny, heroin is an addictive substance, and it's a monkey on your back.'' I couldn't get over that one, so I just said, ''I'm not using anything now.'' She went on with my benefit in mind. ''Have you ever heard of Riverside Hospital? They have a special program for detoxifying addicts.'' I said I hadn't and asked her to get me all the details. I also told her I wanted to know more about her, in a personal way. Then I got her phone number.

The next day right after breakfast, a social worker named Mrs. Wentworth came into the ward looking for me. As I raised my hand to let her know who I was, she approached the bed, and I could tell immediately that this lady had been straight as an arrow for her entire life. When she spoke it was in maple syrup, those sweet tones that only come from years of trying to help people from a long distance. She knew most of the jargon associated with disaster but had never been out on the streets for the experience. Mrs. Wentworth described my future in glowing terminology, as a result of admitting myself for detoxification at Riverside. She said sternly that I had no choice but to get rid of this "horrible habit" because it would eventually kill me.

I told her that I was interested in going straight, cleaning up, freeing myself, starting a career, getting ahead, having a family someday, and other things she wanted to hear. She smiled, deeply satisfied that she had reached yet another derelict kid and headed him on the path toward the great American dream. On her note pad she wrote, "Arrange for Marino to detox at Riverside."

Riverside turned out to be an island in the East River in the Bronx, not far from Riker's Island, the penitentiary. As the ferry pulled away from the 138th Street Pier, I felt like a piece of my life was left behind on the bank, but then I found myself looking forward to the experience of withdrawing from junk with the help of professionals. The first building we entered after docking was called the Boathouse, and we checked in there. After that, we were ushered into a room with about fifteen small stalls inside, only big enough to hold one person. Each booth had two hooks to hang clothes and an oak chair against the wall at the far end. A male orderly instructed us to step into one of the booths and strip down. Then he announced we would be getting an enema.

"Shit, an enema," I thought and wondered why. I learned from some other residents that some junkies would voluntarily sign up to come here and would actually have the balls to bring their dope with them. The trick was called "stalls." They would put the drugs into a condom or one of those rubber fingers doctors use, swallow the bag, and shit out the load for use later. Well, the hospital cut off the stalls at the pass. One of the nurses came into the booth with a bedpan in hand and placed it face up on the wooden chair. I was invited to sit down and finish my watery business, right there in front of God and two female nurses so they could check to be sure it contained no condoms full of cocaine or heroin.

The next thing they told us was that the program was going to take three weeks to complete, and they handed everyone a pair of new white pajamas, loose fitting and comfortable, and a robe. The two nurses led the way to another building and we proceeded upstairs to the third floor, formally identified as the

Detoxification Ward. Inside the double doors, we were invited to sit down in the main receiving area. One of the nurses stood up and gave a pleasant, low-key lecture about how they were interested in our health and welfare and that they wanted us to clean up for our own good. The hospital emphasized "good nutrition," she said, and then gave us the location of a twenty-four-hour juice bar. She told us to drink a lot of water and said they would give out pills for sleeping, and methadone three times a day, in steadily decreasing dosages. She told us to spend time rebuilding our bodies, and they would help in any way they could. I already felt a whole lot better even before I checked into my room.

The three weeks went by without a hitch, really, and almost before I knew it. I must have met thirty different guys while I was there from all five boroughs of the city. We exchanged names, crimes, new methods to work on, all the angles, cons, and capers, sometimes what was in the newspapers, and especially where to score "good shit" in each neighborhood. I was furthering my education at the expense of the state and getting healthy in the process.

Twenty days later I felt like a new man. It was a sunny bright Monday when I had my kiss-off shot of methadone, enjoyed a farewell lunch with some of the guys and staff, put on my freshly washed street clothes, shaved, put a shine on my shoes, and got onto the ferry back to the streets of New York. The first thing I did on hitting the beach was to phone Wanda from St. Luke's and ask her about the picnic, but instead we agreed on dinner the next night at eight. I hung up with a grin, thinking of what I hoped to get into with Wanda. I felt clean and good about myself as I got on a train destined for Brooklyn.

When I appeared at the door, momma jumped up full of happiness and hugged me warmly. She immediately started whipping up a big meal, and Frank wanted to know all about how I was. Even little Joey was there for almost half an hour, holding onto my pant's leg, wanting to play. The old man was out losing it somewhere, but that day nobody cared. We joked around and told family stories, and I felt proud enough to announce, "I'm clean now." They were all so happy I felt like taking a bow. Then I figured to go over and see how Hooks was doing.

With that decision came trouble. I hadn't been out of detox at Riverside for three hours, and here I was telling myself, "Just one shot to feel good." Naturally I promised myself I would not get hooked, as I sent the load in. In my drug-filled stupor, I forgot all about momma's good supper back home, which made her cry hard—one more time.

Maybe you weren't aware of the fact that doctors prescribe dope for ordinary people. All you have to do is prove—or claim—you are terminal with something painful such as cancer and you can get a prescription for a drug called dilaudid, a synthetic heroin. Dilaudid gets you off just like the real thing.

In 1955 federal pressure on dope smuggling was so heavy, they cut off about half of the heroin shipments coming into the city. The addicts literally panicked. You would see them rolling around in alleys, vomiting all over themselves. It was at this time that Hooks and I learned the game called "making doctors," which consisted of doing whatever it took to get some croaker to prescribe the good stuff and staying the hell off the streets.

A junkie I knew named Slick told me about a doctor known to write scrips for heavy drugs if the receptionist-nurse was paid up front in cash. I decided to set up an appointment with a call to his office. The woman who answered sounded like she was going to crawl through the wires and get it on with me, she was so sweet and sexy. "God," I thought to myself, "that woman can sure give good phone."

At ten to eleven the next morning, I was getting off the elevator on the fifth floor of a fancy Park Avenue building and thinking about how nice this receptionist was going to be and how easy the doctor would be with the drugs. Behind the door of the doctor's office in the receptionist area sat a woman in her late forties with a big beehive hairdo, weighing in at over two hundred pounds. Sure, she had big tits, but her face was so round that you would have sworn she had jelly beans stuffed into her cheeks and was sucking out the sweetness on the sly. As I walked in, she sang out, "May I help you?" Miss Good Phone in person. Sorry, wrong number.

"Marino. I have an appointment for eleven," I answered crisply. "Oh, yes," she gushed. "That will be fifty dollars for the first consultation, Mr. Marino." I paid as I wondered what kind of act I should put on to make the doctor. I figured to try on something totally new. I walked down the corridor to his office and knocked, and he said to come in. Inside was a little fudge character, about fifty-five, with shifty eyes and big horn-rimmed glasses. He looked up from his seat and said he was Doctor Perkins and offered me a chair.

He instructed me to take off my shirt and then checked my blood pressure and heartbeat and looked with a light in my nose, ears, and throat. He told me to put my shirt back on and walked back to his chair behind the desk. As he sat down, I was wondering who was to say what next, but the doctor broke the ice. "What's the problem? What do you need?" I leaned forward and gripped the handrests, looking him straight in the eye. "They tell me I'm dying of cancer, and I'm in constant pain. I need dilaudid."

Perkins scribbled on a pad as he said, "Certainly. Certainly. No pain. No pain." He handed me the paper, and I thanked him for the audience. He had written the scrip for thirty dilaudids, which was really nice of the guy, so I thanked him again and backed out, closing the door. When I got back to the waiting room, I noticed Good Phone's purse sitting right down beside her, so I figured to take a shot and see if I could go south with it. I told her the doctor wanted to see her in his office for something. In a thoughtless second she went for it and took off waddling down the hall. Lightning fast I lifted her wallet and a new pad of blank scrips, printed with the doc's name, address, and phone number. I was out the main door and into the elevator before she had even reached his office.

My reward came in two doses. The first was cold cash. I got back my $50 for the office call, plus a bonus of another $125. Not bad for thirty minutes time. The next dose had to do with those scrips. I had memorized and practiced the doctor's handwriting and the way the scrip read. The dilaudid was good, but we ran out soon. Hooks and I had done some, sold some, and gave the others away. I was fairly loose at the time, since money was not a particular problem—drugs were the problem.

Hooks volunteered to imitate the doctor's formula on paper, and I strolled into a busy pharmacy at the corner of Broadway and Fifty—third in Manhattan with the prescription. The pharmacist behind the counter informed me as he took the paper, "There's going to be at least a thirty-minute wait." All I thought was that was the price you had to pay these days, waiting for your drugs to appear as if by magic from over the counter. I walked across the street and into a pizza joint, where I ordered one with pepperoni.

Well who would have figured that this same druggist had been hit with forged scrips three times in the past ten days, each one calling for dilaudid? That tripped his warning switch as soon as he saw it. Then he heard from Good Phone that the prescription was a phoney, so guess who met Marino after the pizza and before he could burp, and who else was back in the slammer?

I started to get spooked when I learned the penalty for forging a prescription for narcotics was not less than one year in prison. But my lawyer and I were hanging onto two technicalities, hoping to save my ass: the scrip was not in my handwriting, and the detective arrested me *before* I took delivery of the drugs. My lawyer recommended that we cop a plea before the judge.

The judge looked down at me hard, then sternly pronounced the position of the state as it related to my position. "Mr. Marino, this is serious business. I don't like what I see on this card about your past, and frankly I am not thrilled with the prospect of having you on the streets to continue with drugs much longer. So I am going to offer you a choice, Mr. Marino. You can go to Riker's Island Penitentiary for one to three years, or you can enlist in the Army and learn some proper discipline from them, in which case I will drop this charge from a felony to a misdemeanor and suspend sentence."

The next thing I knew, I was trading in my tailored suit for an olive-green standard uniform issued by the United States Army at Fort Dix, New Jersey. Before reporting in, I had turned all my available cash and goods into more than seven hundred dollars of the best junk I could find so I could make damn sure the Army didn't get to me either. At times it was tough, because I was anything but ready for what was coming down. That was in March of 1956. Korea was over and nobody knew where Vietnam was yet. I was flying high about ninety percent of the time under the influence of junk, so I didn't need to hear all that "Hup, two!" shit in my ears. They wanted me to run around buildings, do pushups, then pick up butts, play march and run, carry a gun, fix bayonets, and jump in and out of used tires just for the exercise.

Bored as hell, I crawled away one day, heading for the sick bay. The first time in I complained of a fever after running the thermometer up to 102 degrees by rubbing it on my pant's leg. In the end, I conned a croaker into giving me what was called an "L-3 Profile," which meant no waking, standing, or marching for more than five minutes at a time. I convinced the guy that my feet were flat, and with that I ended up in a bunk where I belonged, while all the other booties were out there in the freezing New Jersey air doing whatever bizarre bullshit the Army would order up to keep everybody busy.

Since I became a regular on sick call, I never got through the basic parts of what they had scheduled as an eight-week training session. Instead, I got "recycled" (which meant "send him back through!"), but that didn't bother me because I was usually high, not doing much more than occupying a bunk with my veins full of dope. It got so bad at one point that the base commander called my pop in for a discussion. The brass told pop that I was way the hell behind par as far as military bearing went. Pop cracked my face with a backhand and told me to "act like a man" before he took off. In the end, I was cycled through seven full or partial basics, which took over nineteen weeks, before they finally gave up and handed me graduation papers and some orders, including two weeks leave before reporting for duty at Fort Eustis, Virginia.

At Fort Dix, I saw a lot of easy marks come and go through the basic sessions, and it was easy to get them caught up in a game of craps or cards. Before I left I wound up winning nearly two thousand dollars in cash and a 1948 fire-engine red Cadillac convertible. Even pop's eyes bulged with excitement when I drove up in that Cadillac and parked it on the street in front of our building, but I didn't have a driver's license at the time, since I wasn't eighteen yet. Frank came running out of the house and asked me if he could drive. He got in behind the wheel, and we were off, waving to everyone who was watching and blowing the horn, a little crazy. We were laughing and talking and having a good time. It sure was good to be home. That night I went over to Hook's place to see how he was doing, and we both got totally loaded and sat around drinking Cokes.

When I arrived at Fort Eustis two weeks later, I found quite a few other guys who were into junk like me. One of them was the CO of the outfit, and he would check me in on Friday night for the whole weekend, when I would actually be on a bus to New York where I would cop for the crew and return Sunday evening. But during the week it got harder and harder to stay out of the way. I figured to repeat the "sick call" routine just like in basic, but it didn't work very long, I would show up after getting loaded, but by the fifth day the medics flat refused to see me. The shit hit the fan early one morning when I countered their move by refusing to respond to reveille.

A sergeant came storming into the barracks and started banging on my bunk demanding that I "hit it on the double!" Without bothering to come out from under the pillow, I rolled over and told him, "Look, do me a favor. If there's a war on, call me. If there's not, leave me the fuck alone. I ain't runnin' around no buildings today." Old Sarge couldn't quite believe what he had heard, so he went over his head in the chain of command and called in a second lieutenant. This guy came in with the, "Okay, Marino, up and at 'em" routine. I told him that if they gave me a gun again, I was gonna figure there was a "war on somewhere and start shootin'!" They didn't think my position was very well suited to a career in the Army, so they drew up the necessary papers in two days, and I was mustered out with an undesirable discharge.

I figured everything had come down just fine. After all, the judge didn't say how long I had to stay in the Army, so I was out on that one—and with no parole and no probation.

Just before Christmas of 1956, the heroin fad was catching on like wildfire on the streets of New York. A whole fleet of dope fiends were into the cattle rustling caper, and some were openly heisting cigarettes, which had been our primary source. One night I had just scored some junk on a street corner near a Roman Catholic church in the Flatbush section of Brooklyn. Since I was in a hurry to get off and check the quality, I asked the church priest if I could use the bathroom in the rectory. He didn't particularly like the idea but finally agreed and showed me the room.

I got behind the door and locked it. After shooting up, I put away the works and was into the familiar warm glow-world as I emerged from the bathroom. The priest hadn't waited around to see me out the door, which turned out to be a fatal mistake for the Romans. On the wall near the front hallway was a series of pigeon-hole boxes all full of envelopes. I helped myself to about thirty of them and hustled out the door. When I saw that the haul from them totaled over four hundred dollars, I couldn't wait to get back and tell Hooks. I had just found a new business.

In working a church, the hardest part was getting inside the rectory. Typically, Hooks would knock first and go into his act for the day. Either he was thinking of killing himself, quitting school, joining the priesthood, or some other drastic move that required attention. The priest would invite him into an office for a discussion. Once Hooks was inside, I would knock, usually to be received by the caretaker who would ask me to wait since the priest was "now tied up in a meeting with somebody else." That was like issuing me a license to steal, and I went straight into action.

Just about every rectory we got into had money all over the place. Every drawer of the bureaus in the priests' rooms had either money or jewelry or both. The pigeonholes full of envelopes destined for favorite causes or charities were everywhere. In some of the larger parishes they even had special rooms to count the money, including huge machines that separated coins. Once I turned on a machine like that and walked out with a sack full of quarters totaling nineteen hundred dollars.

We stayed away from synagogues and protestant churches, thinking if one of them nabbed two Italian Catholics, they would pursue it to the ends of the earth. I figured that even if they caught me red-handed, the priests would never prosecute an Italian adolescent, and certainly not a kid from one of their own neighborhood churches. My operating rationale was that Jesus was a carpenter and so was his father, but they never bothered to build a church. Yet, there I was, standing in a huge cathedral with expensive stained-glass windows and matching bells and solid gold chalices when brass would have done just as well. Besides, I figured, those guys had an endless supply of money, stocks, bonds, and real estate, all tax free, so I was just robbing a little from the bigger thieves. Our little business had nothing to do with God.

At the time I was knocking around with a cute girl named Angele. She was a good kid from Brooklyn, but she was on junk, and she liked me to cop for her. Females are notoriously easy to take off, especially in a dope deal. So it was that I planned to work Angela into my church act. She had the face of a saint when she looked right, and it was tough to deny her things when she looked you square in the eye with a sad story. We would get dressed up and ring the bell at a rectory picked at random, right around seven-thirty or eight o'clock in the evening—counseling time.

The priest would typically invite us into the reception area and ask us what we wanted. What we wanted, of course, was his solution to a particular problem. "Well, Father, it seems that we can't seem to agree about children. She wants them now, and I think we ought to wait a while until our checkbook looks better."

At that point Angela would flash her eyes in anger and point her fingers at me, right past the priest. "That wasn't what you said when I married you!"

Most priests couldn't wait to don the cap of fatherly advice. "Listen, my children," he would plead, "let's sit down and talk about this quietly." Angela would come back sharply. "I won't talk with him here. He won't listen to me anyway!" The priest would attempt to relieve the pressure. "Perhaps you should wait here for a few minutes," and point me to a chair, while he went with Angela into another room. Boom, my number was done, and our bankbook sure did look a lot better. I would say we hit about thirty-five different churches in each of the five boroughs over a period of two or so years without ever getting caught. The total in dollars could be well over a hundred thousand, but of course we spent it as quickly as we got it so that's a rough estimate.

5 / Crazed Addict

It was about that same time in 1956 when I made the final turn into a crazed addict—I was totally gone. Hooks and I never thought of morality anymore. Our whole trip was to get into an insulated shell from the outside world using dope and to stay there. We mixed heroin with cocaine, we mixed heroin with disoxyn, and whenever we ran out temporarily, we were not above drinking a bottle of cough medicine with codeine to wash down three or four doridens.

Christmas-Eve of that year my mom was all excited because the family was together for the occasion. She planned for us to attend midnight Mass at the cathedral, then come home for a big turkey dinner. Lots of other family members were going to be there, and mom pleaded with me, "Vinny, this is Christmas and everyone will be here. Whatever you do, stay away from that stuff for me, please?" Actually I had been thinking about getting loaded all night, and my mind drifted onto a possible connection at that hour in the neighborhood, since riding all the way up to East Harlem was out of the question. I reassured mom as I went out the door at about ten o'clock. "I won't do anything, momma, I just want to check on a couple of the guys and wish them a Merry Christmas." I swore on every saint I could remember that I would be "back by eleven" as I closed the door and hit the street.

Dressed in my Sunday best, I walked briskly up to Fourteenth Avenue, where I had heard a new "tip" was forming—a group of guys from another neighborhood who were into the same scene. I spotted a guy I knew named Vince sitting in a diner. As

I sat down next to Vince I noticed how stoned this guy across from us was. Vince said there wasn't much around to cop except what his friend over there had just shot, and he didn't know exactly what that was. There wasn't much time before the family would be leaving for Mass, so I urged Vince to see if I couldn't get three of the pills. Whatever they were, I'd take them.

Vince connected me within minutes to a guy named Antique, whose name fit his face: very old, very worn, and very tired. Antique had all the markings of a fine black walnut, with those deep bags running out from his eyes and lines shooting over the entire distance of his forehead. Even the smile wrinkles at the edges of his mouth were burnt black. He showed me some pills that could have been dilaudid or maybe morphine. I couldn't tell exactly, and Antique didn't "know from nothing" except they were the ones the guy in the diner had taken minutes earlier. I figured if he had taken one, I would need at least three to catch a buzz before Midnight Mass.

Antique sold them for a buck apiece. Since we were in his basement, I cooked up and borrowed his works for the shot. When the unknown dope was ready, I tied off and sent it all in, for Christmas, you know, like a celebration. Nothing happened and I complained. Antique begged for a little more time. We both walked out of the basement and up to the street, where a plastic Christmas caroler was hung onto a telephone pole by the borough.

No more than half a block later a weird feeling hit me, but it wasn't like a junk high. It was hallucinogenic, like acid or the sensation of taking too much speed. Then things started to slow way down, but the sounds were hellish to hear, ringing around in my ears. I must have looked like a zombie. Each slow-motion foot that hit the ground would "slap" the sidewalk, and I couldn't figure out why. When I reached the curb, it looked eighty feet down to the street. God only knows how I stumbled home safety. Finally at my own front door, I could only think to ring the bell by leaning against it. Naturally, momma was the first to respond. She took one look at me and went into deep shock as I murmured, as if mortally stabbed but really only stoned to the gills, "I-need-wa-ter—"

She led me hurriedly past the family parade in the living room with my feet dragging behind. Once inside the bedroom, mom leaned me against the wall and she prayed to God for guidance while she peeled off my dress jacket, and I slid incoherently onto the bed sideways. Mom held back her tears as she picked up both my feet and put me completely on the mattress. After she made sure I was okay, the whole family went off for the Savior's birthday Mass, where they prayed even harder for my salvation. God knows I needed help desperately, but the next day I was looking for a way to score more of Antique's unknown pills.

Addicts referred to overdosing as "falling out," and I fell out in some of the craziest circumstances. Once I went so far as to go out in a "shooting gallery" up in East Harlem. A shooting gallery is a rented room or an abandoned building that some dope fiend opens and then brings in a few sets of works. They rent the works for fifty cents or a dollar to any junkie who wants to use a set. The unwritten law is that you come in, pay up, do your business, and hit the streets. Some busy galleries would entertain as many as a couple of hundred "customers" on a daily basis, so there was absolutely no opportunity to sit around and nod out inside the place. Of course, that rule held for everyone but me one day in February 1957. First I fell down, then I fell out and was dragged down to a storeroom to sleep it off in an empty refrigerator carton.

Once I knew a guy from another neighborhood in Brooklyn named Gino. He was a musician and a fair one at that, good enough to form a small band and get a gig at a club in Flatbush. The band members always seemed to have quality dope around, so one day we headed over to Gino's to see what we could find to get our heads straightened out. Gino was sitting around practicing some songs and waiting for a new load to arrive. He said he'd be happy to sell us some when it came down since he had bought half an ounce.

The junk arrived in about an hour, but Hooks had gotten tired of waiting after about forty minutes, so he had gone out to pick up some cigarettes and soda. Gino and I went into the kitchen and got off. The last thing I remembered Gino saying was, "Wow! This is fucking dynamite!" When Hooks got back five or ten minutes later, we were both out cold on the floor. Hooks damn near panicked since Gino lived with his folks and three younger sisters, but he thought fast and took the works, then stashed the rest of the stuff in his pants before carrying me out the door to a cab on the corner. Two blocks away, he had the cabbie stop while he called an ambulance for Gino.

I slept off the night in a heavy fog, and the next day I learned that Gino was dead. They had found him on the kitchen floor, right where we left him. The obituary read heart attack since the family was obviously anxious to cover his real tracks. Three days later Hooks and I felt obligated to pay our respects, as it would have been conspicuous if we had stayed away. I went with mixed feelings of guilt and concern about myself. Inside the funeral home, everyone was full of grief and open prayer for Gino, who had just turned eighteen. His mother was sobbing openly, and as I reached the coffin to wish Gino well, thanking God or whomever that "there but for the grace would be me," Gino's mom came up and put her hand on my shoulder. "Vinny, whatever you do, don't fool with that stuff, please. For God's sake." I didn't know if she suspected anything.

After leaving the wake, Hooks and I said nothing. What could we say that would possibly make any difference? Besides our guts were wrenching in pain. We jumped a cab to go downtown and get loaded, forgetting everything else along the way.

Right after my DOA and the Christmas incident, my brother Frank started to come down hard on my case whenever he thought I was stoned, pleading, "Vinny, what do you think you're doing besides killing yourself?"

"Hey, I tried some weird stuff for a kick, like everybody else, but nothing regular," I said. I told him he was badly mistaken and frankly full of shit in mentioning "habits." Besides, I intended to end up as a well-connected made-man one day, and soon. Frank came back at me flatly with, "Brother, you know the organization doesn't have anything to do with dope fiends, faggots, or stool pigeons." No, I hadn't thought about it that way. When I did consider my lifelong dream since the shoeshine days on the street, I said to Frank, "Those days are over, like I said." I felt heavy inside with the final gut realization of knowing I was not to be a made-man. But I figured, "Fuck the mob and fuck Frank, too. Just get your head together, one more time."

Two or three days after that conversation, Frank had to break down our bathroom door because he smelled something foul as hell burning. First he knocked hard and fast but got no response. Then he shouted, "Hey, Vinny! You in there?" The odor got stronger as the minutes passed, and he blasted in, using his shoulder.

Frank couldn't quite believe what he saw. Our bathroom had a steam radiator standing up against the wall about two feet in front of the commode. I had lowered the lit to sit down, and after I got off, I immediately knew the junk was much too powerful as I saw the familiar blackness closing in. My first thought was to make it into the bedroom, but it was too late. With the needle still in my vein, all I could manage was a slight lean forward, ending up with my right arm pressed against the radiator, which had just started to warm up.

Forty-five minutes later Frank first picked up the smell. In the next ten, both the shirt and my flesh were smoldering, and he almost fainted with the grim scene and the odor. There was Vinny breathing shallow in a deep overdose, with his arm burning and a needle stuck in it at the same time.

He shook me viciously and nothing happened. He cursed me like hell, but I never heard the words. He splashed cold water on my face, and that made no difference. He hoisted me up and walked me around, after which I fell back on the floor. I don't remember any of this. Four and a half hours later, something finally came into my mind—a sharp pain, and it was everywhere. I couldn't move my body and just barely opened my eyes. From off in the distance an angry, high-pitched voice was lashing out full of fury. "Christ Almighty, Vinny," Frank was intense. "Don't you see what you're doing to yourself?" He held up my bad arm to make me look at it, but I wasn't focusing clearly. Frank shook the burnt limb. "Look what you did to yourself, burned to shit. You're better off dead than to be the way you are now."

Between the hits of the hammers in my head, I thought, "Frank, why don't we just start with a fix, and then I'll die peacefully, later." But I said nothing out loud and faded off to another meeting with total blackness. Apparently, they called a doctor from across the street who put some salve on the burn and bandaged my arm.

In what seemed to me like a flash but was actually more than an hour on the clock, Frank busted back into the room and started banging two suitcases around, with pop right behind him. Even I could see that Frank's emotions were somewhere between total outrage and crying out of love, when he said: "We're going away, Vinny." He turned and walked to the front of my bureau. "You and me and pop, and as soon as we're established we'll send for mom and Joey." I couldn't even raise my head, so I just leaned his way and said, "I can't go anywhere, Frank. I'm sick." Frank opened one of the suitcases, then looked up at me and shouted: "Fuck your bullshit, Vinny! We're going!" And with that he stuffed my belongings into the bag.

I was hardly in a position to offer stiff resistance to anything, yet I couldn't help giving it a try, so I said, "Okay, Frank, let's leave tomorrow. By then I'll feel better." With that pop barked, "We're going away, Vinny, so you just shut up. We're taking you out of this, right now. Maybe you can get your head straightened out away from here." Pop left me with no alternative but the last ditch one-liner. "Pop, I *gotta* go see some guys first, on business. Then we'll leave. I promise." Neither of them bought my bullshit, I could tell.

"No way, Vinny. We're starting a new life, and we're starting it *today*." After loading everyone's bags into Frank's car, they proceeded to stand me up and lead the way out the front door, one on each arm. I thought of bolting, but my feet were dragging, and I just got pushed into the back seat where they laid me down flat. Pop got in front and Frank started to drive headed due south. I sensed the beginning of a long and painful trip.

By the time we reached the Pennsylvania turnpike, I was sick as a dog and emptied my guts in a series of brown paper bags. In North Carolina, I could only remember some signs and my sweat, plus the fact that pop and Frank had long ago stopped listening to me plead for mercy. They turned the radio up so that it drowned out my continuous complaints.

They finally stopped at a burger joint somewhere in South Carolina, and I thought to take off in the other direction for the city and some dope, but the pain was too much and I stayed where I was, sprawled in the back seat. Sometimes I rolled off onto the hump of the floor, as a diversion from the agony. We crossed the Georgia border at seventy-two miles an hour. It was the first time I had managed to sit up and see the speedometer since New York. Then the sign came up, "Welcome to Georgia . . . The Peach State." Just the thought of eating a peach made me each for another brown paper bag. Frank imitated Sinatra while I retched for an hour, and pop whistled along as if he was real happy for one of the first times in his life. The next thing I knew Frank was stopping. From somewhere I heard the pounding surf, and they opened the doors and tilted the seat forward, then jerked me on my feet, urging me to "get out of the car."

I felt like getting back in my shell, with just one more fix, but I couldn't do anything. Somehow they managed to lift me by the feet and carry me about forty feet to drop me in the water. When the first wave hit, I could only crawl back up on all fours, like a groveling dog. Before I could shake dry, the next wave crashed in, knocking me down in the sand. In just under thirty-seven hours, we had traveled from the Big Apple to the city limits of South Miami Beach, Florida. Once there, we started to look for a place to stay. Pop did the driving and Frank did the checking, while I did most of the bitching from the back seat. But Frank was all lit up, bright as hell, and kept saying over and over, ''Hey, you guys! A new life! New lifestyles!''

Within three hours of hitting town, Frank came out of a hotel with a true Marino smile on his face. He beamed into the car. ''It's a real nice setup, with a living room, two bedrooms, and kitchen. Not only that, here's the sweet part. An old lady owns the hotel, so if we take care of the pool and the grounds, it's ours for only fifteen bucks a week.'' With that, pop started to unload the bags, and Frank paid off the room, while I stumbled toward the number he had indicated would be ours.

Except for the whine of the pool filter next door, it wasn't all that bad, and we cleaned up in the process. Two weeks after we got there, pop had signed on as a porter at the hotel, Frank was keeping up about half an acre of grounds surrounding the place, and I was off drugs and on duty as the official lifeguard, swimming instructor, and pool cleaner at the hotel as well. Then, at various opportune times, I burglarized the rooms of selected hotel guests, using a plastic card on the lock while they were busy sunbathing at the pool.

Before a month had gone by, I was familiar with most of the big hotels in Miami Beach, and it was then that I first noticed another breed of shark than the ones swimming around in the water. Sitting at marble tables under sun umbrellas, these sharks played cards, mostly poker. I started watching over shoulders, and saving my money for the $300 buy-in to the game. Within five weeks after we set foot in Miami Beach, things were looking up, and we all felt pretty bright. I was still clean and had $325 in my pocket ready for the poker game. Frank had become a good groundskeeper, and pop enjoyed the hustle of the bellboy job. After work he usually went off to the dog races at the track.

As the eighth week wound up, I was into a winning streak at the game, which I played twice a week at first and then damn near every day. As time went on and the deck got better to me, I neglected the pool more and more, so Frank and pop got out there in the hot sun and did the pinch-sweeping.

One night at poolside under the stars, the deck was hot in my favor. Suddenly I saw this young fox walk in, so full of allure I was forced to dump my hand and beg off to go wash up. When I stood and turned from the table, she nodded and I caught her with my eyes, indicating a meeting in back. She picked up the whole thing and appeared at the hotel bar five minutes later. She sat down first, after sizing up both me and a stool. "You're some player," she said smiling, "and my name is Anna."

It was hard to believe how well her name fit this sultry, Latin-looking girl. I could tell she was mighty young, but her firm breasts pushed hard against the flimsy blouse. Reaching for her hand, I kissed the back ever so softly and said, "Anna, my pleasure. I'm Vinny, and we will see just how good a player I am, especially with you." Anna didn't stop there. In fact, she called to the bartender and turned towards me. "Vinny, would you like a drink to relax?"

"I can think of better ways to relax than over a drink here in the open bar," I said in my sweetest Sicilian-plus overtones. Anna came right along, obviously enjoying the charge going between us as we played that "first time together song." She sang in my ear, "Let's meet somewhere away from here."

"Where and what time?"

She wrote down the name of a place and gave me a couple of hours to get there. I edged my hand around her waist and concentrated on the soft nipples that were plainly visible, since I was kissing her neck and looking down from there. A minute later I sat back down somewhat nervously to play a few more hands with those jokers before shooting off to meet Anna. At nine-thirty sharp, I used an excuse and got out of the game, after silently counting about eight hundred extra sitting with my pile of chips.

Anna was right where she said she would be, which pleased me and I let her know by saying, "Anna, it's so good to see you again. It's been too long." To my amazement, she picked it right up, as if we were lost lovers reunited. "Vinny, with me time isn't important." As she reached out to put her arms around me, the sleeves of her blouse pulled up to reveal telltale marks. I couldn't believe it—Anna was a junkie.

It didn't bother me much after the initial shock, since I confronted her with it, and she copped to the truth. Anna was actually a seventeen-year-old hooker. She had come in with a character from the Bronx because he had paid her two hundred in cash to sit there and look good, then deliver the full evening's pleasures later on. After she met me, she arranged to deliver the following night. He knew she was good for the trick.

She was going to be good for me too, I was thinking as we traversed Miami in search of her latest connection. We were looking for Sanchez, a Mexican who had been her pimp at one point. That was a year ago when she was on the streets before "graduating" to the hotels and developing her own black book, with all the johns and what they paid. We passed a Spanish joint, and Anna signaled me to slow down since she thought she saw someone familiar inside who could point us to her connection. I did a U-turn and left her with the passenger side up against the curb so she could call out. "Is Sanchez around?" she asked.

"If he is, try the pool hall."

Sure enough, Sanchez was inside the pool hall, and Anna emerged in less than five minutes. We could meet Sanchez at his place in a quarter of an hour to score three ten-dollar bags. I was nearly delirious with the thought of the good things that were about to come down. We scored from Sanchez then headed off towards South Miami Beach again, laughing and stroking each other, kissing at all the stops. This was going to be real juicy, I could tell. Sanchez had sworn on his snakeskin cowboy boots that the dope was "pure dynamite." It dawned on me then that we had no works with us, but I had one set hidden in my shoes back at the hotel. Frank had packed it inadvertently when he kidnapped me from my last overdose at our apartment.

When we arrived at the hotel, I was surprised to find no one home since it was 11:30. Anna went in the door before me and headed straight for the bathroom with the bags, which was exactly what I had figured. I headed straight for the closet and my shoe. In less than three minutes we were cooking up, kissing each other over the flame in wild anticipation for any number of warm events. She was kind enough to tie the belt around my arm. I loaded the eye-dropper and got off. Then I tied her arm, found a vein, and sent it straight in. I could tell when the warm glow hit us, square in the pit of our stomachs. Next thing Anna and I were in bed, rolling around up in heaven, maybe even a little higher. We were moving together in a sweet and slow rhythm.

Right then Frank made one of his classic entrances. I thought I heard the door open but was so far away in space with Anna that I didn't even roll over when he pulled off the sheet, revealing the action beneath. Even then I still didn't realize Frank had just been added to the room, but he was totally pissed off, especially when he saw the works and the last bag sitting on a nightstand next to the bed. He picked up the bag and starting yelling, "What's this shit?" And then he threw it at us.

I couldn't do anything but laugh. That did it for Frank. He grabbed a suitcase from the closet, bitching about how much work he had done for me on the pool, plus his own job, and now there I was all fucked up on heroin again, with some "cheap broad" to boot. "I'm going home, Vinny," he yelled. In my stoned condition, I wondered why Frank thought the shit had hit the fan just over that. Anna rose to the question indirectly, taking my mind way off and onto her again. We made loud murmuring noises, and Frank just kept on packing his bags. We exchanged "Oh, Gods!" and "Oh babies!" beneath the sheet while Frank changed his shoes on the edge of the bed. The springs squeaked as we moved in passion, and it was about then that Frank walked out, muttering as he slammed the door.

The next day when I got dressed I found that Frank had left without his keys, but damned if he'd back off that traditional Sicilian pride long enough to ask me for them. Instead, he cabbed it to the airport and boarded a plane back to New York. When I told pop at breakfast that Frank had pulled out, he didn't seem at all surprised. "I think Frank was homesick, for momma, Joey, and the city. "Jesus," I thought, "let's hope so. Surely Frank wouldn't take off just because I slipped up once and got loaded."

About two weeks later things started to come apart for me and pop too. First off, the summer slump was coming on, and the hotel owner sadly informed pop that he was through carrying bags at least until November or December. Then pop was picked up one night by the bulls for "failing to register as an ex-convict with a felony conviction." In truth, the old man wasn't violating any law since his conviction had occurred more than ten years before, but the cops saw fit to hassle him about "falsifying information on the registration card."

At that time in Miami Beach—and perhaps today—city officials tried to prevent "undesirables" from settling in their famous stretch of beachfront. To do this, they issued a "police card" for work clearance and, of course, no ex-con could get one, but you couldn't work on the beach without one either—

Catch-22. Pop's case was eventually cleared, but he ended up thoroughly pissed off with the treatment he got.

Then one night I lost twelve hundred in a one-on-one at table-stakes poker. I swear the opposition had an ace up his sleeve, but I didn't move fast enough to prove anything. I ended up with no chips and sour grapes in my pockets for the long trip back to the hotel. The very next morning I was lounging at poolside, reading over the *Miami Herald* when I noticed a familiar picture. The caption said the man, one Juan Dominguez, had been arrested for "possession of narcotics with intent to sell." I swore that the man was Anna's connection, Sanchez.

That night I arranged to meet Anna, and she confirmed my worst suspicions. Sanchez had indeed been busted, and her name was implicated since her phone number was in his contact book. It seemed that a major drug crackdown was taking place in Miami because it had become the major port of entry for a significant portion of South America's drug smugglers.

It was a Sunday morning when pop and I sat down over brunch to discuss our present condition and plans for the future. First we spoke of the likelihood of jobs. We sat back to reflect on where to go next, since I figured we could survive anywhere. Within minutes, there was a flash of visual communication between us, and I spoke first. "What say we go back to New York, see momma and Frank and Joey." Pop's eyes lit up, and we were ready to go, except for packing and some final farewells.

Anna and I met to say goodbye, although she didn't know it at the time. She seemed nervous and drained when she sat down. "Things are coming apart, Vinny. I don't know why." I could see real problems up ahead for Anna as the junk got harder to score and she went out on dangerous limbs in that desperate attempt to keep up her habit. When I left her off that night at her apartment, I handed her ten bags of Mexico's best heroin to tide her over until her next safe connection could be located. I didn't have the guts to tell her I was leaving so I just said goodnight.

Next morning pop and I loaded our bags into the car. I shot back to the room and cooked up in the bathroom for a fix to carry me partway to New York. By the time I got back into the car I was sailing off in never-never land where reality seemed so distant and meaningless. Pop smiled and got behind the wheel. I got the feeling after a while on the road that pop suspected I was using drugs again but couldn't be exactly sure, so he didn't want to upset our relationship with any hasty accusations. At least not then. He asked me, "Vinny, how are you feeling?" Without thinking, I said as I rubbed my hand on his shoulder, "Great, pop. Never better. And you?"

Pop gripped the wheel with both hands and stared straight up the road. "I'm not sure, Vinny. I'm alright myself, but sometimes I worry about your momma, Frank, Joey, and especially you. What about the drugs, Vinny?"

I told him, "Those days are in the past," just as I reached the height of the junk running in my veins. Pop let it go, as if there was no point in pursuing the subject, and we turned out discussion to the weather in Miami as compared to New York and then onto various games of chance.

In what seemed like next to no time, we got our official Georgia welcome back with the Peach State sign at the state border. Out of the corner of my eye, I noticed the speedometer pushing above the seventy mark. Ten miles farther we picked up a highway patrol car. I turned around to look through the back window and said to pop, "Hey, we have a bull back there on our tail." The old man already knew, but to my amazement he held it at seventy-two as if the cop wasn't there.

"Hey, pop, did you hear me? There's a cop back there." Without a word, pop stiffened his arms as we roared away from the bull wagon behind us. That did the trick. The blue light came on, flashing in a circle, and I thought I could hear the faint wail of his siren. We were hitting at least ninety with the bull about three-fourths of a mile behind when pop jerked hard on the wheel toward a gas station up ahead on the right hand side. The car swerved, bounced once, and then came to a screeching halt. Even before we came to a full stop, pop bounded out his door, moving faster than I had ever seen him go, headed straight for the men's restroom. I looked back through a ball of red dust to see what was coming.

For a split-second I imagined we had lost the cop, but he soon drove up through the dust, sliding into the station next to our car on pop's side. He struggled to get out, holding onto the roof with his left hand as he pushed his heavy weight up from the seat. As he came toward our car, he grinned revealing yellow teeth and hitched his holster belt up but failed to get it over his inner-tube belly. He cocked the hat upwards and held onto the peak as he asked, "Say, son, are yew thuh driver of this heah car?" I said the minimum. "No, sir." The bull looked in the window and across the seat at me directly. "Well, wheah thuh hail is he?" To save the moment, pop came out of the men's room, and the bull turned to question him. "Were yew drivin' this?" he leaned on the fender and looked at pop.

Pop hitched up his belt tight and said, looking down, "That's right, officer." The cop reached for his pad, but before he could get it, pop broke into an anguished, "Ooooooo!" and held his ass, as if in terrible pain. Then he whirled and returned to the safety of the men's room. The cop looked at me again, puzzled. I threw my hands in the air and shrugged, as if I were a hitchhiker and knew from nothing.

Within two minutes, pop came out again, looking apologetic and fumbling with his belt, as if to buckle up. The bull started to recite the violation. "Yew wuz doin' seventy-seven miles an hour, an' ah can't let that kinda thang happen in mah county." Pop looked as if he was going to give his excuse, but instead he spun again and ran for the restroom, holding onto the seat of his pants and moaning.

Pop came out the third time, pulling his belt tight with one hand, while the other was covering his backside. Before the cop could say anything, pop cut in with, "You see, sir, it's a bad case of diarrhea. I was just making a run for the men's room."

The cop's whole case deflated like a pricked balloon. "Huh?" was all he could manage before pop went into his wail one more time and bolted for the restroom, slamming the door. Meanwhile, I was cracking up behind the windshield. It was all I could do to contain a burst of open laughter. The bull started shifting his weight from one cow-leg to the other, not really knowing what to do. Bang on the door? No. Shoot through it? No. He finally just took off his trooper hat and the dark glasses, then proceeded to wipe the sweat off his face with one of those bandanna hankies so popular down south.

Pop came out into the open air again and looked straight at the bull. "Well, officer, you see, I hope, why we were in such a hurry." Pop displayed his most convincing smile, his eyes pleading for mercy to a fellow man who might understand this human condition. The cop had no real comeback so he muttered, "Wail, no mo' speedin'. Yew okay now?" he asked pop. Pop said he "was better" and then asked the cop where he could get some Jockey shorts in the area since his were ruined by the runs. Incredibly, the bull gave pop some directions to the next town, "first light, then left," and sped off. Pop and I doubled up in laughter, then bought a cold soft drink. After filling the tank, we continued our voyage back to the city, which took less than thirty hours.

Face-to-face with that familiar skyline, we both felt really good and talked about a special meal in Little Italy to celebrate. Secretly, I was planning to look up Hooks and get loaded, find a broad, get a little fruit from a street vendor, and boost enough cigarettes to buy some new clothes for the occasion. It really felt good to be home.

6 / If You Can't Do the Time

The fall of 1958 the streets of New York were hotter than Miami's with pressure coming down from the Feds on drugs. Another panic hit the city, this one a lot heavier than the time before, and people were being sent to the joint like flies. The last straw came when the bulls instituted a clearly unconstitutional statute called a 1533: "loitering for the purpose of obtaining narcotics." It was hard to prove and sounded like nothing— which it was—but that was *after* you spent ten or twelve hours in a lockup, just long enough for an average addict to start getting real sick. The precinct bulls got a big kick out of it. The final irony was that even when people did manage to score some junk, dealers "stepped on it" so heavy with quinine or Manita it wasn't worth buying.

Hooks and I decided to get off the streets altogether. We went into the business of buying written scrips and stealing blank pads full time. Dilaudid was better than the street heroin at that time and a whole lot easier to score. We would shoot for the greedy side of a pharmacist and see what happened. I would take the first legitimate scrip in, and the pharmacist would usually call to verify it with the doctor. Then when he filled the prescription, costing four or five dollars, I would drop a twenty dollar bill and leave the change.

Next day I would come back with the empty bottle and no scrip, saying, "the doctor wasn't in yet, but I need this filled right away. The scrip for it will be ready later today." Again I'd leave a twenty to pay for a five dollar prescription. The third time I'd tell him, "I lost the scrip, but could you please fill it one more time,'' as I waved the twenty before placing it under the bottle. From then on, I would simply walk in, tell to fill it up.

We nicknamed one guy who owned a drugstore on Fourteenth Avenue in Brooklyn ''Dan the Connection.'' He wound up selling us thirty dilaudids a day with no scrip. Finally he couldn't get any more shipped to him until he showed records accounting for the first two thousand tablets. Dan tried to back out of our deal, threatening to call the cops, but he couldn't because of all the drugs he had sold us without prescriptions. He was caught in the swindle and couldn't move. We demanded and got pharmaceutical coke, dilaudid, tuinal, dolophine, desoxyn, methadone, seconal, and benzedrine, plus all the new needles we wanted.

Dan wound up holding a ''Special Storewide Sale'' for two weeks, then apparently absconded with whatever cash he took in. When Hooks and I saw the closed sign on the drugstore for five days running, we looked for angles in another direction.

In the drug world, whenever a caper started to work for a few people, word would spread like lightning. It was like that with our cattle rustling and cigarette boosting, and now with forging prescriptions. Official blank pads were getting stolen like hotcakes. In the beginning, you could cash in a forged prescription like you wound an American Express Traveler's Check. They were as good as gold.

I preferred the game of ''making doctors,'' however, since then it was totally legitimate to carry around dilaudid or whatever. One day I ran across a junkie named Ace cast in the same mold as me—keep your act together and dress well at all times. He told me about a certain doctor who was inclined to write heavy drug prescriptions, but you had to have a story and pay the nurse up front. I figured to give it a try. The next afternoon just before two, I opened the door to Doctor Leachman's office on Fifty-fifth Street in Manhattan. A young receptionist smiled and offered me a seat. She asked my name, address, and phone number, and told me, ''the initial visit will be seventy-five dollars.'' I thought about inflation and the murderous cost of maintaining the lifestyle but not for long. A white-capped nurse emerged from one of the doors off the reception room and said, ''Marino.'' It was time to sell Doctor Leachman.

I followed her into a smaller cubicle, where she asked me to have a seat on the examining table and told me, ''The doctor will be right in to see you.'' Within five minutes the doctor appeared and sat down opposite me and looked directly into my eyes.

"What seems to be the trouble, Mr. Marino?" I figured this had better be real good, with seventy-five bucks riding on the outcome, so I grabbed the edge of the bed and leaned toward him. "Doc, I gotta get this weight off my chest, I gotta tell someone." He crossed his legs and took the bait. "Go on," he said.

I shook my head while looking down and said, "Well, Doc, it all started in Korea. I was stationed there for nineteen months." The doc nodded with sympathy, and I continued, "I was in a foxhole one night with my three buddies. We were up in the frozen part of the north. All of a sudden a mortar shell came whining in and exploded right on the edge of the hole. All three of my buddies were blown to bits. One of them was decapitated." I wrung my hands and dropped my head, shaking it from side to side.

"Jeesus," the doctor whispered, "you must have been . . ."

"Yeah, I was badly wounded, Doc, but no one could reach me for two days. I had a severe concussion and was in tremendous pain. All they could do was give me morphine since they couldn't evacuate me to a hospital for another three days, and they had to keep me quiet because the enemy was all around us. I was in a stupor. The pain was awful, so they kept giving me more morphine," I said as I hung my head even lower. I regained some composure and went on, "To make a long story short, I got hooked on morphine by the time I got out of the hospital. I've almost got it licked now, but I need some help. I can't go to one of the institutions because I have a wife and three kids. Jesus, Doc, what am I going to *do?*"

The croaker had heard enough and came back with, "I can help you." He picked up his pad and wrote me a prescription for thirty-six dilaudids and gave me a nice little talk about the "debt American owed her veterans." As he put his hand on my shoulder to show me the way out, I saw the perfect opportunity to pick up the prescription pad sitting on his desk. Then I was out the door, on my way to a drugstore to cash the legal scrip.

Three weeks later I showed up with a new sheet of Leachman's paper at a Brooklyn pharmacy I had picked at random and had never been in before. What I didn't know was that it had become popular with other paper-hanging junkies, and the bulls had two detectives hiding in the wings, checking out every prescription for dilaudid directly with each doctor before it got filled. Naturally, I had the wrong number. I was arrested and couldn't do a damn thing to get out of it. They had me cold, and I was headed directly to jail.

Some good luck fell in my lap when I got out on bail, but then the other shoe fell when I drew Judge Samuel Leibowitz of Brooklyn Felony Court, the most notorious man when it came for sentencing. My case was set for ten weeks later. I spent most of that time just drifting around from place to place, quietly scoring whatever dope I could and staying off the streets. I didn't want any complications added to the predicament I was already in. And so I was shocked to learn the cops had circulated my mug shot to every pharmacy holding bad paper in all five boroughs. No less than ninety-nine pharmacists positively identified me. That was all it took. I was looking at a formal indictment charging me with ninety-eight counts of "forgery in the third degree: prescriptions for narcotics."

Through the maneuverings of some clever attorneys, I had managed to avoid Leibowitz five times in the past, but when I drew him this time, my lawyer told me there was no way out. I had to get ready to spend some time away from the streets. After all, I had caught the breaks of nine guys till then. This time they caught me in the act, plus another ninety-eight positive IDs from mug shots. I was gone. The feeling was frightening as hell as I became certain I was going to the can. I made a plea bargain with the DA's office to cop to "attempted forgery in the third degree," including "all known and unknown counts." That meant that any other scrip they said I forged prior to my sentencing they could prosecute me for later.

It was also obvious that there was no sense going into the can with a bad habit. I knew the joint was no place to kick a Jones—they had no tolerance and actually treated an addict like an animal there. I went through a connection to see this Doctor Grossman about his Twelve-Day Out-Patient Detoxification Program, which was guaranteed to get you clean for only $250 in cash. All I had to do was show up at the doctor's office once a day for a shot of some unknown substance, then make a short trip down the block to the corner pharmacy for two unnamed white capsules per day, and that was it. It seemed that no one ever questioned the parade of prescriptions that Doctor Grossman was writing every day, but I did hear later that he was arrested for various reasons.

As the courtroom clock stood at ten my next day in court, three junkies, all from different boroughs, waited for sentencing—all on the same charge. It was January 16, 1959, dreary and cold. Not even a month had passed since my twentieth birthday as I sat wondering what kind of a mood Leibowitz was in.

The first junkie was nicknamed Dapper, and he drew a "bullet," slang for one year. I came up next. Incredibly, Leibowitz asked if we didn't want more time before sentencing, in effect offering me another two to three months of freedom on the streets. I just figured, "No, I've had enough of this uncertainty. Let's get it on or get it off." I told my lawyer to go with it right then. So the judge banged his hammer and came down with a call for, "An indeterminate sentence of one to three years at Riker's Island Penitentiary." That meant one year minimum and, depending on behavior, up to three years maximum. My heart sank and my head pounded with fear. The last guy's name was Teddy, and he picked up a five-year stretch at Elmira.

Before we were taken away, I had a free moment with my mom and pop. Momma was crying, and pop didn't know what to say. I figured I wouldn't need my $250 cashmere overcoat, so I handed it to pop and told him to take care of it for me. I told them I was sorry for what happened and would make it up one day. Right then I was looking square in the face of three years behind bars. The feeling was close to that black wall called overdose, and my mouth was dry as I walked to the bull pen ahead of the bailiff.

When Dapper, Teddy and me were together again there, I started bitching about being second. Teddy came straight back and said, "Hey, what about me, Vinny? I drew five years, and I was only looking at fourteen counts. You had over ninety, right?" Yeah, I admitted without saying it out loud that he was right, but my tough-guy image dictated that I not show these guys anything—especially no emotions. The game to play out was, "I'm gonna do the time, not let the time do me. If you play, you gotta pay, or if you can't do the time, don't commit the crime," and other such street bullshit.

After a short while we were handcuffed in pairs. When about ten pairs were ready to leave, we were ushered out the back door of the court to some olive-green vans. The hacks loaded us in, locked the door, and we were on our way to the Brooklyn House of Detention for Men on Atlantic Avenue. The only notable difference between this place and Raymond Street was that the walls weren't four feet thick here, and an elevator took you from floor to floor. Other than that, the general feel and the patterns were the same.

Once again we went through the ritual of ID cards, fingerprints, and "spread 'em." In the cold showers, when the water hit me in the face, I started thinking hard. "Three fucking years of my life.'' It scared the living hell out of me, and my stomach went queasy. I figured I could have accepted a stretch that long for some of my real crimes, but not for a bullshit forgery of prescriptions. Then another lightning bolt of fear hit me as I rode up the elevator to my designated floor. Before long I was in front of a six-by-nine bar cage, and I had just started to consider it when the buzzer hit to admit me and lock me in.

It was Friday night and no way for me to get transferred out to Riker's until at least Monday morning. I paced around the cell, fear-filled as hell, wringing my hands behind my back. What would happen to my mom? What about the rest of the family? How could I keep my sanity? And then I thought about the worst—since I was known as a wise guy, I could get killed in there if I wasn't careful. I started to count up my mixed blessings in a desperate attempt to balance out before I went crazy. ''Well, it could have been five years.'' It occurred to me I might get time off for good behavior, and I thought about maybe twenty months. Of course, that was still six hundred days.

The days of waiting at Brooklyn Detention were boring as hell and a little bit jittery, as I was still kicking a habit. Visitors were allowed from 6:30 to 8:00 nightly, a half-hour session per person. The whole family took turns coming to see me. The visiting room was a series of phone booths open at the back end, with a glass shield up front that blocked any physical contact with your visitor. Each person would pick up a phone and speak through it, but the entire conversation on the prisoner's side was heard by all the hacks in the room, so the talk centered mostly around the family and who-was-doing-what.

As each morning came, I was anxious about them calling my name for the transfer to Riker's Island so the time clock on my sentence could start running. The daily routine was breakfast in your cell, out to the day room for a couple hours to rap, play cards, or sing, followed by lunch and back to your cell. We came back out around two o'clock and stayed until almost four, and then back in our cells for the four o'clock count. The same thing happened after supper, around six. They locked us out again for the day room, where I met several guys I knew or heard about from different neighborhoods.

Each day from Monday through Friday of the following week, I was up at five or six in the morning, hoping to hear I was leaving. But nothing happened all week, and I was facing the possibility of going through another weekend. ''Maybe I'll get a break,'' shot through my mind, almost as a saving grace. Then I switched to, ''Fuck it. I'm a stepper, I'll handle this bit just fine.'' Monday again. On the ninth day of dead time in Brooklyn, a hack came to my cell and whacked the bars with his stick. ''Hit it, Marino. You're leaving today. Roll up your blankets and bring 'em with you.'' Time to ship out for the island in the middle of the East River and the beginning of my three-year bit on the ''Rock.''

It was freezing cold that Monday morning. Since I had given my overcoat to pop, I had nothing to wear but a light sports coat and a white shirt. Handcuffed and waiting for the ferry, the chill ran right through me, and nobody even blinked. As soon as the ferry was away from the dock, they had to open the doors of the van we were in and take the cuffs off. Once a ferry had sunk in the middle of a trip, and twenty inmates drowned because they were handcuffed together inside a van, so a new law had been passed. With that first blast of frigid air out on the open water, reality hit me and everyone else like a ton of falling bricks. Silence was king in the air. Every guy in the van was on his way to opening a new time stretch in the pen. After about twenty-five minutes, we slowed down and pulled up in front of a huge sign at the waterline—''Riker's Island.'' My body temperature felt like it dropped ten degrees as we hit the dock.

After the boat was tied up, we were directed to board some waiting buses with no talking—about sixty guys in all. I sat down behind a wire cage window with my handcuff partner, and we were driven to the main receiving room where everyone was told to sit down and wait for the standard processing. It was the same old shit except for a new one on me. They sprayed us with a foul-smelling delousing liquid to be sure no one carried a disease into the joint. After the spray, it was off to the showers, and after the showers came the uniforms to make our visits official. The adolescents were issued brown, and the adults got prison-grey pants, shirts, and socks. We were then taken to a wire cage and given a choice between clodhopper boots and shoes that looked like toolboxes. I took a pair of shoes.

As I got dressed, it hit me that these guys were dead serious and not in a mood to screw around. Up to that point, I kept thinking that ''something would work out and get me off,'' or ''this ain't real, it's a dream.'' But it was all too real. Vinny Marino was gone—replaced with Marino, Carmine Vincent, #102129. When they gave me that pen number, it hit a string of fear from those ugly toolbox shoes right to the tip of my head. We were led back into the receiving area, and by then I was starving and colder than hell. The hacks came out and announced lentil soup was available. My head thought that all lentil soup was shit, but my stomach ruled and I went for it, eating the whole thing down to the cut-up frankfurters on the bottom. Then they brought a cup of tea, which hit the spot even though I normally drank coffee.

After waiting for the next hour or so, I found myself with seven other young guys being escorted to check in at the adolescent dormitories. The only way to reach our dorm was to pass through the main cell block, and that moment was one of the scariest of my life. The sounds were weird and eerie, like four or five hundred guys crying. And it built to a crescendo of moans and low groans, as if everybody was being tortured. I thanked all the gods for not sending me to serve my stretch there.

My new place of residence was Dormitory Number 3, and it slept about seventy-five guys on bunkbeds in one big room. For a whole bunch of reasons, I felt relieved when my bunk number was finally assigned. All the processing was over, and I could relax for a minute and think about things. A real treat came my way about twenty minutes later when a guy named Angelo appeared and handed me a package, telling me it was from some of the guys. I remembered as I came in I had seen some familiar faces from the different boroughs, but I never figured they knew who I was. They had arranged for a box filled with cigarettes, candy, a toothbrush and toothpaste, razor blade, soap, peanut butter and crackers, and some coffee. I felt like royalty for a minute and began to get more comfortable with my new surroundings.

The first thing each man had to do was find a job within the facility so that the hacks could get ready to give you their "marks." Marks were assigned after you were on the job for 90 to 120 days, and they depended on your involvement, performance, behavior, and attitude toward the joint's standards. If you were sentenced to three years, the marks you got indicated your maximum and minimum stay: for example, 24/18, which meant your maximum time would be twenty-four months, but with good behavior you could get out in eighteen.

A job was open for a captain's clerk, a status position because it was directly under the hack who ran all the adolescent dorms. Dapper, the guy who got sentenced with me, urged me to go for it, saying, "it could help the good people." When it came time to interview for the job, I only had one thing in the experience column, not much at all. I had memorized the standard typing test line of, "Now is the time for all good men to come to the aid of their party." I could rap that out like an electric transmitter but nothing else. Well the captain didn't dictate anything original, so I got the position based on that.

The assignment turned out to be sweet, indeed. Like most hacks, all the guy Watson wanted was no trouble, so he gave me a free hand, and I took over. Within a month, I had changed all the bunk assignments in the four dorms to reflect what the guys wanted, which was strict segregation. There was one group of blacks (or "yams" as we called them), another of Puerto Ricans, and then white guys. We also sat in these groups in the mess halls at separate tables, and everything was going real smooth. It wasn't long, however, before a certain hack, a black guy named Spiker, got a bug up his ass that he wanted us to "cut out this separation and mix it up." He gave that order one night at supper and nobody liked it at all. After the meal when we were back in the dorm, the leaders of each group met and everybody agreed, "Fuck it. We can't go for this. Let's go on strike in the morning."

We sent out word to the other three dorms. The plan was to line up for breakfast as usual with our friends—blacks with blacks, whites with whites, and so on. If the hacks gave us a beef, we would refuse to eat. We came out of the dorms at seven and fell into the unspoken color codes of black first, Puerto Rican second, and whites last. Spiker spotted the segregation and started raising all kinds of hell, demanding that we "shift all around and mix up the colors." We did what he said and passed the word to skip the meal.

Each guy passed through the food line, picked up a tray and a spoon but nothing to eat. Ten minutes later, when the hacks realized what was going on, the bells went off. We were mustered out of the mess area and taken on the march back to the dorms to sit and wait for the trouble we knew was on its way.

Just after eight, a full-blown riot squad came barging into the adolescent wing and hit Dormitory Number 3 first. They came straight to my bunk as if I was one of the ringleaders. One mean looking hack with a big stick walked slowly to the front of my bunk and asked me directly, "Okay, Marino. How come you didn't eat breakfast?" I grabbed my chin and said, "I have a helluva toothache, and the pain's shooting right through my head, so I didn't feel like eating anything." That wasn't good enough because the big hack told me to follow him outside and stand up against a cement wall. About ten other guys from my dorm and ten from the other three dorms were all lined up against that wall, where we waited for what the bulls had up their sleeves. It struck me funny that we were all white and mostly Italians—or if not Italian, then Irish.

They led us in a short march from the adolescent division to the cell block. We were each deposited into the "bing," solitary confinement. Twenty of us were each looking at four walls and nothing else worth commenting on. I cooled my heels and sat back on the floor against one of the walls, waiting for the next step from the bulls. In less than twenty hours, I had a fair picture of life in the bing, and I was certain I didn't need anymore of it. Breakfast was a cup of black coffee and two slices of bread. Lunch was tea and more bread. Supper was a choice between cocoa, coffee, or tea—and bread.

Sometime during the afternoon of the following day, the buzzers went off. I heard a general clamor as the other nineteen guys were released from their respective cells. Mine failed to click. As Dapper passed my cell, I asked him to tell the hack that they forgot to hit my button, that I was still locked in. Dapper disappeared and I heard nothing for nearly two more hours.

Then an abrupt "bzzzzzzzt" sounded in my cell and the door opened. A hack came in, followed by two plainclothes cops. Without giving me any idea of what was going on, the hack jerked me up, turned me around, and slapped a pair of cuffs on my wrists. Then the two black-suits started to lead me away. "Hey, what's happening?" I should have known before asking that in the joint you have no right to anything, especially information. The hack looked back and told me bluntly, "Just shut up or I'll break your fucking face." They led me into an open yard area where a gray, unmarked four-door Dodge sedan was sitting on the grounds. They shoved me in, then locked the door. We drove to the pier where we sat waiting for the ferry back to New York. The boat pulled up within fifteen minutes, and another fifty or so guys were unloaded.

Naturally, we were headed in the opposite direction. As we boarded the ferry and pulled away from Riker's, I wondered about where this whole new adventure was leading me. The ferry pulled into the 138th Street Pier, and we were ready to go.

Our next stop was King's County Hospital. Inside, an orderly signed a receipt book for me, and the cops departed the scene to be replaced by two orderlies dressed in faded green smocks. They seemed somewhat uncomfortable with me in handcuffs, so the guy with the key unlocked them. We got on an elevator, and as the automatic door opened, I faced a sign reading Maximum Security Psychiatric Ward. "What the hell did that mean?" I was led inside and told to take a seat in a small cubicle. In short order, an official looking white-coat appeared, tagged Director of Admissions. He sat down and informed me that I was there for "observation," since the hacks had circled me as the ringleader who had incited the riot.

A lot of weird people were in that maximum security psychiatric lockup. They must have had at least ten murderers—one was a guy named Cavanaugh. He was about twenty-four and so strange they kept him in a straitjacket all of the time. Even with that, he would shake violently back and forth, as if to pull a Houdini. His story was that he once asked his mother for ice cream money, and she refused him or didn't have it. Either way, he didn't like it, so he picked up a ball-peen hammer and bashed her over the head repeatedly until she was dead. When I found out about that, I was relieved that they kept Cavanaugh in his own special wrapper.

In the end, I spent three weeks in that ward and never did find out what they were looking for or what they found. But I didn't mind the place since nobody messed with your head, and the food was better than on Riker's.

One night after supper they brought us all into the day room for a movie. When we were seated, they brought out the "hard cases" including Cavanaugh. An orderly must have figured to give him some space to stretch because he opened the back straps of Cavanaugh's white canvas jacket allowing him to move his arms. The movie credits rolled onto the screen, revealing the title, *White Heat,* starring James Cagney. I sat up on the back of the bench for a better view. Just as Cagney was proclaiming to his film momma, "Look, ma, I'm on top of the world!" I got a blind-side blast from Cavanaugh, who had snuck up behind me without warning. He knocked me off the bench and hard onto the floor. With my head spinning, I looked up to see no less than six massive hacks coming down on Cavanaugh, holding him absolutely still, although he was shouting at the top of his lungs something about "killing everybody." A nurse came in to hit him with a quick shot, and within three minutes his lights went out and they carried him away.

I was still on the floor, watching all the action and wondering if Cavanaugh had done me any damage. One of the hacks came up and asked how I was. Without thinking, I said, "Ah, I'm okay. It's cool." If I had been quicker, I could have said, "Oh, my head," or "I can't hear and my back hurts." The claim might have been good for some reduced time or an early parole, but I missed it.

On my thirtieth day in King's County, the same two plain-clothesmen came back to pick me up for the reverse ride to Riker's. As the boat pulled in under the sign, I wondered how life was going to be back in the dorms, but we skipped the receiving area, and I was driven directly to the bing reception room. I couldn't figure why the hell they put me back in solitary confinement, but the hacks didn't need any reasons for what they did on the inside. I was looking at three weeks down there all by myself with nothing to read and nothing to do but think. I thought about better junk and pretty ladies, Miami Beach and freedom, and then mom and Hooks back home. I wasn't going to let it get me down, even though they came two days straight with bread and coffee or tea, three times a day. On the third day I got three square meals. Showers were once a week, and I didn't even bother to shave. Who the hell was I gonna see? Meanwhile, the bing time taught me nothing.

On the morning of the twenty-second day, I saw my first light when they brought me up out of the hole. I was thinking about which bunk in the dorm I would have, when we stopped right in the middle of Cell Block One-A. The hack opened the door and edged me in, signaling the buzzer-pusher to close it. I wasn't going back to the dorms. I had a terrifying fear of what it was like in the main cell block, remembering my walk through on the first day and the anguished cries from the men. I wondered what the hacks did to make it that way.

In order to understand a prison hack, you have to understand their mentality from the start. In other words, what future was there for a guy when all he knew how to do was put a key in a lock, then open or close a door? That was where the hacks were, and that was where their level of intelligence was. Most of them were capable of almost anything to mess with your mind, and many didn't have any problem doing a tap dance with their billy on your head either. They spent eight hours a day locked up with you, so they were the big peckers while the cons were the hens.

I found out quickly that my new cell block was reserved for the more defiant adolescents, and most of them had heard of me as the "riot ringleader." That got me some immediate respect. It wasn't long after that I gained some more notoriety as a result of my shoes. I had arrived on Riker's with a forty-nine dollar pair of Stetson's, but of course they took them away at receiving. Then I noticed another guy wearing a pair of street shoes and asked him how he had managed it. He said he had foot trouble, and the croaker okayed his special shoes.

Later I put in a request to go to the infirmary and pitched the guy a story about my flat feet. I explained my army profile and that the particular shoes I wore had a special built-in lift in the heel. He told me he'd get back to me," but my instinct told me I had the sucker. Ten days later a hack told me I was wanted in the receiving room. I knew right away that meant I got my own shoes, but not wanting to show how excited I was, I put on a straight face, went down to the receiving room, and got my street shoes. From then on, everyone figured I had one hell of a connection in the joint or I must have been somebody.

As we drifted along with the boring routine, the hacks picked on more and more trivial stuff all the time—we weren't staying in a straight line going fast enough to suit them, or some other bullshit good only for a hassle. One hack named Warfield decided to start attacking segregation again. None of us could see why they wanted us integrated, but that time I saw the handwriting on the wall spelling big trouble, and I wanted no part of the action. If anything went down, they would tag me as an instigator or ringleader.

Warfield gave the entire block a threat: "If you guys don't come out to the mess hall integrated by tomorrow, the shit is going to hit the fan." And all the while he was talking, he seemed to be looking straight at me. I decided that some drastic action was in order. That night about one or two in the morning, I took my razor and cut open an artery on my upper left arm, enough to produce some obvious bleeding but no permanent damage. To finish the scene, I put in a weak call, "Off . . . i . . . cer, Off . . . i . . . cer." When one of them finally approached, he was ready to bitch about my complaining for nothing. "Whaddya want, Marino?" I slowly showed him my wound and whispered, "I'm dying. You gotta help me."

The hack had no choice so he signaled for attention, and I ended up going by stretcher to the third floor of the hospital wing. They tied a bandage around my arm to stop the bleeding temporarily and pushed me through a door marked Mental Observation. At least I was out of the cell block and what looked like certain trouble.

The time I spent in MO wasn't all that bad, considering the alternatives. We spent most of the day locked up, but the food was better (including fresh eggs and fruit), and best of all, there were no hacks to mess with me. As time went on, I rose above the psychos rather quickly and landed myself a job as an orderly on the sixth floor of the prison hospital, where I felt pretty good about things. I had my own white hospital outfit, and, sure, I had to take some temperatures and change the sheets, but what the hell, I had the run of the place and wasn't locked up except at night. The bonus was that some drugs were available from time to time, especially valium and librium.

After a while on Riker's I got good at transferring between the cell block and the mental ward. When the time on the cell block got dull, I made an appointment with the psychiatrist and told him that I was hearing voices. Next thing I was back on the sixth floor doing my orderly work, then playing cards on valium after hours. Every once in a while some junk would come in because, unlike the main pen, visits there were right across an open table. Each time I went back to the joint, they assigned me a new cell block, which also helped to break up my bit with a change of scenery and people.

On one occasion I was assigned a job in the commissary, which was near the height of insanity since every con working there was a known thief. But that didn't seem to matter—everyone in the department was stealing from the state in one way or another including the boss hack, Fioro. At the time, I was in Block 8, which included the library, commissary, and transportation operations. Transportation carried out all the garbage. We worked out a deal to stow cartons of cigarettes and cases of candy bars in the trash cans, then retrieve them later and share the haul after we finished working.

All things come to an end, however, especially the good ones, and that caper was done for when the prison warden ordered an inventory. After that the cons all got transferred to other blocks, and Fioro faded from sight. We heard he was indicted for embezzling $80,000 worth of goods. He caught all the heat for the missing goods.

We were treated on rare occasions to junk, pot, or booze, all provided by greedy hacks who made underground contact with someone on the outside for money. Also as your seniority built, it was not unusual to gather several valuable things that couldn't be bought—a pillow, bedspread, a decent hairbrush, or a larger mirror. These were officially ignored if you paid your way with cigarettes. The same was true about being certain of good food as you passed down the line. Three packs a week bought you a better breakfast of either french toast, bacon and eggs, or pancakes. Four packs was the price of steak sandwiches for lunch, and five packs got you either steak or pork chops for supper. If you had no money to buy cigarettes, you were a definite loser since the joint gave no allowances and paid no wages. And the chicken they normally served had the distinct taste of seagull, that is, of course, if you could get past the feathers left on it.

We all played cards regularly, but it wasn't kosher to gamble out front, so we just kept track of the money on paper. The limit was put at ten dollars a week, which was all that anyone could spend in the commissary. The losers took a list from the winners and picked up what they wanted from the commissary. I once beat an Irish smartass named Kelley, and he ended up owing me eight dollars so I told him what I wanted, as we only got to visit the store once a week. I was out of some stuff and was also helping a kid from the Bronx whose folks had disowned him, so he was flat broke.

Kelley went to the commissary all right and bought what he wanted, then put the word out that I could go to hell for what he owed me. No way could I let Kelley's challenge ride, so I approached a bull I knew who sort of liked me, maybe because we were both Italian. His name was Perino, and he had the night duty. I told him straight, "I have a beef with a guy I want to take care of myself, so could you stay out of the back of the block in the square for ten minutes?" Perino didn't seem to mind the idea at all once he found out the guy was Irish. He told me the conditions flat out: "Marino, no weapons, no blood, and make it quick."

I felt good that he had given me a pass to handle my own business, so I sent a friend to tell Kelley I wanted to see him in the square. That was where most of the guys worked their beefs because it was out of the view of the hack on duty. Kelley was bigger and heavier than me, so he probably came just to see how hard I might push before he took action himself. He walked up to where I was waiting and said, "You wanted to see me . . ." I cut him off with a round-house right under the chin, which stopped him cold but broke my hand. I couldn't report the condition then since Perino would be involved in an investigation and the grief of at least two extra hours of paperwork.

I lay up with the unbearable pain until the next morning when we were locked out again. Then I went in with a story that I broke it playing handball on the back wall. I think the hack there knew, but he was cool about it and sent me to the hospital. They sent me to the prison ward at Bellevue to have the hand set, and I complained so loud of the pain they treated me to a free shot of morphine before they set it. I felt like I was back on the streets, sailing around in heaven somewhere.

The months passed by, and I found the calendar drawing closer to my marks. They were 30/24—thirty months at the outside and twenty-four months for good behavior. Since I hadn't heard anything to the contrary, I assumed that I was getting out at the two-year mark. To get ready, I began to give away some of my prized possessions. Two days before I thought I was going out the front door, I got a call to report to the preparole division. I went down with a hack and waited while he went in to tell them who was outside. After ten minutes they called me into the room, where I found myself facing three men each about sixty years old with a big pot belly and a suit way too small. They all had their hair greased down, and each was outfitted with a prison legal pad and ballpoint pen.

They asked me to sit down, and one of them opened my file, then followed it with a proclamation. "Mr. Marino, because of your improper behavior, most notably participating in a riot, your marks have been extended by three months." I could not believe it, and of course they had nothing to say. It burned me to the extent that when I walked out, I slammed the door good and hard behind me. When I was returned to my cell block, the other guys refused to believe that I wasn't getting out on schedule too. Then the morning of the day I was originally due to be paroled—before they handed me three more months—I was called to go to the preparole division again. I was excited since I figured that maybe the jerks had seen the light and decided to let me go on schedule. When I got into their special room, the same trio handed me a piece of paper good for another week in the bing. That was my specially designed sting for slamming the door.

As my time on Riker's Island finally dwindled down to the last sixty days, I got myself one of those cheap ball chains you normally wear around your neck. Each day I clipped one of the little balls off, maybe into the crapper or onto my cell floor, but always somewhere. The chain showing my time got shorter and shorter. I kept my mouth shut and stayed in line so there was no chance that they'd extend me again. My inner clock was off and running already, and I had a clear picture of myself on the outside, looking in—a free man after almost twenty-seven lousy months.

7 / My Summer Job in the Country

My release day was a bright sunny Monday in the latter part of April 1961, but it only became real when the processing started, this time in reverse. We went through receiving, returned the ID cards and the uniforms, then got our civvies back. Frank had mailed me a new outfit, and as I got into it I felt like a million dollars. When I stepped into the freedom of the open courtyard, I took a deep breath of the fresh spring air and stretched my arms as high as I could over my head. No more handcuffs.

We boarded the same buses that had brought us into the joint, and I didn't even bother to wave goodbye since I had some serious thinking to get into about my schedule for the day. How was it going to be back in New York? I knew they were going to take us to the Tombs to meet our parole officers before final release. Mine would probably give me some orders to follow since I still ''owed'' them nine months on the three-year sentence. He'd also want to know where I was going to work and live, so I had to make up some good stories.

After that, I absolutely had to go up to Mount Sinai Hospital and visit momma. She was in for a couple of days for a ''female'' operation, but it was only minor and nothing to worry about. She had finally divorced pop and she'd been in a much better mood since then. Next, I had to get laid. I was a young man in New York and had spent over two years behind bars laying up on my ass, alone. So I was going to turn over a new leaf and beneath it you could bet she was going to be beautiful. Finally, I had to get into some serious thinking about my future and the junk and what I was going to do—go back to the streets or what? Above all else, I could not get into a position where I had to go through all this, not again. If I violated my parole with more trouble, I was liable to get five or ten years. No way could I take that.

The bus we were in drove on the ferry. I got out on the deck to look over the situation and do some more thinking. When I had reached the handrail amidships, I looked down into the East River, filled with debris and other crap floating around, all being churned up in the wake of the boat. It was then that I thought of getting loaded—maybe once. But there was no way I was picking up a habit, not then. I couldn't go backwards—not anymore. As the boat pulled up to the pier on the Bronx side, all the guys aboard my bus let out with yells and cheers. "Hey you guys! Females!" "Look! There's a dog and a little kid!" "Hey, a beer joint!"

You could feel the electricity in the air as we drove down the East River Drive, heading for the Tombs in downtown Manhattan. The bus ground to a stop, and we entered the building and took the elevator. During the ride up I wondered about how to play it with the guy. Then the door opened and we were led into the reception area. One by one we approached the desk and gave our names, then were shown into the waiting room. Soon a young Jewish guy came out and held up a file of legal size paper and read off the name, "Vincent Marino." I raised my hand to signal I was there. As I got up he shook my hand and said, "Hi. I'm Phil Goodman. I'm going to be your parole officer."

"Hi. I'm Vinny Marino." He told me to follow him, and we walked over to his desk. He offered me a seat on the right side of it and opened my file. After looking it over, primarily at the list of charges, he asked, "Vinny, where are you going to stay?"

"At my mother's for the moment, since she'll be coming out of the hospital and will be recuperating," I told him.

"Okay, and what do you intend to do with your time?" I thought to myself, "Open a heroin processing lab in my basement and sell dope on the streets," but I held that in check and said, "Well, I can't really say, Mr. Goodman, until I see how my mom is. But as soon as she's on her feet, I'm hitting the streets to find a job. You can bet on it."

As Goodman reached for his pen he said, "I'm not a betting man, Vinny, but that sounds acceptable for the time being. Now, in the beginning until you can get a job, I want to see you in here every Monday, at ten in the morning. After you find work, we'll move it to every two weeks, and then maybe only once a month after you prove yourself."

"That sounds fair," I said.

He picked up a small card and started to read me the rules, "You are not to associate with any known exconvicts, drug addicts, or drunkards. You will not become inebriated or involved with any drugs of any kind. You will be in your home by midnight every night unless you get written permission to the contrary." I just nodded in agreement while thinking, "Jesus. These guys want to make a monk out of me."

Goodman then made a move that caught me completely off guard when he said, "Look, Vinny, God forbid, but if you *should* get involved with drugs again, tell me. Whatever you do, don't lie to me. We can always get you to a detox ward. Now, I'm not suggesting that you are going that way, but if you should fall, I'm not such a rigid person that I can't deal with it."

I thought maybe I should believe him, but my cynical side grabbed hold. "I'll keep you posted with everything I'm doing, I promise." Goodman nodded and reached into his top drawer where he picked out a twenty and handed it to me saying, "This is carfare to get you where you need to go and maybe a bite to eat." I thanked him out loud and thought to myself, "No shit. Twenty bucks for twenty-seven months of living like an animal." I stood up, shook his hand, and said, "Goodbye. See you next week." With that I hustled out the double doors. I knew I was free when I hit the street, and I felt like doing a dance.

Stepping down into the subway station was weird, the sound of the oncoming train and the warm air pushing past me in the tunnel. It had been nearly three years since I'd been down there. As I boarded my train, it occurred to me that I looked pale as hell from all that time in the joint. So when I reached the station, I shot up to the street and into a pharmacy where I bought a bottle of Man Tan with the state's twenty and rubbed it on my face and arms in a bathroom at Mount Sinai Hospital. After it was on, I peeked in the mirror, and thought, "Holy hell, I look like a Mongolian mugger." But it wouldn't come off. "Screw it. Momma's looking for me, not the color of my skin." I straightened my clothes, then drifted out the door.

The first sensation to hit me in the hall was the sweet smell of flowers combined with the nasal burn of rubbing alcohol. I rode the elevator to the second floor, then walked briskly down the corridor looking for room two-four-two. I was definitely noticing all the neat little nurses in their lily-white uniforms. When I got to momma's door, I knocked before I went in. Two ladies sang out, "Come in." There was my momma, with her arms opened wide, reaching out for me from her hospital bed. I ran over and gave her a big hug and a kiss. "Hi, ma. Gee, you're looking great."

I could feel her sigh with relief and almost cry as she said, "Vinny, my son, my son." At once I knew I loved my mom, and she was still the most special person in my life. Yet I had done so much to hurt her, and I felt sorry about that. Well, I didn't intend to do anything more, not if I could help it. Momma said that she was so proud I had been good and learned my lesson. I told her about how we were going out to Vincent's Seafood House in Little Italy as soon as she got released. She laughed, and the other Italian lady in the room laughed right along. I looked over at her and said, "Hello." She smiled and said, "You musta be Vinny. I'ma Mrs. Ferraro."

"How are you?" I said.

Just then Frank walked in. "Hey, Frankie!" I said and hugged him like a bear around the shoulders. "Hey, you're looking great, Vinny!" With that, Frank and I sat down on the edge of momma's bed, and we all chatted for another twenty minutes or so before I called Frank out of the room to talk to him. "Hey, Frankie, I gotta go and get laid. Tell you what, though, I'll call you later and we'll shoot out for dinner." Frank could tell I was clean, and he was obviously pleased since he generously reached into his pocket and came out with a roll and peeled off five twenties, telling me, "Here, Vinny. Go out and have a good time. We can meet tomorrow, right here, to pick up momma in the morning. She's being released at ten o'clock." I took the money. "Hey Frank, you don't have to do that, but thanks, brother."

I rode down the elevator, thinking about the nearest cab. It was a yellow, and it went streaking by at about forty, but a quick whistle hailed him over. As I got in I couldn't think of anything but the order, "One Hundred and First, between First and Second." The cabbie tripped the meter, and we were on our way. As we passed the light at 99th Street, I happened to spot a black dude named Chuck, who had less than two months left on Riker's just as I came in. In the month or so we had known each other, he gave me some real good tips. I told the cabbie to pull over and paid him as I called out the window to Chuck.

He stopped, and I noticed that he wasn't moving too fast. When I got closer, it was easy to see he was strung out on dope. He shook my hand though and said, "How ya doin', man?"

"Great. Look, I got two things in mind, and I'm in a hurry. First I want to get laid. And second I want to get loaded. Are you my man or not?" Before he could answer, I looked up at a clock in a bank and noticed that it had been exactly four hours and twenty-three minutes since we had landed at the pier in the Bronx.

He tripped back with, "Jesus, you're serious. Slow down, man. Things are happenin'. I can fix you up right away on both issues. What's new?" I told him, "I just got out," and asked "which way to the action?" He started walking as he said, "I'll take you to Theresa's, you'll like her." Theresa turned out to be a sweet little Puerto Rican girl of nineteen. She opened the door and invited us in. I caught her with a smile, and she didn't back off an inch. Chuck gave me the only come-on line I needed when he said, "Theresa, this is a friend of mine, Vinny. He just got out of the joint, so I want you to treat him like he ain't never gonna forget."

She smiled and said, "I sure will," as Chuck turned for the door. I stopped him aside from her and whispered, "About the money?"

"Aw, I dunno, Vinny. Just give her twenty bucks, and she'll show you a helluva time. She's in my fifty-dollar a trick book, so you're cuttin' a deal. Then come look me up when you're finished, and we'll see about that second issue. Take all the time you want, I'll be around."

I let him out and closed the door, then hitched up the chain lock for tighter security. Out went the lights and on came Theresa. We both fell down on the bed, and neither of us got up for the next three hours. Theresa finally fell asleep, so I got dressed, left her thirty dollars, and slipped out the door figuring to find Chuck again and shoot up into seventh heaven one more time.

Well, I found him just about where he had been three hours earlier on the street. Within seconds we arranged for a score. The price of bags had gone up from two to three dollars each, and I asked him for five, handing him a twenty. A few minutes later he came back with the bags. I offered him three, "for the use of the works and your time." He was delighted and started to cook up the junk. I asked what he knew about the quality because I was clean.

"No way two bags goin' to kill you, man," he said as he loaded the eyedropper. I tied up my arm with his belt. He handed me the spike, and I found a vein straight off and sent it in. The glow hit my stomach with a turn and a twist, and I knew I was home. My head lifted off in the next twenty seconds, and I was away into a world that can't be described. The amount was just right. I sat around with Chuck after he did his up, and we drank Cokes and nodded somewhat, then talked intermittently.

Then I thought it was time to scoot over to Brooklyn and see my old paisan, Hooks. Hooks was at home and answered as I pushed on the doorbell. His eyes lit up as he opened the door, but the rest of him looked like a dishrag. He was strung out all the way to the corner pharmacy, I could tell even in my own stoned condition. He shot at me with, "Hey, Vinny! How the hell are ya? Now why dincha tell somebody you were comin' home? Hell, we'da thrown a block party!" Hooks laughed and pointed me inside. "So what's new, you old sonofabitch?" I asked.

"Aw, not much of nothin'," he twitched, "same old shit. But you're lookin' real good, Vinny. The joint didn't wear you out, that's great." Then we circled around some of the names in the neighborhood. I found out that three guys in our old group had OD'd and died one night not long ago, and so there was heavy heat on the street with detectives all over the place.

"You got any dope?" I asked him.

"Nope. But I can sure cop, if the guy's still at home." I slapped him on the shoulder and slipped him a twenty as I said, "What the hell are you waiting for? I'll sit here, I'm kinda wasted." Within a few minutes Hooks was back again, breathing heavy from the run. He dumped four candy bars, five three-dollar bags of heroin, and a five dollar bill onto the kitchen table, grinning as he did it. "You go ahead with what you want. I'm already loaded and only need a bag, maybe two. Take the rest," I told him.

His eyes lit up again, brighter than before, as he went for the works. "Right on, Vinny. I'll take three and leave you with two." He tied up and got loaded, and I did one bag. It turned out the stuff was better than what I had done up at Chuck's, and it put me in a place even higher than before, where all I did was nod my head, up and down. I was totally out of it for the rest of the night, and crashed at Hooks' place, but I did manage to get up around seven-thirty the next morning, just in time to phone Frank. "Where do we meet to get mom?" I asked him.

"Well, since it's eight now, why not I just meet you at the hospital at nine-thirty. How's that?"

"Great, Frank. I'll see you in mom's room."

I hung up, then dragged my body into the bathroom for a shave and a shower. As I dressed, I saw Hooks sprawled on the bed in his room, still out of it. The sight brought me straight back to another conversation with myself about junk. Hitching up my belt buckle, I swore that this time I am *definitely* not going to get myself hooked. I could not afford to violate parole or do anything crazy. During the train ride to the hospital, I continued to tell myself, "No way. Not this time. In fact, no drugs at all today. You gotta be with momma and Frank." I made it through that day, but of course it was busy as hell with mom just getting back home. We had to go out and shop to stock her refrigerator, then Joey came home, so we talked, plus Frank and I had a lot to discuss.

At around seven o'clock Frank drove us to Vincent's for a magnificent dinner of shrimp, scungiles, and mussels. It was one of those days that stayed in my memory, with the family together—except for pop—and everyone having a good time.

If I had been smarter then, I would have known that returning to Hooks' place on the third morning out was a bad move. He had a full-on habit going, so he *had* to be in action every day. He said he was "doing a little of this and a little of that, whatever comes along, I take it day by day." And so, true to our historical pattern, we teamed up and started taking whatever came along, every day. First we dabbled in the cigarettes, next we rustled some cattle, then we burglarized a few places, and finally we remembered the churches and went into rectories with a vengeance, sometimes hitting two or three a night. By the time I had been home from Riker's a little more than two weeks, I had gone right back to the point where it was costing me a minimum of fifty dollars a day for my habit, and I had already overdosed a couple of times.

Every Monday, when I went in to see Goodman at the Tombs, he would ask, "You using drugs, Vinny?" I would lie and say, "No way, Phil," then hope to God that he didn't notice the skin-colored make-up I had rubbed on to cover the tracks in my arms. Goodman would also ask, "What are you doing about a job?" I would put off with something like, "I'm looking." As I walked out of his office on Monday, it hit me right between the eyes. "Hey, dummy. If you keep going on this merry-go-round, you're going to end up with a free ticket right back to Riker's Island. You violate this parole, and you still owe them eight months and change. They'll jerk the rug right out from under you and your habit, slam you back in a cell, and leave you there for a long time."

Those same kind of thoughts were shooting through the fog in my head when I woke up one day and found myself groping on the floor next to the bed for a set of works. Before I could find what I wanted, the phone rang, loud and clear, rattling my already shattered nerves in the process. I managed to sit up in bed and look around for the damn thing. With some concentration, I located the phone under a sweater and mumbled hello as I picked up the receiver. Pop shot back from the other end, "Yo! Vinny!" so loud in my ear that I held the phone back about eight inches for a minute, trying to determine if someone had turned up the volume. I figured to hold this conversation about that distance from my aching eardrum, so I barked back at it, "Hey, pop. What's up?"

He came through with an audible concern. "How you doing, Vinny?" I could only think to say, "So-so, pop. Why?" That made him bellow through the horn: "Because I'm worried about you. We need to sit down and have a talk." I said to myself, "Yeah, right after I have a fix, pop," and then told him on the phone, "Okay, pop, we'll do that, real soon." He roared at me like a loudspeaker. "No! Not real soon, Vinny, *today!*" I never realized pop had such power, so I agreed. "Alright, pop. When and where do you want to meet?"

He directed me to Vincent's in Little Italy at noon. I thought to myself that the place was turning into a regular family haunt. But they sure had good food, and with that idea I got a little excited as I said, "See you there at twelve sharp, I promise." He said, "You had better keep your promise!" and hung up abruptly. The receiver burped back to a dial tone, so I knew the conversation was finished.

I dropped the mouthpiece onto its cradle. Meanwhile I was already across the room loading a cooker with junk, thinking about what pop might want and how to clear my head for the day. I sent the dope in, nodded out for an hour, then got up and showered, still in a stupor. It must have taken close to forty-five minutes for me to find the right clothes. That only left me twenty minutes to make it on time as I left the hotel in midtown and jumped in a cab. When I got to Vincent's at ten past the hour, pop was already there, sitting at a table, all dressed up. He looked good to me, and I smiled broadly as I walked over to him saying, "Hey, pop! How you doing?"

He stood up and hugged me and said, "Good, Vinny. Good. And you? What you been doing these days, huh?" Pop was trying to look at me directly from the hug, but I wasn't ready to do that, so I pulled him in close and whispered, "Nothin' much. Looking for a job, that's all." He pushed me away to arm's length again and tried to look into my eyes. I could tell he knew something was up, because even though I wasn't strung out yet, I wasn't looking nearly as good as I did when I first came out of the joint.

Without accusing me of anything directly, he strongly hinted at his suspicions. "I've been thinking about you, Vinny. What you should do. Maybe you could get away from the city for a while, it'll be better. Fresh air, the country. A chance for you to think. You know, you were good at the lifeguard job in Miami, so why not get a job up in the Catskills or the Adirondacks? It's May now, and they'll be hiring for the summer season." I thought about stalling him as usual, as I would anyone, but the idea struck a chord so I said, "Sure, pop, I'll check it out." Pop wasn't through with me, however, and I sensed that he had thought this one out a little bit more than usual when he said, "Why not finish lunch, then drive over to Warren Street and we'll have a look?"

At first I thought, "Dammit, there goes my afternoon fix," but then the idea came that "maybe this isn't so bad after all. It'd be like a vacation. I'd get to meet some new ladies, the work as a lifeguard isn't all that hard, plus it would be a break from the routine, which I need because of this goddam junk anyway." So I proudly told pop, "Sure, pop, that would be great. Right after lunch we'll check it out." Pop smiled and returned to his plate of scungiles. He insisted on paying the tab and left a generous tip, typical of someone who was active in the business. Then we were on our way towards Warren Street, right near City Hall in Manhattan. The area was famous for its long lineup of various employment agencies, mostly private, where you went along glass cubicles reading the lists of openings. If something looked interesting, you could walk in.

Pop parked the car and we started down the street, looking the situations over. Before too long, one in particular caught my eye. It said: Lifeguard and Swimming Instructor, Adirondack Mountains. Go to Room 202 and ask for Mr. Martin. I turned to the old man with genuine excitement. "Hey, pop. Look at this one. Right up my alley. You wait here and I'll go see about it."

"Sure, you go on," he said and leaned back against the wall. He watched where I went, which was straight in the front door of the 202 place. Ten or twelve desks were crammed into this extremely small office, and every desk had someone behind it, and eight of them were on the telephone. The lady right in front hung up her receiver, so I walked over and asked, "Ma'am, is Mr. Martin in?"

"Sitting right over there, sir," she said and pointed her finger to a far corner position. I looked and saw a fat guy about fifty-five with not much more than a third of his hair left. I shot over to his desk and said, "Hello. I'm Vinny Marino." Of course he was on the phone, too, so he gestured I should have a seat. I couldn't see his eyes behind bifocals as thick as the bottom of a Coke bottle. I was grinning to myself about this guy interviewing anyone for a lifeguard job. Soon he got off the phone and into a discussion with me about the opening.

"I'm here about that lifeguard and swimming instructor job in the Adirondacks. Number thirty-eight on the board." He shuffled some papers and said, "Gee, kid, I'll tell you the truth. I just got rid of that job. Somebody took it this morning. But, there might be something else. Let's see. Can you water ski?" I had never been on water skis in my life, but the question rang straight to my act. I thought fast and came back with, "Can I water ski? Yes, sir, I can water ski on two skis, I can water ski on one ski, or I can water ski on my bare feet. I'm so good at it that I was just last week thinking of turning pro, if I caught a break."

Martin looked like that sucker that is born every minute. I knew he was sold on my credentials when he said, "That sounds great. I have this other job opening at a resort in the Adirondacks. I think you'll fit the bill. By the way, it pays sixty dollars a week, plus room and board and tips."

"Great," I said, "When does it start?" He looked down at the description again to discover, "Monday. This Monday. They want someone up there by then, so he's got a week to get ready for the first busy weekend. That's Memorial Day, you know." I hadn't thought about it, but it was already Friday. That only left the weekend before my departure.

Martin said, "It's a nice place," and went on to tell me which bus to catch at the Port Authority Building and that he would send word ahead to have the resort van pick me up at the bus station Monday night. I stood and smiled, then shook his hand as I said, "Thanks, Mr. Martin. I won't let you down."

When I told pop, his eyes lit up like Christmas bulbs. He smiled all the way from ear to ear, saying, "I told you things were gonna look up. Hah! Good for you!" Pop held me tight and shook my right shoulder, saying in celebration, "Come on, let's go have a beer, son." I smiled and thought, "A beer? Who needs a beer? I need something for my veins," but looked straight at pop and said, "Yeah, sure pop. One beer. Then I gotta go meet somebody, by four." He was laughing and so excited, I didn't think he heard me as we headed across the street to a sign that said Tony's Bar. We went inside into the dark. I couldn't see where I was, and pop ran into me when I stopped. "Whoa. Dark in here, I can't see."

We adjusted in about a minute, then grabbed two stools at the bar and ordered. As the bartender moved off to a chillbox to get the beers, I was thinking about getting back to my room for a fix, real quick. I was sipping the beer and bullshitting along, when it dawned on me. "Oh, no! My parole. Goodman's got to approve a move like this." I told pop about the predicament, then decided I'd call Goodman before going over. I pushed a dime into the slot of the pay phone and got Goodman who agreed to see me at four o'clock. Pop drove me over there in less than fifteen minutes, after he finished his beer and I left mine. It was five of the hour when I reached his office, and all I could think of seriously was my next fix. Goodman was waiting with his handshake all ready.

I put on my best act, "I got a job!" I told him and explained what it was, pointing to my "need for a change of scenery. I was starting to get depressed, so this would be an opportunity to get away from the neighborhood and out of the city for a while. The fresh country air should help me with my thinking, especially about what to do with the rest of my life." At that point I wasn't kidding, and Goodman could tell.

He smiled and said, "I agree, totally. You have my support. While you're up there, you don't have to report in down here, but I do want you to call me, every two weeks, starting with

Monday, the fourteenth of June. I want to hear about the progress, and how you're doing.'' I saw no problem with that, so I said, ''Yeah, sure, Phil. Will do.'' He asked a final question with a slight tug on my sleeve and a look in my eyes. ''You're not using drugs, are you Vinny?'' I gathered up every straight inch of my being. ''No, Phil. I'm clean.'' He let go, and I turned and went reversing out of there in a hurry.

Once out on the street, I scanned the scene for a cab. With none in sight, I started moving toward my hotel, but it was a long distance away, too far to walk in my condition. Finally a cab appeared and I signaled him over. I gave him the hotel's address and doubled over as he put it in drive and shot forward, simultaneously flipping the switch on the meter. We got there soon, and at the sight of my room, I breathed in relief as I dipped for my key. In seconds I was sailing away, and mellow as hell.

My first clear thought after that was about the clothes I would need for resort work as a water skiing instructor. ''Did I say water skiing instructor? Oh, God!'' flashed in my mind. I thought about taking some lessons before going—but where, on Coney Island? Then I thought of the six hundred bucks I had stashed—mostly for maintaining my habits, but also for emergencies like this. I took the bills from the hole behind the bathroom mirror, counted off four big ones, and put the rest back.

Switching off the lights, I headed for a quick shopping trip around town. I bought a whole new set of beach outfits, stuff that would be appropriate for the occasion. Three sharp cabana tops with matching swim trunks, a couple pairs of sandals, a blue nylon windbreaker, several pairs of slacks and five or six sporty summer shirts. Just like with the junk, I kept spending the money until it was gone. Then I went home and retired for the night.

Saturday morning found me heading off for Hooks' place after fixing up for ''breakfast.'' We shot straight for the nearest A&P where we rounded up enough cattle to sell for about $150 in less than two hours. Later that morning, we struck an appliance delivery truck for our first ever color television set. It was worth $300 in cash. With that caper completed, we cabbed it to Harlem and reloaded our pockets with bundles of junk. After shooting up to test the quality, I was flying high but figured I had to go over and see momma before I took off for the mountains. When she appeared at the door, I could tell right away that she sensed something was wrong, like I was using again. When I told her about the change, "Ma, I need it and it'll be good," she agreed. Just then Frankie walked in. He was excited with my prospects for the future, and even saw some opportunity in it for himself. "Great, Vinny. Maybe I'll come up for a visit one weekend, after you're settled in."

Mom made us all sit down for a traditional meal, which was finished in a little over three hours. With that, I said my good-byes and shoved off for Hooks' place in Brooklyn and my evening fix. Sunday went by in a stupor, more or less, maybe even an overdose. I finally woke up in a slush, with everything swimming around, only to discover from the desk clerk that it was already ten o'clock Monday morning. I told him I'd be checking out at noon.

I had other things to do, like look up the number of one of my old croakers to see about an appointment that day. I set the appointment with his girl for two that afternoon. Next I hopped in a cab and headed for Harlem to be sure I had enough junk to take along with me when I hit it for the mountains. At two sharp I entered the doctor's office, and after a little dramatic act, he wrote a prescription for thirty-six dolophines and thirty-six doridens. I thanked him and raced to the pharmacy to get the scrips filled with less than an hour before the bus left the station. Back at my hotel, I added two sets of works to my bag and said farewell to New York City for a while and jumped in a cab for the Port Authority Building.

The bus pulled out as scheduled at four o'clock, and the timetable called for a five and a half hour trip, so I sat back to watch the change of scenery I had been telling everyone I needed. It was springtime, and green hit me from all angles—I was used to the gray of concrete or a cell. I thought about how good this change was going to be, and then my eye caught the sign above the restroom on the bus. I decided to make the pace of the changes a little bit faster and more mellow, so I slipped two bags of junk and a set of works from my suitcase and went to the bathroom to get loaded and experience the sunset.

As the warm glow took hold, I slid back into my seat, where I drifted between nodding and sleep for the rest of the trip and only woke up when the bus stopped at my destination. I shook off as much as I could before grabbing my bag to get off the bus and look for the resort van. Only three people had debarked at this station, and the rest of the town was empty except for a white van with Katzef's Resort painted on the driver's door. The driver held out his hand, saying, "Hi, I'm Tom Benton."

I said, "Hello, Tom, I'm Vinny Marino," as he showed me where the baggage was stowed. I climbed in on the passenger side up front. He wanted to talk on the way over, but I wasn't much for it so I mainly answered with nods and nopes. In fifteen minutes we pulled up in front of an enormous old Victorian style house nestled into a neat little valley in the mountain under a full moon. Tom carried my bags as we went in the front door then down the hall and into the kitchen. I met the owners, Mr. and Mrs. Katzef, a nice Jewish couple in their fifties, both slightly fat. He was balding, I noted as he said, "Hello, Vinny. Welcome aboard. Listen, I should tell you that this is a family-type operation we run here. Everybody is cordial to the guests, at all times. Now, since you are going to be involved with the water sports, we'll have you eating with the guests in the main dining room. We would like for you to be seen as a host for the hotel."

Suddenly I felt like I was really going to like the job, so I said, "Thank you, Mr. Katzef, and you can be sure I'll do my best to give all the guests the service they deserve." Katzef took my left arm, and we went all around with introductions, but I only recalled the name Benton, the driver of the van, and Sally Ann McQuistin, who was a pretty blonde waitress from Poughkeepsie. Katzef was on his way out as he told me, "Mr. Benton will show you where you'll be staying, and he'll also show you the ropes down at the lake tomorrow."

"Thanks, Mr. Katzef." I waved with my hand as he walked out through the swinging doors of the kitchen. Benton pointed toward the back as he opened a door. We were headed toward the staff cottage. Inside a central hallway had ten rooms opening into it, and a shower and toilets for both sexes were located in the middle on each side. My little cubicle was third on the right. Benton turned the key and opened the door. It smelled a bit musty, but there was a nice single bed with a flowery spread and pictures all over the walls. Benton lowered the boom with, "About the lake, Vinny. I'll show you all the equipment at around eight in the morning, how's that?"

I looked for a way out, but none came to mind, so I said, "Yeah, sure, Tom. Eight will be fine." As soon as Benton left I damn near panicked with the thought of "tomorrow and water skiing, no shit," so I frantically searched through my bag for some junk. I emptied half of my suitcase before I found what I wanted, then headed straight out the door and down the hall to the bathroom for a glass of water.

Back in the room, I got off, then picked up my clothes and put them away in the closet and drawers of the bureau next to my bed. Next thing I dropped onto the mattress. When Tuesday morning came I was lucky to wake up early since I hadn't set the alarm, and through the fog in my head, I thought, "Just one shot to clear it, then I can move." I reached down for the works in my shoe by the bed. I punched through two misses, then found a way and sent it all in. When it hit, I stopped thinking about the lake and the water skiing and calmed down. I kept going in a glow through a shower down the hall, although I was sort of banging off both walls as I came back. No one happened to notice though. I went over my selection of cabana outfits, dressed, and went off to see who was around the main hotel—anything to avoid getting near that damn water.

I drifted in the back door to the kitchen and spent the better part of an hour meeting all the neatest waitresses. I looked at the breakfast food sitting all around me but passed on it since I was too far above in my head. When the clock pointed to ten minutes of eight, I thought about my meeting with Benton and got cold feet first, then the chill ran all the way up to my eyeballs and higher. I didn't know how I was going to beat that one.

Reluctantly heading for the edge of the water, I noticed signs all over the place saying See Lifeguard Before Using Canoes. I couldn't figure why anyone would want to speak to me before taking out a canoe—I had never been in those aluminum things either. I was impressed with the sight of the lake—a sparkling blue-white glass color. Then up walked Tom Benton. "Morning, Vinny. You ready to look things over?"

I thought, "That's *all* I want to do, Tom," but said, "Sure. Let's go. Where do we start?" He took a step without looking and tripped on the gunnel of an upturned canoe. He laughed at himself without falling down and said, "Let's start with the canoes." I gave him an encouraging slap on the shoulder. "Maybe you should start with a swim in the water to wake up." Look who was loaded. He walked along, and I followed behind, trying to listen as best I could.

"There are a dozen canoes, and it's damn funny to watch people turning them over all of the time. Last year the guard had five people in trouble, all at once. It's only pure luck no one drowned. He buzzed around with the motorboat and dropped them all life rings. That kid sure was a fast thinker,'' he concluded. I felt I was losing it, right in the middle, and would never get back. He headed for the pier that ran ten feet out into the shallow water. Alongside the dock was a speedboat with a seventy-five horsepower outboard motor. Benton started messing around with different parts of the engine, telling me about the ignition and such. After some unintelligible words smothered by the roar of the engine so I had no idea what he said, he shut her off, to my amazement, without even suggesting a trial spin.

As we got out of the boat, I saw two sets of water skis chained to a rack, and my stomach turned weakly again. Benton looked at me as if he was finished, and sure enough, he said it. ''Well, that's about all I can think to tell you. Anything else you need to know?'' I thought about asking him if he could teach me to water ski but just shook my head. ''No, thanks, Tom. I'll just start and if anything comes up, I'll come and find you.''

He started toward the hotel. I waved him off and looked back at the water and over the equipment. I thought about going to the nearest resort and taking some lessons on their skis. I walked over to the boat again and thought about hanging myself with the tow rope or starting the motor and going out for a trial run. I moved to the canoes and wondered about when to get into them and how then hell I was going to balance the things with all the ringing I had coming down in my ears. ''Not today,'' I concluded. ''I need some more time to get my act together.'' So I crept back into my room.

At lunch time I met more of the staff and went walking all over the property to get a feel for things. Around two-thirty I went back to my room, got off, took a nap, got up at five, showered and went for a light dinner. I stood around for a couple of hours chatting with the girl from Poughkeepsie. Then I figured to go back to my room and read for a while before calling it a night. The next day I played it sick as a dog and shot up in bed, spending most of the day in my room nodding and reading. I only left to eat. Late that night I got off again, took a couple of doridens, and went to sleep.

Thursday I stumbled down to the water and started the boat up for a run but then chickened out at the wheel, shut it off, and returned to my room for a fix. No one seemed to notice anything unusual, so I got away with my act until Friday at ten in the morning when I ran out of heroin. As I sent in the last hit, I figured to myself, just like an addict, ''Well, I'll start this job off clean. I'll just take dolophines during the day and doridens at night to sleep." With that combination I thought I had it made, so I headed down to the water to get in some much needed practice.

I walked to the water and stepped in knee deep before I realized the insanity of my position. There was the lifeguard and swimming and skiing instructor of the luxurious Katzef resort, stoned to the point that he thought he could stay on top of the water, with heroin, like Christ. I was decked out in my finest suit, with a diamond pinky ring for dazzle, an expensive gold watch, and some sharp sunglasses. I got the hell out of the water before anyone saw me and headed for the canoes. As I turned one right side up, I noticed that Benton was pulling in at the hotel with a whole vanload of people—paying guests. I pushed the canoe out into the water, grabbed both sides, and tried to hoist myself in, but it wobbled somewhat and I missed. Finally aboard, after five minutes of struggling, I noticed some guests coming down to the shore to have a look at the lake—or at me. So I paddled away, thinking "just like a pro."

Up ahead I could see a big raft floating on pontoons in the middle of the lake. "Why not head for that?" raced through my mind, and I did. Within twenty-five strokes, I thought I was master of the canoe and that "any moron could do this." I was laughing as I turned into the wind.

The canoe turned over before I could move. Down in the drink twice in one morning, I could only think about my glasses and cigarettes heading for the bottom. I dived and by magic found the glasses. When I returned to the surface, the canoe was still upside down in the water, and on the shore I could see that a whole group of clowns had gathered there for a laugh at the (junkie) instructor, now struggling like hell to right the canoe in the water. It took me over an hour to get that canoe back on the shore. Two waiters had been watching the whole episode and were there laughing their asses off. As I slowly dragged everything out of the water, they came up and started with the jokes. "Hey, Vinny, what the hell happened to you?"

"Fuck you two guys," I thought, then came out with, "Nothing, why? I was just testing the canoe to see if you could breathe under it when it turned over. You know, what if a guest loses it out there in deep water?"I thought I had them, even stoned, when the first kid shot me down with his index finger. He pointed at my soaking wet cabana jacket and said, "For that all you had to do was ask me, I always ride 'em."

I said, "Fuck you. You weren't here." The second hired hand pointed at my watch and got me again. "Why the hell would you wear that, if you knew you were going over?" They both laughed as I shook off some water. I headed to my room for a couple of dolophines to keep the act going and to change my wet clothes.

I thanked God and my stars when Saturday came that it was cold and dreary so almost no one came near the water. I stumbled through the formal meal with a couple from the city and remembered nothing about the content of our conversation.

The next day at the peak of a pill high, I thought of going down to the water, a blind move straight towards disaster. Standing on the dock in the morning sunlight was a young newly married couple. As we talked I found out they were both schoolteachers, and the guy said, "We only have today and tomorrow before we have to go back, so we want to do everything. Let's start by you teaching me to water ski." I groaned to myself and took the keys to unlock the skis from the rack when Benton came up and started to give me a hand by untying the boat. He also pointed out a couple of places in the lake and asked, "You do know about the shallow water, over there?" I squinted to look, stoned as hell. "No. Where?" He pointed again and I thought I had it down on the map in my head, as he said, "You can't go near there or you'll screw up the props on the boat."

Well, I had never even driven the boat up to that point, but what did that matter? I had a water ski lesson to give. I had seen some pictures, like movies and sports news, and that was all I was operating from in the fog of the pills. I told the schoolteacher to put on the skis, and hold onto the bar. I turned over the boat's motor, and when it roared, I started getting into the idea of racing around on the lake. I looked back at this dude up to his neck in the water, with the tips of the skis sticking out, holding onto the tow bar at the end of the rope. I got out of the boat and made up some lessons as fast as I could. "Just relax and let the boat pull you. Keep your knees bent. When you're ready to go, yell out 'Yo!' and if anything happens and you fall, just let go of the rope and I'll come and pick you up." He was shivering somewhat as he said, "No problem, I got it."

I waded back to the boat and climbed in, then eased into the driver's seat. I dropped her into drive when he signaled OK, taking off on the water as well as up in my head. The breeze was blowing by and I was flying. I looked back at my rider and to my amazement he was still up, skimming the surface but with a weird look on his face, like it was frozen. We went along a minute or two more when I realized that we were pointing to the shallow water Benton mentioned. I looked over the side and, sure enough, it was shallow enough to see the bottom.

I threw the wheel over into a hellish left turn, thinking only about the water and nothing about the guy on the rope. Because of my sharp turn, he found himself looking at a tree hung out over the water as he swung around in a much wider circle. Now, a normal novice who faced that kind of predicament would have simply dropped the towline and taken his bath, but that yokel couldn't hear me yelling, "Let go!" because he held on for dear life—right to the end when he cracked his leg smack into the tree.

His wife was screaming bloody murder all over as some people came down and pulled him out of the water, while I headed the boat back to the dock and cut the engine. I figured to bluff my way out of this one and ran straight back to the scene and started my act, with him moaning. I screamed, "What the hell happened? I told you to let go. Don't you know how to listen at all?" The guy kept moaning as someone left saying, "I'll call a doctor and an ambulance." At about the same time, the owner of the resort, who had obviously heard about my canoe caper, got wind of the crash down at the edge of the water. He came huffing along as fast as he could.

Katzef almost fainted with the sight of the blood and the bones sticking out of the man on the ground. Luckily for him, the ambulance arrived and took his attention away from the wound. The crew did some first aid, then took the guy away for emergency treatment. Katzef took me aside for some private questioning. "Vinny, how on earth could this possibly happen?" I looked at him as straight as I could. "By God in Heaven, I swear that the guy didn't know what the hell he was doing on skis." He looked down, then directly at me. "I thought you were teaching him to ski. Vinny, how long have you been water skiing, may I ask?" I never hesitated. "For years, Mr. Katzef." He didn't hesitate either. "Well then, Vinny, you wouldn't mind giving me a demonstration?" There was no way out, so I came back with, "No, not at all. Who's going to drive the boat?" My heart sank down to my ankles, and the drugs were past giving me any assistance.

I took off my latest cabana jacket and hung it on the ski rack. I closed my eyes, hoping for a miracle, but none came as I waded in knee deep with the skis and splashed around getting them on. The smartass waiter who had poked fun at my canoe turnover gunned her twice, and the roar hit me as a warning, but I couldn't back out. I tucked my knees up under my chin and yelled, "Yo!" The curtain was up on my showtime. I shot straight up out of the water about two feet and straight back down, head first. The boat dragged me about fifty or sixty yards before I let go of the bar and went under. When I surfaced again, I knew it was all over. Half of the staff and more than two hundred guests were watching with a giggle from the shore.

Old Mr. Katzef was looking too, shaking his head. As I dragged my amateur act out of the water, Katzef approached with my formal walking papers. "We won't be needing your 'services' any longer, Vinny. Please pick up your pay envelope and be off the premises before ten o'clock tonight." Feeling all washed up, I walked weak-kneed to my room and ate three more doridens to even things out while I packed—after less than a week on the job.

Somehow I managed to get out of the resort without much more fanfare. Benton brought my termination envelope with sixty dollars to my room. He had gotten a kick out of the show and was grinning as he told me, "Katzef asked me to take you to the station for the seven o'clock bus back to the city if you want."

At six-twenty, Benton pulled up in front of the staff cottage. As I walked out the front door, I could see a slice of the lake silhouetted in the sunset and some giant pine trees but no boat or water skis to spoil my last glance at the country. I took my last deep breath of mountain air, threw the bag in the back, and climbed aboard. When we were on our way, Benton started questioning me, somewhat amused, "How in the hell did you manage that one, Vinny?" I wasn't interested in discussing the disaster, but said, "I was trying to avoid that shallow water you pointed out and forgot I had a passenger behind." He laughed and went into telling me how that schoolteacher had in one day made himself known all over the resort as someone who demands "instant everything," then tips next to nothing. He said that most of the waitresses and the guys at the golf shop got a real kick out of the incident. Too bad I had to get booted out of the story so soon.

At the bus station, I thanked Benton for the rides plus the help at the boat dock. I went in and bought a ticket, then waited for the boarding call that would take me back to New York. Once the bus pulled away from the little mountain town, I started coming down hard as the full weight of the day's disasters landed in my head. I thought, "How could you be such a fuck-up?" That wasn't enough, so it went on. "A peach job and you blow it, asshole." Conscience was riding me hard and finished with, "What the hell do you expect to get out of being back in the streets?" In a desperate attempt to avoid that kind of inner conflict, I put my arm under my head and leaned against the bus window, trying to sleep for the rest of the ride.

8 Scams, Heists, and Legitimate Business

When I opened my eyes again we were barreling down the final stretch of the West Side Drive, and I could see the familiar lights and outline of the city. A little after midnight we pulled in. I grabbed my bag and took a cab over to mom's place, where I figured to spend the night. I went to her door and knocked, wondering about a storyline to cover my catastrophic tracks just as momma opened it. She was shocked. "My God, Vinny. What are you doing here? Come inside." She hugged me, then pushed back to arm's length, as she stood there and demanded an explanation. "What happened to your job in the mountains? The resort? Are you alright?"

"I'm fine, momma. And nothing happened, that's what happened. It turned out that I didn't have the right licenses to operate the equipment, and they had to let me go because the state wouldn't issue them soon enough." Mom plopped down into a chair at the kitchen table and held her forehead in the palm of her hand. "Oh, no," she said, "now what are you going to do, Vinny?" I thought to myself, "Get some more drugs and forget about it," but told mom, "Get some sleep and think about it tomorrow."

While I was still sleeping the next day, mom decided to take my future into the family's hands. She called my Uncle Bobby, dad's oldest brother, who had made a lot of money in his day, first in selling rationed goods during the war and then later by acting as the stick man in some high rolling crap games at the local clubs. I had looked up to him in my earlier days, and momma knew that. Bobby agreed to talk to me since, after all, he was my godfather. We agreed to meet, and when we did he gave me a pep talk warning me away from stealing and the mob. "The same is true of that babania. No one wants anything to do with a junkie. Remember that."

I told him I would remember, and that I appreciated his concern for me. As he got ready to leave the restaurant, I suddenly felt him pressing two crisp hundred dollar bills into my hand. I smiled with a nod of gratitude, and he said, "Be good to yourself, and treat it like seed money, to get a new start." I waved goodbye and felt good about that meeting with my uncle. As soon as he drove away, I grabbed a cab for One Hundredth Street and First Avenue. Within fifteen minutes I had bought fifty dollars worth of heroin, and then I shot back to rent a furnished room on Forty-second Street in Manhattan, which cost me another thirty-five for the week.

Once my mind was in that familiar cloud, I drifted downstairs and used the pay phone to call Hooks and see what was new at his end. As it turned out, Hooks was in bad shape. He had just been taken off by three other junkies on a rooftop for eighty dollars. Hooks said he had pushed one backwards far enough to get a head start down the stairwell and had gotten away, but with no money and no dope. "What a bummer," I told him and remembered all the times he had saved me. "Yo, Hooks, get your ass over here. I got what you're looking for." He got the location and hung up, heading straight for me and a fix.

I stumbled back up to my room to wait for Hooks to show up. I was nodding out when someone started to bang furiously on my door about thirty minutes later. In my condition I thought a goddam cannon had gone off, but then my paranoid mind settled on the truth. "It has to be cops! Jesus, I gotta get rid of the dope before they break in!" The door got pounded hard again. I didn't say a word but started stuffing the junk into a brown paper bag. As the door thunder went off again, I tossed the bag out the window and felt relieved to have beat the heat one more time. "Let the bastards find it now," I thought as I strolled towards the door. It banged again and I threw it wide open. Hooks was standing there. "What the fuck," he said. "Where have you been?"

"There were cops here!" I told him, wondering to myself. "You're crazy. It was me. You must have hallucinated." Hooks pressed on, "Where's the dope?" I thought, "Oh, shit!" and hustled for the door, then down to the street. Hooks figured I was totally gone when I went looking around in the trash. The brown paper bag of heroin was nowhere to be found. Some junkie must have thought he had died and gone to heaven when he saw that package come down from the sky.

So Hooks and I grabbed another cab and shot back to score another two bundles, which cost me fifty dollars more. But what the hell, it was only seed money from Uncle Bobby for getting off to a "new start."

When Hooks and I came back down somewhere close to reality the following morning, we washed up and sat down at the creaky wooden table in my room and talked. Hooks said that more junkies were out there now than the bulls could hold in all their joints, and he knew several addicts who made a point of turning on two or three new suckers every week. That was crazy because we never turned anyone on to junk and never wanted to. We had enough trouble getting our own without having a bunch of new assholes to deal with, plus their parents, if they were young.

By then a fleet of junkies was drifting about the city wearing oversized coats for rustling cattle from the supermarkets. The papers had run the scam on the front page a couple of times, so most stores had added stiff security to their operations. Of course, that cut into our cigarette action as well. Things had changed in the rectories, too, probably as a result of our earlier multiple strikes. Hooks and I were wondering which way to turn when a perfect new scam came our way.

I met a Puerto Rican junkie in Harlem whose brother worked at the post office but still lived at home. The guy told me his brother would on occasion hold aside a letter from American Express or Diners Club so he was getting the credit cards before they were delivered with no signatures on them yet. Then he sold them for twenty-five bucks a piece. This junkie had no idea what the hell they were good for, but I knew how much gold there was in those tickets. I told him to have his brother Santos put an order in for one of each.

Over the next six weeks, I got tight with Santos to the tune of paying him $150 or $200 per week to get me new cards. It was simple for him. At that time, the companies were just starting their big mail-order campaigns to get people to carry them, and Santos worked in the main sorting room at the Times Square Station. Santos was happy with his end of the deal, and Hooks and I had no complaints. I had cashmere coats, expensive sports jackets, mohair slacks, silk shirts, and Countess Mara ties. At times, I would charge a case of whiskey or champagne and sell it cheap to winos down in the Bowery. Those guys were in love with Hooks and me after a while. Hell, we loved them too. Everybody got an even break.

After serving our apprenticeships in the charge-card business, Hooks and I got hip to the Bad Card List issued by both Diners and American Express, and we managed to get a copy for ourselves each time they were issued to merchants. Then I started to phone people getting new cards, telling them, "we just want to check your current address, age, and occupation before we send your card." That way I knew something about the real cardholder in case a store clerk got suspicious. We would run up a modest amount—say $500 to $1,000—on each of the cards, limiting our purchases to $100 in each store, and then dump the cards in a sewer.

I had just gotten a fresh Diners card when I thought about the cash a piece of fine jewelry would bring. I went into a jewelry store on Madison Avenue and looked around like a seasoned tycoon, asking to see various pieces. Each item I inspected was more expensive than the last. In five minutes, I had picked a $2,900 diamond ring with a platinum setting. "I'll take it," I said to the clerk. I was king of the mountain as I handed him the card. He disappeared behind a red velvet curtain, saying, "I'll be right back, sir, as soon as the charge is verified, and I'll get a nice gift box for the ring."

The store owner apparently decided to check with Diners for approval. Diners had their doubts, too, so they dialed up the card's owner and asked if he had lent his card to a young chap who was purchasing a diamond and platinum ring, costing $2,900 plus tax. The Diners Club representative heard a "No, no, no!" to all questions. With that he hung up and dialed the cops.

The precinct sent a guy named Walsh, who was obviously delighted with the opportunity to bust someone dressed ten times better than he was. He made a point of flashing his handcuffs to some customers in the store before he slapped them on my wrists. Outside I was offered the familiar back seat for the ride to the station and after booking was sent to the Tombs, since that's the joint with jurisdiction over crimes committed in Manhattan. I had never been to the jail there before and was not thrilled with the prospect now since it had been almost nine hours since my last fix. Then the worst part dawned on me. Since this incident was a clear violation of my parole, no bail would be available. I was going to sit it out in the can.

I said when you've seen one joint, you've seen them all, but I must take that back when it comes to the Tombs of Manhattan. The entering process was the same, though I felt out of place with over five hundred dollars worth of clothing on my back, given where I was. Then a group of us got ushered into an elevator, headed for the "cattle floor," where they put dope fiends when they got arrested.

As the doors slid open, I could not believe what I saw and heard. My stomach crawled with the human misery all around. It was God-awful, and I was so scared I couldn't move. I tried to back up into the elevator, but the hack pushed me out with the butt of his stick. There must have been two hundred men on that floor, about ninety percent of them kicking habits. Guys were bent over in pain, others were yelling, crying for help or their mothers. The place smelled like a sewer, and it didn't matter whether a man threw up on the floor, urinated in his pants, or whatever, it stayed right there. The hacks didn't even seem to notice, and they were not about to do anything to help. I got sick to my stomach because I knew that in just a few hours I would be right in there with them, kicking cold turkey.

On the way to my cell, I saw a huge rat walk down the corridor as if he were the warden. Once inside, I looked around for more vermin. The dirt on the floor must have been there for years, and cockroaches as big as your index finger were running everywhere. When you slammed one, they all stopped as if to mark the memory of Cousin Bill the Roach but not for very long. I also found lice in the blankets, but the real bitch was that no one was interested in my discoveries. I was so dejected I sat down on the steel bunk and ripped my silk shirt wide open, popping the buttons.

Then the pain came, and it stayed. I was doubled up on the cold steel for hours, then down on the floor with all my animal friends. They didn't care and I didn't care. How could anyone care when you were freezing with pain, and at the same time it was too hot for blankets? I dragged myself up off the floor and slumped over the white porcelain commode, looking down at the water. I felt this strange urge to sneeze and vomit at the same time, and then it happened. The spasms caused me to throw up violently for at least two hours. It seemed like eternity before my gut relaxed.

At suppertime, they shoved a tray of mush under my cell door, with plain white bread and black coffee on the side. I pushed it back out in the corridor, figuring to let the rats eat the shit since I couldn't bear to look at it. Within minutes the roaches had found the dish. They were crawling all over the food, and four of them drowned in the coffee. The sight made me vomit uncontrollably for the next half hour. Then I started pacing in circles around the cell, holding onto my gut and squeezing hard, trying to get rid of this horrible monkey kicking the shit out of me.

Suddenly, this character in the next cell started shouting. "Get me outa here! I can't stand it, I'm dying! God, somebody help me!" A hack yelled for him to shut up without getting off his ass at the opposite end of the lockup. The guy kept screaming and moaning. It was taking my mind off the pain of my body, so I just listened. The guy picked up his plate and banged the bars of the cell with it. The hack had heard enough, so he came over to the cage and warned the junkie, "Shut the fuck up or I'm gonna tap your head with this," and he cracked a row of bars with his billy stick.

I figured this must have been the jerk's first pinch or he's not from New York because he told the hack, "Fuck you and your tap dances, I'm dying!" The hack's eyes lit up with a mean streak you could actually see, and he shoved the stick through the bars into my neighbor's gut, knocking the air out of his system and landing him on the cell floor. The guy shut up.

Later that night, he started talking to me. "Hey. You over there." I asked if he meant me since we couldn't see each other with the steel partition between cells. I didn't want to cause any more trouble than I already had on my hands, so I whispered, "Yeah, what." He paused for a moment and then said, "Aw, nothin'. I'm gonna hang up now." I said, "Yeah, right." Five minutes later I heard his throat gurgle for a split second and then the sound of a rhythmic thump—thump—thump against the bars of his cell.

I figured, "This fucking maniac is for real!" and called out loud, "Officer! Hang up!" The hack who responded was bent out of shape with having to walk fifteen feet probably for nothing. "Yeah, where the hell is it?" he said as he approached, slapping the club into his palm. His face went white as a sheet when he saw the guy next door hanging by his neck, dead. I turned away and didn't look when they brought a sheet and a stretcher to cart him off to the morgue. Within an hour, they brought another junkie up to fill the dead man's space, and it was as if nothing had gone down. I was stunned and wondered, "What the hell is the meaning of all this?" Of course, no answer came.

The next morning I was still sick and the memory of the sounds of death stuck close, as if I might be involved personally before long. I tried not to think about all the close calls I'd had, but I wondered what caused the guy to hang it up. Again, no answers, just haunting questions.

At ten or so a hack came out with a list and started calling names. It was arraignment time for last night's arrivals, and Marino was among them. They brought us to stand in front of the elevator, with a hack on each side and one more bringing up the rear. They were nervous and always carried their clubs in hand, never in their holsters. We zipped down to the first floor and were shown the inside of the bull pen to wait for a courtroom assignment.

My one phone call the day before had been to my bail bondsman, which was standard practice. He called my lawyer, and the lawyer called my brother Frank, who brought a change of clothes for me and was now waiting with the lawyer in a courtroom on the second floor. That's where I ended up, about twenty minutes later.

I was charged with attempted grand larceny and remanded into custody without bail until the trial, set for three weeks later. I told the lawyer to get in touch with Goodman, my parole officer up on sixteen and tell him I was in. Maybe he could do something. Frank came up to me and gave my beaten body a quick look. My habit was visible, and all my clothes were crumpled to hell. Frank said something about "how much shit can one man get into?" and shook his head before asking if I needed anything. I told him to send me the key to the front door if he got the chance. Frank grinned and said he'd "see what he could do to help." Even in the shape I was in, I could still appreciate my brother in tight situations.

My lawyer and I came up with a strategy to fight the case. I hadn't signed the charge slip—mainly because the detectives arrested me before I could—so we were going to try that technicality on a jury. Then Frank told me during a visit that he knew someone at Diners Club who might be convinced to drop the charge, but he needed more time. I decided to stall as much as I could, so at the first trial my lawyer asked for a month's delay to "gather more evidence." At the second session we asked for and got another three weeks to "prepare the case." When they brought it up the third time, I had a new lawyer there and told the judge I needed time to brief him. That bought us another twenty-day delay.

At each of these court sessions, Detective Walsh was there, and he didn't like me any better than when we had first met in the jewelry store. He persisted in questioning me. "Where did you get the card, Marino? Tell us and we'll see about a deal." I kept giving him smartass answers, which only made him madder.

Goodman took a special interest in my case and came down to see me once or twice a week. He was an all right guy, and he tried to steer me straight with his talks. "Surely you're good at *something* besides stealing, aren't you?" I couldn't think of what exactly, but I gave him my water-sports routine time and again, telling him that I was planning to get myself together this time, dry out totally, and stay on the straight and narrow. He suggested that we might get a deal from the judge to get me a reduced sentence if I would voluntarily commit myself for treatment at a federal facility in Lexington, Kentucky. Hooks had been there once, so I sent word with Frank to have Hooks come tell me about the place.

When Hooks finally showed up, I was surprised they didn't arrest him on the spot. Jesus, he looked awful. His face was sunken and shallow, his weight was down to maybe a hundred and ten pounds, and his nails were bitten to the knuckles. I told Hooks he should slow down, and he said, "Sure, Vinny. Tomorrow." He sounded so much like me that I had to laugh. Hooks also told me a very interesting piece of information about Lexington. Even though it was a federal penitentiary, when an addict came in on a voluntary basis, all you needed to get out was give forty-eight hours notice, and they opened the gates. At that point I made a decision to go for a stretch in Lexington if there was any way to work the deal.

In the end, I stayed over six months in the Tombs and saw more than two thousand junkies come and go with their complaints and withdrawal pains. One thing that always amused me was the number of guys who listed their home addresses as the Tombs because they knew they would be back shortly and didn't want their mail to get lost.

Then the word came through Frank that he had reached a

central figure at Diners Club headquarters and told the guy that I was addicted but had kicked and wanted to go straight and wouldn't they help me out. He must have done something right because the Diners' people allowed the charges to be dropped to attempted petty larceny. My lawyer arranged to go through the sentencing before a judge, who handed me six months, the maximum for my charge. The Tombs' time counted so I was due for immediate release, or that's what I thought. Goodman was also back in the picture with a deal to get me off the parole violation if I would voluntarily go to Lexington. That became part of the parole condition, when they shipped me back to Riker's Island Block 2, where I sat for two days waiting to see the parole board.

When they called me in to the hearing, the head man wasted no words, "Mr. Marino, your case seems to be going from bad to worse. Now, Mr. Goodman is recommending that you be granted your freedom based on a voluntary commitment to enter the substance abuse program at the federal facility in Lexington, Kentucky. Is that correct, and if we approve this recommendation, will you go to Lexington?"

I looked at the man in earnest and said, "Sir, I realize how my record looks. It stinks. But now I know where I went wrong, and I want to straighten out—for good. Yes, if you say the word, I will be in Lexington in the morning. I have already arranged for my family to buy me a plane ticket."

The next morning, I went to Lexington, and two days after I checked in I put in a chit to get out because I felt like getting high. After all, the parole board had said nothing about how long I had to stay in Lexington; they just said I had to go there. At the end of the fourth day, I checked out and got on a bus back to New York.

Not long after that, Goodman got wind of my fast move and came to my mom's place when I happened to be there on a visit. He banged on the door and called out, "Vinny, I know you're in there. Open up." I didn't know what to say to him so I sat tight and waited for him to go away. Mom was out shopping, or she would have given me up. But Goodman kept on banging, so I opened the door and invited him in. He was sweating profusely, and the white shirt was soaking. Goodman leaned forward, almost in pure exasperation, pleading, "What the hell happened, Vinny?" I told him the eggs were cold at breakfast, so I left. He dropped his head in his hands, as if to cry.

I heard three months later that Goodman had dropped dead with a bad heart attack. For a minute I wondered if I had anything to do with it, but then I took off for Harlem and another load of junk.

A week after my return from Lexington, I got settled into the Flander's Hotel in Manhattan, then set out to find Hooks. His folks were visibly proud when they told me he voluntarily checked into Riverside for detoxification. It was hard for me to believe my eyes when, two days later, Hooks showed up at my room, soaking wet and obviously straining from some heavy exercise. When I asked him what the hell was going on, he told me he had just made it off North Brother's Island by swimming. I told that he had to be full of shit or high as hell, which he denied. He stuck to his story of swimming away. The next day his version was confirmed by the newspapers with a third-page story. "Man swims from Riverside Hospital on North Brother's Island—Fate Unknown." I laughed and waved the paper in front of Hooks.

I was amazed that Hooks had made it, looking as bad as he did. His eyes were sunk so far back in his head I didn't know how he managed to see anything clearly. Of course, neither one of us was seeing anything clearly at that time.

I was over at his place in Brooklyn about three days after he had paddled home, and we were back to the old game of talking about ways to make money right after we had both gotten off in a combination shot of heroin and desoxyn. We were out of cigarettes so I volunteered to drop downstairs to a nearby mom 'n pop store and get some.

When I hit the street and looked into this little store, no one was behind the front counter. Looking again, I saw an old lady eating a sandwich in a small kitchen in the back. Something told me this could be an opportunity. I eased the door open and got down on all fours to check things out as fast as possible. Behind the counter was a gallon-size jar filled with loose quarters. Without a second thought, I cradled the jar and crawled back out the door, then ran in a flash up to Hooks' apartment.

I told Hooks where I had gotten it and not to worry because no one had made me, and no one even knew that it was gone yet. We didn't waste any time getting out of his place, since his folks were due home from work, and we had to get rid of the change in a hurry. Hooks grabbed two paper bags, and we emptied the money into them, then hustled down to the street. I waited in the foyer of his building while he hailed a cab. We got out on Fifth Avenue and started looking for a bank.

I couldn't believe my eyes when two narcotics detectives came out from a theater lobby and pulled us inside to frisk us. I set the coins down on the lobby floor as I turned to face the wall for their frisk. Luckily we were both clean, except for the obvious question that came when one of the bulls looked into the bag. "Okay, where the hell did you clowns get these?"

Without blinking, I said, "I work as a doorman at a restaurant, and those are the tips I saved." The cop looked at me like I was nothing more than a bold-faced liar and said to stay put while he went to his car and radioed the precinct. Incredibly, our good fortune prevailed since the victims had not yet called in their losses. The cops had no choice but to let us go.

Once inside the bank, I noticed that they had done some fancy redecorating to include low, open counters for the tellers in place of the standard cage with bars. I asked one if she could change the coins into paper money. "We can't take them unless they're in rolls and marked." I thanked her for nothing, and we left the bank to look for another place willing to do business without the formality of rolls. We ended up stopping in at least seven or eight different stores to get rid of it all. But when everything was finished, we tallied the take at just over six hundred dollars.

"Not too shabby," I said, "for a cigarette run." Hooks was shaking with laughter as we boarded a cab heading for Harlem to cop.

Within four days we were broke again, as a direct result of the outrageous cost to maintain our drug habits. I recalled the bank with open counters and said to Hooks, "You know, that bank is worth a shot if we can our act together." We agreed to meet at the corner near the bank three hours later in our working clothes. I went back to my room and slipped into my Sunday best, including a dress shirt and tie with a sports jacket for the occasion. Hooks showed up looking like a derelict, exactly as we had planned.

He went in about eight paces ahead of me. As soon as he was inside, he doubled up as if in some kind of hard pain and headed back toward the assistant manager's desk. As he walked, he started groaning so everybody could hear and fell down on his left side, then rolled over and over as if he was caught up in an epileptic fit or something. All the bank employees focused their attention on him just as I reached over one girl's counter and dipped into her cash drawer. I quickly lifted all the ones, fives, and tens, and was reaching in for the twenties when she started to turn back towards me. I figured to get out while the getting was good. Two blocks away, Hooks rejoined me and we got into a cab for the familiar ride to Harlem. In less than five minutes, with no hassles at all, we had made off with a little over eight hundred dollars. I thought it was too good to be true.

We walked back into the same bank no less than two weeks later. This time Hooks dressed differently, and he went up to a teller's window and threw a loud fit, something about not being able to find his mother and "God can't somebody please help me?" His act drew all eyes for that one split second. This time I skipped the ones and grabbed all the fives, tens, and twenties for a grand haul of $2,205. From that point to this day, I never set foot in that bank again. No use pushing your luck, right?

By the fall of 1962, I was widely known in Brooklyn and Little Italy as an accomplished mover, hustler, and all-around thicf-at-large. I always seemed to have some swag for sale—a TV set, stereo, air conditioner, cigarettes, what have you. I never liked to hang onto the stuff for long because anything but cash involved the risk of getting caught twice—once when you stole it and once again when you sold it. Hooks and I solved that little problem by getting enough money together to buy an old '55 Chevy hardtop. We started cruising around the streets behind delivery trucks, stealing to somebody's order.

One time we were in a cab stuck on a side street behind an appliance store truck. I asked the driver if he wouldn't like to make a fast twenty. He said sure and never asked what he had to do, which was nothing but sit there and watch. We waited until the deliverymen went in the store with a huge refrigerator and closed the door behind them. Then Hooks and I jumped from the cab into the truck lickety split and came running back with a portable TV and air conditioner. We threw the air conditioner on the front seat of the cab and the TV in back, then told the driver to, "Jump the damn curb and get the fuck outa here!" He couldn't say anything but, "Jeesus! What the hell did you guys do?" as he sped away from the scene. He was still shaking his head when he got out of the cab downtown next to my favorite swag buyer's place, and I tipped him five more.

The guy who ran the wholesale swag operation bought almost anything I had, but the catch was his conversion rate was a lousy twenty to thirty percent of the retail price. The owner's name was Maxie Berger, and he was every bit the thief that I was. He operated a "legitimate" storefront, that's all. We settled on $250 in cash for both pieces. After the transaction we were just looking around his joint, relaxing for a moment, when I noticed about a hundred cardboard cartons, all marked with various prestige brand-name perfumes, like Arpege, Chanel, and My Sin. I asked Berger what it was all about, and he muttered something about a special buy he had made, such that he could give us a "real deal" on them.

"Just fifty cents for the one ounce bottle, or if you want a gross at a time, it'll be even less—like forty cents a bottle. Hell, that kind of stuff is real expensive." I bought about a dozen of each, paying him with the same cash he had just given me. Back in the cab heading for Brooklyn, Hooks thought I was crazy for going into the perfume business and poked fun at me. I told him to just sit back and wait. We were going to conduct a little "field test" of the neighborhoods.

Even I couldn't quite believe the way most of the guys took to the stuff, once they were convinced it was legitimate and not bootlegged. I reassured everybody. I told them that "we had just hit a ship," or that "someone had taken off a shipment," and they went for it. At first I was selling the bottles at two dollars a piece or three for five. As Christmas came closer and business picked up, I jacked the price to three dollars each and two for five.

Within a month I was traveling to Berger's three or four times a week, buying two or three gross each trip. I had a regular list of local clubs that would take a case or two. It even amazed me the way that fake perfume caught on in no time. Everybody reordered, and I figured they must be reselling it at four to five dollars per bottle. That was fine with me. I was making $800 to $1,200 a week, and it was a legit business—I could always claim someone had sold it to me as the real stuff if anything went wrong.

The bottom of the whole business fell out when the newspapers did their own investigation of this phenomenon and exposed the story on all the front pages. A couple of television news shows did features on the subject, too, which showed the similarity between the bogus stuff and the genuine thing. The news dubbed it the "Bathtub Perfume Caper" and several dealers had been busted, but not me or Berger. When the lid blew off, I took my last case back to Berger and got a refund after a short hassle. I threatened to withhold future swag deals, and he ended up giving me the cash.

However, getting cash was not a particular problem for me in New York—drugs were the problem. My habit inevitably ended up costing whatever cash I had, almost down to the penny. When Hooks and I were flush, we shot speedballs—that incredible combination of going both ways with cocaine for the up charge and heroin for the real smooth feeling. Of course, there were days when we had to get by with only fifty or sixty bucks between us, and we would be on the edge of sickness. The whole thing was a vicious circle, but we were usually too high to do any serious thinking about it.

As the wheel turned, I found myself looking into another new business, which involved the appearance of zircon stones—the ones that look just like diamonds. I grew up right around the corner from the jewelry exchange on Canal Street, so most of the employees were from the neighborhood, and from time to time I would hear about some deals that went down involving swag or phoney goods. I decided to check out the exchange scene again for myself, and I noticed as I walked through the various stores in my finest outfits that those guys didn't operate like small jewelers did. When you wanted to see a certain piece, they brought out the whole tray instead of just what you asked for. Since most of them were fairly big dealers, they didn't seem to pay strict attention to the risk of the merchandise being out on the counter for close inspection. Part of it, I was sure, had to do with my appearance. They probably figured I had the money to be in the place and could afford to buy whatever I looked at.

My next step was to check out the prices of the zircon settings. It blew me away when I found out that a zircon might sell for $20 to $30 for a full carat, when the real diamond went for $1,500 to $2,000. You could buy a zircon and have it set in 14-carat gold or platinum for about $100.

I would take an inspection trip through the exchange and visually pick out the item I wanted. Then I would head straight for the zircon dealer to describe the match-up of the expensive thing with a zircon fake. Within a matter of hours, certainly not later than the next day, the zircon would be ready, and I went into action. Returning to the exchange, I would ask to see a piece on the same tray as the one I had marked for the caper but not the actual piece I was ready to switch. I got very adept at switching my fake for the diamond right under their noses.

Unfortunately, it wasn't long before the store owners began to notice the switched pieces in their inventory, and they put one and one together with my reputation around town. At that point, a lot of them would simply refuse to let me in the place, or they would put two clerks on my tail, so I couldn't make a move.

I adjusted and went into phase two, accompanied by beautiful women to distract their attention. Most of the girls were hookers made up to look stylish and conservative, like a neighborhood girl I was about to marry. And that was the story we used. We needed an engagement ring. Typically, I already marked the one I wanted and had the switch ready in my hand when we would ask to see another ring. At the critical moment, I would tell the clerk, “That's the one. Let me put a deposit on it.” I would reach for a wad of bills, always flashing a couple of hundreds and fifties. As he removed the ring from the tray to mark it sold, I would switch my fake for the piece I wanted, then hand him a fifty. Naturally, I never returned to claim the deposit or the ring we had put on hold.

It went along that way for at least a couple of months. I made a successful hit once a week, sometimes more often. One hot, muggy day in August, I was sweating like a hog and didn't feel well since it had been about eight hours since I had shot my last fix. I was making a switch, but my timing was horrible, and the clerk made me with no difficulty at all, but I didn't notice. Thinking I was slicker than owlshit, I put the ring in my mouth and turned to head for the door. Without the slightest hesitation, the clerk started up with, “Stop! Thief!” at the top of his voice, raising every eyebrow in the place. He ran toward me at the exit door, and I flashed on whether he might have a gun since a lot of guys carried a piece at the exchange. I bolted out the door, figuring to make it to grandma's place three hundred yards away. As soon as I hit the sidewalk, I saw a cop on the corner of Canal and the Bowery, and before I had made half a block, the clerk was sicking thc bull on mc. “Thcrc hc gocs! Thicf!”

The cop decided to become a hero, pulled his gun, and came after me yelling, “Stop or I'll shoot!” I didn't think so, not with innocent people out on the street who might get hit, so I took the adrenalin for what it was worth and turned on the speed right up to the maximum. I rounded Hester Street and made a right. Within five seconds I was at grandma's front stoop, which was eight steps up. I hit the top step in two jumps, opened the foyer door, and slipped inside. Panic was still slapping my insides as I saw the cop coming after me only about fifty yards away.

Grandma's apartment was on the first floor, first on the left. I shot to the door and tried to open it, but in a flash remembered that she had three deadbolts for extra protection. I banged loud as hell on it, yelling, "Ma! Open up! It's me, Vinny. Hurry up, ma!" As she fumbled with the locks she was concerned, saying, "I'm coming, I'm coming."

"Please hurry, ma. I'm in trouble," I pleaded.

Just as she opened the door to let me in, the cop pulled open the front door of the building and saw where I went. After bolting one of the locks, I handed the ring to grandma and asked her to hide it for me and not to say anything. I opened the window in ma's kitchen and jumped ten feet to the ground right after I heard a loud triple knock at her door. I was in an Italian neighborhood, and all I needed to do was knock on virtually anyone's door and say in Italian, "I need some help, I'm in trouble. The law's after me." But I wasn't thinking and I tried to make a run for it on the street.

The cop got close enough to point his gun and make it stick four blocks from grandma's place, and I was in handcuffs again, heading for the end of another fast run. I knew that I would be going to the Tombs, and my stomach crawled with fear as I thought of the cattle floor and the junkies going through hell, with me about to join them for another round of gut-wrenching misery. Within an hour of my arrest, I was mugged, fingerprinted, and booked, then led to the tank. Early that evening I went to night court for my arraignment, and the judge slapped me with a ridiculously high bail, probably because of my record. I couldn't make it since I couldn't reach my bondsman at that hour, so I was processed, showered, inspected, and off for the lift ride to the ninth floor. The thought of it sent a bolt of horror straight through my body, but when we got there and the door opened, conditions were even worse than I had imagined.

There used to be one man to a cell, now it was two or three. The roaches and rats had increased their populations in similar fashion, and nothing had been done about the filth of the place. The only thing different was they had added one more steel slab to each cell. As I entered the six-by-nine cage, I wasn't ready for the guy who was laying up on the bunk to my right, all wrapped in wool blankets, sweating and doubled over in pain. He was moaning real low and rolling from side to side. No way could I handle it. I considered calling and asking the hack for another cell but thought better of it and just sat down on the cold steel to watch what my new roommate was going to do next. In my condition, I didn't need any surprises.

That night in the Tombs taught me something new about self-discipline and willpower. At first I felt the guy lying right above me might be dangerous, so I couldn't take my eye off him. It helped to imagine myself as a hack or his shrink, sitting there with him as my patient. Then I thought how I might be his father or his brother, just watching to see that the pain didn't get out of hand. My cellmate started heaving, and I knew in an instant he'd be tossing his cookies, but I didn't want the mess or the smell, so I told him straight, "Make the crapper, man!" He got louder with the moaning, so I said it again. "Yo! Make the crapper, not on the floor!"

He slid down off the top bunk and went on all fours to the crapper in the corner, where he draped his arms over the sides with his head partways down in the bowl. He retched for over an hour, and all the sounds were magnified by the flushing bowl. At one point I felt like telling him to "Move over!" so both of us could hang in there. I hung my head in my hands and thought it must be like this down in hell itself.

As morning came on, it struck me that a whole night had passed but I hadn't lost it like I thought I would. I had gone through some horrible physical pain—mainly in my stomach—chills, hot flashes, dry heaves, and spasms, but I found that I could ride most of it out mentally and leave a lot of the drama behind. I saw right then that most times in the past I had put on the physical act to make a point, especially if it could do me some good, like in a hospital where you could get methadone or some other drug. But the Tombs didn't carry methadone; all they had was hacks with big sticks. I was better off concentrating on my cellmate, neglecting my own situation as much as possible. To my amazement, it worked.

The court set my case for eleven that morning, so I was called down to the first floor at about nine-thirty, after shoving my breakfast back out in the corridor where it belonged. My cellmate did the same. At ten past eleven, the bailiff called my name, and they read out the charge of grand larceny. I pleaded not guilty, looking over at brother Frank as I said the words. He was leaning forward with his hands on the back of the bench in the first row of the courtroom, obviously concerned. Bail was continued at $25,000, and my bondsman was on hand to make it. I figured in about an hour I'd have to lie my way out of a discussion with Frank so I could make it up to Harlem and shoot up to get my head straight and my body back in shape.

Frank was waiting outside the courthouse when I was released, just like I figured he would be, but there was no shaking him that time. I stuck my hands in my pockets as we walked along, and he stuck his arm through mine to be sure I didn't get away. "Where the hell are you going, anyway?" he said. "I just want to lay down and sleep for a while," I finally said. But he didn't buy that. "Bullshit, Vinny, you're looking to go and get loaded again, that's all," he said shaking my arm. I stopped cold and looked him straight in the eye. "No, I'm not, Frank, really. I just want to clean up and take a shower. Then get some sleep." He tried to turn me into a restaurant, suggesting, "Hey, I'll tell you what. Let's get a bite to eat. I want to talk to you about something important."

I thought, "Eat, shit. I don't need to eat, Frank, I need a fix." Instead I said, "You order, Frank, and I'll be right back. I gotta go see a guy on some business. It'll only take fifteen minutes. Promise. I'll meet you right here." I backed out of the restaurant door and grabbed a cab before Frank had a chance to block my move. I made it to my room and my money stash, then had the cabbie take me to Hundred and First and First. By the time I scored, shot up, and got back to the restaurant, Frank had been waiting long enough to have a hamburger and two cups of coffee—maybe an hour and ten or fifteen minutes. He was not overjoyed with what I had pulled or the fact that I was stoned again.

"Damn, Vinny. I don't understand. Don't you ever learn anything?" I mumbled something, but he went on to describe a problem he was facing that might turn out to be an opportunity for me to make an honest buck and "get the hell off that junk." It seems Frank had a minor problem with his spleen that required surgery and three to four weeks off work to recuperate. At the time, he was a doorman at a classy restaurant, parking cars. He told me that on normal nights there would be as many as thirty or forty cars, and busy nights even more.

He figured that each of them was worth at least a buck tip, which meant that in a six-day week he was making around $200 to $250. "You don't have to go to work until six at night, and you're done by 11:30, latest 12:00, with a meal included." I didn't quite know how to react to everything he was saying, but I figured to tell him "yeah" no matter what he said. I also figured that I might just do it since I did owe Frank. He smiled and said, "Hey, that's great, Vinny. I sure do appreciate it. Why don't you come down tonight and I'll show you the ropes?"

The ropes turned out to be on the sidewalk in red velvet, under the canopy of the San Marino Restaurant. Through the dense fog of drugs, I somehow got it together to move three or four cars around for Frank, then met the owners of the place, a nice family named Sergio. Just after eleven, one of the brothers came out and asked us to come in for dinner. I didn't feel much like eating, but I changed my mind when they put on some special fettucine. Nothing like good Italian food, even if I couldn't see straight.

Two nights later I was on the front line alone, and I really did go in straight. I hadn't done anything in about six hours, although I had some junk stashed in my locker at the restaurant for later that night. Inside of two hours, I had about thirty-five customers' cars strung out over a three-square-block area, and I was running my ass off trying to figure out how to bring the thing closer to home. Besides, I soon discovered the tips were a lot better the faster I got the man his car. It only made sense. So the first new move I made was to put my cars at the three fire hydrants, two bus stops, an alleyway, and two red zones, all between Second and Third on Fifty-third. Then I double parked the whole left side of the street since it was one-way. I watched my block for cops and hustled over to talk or buy them out of the fifteen dollar ticket the car was due.

Within a week I started to steal parking tickets from their rightful owners on my way to work. I just lifted them off the front windshields. A parking ticket was one thing you could steal in broad daylight, and nobody seemed to mind. I took them to work with me and kept them inside my huge doorman's coat. About nine every night, I would ticket the whole block, maybe fifty or sixty cars in total. The scam was to hustle a guy by telling him that you had put the false ticket on the car, which caused the cops to pass it by. "Hey, man, I saved you fifteen dollars." The line was always good for a couple of bucks, maybe three, sometimes five. It was getting to be a real interesting job. The pay was up in the range of $250 to $500 a week. My habit was taken care of, and the action was legitimate for the first time.

During the second week I noticed a new building going up nearby. They had just finished the ground floor, and it would make a hell of a parking area if someone could talk his way into the grounds. The night watchman turned out to be an Italian guy named Joe Delvecchio from Brooklyn. In no time we agreed that he'd let me in to park cars for fifty cents a piece.

I looked the place over and came to the conclusion that it would hold a hundred cars, maybe more in a pinch. Then I figured I would need a runner if it was going to be a regular parking operation, which was exactly what I intended. Two days later my runner was in place, and we were soliciting business right off the street. I started telling the restaurant customers, "I might have to put it in the garbage because the street is tight and the cops can't be bought. A ticket would cost you $15." Most customers would tell me to "do what you have to," and that naturally meant their car went straight to my garage on the corner at $2.75 for the first hour and $1.00 per hour after that. We had an elaborate keyboard with color codes to locate the cars, since it got so busy we had to let some customers go and get their own.

By the third week, I had hired a second runner for the "garage" and started taking some of the cars for rides up to Harlem. That was, of course, after making sure the customer was comfortably seated in the restaurant. In Harlem I would score the junk I wanted, get off, and drive back to the garage. Once I took a couple's car after they had been in the restaurant ten minutes, but they decided to leave about five minutes later. Lucky for about an hour after that, I saw them at the corner before I turned left so I shut the car off right there. I rubbed my hands in the dirt before hustling up with the line, "There was battery cable trouble, but I finally got it fixed." The guy wasn't too happy about his missing Jaguar for that hour, but what could he really do? I put my hand out for a tip as I opened his door. Again he didn't know what else to do, so he gave me a buck. I gave him a grin and a big, "Thank you, sir."

Trouble came in the form of a strange car sitting in the driveway to my garage one night, three and a half weeks into the gig. The driver was the owner of the building, with "What the hell are all these cars doing here?" Delvecchio came shuffling up and went into a classic act: "Hey! What the hell are all these cars doing here? Get these cars outa here!" It started to drizzle as my two runners and I moved each one of those cars out of the ''garage'' and back onto the street since the owner had so rudely closed down our swank operation.

Frank recovered and came back to work two days after we had to close the garage. He couldn't believe how I filled up the whole block with our cars. I told him, ''Don't worry, Frank, it's cool.'' When he saw the tips, he just kept doing what I had started. With Frankie on the job again, we let one runner go, and I started to drift away from full-time parking and get more into drugs.

After a month or so, I would only show up on real busy nights, like Friday and Saturday, and every once in a while I would put in a couple of hours at ''showtime,'' when the curtains would go up on Broadway. It was a real phenomenon in New York. The plays used to start at eight-thirty each night, and when it happened, traffic from the east to the west side was tied up tighter than a drum. No one could move, although you wouldn't think so if you heard all the horns. The whole city went off like a bell at that hour, and people who were otherwise fairly normal started screaming, ''Come on, you jerk!'' or ''Get the hell outa my way!''

One Thursday night at showtime I went down to the restaurant to see Frank. It was raining and chilly, and I felt nervous and rotten since I had just spent fourteen days at Metropolitan Hospital where I had voluntarily entered their twenty-one-day detox program. I couldn't take any more so I had left that morning, and I thought of Frank in terms of borrowing fifty or a hundred dollars, naturally to use for scoring.

As I approached the street, it was an absolute standstill, and the sound of the horns was magnified by the buildings. Pop was standing talking with Frank since he was a doorman at a restaurant right up the block. Just as I walked up, a black guy in a Cadillac limousine had gotten as far as the restaurant, and he was leaning hard on his horn for no apparent reason. I had a hellish headache, and that jerk was interrupting my plea with Frank for money. I walked over to his car window and was real humble as I said, ''Look, pal, it's showtime and this traffic here is straight up to Eight Avenue, bumper to bumper. Blowin' your horn ain't gonna help anything. So please, do me a favor and lay off, huh?''

The driver pushed my hand off his car door. ''You can kiss my ass, white boy. I'll blow this muthafuckin' horn as much as I want,'' and he leaned on it again. The monster in me exploded. I put both hands on his door and spoke out in real anger. ''Look you liver-lipped, rubber-gummed black motherfucker, I asked you nice the first time, and now I'm telling you, if you wanta be a tough guy, come on out of the car."

Instead of reaching for the door handle, the dirty bastard reached under the dashboard for something. "Damn," I thought, "gun!" I whirled to grab the big black restaurant doorman's umbrella from Frank. As I turned back to face the driver again, he had opened his door and showed me his weapon—a wooden bat about eighteen inches long. I turned the umbrella into a spear and jammed it hard for survival right at his face. He moved slightly, and it struck him in the left cheek, where blood shot out. I pulled back to see what he'd do and noticed that this dude stood about six-three—mean and ugly and mad and bleeding. He was swinging the bat like he could murder somebody.

I jabbed at his head again, but the blow glanced off his skull, and I backed off, then turned the umbrella around so I could swing it and hit him with the wooden handle. I got into some fast footwork on my way backwards, and he took a swing at me but missed. I swung at his head as hard as I could while he was off balance, and I caught him alongside the left ear, knocking him to the pavement. My hit also broke the umbrella handle.

By this time a whole crowd of people had gathered, from the street and inside the restaurant. Frank ran in to grab the other doorman's umbrella, since mine was shot. The black was up and coming at me with bat in hand, although he was somewhat wobbly and bleeding badly. One of the Sergio brothers from the restaurant had run back in to call the cops. The black guy swung at me but missed and hit a fender with a bang! I came up from the ground with a right and clipped him under the chin, and Frank cracked him on the head with the back-up umbrella. That put him down to stay, and by then I could hear the sirens off in the distance.

The cops arrived about twenty seconds later and arrested me and pop. They called an ambulance for the black cat. That was a new precinct for me, and we got a lucky turn on the way to the station when one of the cops turned around and said to pop, "Don't I know you?" Sure enough, pop know him since he'd been working as a doorman in the area for the last three or four years. When we got to the station, I knew several of the beat cops standing around, and they knew me as the doorman at the restaurant, Frank's brother, not as a junkie. After we had been booked for assault, the cops started to talk to us about strategy.

One of them suggested that we file a countercharge against the black, charging him with assault as well. I told the cops that he had verbally threatened and abused me and had taken the first swing.

They drew up our papers, and one of the cops called the black to tell him that countercharges had been filed. As a result, he would have to be locked up until bail could be set and made, unless, of course, he wanted to drop the charges against the Marinos.

It turned out that everything got dropped, including the hammer. Pop and I were released and went back to the restaurant looking for Frank, but Frank had already been fired. For what? Well, the restaurant owners had come out to witness the fight, and in the process they saw where we had all the cars parked, with parking tickets on every one. Then they found about four hundred more tickets in my lockers so they must have figured something like "lawsuit," and they blew the Marino brothers off Fifty-third like so many Italian salamis in a windstorm. I found out later that the black guy we hit sued the restaurant, and they made an out-of-court settlement.

9 / SYNANON FOR LIFE?

Just after my twenty-fourth birthday at the beginning of 1963, the United States government enacted a new law about illegal search and scizure based on the *Miranda* case. To me it was like catching an ace with a face card in a blackjack game because it involved the suppression of evidence gained illegally. I could now get caught with heroin or some works on my person, but the cops couldn't present it as evidence because they had no legal reason for stopping me in the first place.

Miranda worked like a charm for me. I was stopped twice in one month, on the street for no reason, and the first time the detective found a bundle of junk in my shirt pocket. The next round, I got caught when I was high, nodding out on a corner in Brooklyn, and they found a set of works plus three ten-dollar bags of junk. In both cases I played "delay" and *Miranda* to the hilt. To postpone, I claimed we needed more time for evidence or that I was in the hospital to detox, my lawer couldn't make it, or I had just changed lawyers.

Each time a case is postponed, all of the witnesses and the arresting officer have to come back again, or it ends up being dismissed. I had postponed the two junk cases four or five times each, until one day the cop who arrested me didn't show so the judge dutifully dismissed the case. From the center of the courtroom, the district attorney stopped dead with a look of total disbelief on his face. I laughed to myself as he threw his whole sheaf of papers onto the courtroom floor and turned up to the judge at the bench. "How can you release this man? We *know* he's a drug addict and a criminal. He was arrested with heroin on him both times. How is this allowed to happen in a legitimate court of law?'' I didn't feel like sticking around for any reversals, so I saluted the bench and walked out the door, a free man.

I should say free from the joint, but not the junk since I was using both heroin and doriden heavy. I had two habits going, and the overdoses were getting more and more frequent. When the case of the stolen ring from the diamond exchange came up for the fourth time on the docket I was really in bad shape. By then, the clerk from the store had quit his job and left town, which seemed like a miracle. The judge dismissed that case, too, based on the missing witness plus the fact that they had never found any evidence. (I later found out my momma had given the ring to the Catholic Church one Sunday morning at High Mass.)

I was soon back on the streets, mainly in Brooklyn, dealing drugs and using the leftovers to support my habits, which were vicious. One night I went to Harlem, where I bought one hundred dollars worth of junk and went up a stairwell leading to the roof to get off. I overdosed there, and somebody relieved me of about sixty dollars, all the junk, my shirt and jacket plus my shoes. That was March and a long way from summer. I stumbled six long blocks to my connection's place, shivering like hell in my stocking feet. I bummed a dime and called Hooks, begging him to bring a cab and save my worthless ass. My life was just dragging on, near disaster with the drugs, and with no other real purpose.

Hooks and I knew most of the guys from the old neighborhood, so we ended up both dealing and doing drugs with them. One of our favorite hangouts was the Lowe's Theater on Forty-sixth Street. It had a big covered foyer where we could stand back off the street and still see all the action without loitering in front of a store. Hooks and I made it a special point to go see the manager of the theater, where we pitched him on our value to him as we could stop any trouble before it got started with unruly kids. All we wanted in exchange was the right to see the movies free. He said he already had one security cop but, ''What the hell, okay. You guys keep everything cool and go ahead into the movie whenever you like.'' So we hung out there, usually high as hell, doing our deals from a car parked in the alley next to the place.

One night late, when Hooks and I had just gotten off, I was out of it and barely able to walk as we passed the theater. It was after eleven, and the box office was closed. I told Hooks I was going to catch what was left of the picture. He didn't feel like it, so he wandered off. When I reached the foyer, I opened the door to the lobby and was confronted by a guy in a security uniform, someone I didn't recognize. I felt this mean streak running right up my back and didn't like the fact that he was in my way.

"Where the hell do you think you're going, man?" I stepped right up and said, "To see the maanager." He shot back, "You can't see the manager. He's in the office, countin' receipts." I brushed him aside. "That's alright. I'll knock first." With that I turned and took two steps toward the office door, when the guard pulled his stick and came across with a full swing aimed at my right eye. The blow sent me reeling toward the door, but he wasn't finished. He hit my eye twice again, and as I was sliding to the floor his fourth swing missed me and shattered the glass door to the lobby.

I went down for the count, with the whole right side of my face blown up, my right eye completely closed, and blood everywhere. The manager came out, but he didn't recognize me, so he ran back to his office to call the bulls. Ten minutes later two cops handcuffed me even though I was semiconscious.

While the cops were getting ready to take me away, a neighborhood kid who had heard the ruckus came out of the movie and recognized me. He shot over to tell my brother what had gone down, and Frank got to the station house within fifteen minutes, and insisted they take me to a hospital. After a delay, they booked me for malicious mischief and assigned another car to transport me with Frank to Isreal Zion Hospital. The people in the emergency room took one look at my face and the cops and said, "We can't do anything for that eye here. It's too bad." Another forty-five agonizing minutes in an ambulance got me to King's County Hospital, and then all they did was clean up the blood and try to slow the swelling.

Over the next two days, the medical team diagnosed a "concussion with a blow-out fracture of the floor of the orbit beneath the right eye." The eye couldn't even be seen because the entire right side of my head was closed for reconstruction of the worst kind. The morning of the third day they finally opened the eye for inspection and found out it was bad. They operated on it twice that week. By the end of the second week, I was getting methadone for a habit, and my eyesight was 20/200. I wore a black patch to keep my right eye under cover and out of the way since it was useless anyway.

As I came slowly back into full consciousness and the realization of what had gone down, my feelings ran from total outrage with that theater guard, the theater, and the cops to a down-in-despair-fuck-living feeling with who I was and everything I stood for. Then my problems got compounded. At my arraignment, the bullshit judge hit me with a bail of five hundred dollars on the charge of malicious mischief. I should have been let go on my own recognizance for a penny-ante charge like that.

At the appointed hour, my name was called and the judge noticed the absence of a lawyer. I told him, "That's okay, Your Honor, I can defend myself on this one. I'm ready for sentencing." Incredibly, the judge asked, "Now, you have no previous record, is that right, Mr. Marino?" Jeesus! I couldn't believe it. I had been in every joint in four out of the five boroughs. Without thinking any further than, "Well, he didn't look, damned if I tell him what's right under his nose," I said, "Yes, Your Honor." He banged hard with his gavel on the wooden bench and sent down a sentence of thirty days, suspended. I got up with a smile and said, "Thank you, Your Honor," and turned for the exit sign at the back of the room.

As the judge looked down at my file to sign the order, he saw a whole string of charges typed out under my name, and the shock hit him. He yelled out, "Mr. Marino! Wait a minute." My heart froze as I stopped dead on the rubber mat laid down the aisle of the courtroom. I turned around slowly. "Yes, Your Honor." He glanced down sternly over his bifocals and said, "I thought I heard you say you had no previous record." Standing there halfway home, I figured to go for the drama. "Well, I don't, Your Honor, not for disorderly conduct. This is the first time I have ever been picked up for that."

I knew the act went down when everyone in the courtroom broke up in laughter. Then I couldn't help laughing, and finally the judge cracked a smile. "Go on, Marino. Get out of this room before I change my mind." I couldn't exactly figure out who was blind that day, me or the judge. To avoid the confusion of too much thinking on the subject, I grabbed another cab and rode off to get loaded in Harlem.

By this time, it had been more than ten years of full or part-time heroin use for me, and I was feeling the toll. Most days dragged on in a round of blurry stupors. And now I had a black patch over my eye, which made me look suspicious right from the start in most stores. Whatever novelty the lifestyle had died a nasty death and went straight to hell. Nothing was funny anymore because my sense of humor was buried in junk, and it took a lot of stealing to support the dead-end swindle of my daily habit. Both my old neighborhoods—Brooklyn and Little Italy—had me marked as a ''living legend'' in terms of thievery and drugs, so naturally whenever anything happened the local cops would come looking for me.

Most times they found me high as a kite, standing on a corner or sitting on a stoop, which made me an easy target anytime a cop had a particular frustration he wanted to vent. I was always good for a couple of free cracks across the face. Then there was always the option of handcuffing me and hauling me off to the station for ten or twelve hours in their bull pen. Everybody with any power took advantage of me, and I was getting sicker and more tired of the doped-up routine every minute, especially since I couldn't see any end to it.

I could only see one thing clearly—eventually I would do a life sentence behind bars, only on the installment plan. If I stayed lucky, it would be a six-month bit here, two years there. Then sooner or later a stretch of five-to-ten. And if I wasn't lucky, I'd get a sentence that equalled a football score with my existing record. None of this looked too good, but I didn't see any real alternatives in my condition at the time. My trial runs with the detox places had all fallen flat on their asses, and I had some serious questions about any difference between a habit on heroin or one on methadone, which the state was unofficially sanctioning.

The gut realization hit me hard—I wanted to give up drugs, but my habit had me wired. It seemed I had no choice if I wanted to keep on living. The only solid thing I could think of in terms of a solution was to get the hell out of the neighborhood for a while, if only to avoid all the hassles with the heat. So I drifted to Manhattan and located a hole with four walls at the Stanwick Hotel on the west side.

In a dense fog one day while I was loaded, I thought of pulling a quick caper, just like in any other neighborhood. I called Hooks and asked him to meet me on Broadway and Seventy-second Street. He drove up about an hour later in a borrowed car, and we went uptown. I had him stop at an A&P,

and I got out of the car and walked in. I grabbed an empty toilet paper box, filled it with about twenty cartons of cigarettes, and walked right out to the street with it. No less than six people made me, including the manager. Somebody even wrote down our license plate number before we took off. Less than a mile away, two squad cars boxed us in, so we gave it up. I copped to taking the cigarettes and said Hooks wasn't in on it.

They let Hooks go on the spot and took me to the police station. I was booked and later released on $1,500 bail after spending one night in the tank sick as a dog. Within a week I tried to make the same move with cigarettes and got nabbed in the process. That bail was set at $2,500 and once again my bondsman Tony was there. Within three more days, I made four churches and paid him off.

Things were so drastic that even my mother was up in arms. She was talking to everyone she knew about me and what they could do, "anything to help with my son Vinny." In desperation, she remembered an old neighborhood friend of mine named Al DiPrimio, who was now an up and coming lawyer with a downtown office. Momma arranged for a meeting between the three of us. The morning of the meeting momma came over and made sure that I only went where she could see me except for my shower. I got dressed in the best I could find and followed behind as mom led the way to the street for a taxi.

DiPrimio asked questions instead of having all the answers, and I liked him for that straightaway. He didn't lecture me on the past, but he was intent when it came to focusing on the future, which was something I could listen to for a change. My past was full of shit, as far as I was concerned. Show me the way out, was what I wanted. DiPrimio agreed to handle the latest two busts for me.

When the first case came up on the court docket three weeks later, DiPrimio was at my side, armed with his briefcase and dressed up in a Brooks Brothers suit. After the formalities, DiPrimio sent me into shock as he started to talk.

"Your Honor, my client is not really a thief, in that he comes from a very decent family in this city, and he really wants to become a responsibile citizen, but he is sick. He is a drug addict. We admit that, and we also admit to the horror of a human being caught in this position. This man has seriously tried to detoxify, Your Honor, at several facilities. None of them has worked, but Mr. Marino is not willing to give up yet.

"We have learned of a new rehabilitation center called Synanon, which was started in California and has a very high success record. My client wants to go there and commit himself to their program, and frankly, Your Honor, it is my professional opinion that the City of New York will be infinitely better off if we get this man off the streets and into the hands of an organization that can truly help him find the way. This Synanon program, I should mention, is one that lasts a lifetime, and so if it does work for my client, it is undoubtedly the best solution we can offer the court at this time."

This was all news to me. I looked at DiPrimio and wondered what the hell he was talking about, while the judge looked at me, wondering if I was ready for a lifetime commitment to anything except junk. He asked the two lawyers and me to approach the bench. When I was less than three feet from his face, the judge looked down and asked, "Mr. Marino, are you serious about this?" I said, "Yes, Your Honor," and looked up at him with my one good eye.

"Very well, then, Mr. Marino, if you do get into this Synanon program, I will suspend sentence on this charge." As I walked out of the courtroom, once again a free man, I had no intention of doing anything except shooting off to Harlem and scoring. But my mother was there, and DiPrimio was hanging on my right arm from the time we left the bench. The two of them damn near forced me into a nearby restaurant, where we got a booth. DiPrimio proceeded to pick me apart relentlessly. He talked about my past and drew the inevitable conclusion that I would die soon if I continued my lifestyle. Then he went on to say that prison was the only real alternative to Synanon and that was why he had come up with the idea. I was so run down I could only nod along in apparent agreement. Momma made a passionate plea. "Vinny, my son, I don't know how or why you got into this, but please, for me, do this and get out." They reached me, so I said, "Okay, I'll go."

I was thinking at the time that I could kick the junk cold, but I didn't know what to do with the doriden habit since I had already had three convulsions—I never knew those pills could be so dangerous. With that realization, I thought to myself that this Synanon place could work, so I agreed to check it out tomorrow."

DiPrimio gave me a last piece of positive reassurance. "Look, Vinny. They say a lifetime, but just go in and get yourself straightened out, stay a year, maybe two. Then, if you choose, come out and lead a normal life." Again, the easiest way with all that pressure was to agree. Momma insisted that I accompany her and spend the night at her apartment. I agreed but first went to my place to pick up a change of clothes, some junk and the works, and a few dolophines and doridens. After we got home, momma fixed me some spaghetti and meatballs. Later, she laid out a pillow and blankets on the couch, and I went into the bathroom, got off, then crashed for the night.

At ten minutes to nine the next morning, momma was shaking me awake. She brought me a glass of fresh orange juice, which I used to wash down a couple doridens and dolophines when she left the room. I could smell the good food as I brused my teeth and shaved. When I came out of the bathroom, DiPrimio was there eating breakfast, and obviously enjoying it tremendously. I didn't know what the hell was going on. After we enjoyed mom's cooking, DiPrimio asked me if had what I needed for a month, packed up and ready to go. I was caught short and asked, "Where are we going?"

"To Synanon, like we said to the judge," he came back with.

We went back to my place to pack a suitcase full of my belongings. Then the three of us sped down the West Side Highway and onto the Connecticut Freeway. We were heading for Westport, a community of white collar commuters. In less than three hours, we pulled up in front of a huge three-story old colonial house on the outskirts of Westport. DiPrimio said, "Let's go in," as my heart sank to my knees. I made a quick move and swallowed the last three dolophines I had. As we walked in, a smiling face greeted us with, "Hello, welcome to Synanon. May I help you?" DiPrimio offered the first response. "We have an appointment to see the associate director at two o'clock." The young girl looked to me like a hooker, at least once upon a time, but she was calm and collected as she replied, "Let me call him and confirm the appointment." She asked our names, and everyone got logged in on the roster.

A guy named Ted Brown and his wife, May, were in charge of that particular place, and the minute I laid eyes on them I knew they were knockaround people. Brown was simple yet firm with everything he said, and I liked him right off. He invited me to come into his office alone and started in with very direct questions. "How long have you been using drugs?"

"Ten years, give or take," I told him.

"Why do you want into Synanon?"

"I have no place else to go, and I need help."

He tried to push my buttons as he replied, "You don't know what the word means, Marino. You say you need 'help,' and I say go to a fucking employment agency. This is our *home,* and here you come barging in like a wise-ass kid, holding your mommy's hand with your lawyer on the other side. You're a baby, Marino, an asshole, and you're not worth a shit."

Well, Brown had me dead to rights, and I was in no condition to argue. I said humbly, "Look, I've tried everything, and I know I need help." Brown was not kind as he came back with, "Bullshit, Marino, you haven't 'tried' anything. All I see is a loser on the run, calling himself a big man, sticking needles in his arm, and stealing anything he can find to keep his habit flowing."

His dialogue struck my conscience in a very clear way. I knew deep down that whatever else happened, no way was I going to be able to bullshit these people. I settled into the candid conversation, and Brown started to relax somewhat from his heavy come-on talk and spoke openly of his methods, saying, "All we wanted was to be sure you really wanted some help, and that's why we're here. Welcome to Synanon." He went on to tell me the "ground rules" at Synanon—no drugs or alcohol, no negative talk, no violent behavior, no sex, no coming or going without permission, and no discussions of the highs or the lows associated with past drug trips. I nodded my head in agreement, figuring that I'd have to see what subjects could possibly come up once all the above had been eliminated.

Brown called momma and DiPrimio into his office. Momma smiled broadly and took my hand when Brown said, "We think Vinny can help himself here at Synanon, Mrs. Marino, and we have accepted him into our home." A wave of relief swept over my body when I heard that I was accepted, but still I wasn't feeling good, and it was getting worse by the minute. Brown sensed something. "By the way, aside from heroin do you use any stumblebuttons, idiot pills?"

I decided if I was going into Synanon, I might as well be honest, so I said, "Dolophines and doridens." Brown shook his head. "Oops, around here we have people kick cold turkey right on that couch, but we do not mess with barbiturates or hypnotics. You could have a convulsion. You're going to have to go into a hospital first and clean up that pill habit."

Momma looked dejected with the prospect of having me back

on the streets, and then she asked, "Isn't there a hospital near here that could help him?"

Brown said there was and put a call through to Fairmont where we hit a jackpot. They could take me right away, and I was eligible for federal rehabilitation money. That saved $1,200 a month, which we didn't have anyway. Fairmont had some very wealthy people as clients, primarily alcoholics who were drying out. Momma and DiPrimio drove me there in less than half an hour.

On the way I was getting dizzy and beginning to feel like I was going to have another convulsion. I got real scared. A little after we got there I looked out the barred window of the reception room and saw momma waving with tears in her eyes as she and DiPrimio drove away. Fortunately a nurse from admissions was standing beside me because I felt an awful weird sensation sweep over my body. She showed me to my room and as soon as I entered it, I had a violent convulsion. My body cracked in a giant uncontrollable spasm, and then I blacked out.

I woke up enough to see where I was again three days later. Tubes were in just about every pore of my body, and bottles were hanging overhead. A middle-aged blonde nurse was the first person I recall. Her job was to keep all the tubes open and my juices flowing. Her name was Mrs. Beatty, and she seemed pleasant enough as she passed by each day.

When she thought I was well enough to absorb some solid information, she told me how lucky I was getting to the hospital when I did. If I had had the convulsion at Synanon, I would probably be dead or else a vegetable. She said that I was choking on my tongue, and it took more than nine hours of constant treatment before I was out of intensive care. Most of the staff had never seen a convulsion that severe, and it had everybody around talking for days.

Around the fourth day there, I was getting the sense that something they were giving me was just like the high of junk or doridens. I asked Mrs. Beatty about it. She picked up my chart and said, "You're getting methadone and doriden on a daily basis." Then she looked up, "I would guess they can't let you go off all at once, not with the condition your body is in."

Well, that did it, because the food was good and they had steam rooms and sauna baths, plus a wide open day room with TV and card tables, and everybody in the place had his or her own private room, complete with bed and bath. I made friends with the other people there, including an artist named Flicker who was kicking goofballs too. He said he was "determined to beat the damn drugs."

I figured to myself that there was probably no way to *beat* drugs, but I would be quite happy to just *abandon* the goddamn stuff. I knew deep down there was no way in hell to "join" drugs and win. Brown's talk at Synanon stuck with me so much that I spent thirty days there and got healthy, clean, and picked up a positive mental attitude in the process. When I was all dried out, the director called Brown and said I was ready to be picked up. Two residents came over to pick me up on a bright Monday morning in May of 1964.

As the car pulled up in front of the Synanon residence, I noticed the enormity of the place. These people were living in a mansion. The huge living room had a fireplace with a marble mantle. The dining room was decorated with a formal chandelier that had a thousand pieces of cut crystal. I thought, "The Duke of Synanon must eat in here," as my guide led me through the dining room and out into the kitchen, where there was more space for food than an army could eat in a year. Two huge refrigerator-freezer combinations stood against one wall, and two ten-gallon coffee urns brewed on a counter next to the chillboxes.

They took me upstairs to the sleeping area, which was made up mainly of large and small bedrooms. "These are the male dormitories, and the other side of the house is where the females sleep." There were single beds and bunkbeds. A resident named Tommy pointed to a top bunk and said, "You can call this home."

Then he told me a little of Synanon's history while we passed by the single rooms, which were all occupied by the staff. "A guy named Chuck Dederich started the organization in Santa Monica, California. Now we have houses in San Francisco, Oakland, Tamales Bay in Marin County, one in Reno and, of course, this one here in Westport." I asked him if the different houses worked together in any way. He told me the units were all self-sufficient, but residents would be reassigned to different locations at times for different reasons, like when individual talents were needed. This provided a diversity of scenery and experience.

Tommy told me I had half an hour to clean up before meeting everyone in the living room. I took opportunity to shower and then laid down on my bunk, when it occurred to me that my suitcase wasn't around. As I walked into the main room, twenty-five minutes later, about fifty people were sitting around the room. Most of them were smoking cigarettes, and they all seemed rather glad to see me. It seemed they had heard about the trauma I had gone through at the sanitarium, and they were happy I had made it. Each one stood up and said who they were, but I only got three or four names at that time. Then I remembered that these people could only speak in positive words so no wonder they were all smiles and handshakes.

Next I saw my suitcase in the middle of the room. Tommy told me again about the cardinal rules, and that the penalty if the staff chose to excommunicate you for an infraction was instant exile from the program. He explained about "my" clothes and said, "We don't have 'personal' possessions in Synanon since everything is community property. You can use all those fancy colognes along with everyone else in the male bathrooms, Vinny, but forget about the clothes."

My heart sank and almost hit the soles of my feet. I must have laid out a thousand dollars worth of the best threads available in New York, and the thought of losing everything hit me hard. I wanted to ask for my favorite cashmere sweater but kept quiet and figured maybe I'd be able to buy it back later when I saw someone wearing it. Tommy told me I could draw a new issue of clothing from the free community store.

The next step was, "Please come up to the attic with us, for your formal initiation. "Uh-oh," I thought, but halfway up the stairwell I remembered one of the ground rules was no violence. That calmed me down somewhat. The attic was empty except for one solid oak chair, sitting smack in the middle. Tommy invited me to have a seat. "We want your wig." With that, a guy named Eddie plugged a cord into an outlet and turned on the barber clippers he had in his hand. I got a military crewcut in less than five minutes and was then unceremoniously handed a broom and a dustpan with the instructions, "clean up your mess."

The first couple of days there were real tough on me. I got fed up with the positive bullshit all of the time since there was next to nothing positive about me, and I knew it. Almost everything I said brought the same response, something like, "We don't do that here." I would meet a guy from the Bronx, shake his hand and say, "Hey, I used to cop in the Bronx," and two people would shoot in with, "We don't say that here." My whole past life was out of bounds from Synanon conversations, and I felt like an orphan. I walked around mumbling to myself, "Jesus, what the hell else *is* there to talk about."

The night after I arrived I was busy doing my after-super duties as dishwater and general cleaner-upper for fifty-two people when Tommy walked through the entire house shouting, "General meeting at seven o'clock." I looked at my wet, soapy hands and thought, "Now what. I was planning to watch TV," but I went upstairs to shower and change clothes before the meeting started.

Everyone showed up a few minutes before seven in the living room, and I noticed right away that no one was talking, almost as if something serious was about to happen. Ted Brown stood up to announce each person's room assignment for what he said was to be an "encounter group." I wondered what the hell an encounter group was as I followed fifteen people into a room. Inside, all of the chairs were in a circle, so I sat down in the only seat left and looked around silently, waiting for what was next.

Well, no way could I believe the words I heard. The rule was that "anyone could say anything at anytime," but I wasn't used to that kind of talk, not coming from the streets of New York. If that kind of thing came down on me out there, I would have had to break the person's jaw. You simply did not talk to anyone like that without asking for trouble. People were verbally tearing each other up like dogs on the street, and I didn't get it. It was scary, the way someone would attack a person verbally, along with everything they seemed to stand for.

After an hour or so of watching this abuse being thrown around, I started to get the message. Aha! The game was beating people up with accusations and putting them down with nothing more in mind than having them take a careful look at what was said. A person could say anything, and it didn't matter as long as you listened to it and didn't get violent. Then I noticed that most people looked no different after their turn in the hot seat, so I got more used to the idea. But that was easy since I had no history in the place yet, and no one was ripping at Marino during that first encounter session. Under it all, I began to see a dimension that was totally missing from the streets—some kind of genuine caring. The comments were all made to help.

One guy named Reed announced his intention of leaving Synanon the next morning. Someone was always "on point" at the residence, which means standing sentry at the door. Absolutely no one could come or go without permission and signing in or out. It was a lifetime bit we were doing, so if Reed did leave the next day, he was out, like in exile. It was obvious to me that the others cared about what was going to happen to this guy out there. I didn't have much to say during that first encounter session, but I sure was listening hard. It was a good feeling when I got the idea people there still cared about another human being. I remembered being in various hospital detox wards when someone would say, "I want to leave," and the official response was more or less, "Yeah, go ahead."

I warmed up to the idea of caring for other people, and I found I liked most of the residents in Westport. Then I started to like the place itself and the lifestyle. It wasn't long before my sense of humor was back in full swing, and I got to be known as a general knockaround character. But this time I was going in a different direction for once in my miserable career.

The founder of Synanon made a point of emphasizing how we were to view the place: "Synanon is an island of sanity, and the world is an ocean of insanity, and if you step off this island of sanity, you die." That's where he came up with the lifetime commitment rule, and it was symbolized in the house with a life preserver on a painted raft that read *USS Synanon*. Inside the raft was a sign indicating the number of "clean" man days credited to that particular facility, and it was changed on a daily basis.

As the days came and went, I got more and more familiar with the rules and the routine, mainly by asking the people who had spent some time in the facility. Communication was open, and I was enjoying living there. I started to believe deep down that this place could work. What I didn't realize at the time was that I was on what they called a "honeymoon," which was somewhat easier treatment granted to the newcomers. I guess they knew that heavy pressure on someone just off the streets might cause a person to bolt out the door.

Once after I had been there two weeks, the entire house went on an outing, down by a very beautiful lake nearby. After we got out of the vehicles and started strolling around at the water's edge, I noticed a Synanon guy dressed in funny clothes, sporting a shaved head, who was doing all the work. Since I was already on the service crew at the facility, I figured to give the poor guy a hand. Tommy pulled me up for it right away, telling me, "He's considered spare parts, leave him alone." I guessed that he was more or less serving their equivalent of time in the bing. Then I learned later that he was on what they called a "contract" and would have to do anything he was told to do from six in the morning until around midnight.

Inside the facility, they made a special point of breaking up the day to avoid boredom. First was breakfast, after which we would go back to the dorm and clean up. That was followed by the morning meeting where they talked about the schedule for the day, people who might be up for transfer (or, as they called it, rotation) to another facility on the West Coast. Then we would either sing songs, tell jokes, do skits, or something like that. One of my favorite activities at those morning sessions was the "liar's contests." You would have to tell a total lie, and the winner was the most believable person. Before lunch, my duties as part of the service crew were to do the dishes, sweep, mop, and clean the shitters.

Lunchtime was around noon, and then a seminar was held at one o'clock. Sometimes we had guest speakers from the local community or one of the directors would simply throw a subject open for discussion, such as euthanasia, abortion, or the ideas of famous people—anything so long as it wasn't drugs. After dinner on Monday, Wednesday, and Friday evenings we had encounter groups or "games" as they were called. On off nights we usually had some kind of special event. Then, on Saturday nights we hosted an open house for the folks from Westport and surrounding communities. Sandwiches and coffee were served, and one or two of the residents would volunteer to relate their typically horrendous past history and then speak brightly of the future as a result of entering Synanon.

Anytime someone had an anniversary, a year or two or three years of residency in Synanon, we celebrated that towards the close of open house. They really made a big deal about it. The guests, or "squares" as they were referred to, were generally impressed with the turnarounds some of us had achieved. The term *square* was used to differentiate nonresidents, but it was meant in a derogatory way because some of those squares were real down-to-earth people.

Of course, at times I had second and third thoughts about the whole trip. In addition to "no drugs," which I could understand, they also told us "you will never have a drink again in your lives." I remember thinking to myself, "That's heavy. Am I ready for this?" Then Ted Brown looked at me funny one day, and I wondered if he had just shot up, and if so, where he kept the junk and his works. I wondered if anyone there ever got loaded on the side. I mostly wondered if I could commit myself to Synanon for a lifetime.

Most of the trouble in my head at that time, however, came from the no-sex rule. A couple of sharp looking young women were in residence, and I was more than just a little horny, particularly since I had recently kicked. That was fairly normal with dope addicts after withdrawal because so many sexual feelings were repressed when you were on drugs. The same was true of eating. On the tenth or eleventh day of a dry-out period, a junkie usually got what we called "the chunks," which meant you felt like eating anything and everything in sight. During that time you took your ribs out of hock and made up for all the skipped meals.

Back on the subject of women. Within two and a half weeks after my arrival, a newcomer came through the door. She was long, lean, and beautifully featured black broad from Manhattan named Barbara. I caught her eye as soon as she came into the kitchen, and she stayed on me long enough so I could tell we had made a point. The second or third day we had coffee together, and the fourth day she hit on me directly. "Fuck these people, honey. We don't need Synanon. You come by my man, and I'll take good care of you." Believe me, Barbara made me think real hard about what she was whispering, but somehow sanity prevailed and I stayed and didn't even get down with her then.

Just after my first month in the facility six names were called out at a general meeting one morning, and mine was one of them. Ted asked us into his office after the meeting and told us that we were being rotated to the San Francisco facility called Seawall. I was immediately elated with the idea of a transfer, plus I had never been to the West Coast. He showed us six one-way plane tickets and let us know they were nonnegotiable. The flight was scheduled for departure at 11:55 the next morning. We all started laughing and talking, and I noticed that Barbara was in the room, so we would be winging our way across the country together.

Ted topped the small talk on a serious note. "Okay, knock it off. Because you're relatively new, we're going to ask you to raise your right hand to swear allegiance to Synanon before you make the trip." I thought it was somewhat bullshit, but I said the words anyway: "I swear to abide by Synanon's rules. I have no intention of leaving and no intention of using drugs or alcohol ever again.'' Ted then turned in his chair and looked directly at me. ''Vinny, I'm appointing you as the leader of this group.''

I thought, ''Damn,'' as he handed me all six tickets, and I asked what that meant. ''It means you're responsible for delivering the group intact to the San Francisco airport with no interruptions.'' I reluctantly took the tickets. ''Oh, okay. I got that.'' As I walked out of the office, I thought that it must have been double reverse psychology on Brown's part. He knew I was the craziest guy in the place, so he probably figured if I was the leader, I'd keep myself in check.

After supper that night we packed up our things and said our goodbyes at a coffee and donuts party. Before everything broke up, Barbara eased over to me. ''Honey, maybe we can get a trap set after we're in San Francisco for a while.'' Then she asked me to make sure that we sat next to each other on the plane. I smiled, then moved away thinking, ''Boy, this broad's god some big balls.''

Drifting into the kitchen for a refill, I approached an older guy named Manny and asked him, ''How long do you have to be around to get a trap?''

''Forget it, Vinny,'' he said as he turned to fill his cup. ''You have to wait for about a year.'' I was still puzzled so I pressed him further. ''Yeah, but why so long?''

He was slightly disturbed and shot back, ''Vinny, you didn't come here to get laid, you came here because you're an asshole, a runner, a junkie, and a thief. Forget about traps.'' Manny turned and walked away. I approached Tommy, who was a coordinator and had become a friend. I asked him to explain the whole trap concept and why it took so long to get one.

''In order to be eligible for a trap,'' he began, ''you have to be around for about a year, and so would the female. Then, if you've got eyes for someone and she's got eyes for you, you go to the male director and ask for permission to get hooked up. She, in turn, goes to the female director and asks her permission. Then the directors get together and weigh up your growth, attitude, progress. If they think it would be healthy for each of you, they give you what is called a courtship. That means you're recognized as having a relationship but no sex yet—no petting, no touching, but you would be allowed a respectable kiss when you walk her to the girls' dorm at night. This courtship goes on for about a month.

''During that time, you'll go out with older traps to movies and such. Then if both your attitudes are okay after a month you'll be given a trap. That means you get to go to what is called the guest room. In the beginning it's once a week for four hours. Then it goes to twice a week, then it goes to twice a week overnight. Of course, prior to giving you the trap, a female would have to go to family planning for some form of contraception.

"To tell you the truth, Vinny, you're considered chopped meat as far as the length of time you've been here. You're really wasting a lot of psychic energy worrying about things that will happen naturally down the road. Why don't you put more emphasis on doing what we do here? That would be a lot more important than worrying about something that won't happen for probably eleven more months."

"Okay, Tommy," I said and thanked him. On my way up to the dorm I started to think what a nice guy he was and that I'd miss him.

Sunrise was a little after six the next day, but I was up with the first light of dawn, finishing my packing and straightening my bunk area. I drank a lot more coffee than I should have at breakfast and was jittery as the six of us boarded the van outside the house where everyone exchanged final farwells. The drive through Connecticut was beautiful, and when we passed the city, it was dark and gray in contrast. Heading toward LaGuardia Airport, I actually felt a different kind of high rush through my body, and I thought to myself as I looked out the window, "I can't be feelings this good without drugs, can I?"

We pulled into the terminal at 10:32 a.m. "Plenty of time," I thought and the departure board said our flight was on schedule. Knowing what junkies were capable of, I pulled Barbara aside and told her to keep an eye on Mimi. Then I went up to a guy from the Midwest named Don and told him to keep his eye on the third guy, while I watched the fourth one. We stuck together that way through a trip to the john and the newstand before we boarded the plane. In the coach cabin it was two-three-two seating in each row. I let everyone go in before me, then handed the stewardess the tickets.

Barbara ended up with me, in the two window seats right by the bulkhead separating us from the first-class kingdom. I had an even better ride because Barbara went under the blanket and gave me a treat no less than three times. I must confess that I fell right into it, then started thinking I'd probably get in trouble if it ever got out. "What the hell," I thought to myself, "at least I got permission from the group leader."

San Francisco was covered in a creamy cloud of fog when we landed, and the city looked white from the air, whereas New York always hit me as basically gray. As soon as we stepped off the plane, I saw a sign being held up by two guys back in the crowd. It said Synanon in big white letters, and below that was chalked in, Seawall Welcomes Westport. I waved and went over to introduce myself, checking on both sides to be sure no one was bolting. We got our baggage loaded into the van and headed for the Seawall facility.

I walked in the front door of the facility—a huge building that was once a paint factory or something, but now over two hundred people lived there—and saw a massive crowd of bodies, all moving every which way. We approached the point man and checked in. Then right over my shoulder I couldn't believe my eyes! It was an old friend from my old neighborhood. "Hey, Vinny! That you?" I cried with delight.

He looked at me directly. "Vinny Marino?"

"Yeah! Vinny Ferratino! I'll be damned!" Everyone had called him Vinny the Animal. The last time I saw him, we were seventeen and on a heist together. We were higher than kites and were sticking up a Thom McAn shoe store on Flatbush Avenue. I was tying the clerk's hands behind his back with a rubber hose before we got the money when I looked up to see Animal climbing up the ladder looking for a pair of shoes in his size. I rang the no-sale button, grabbed about seventy dollars, and bolted out the door, yelling, "let's hit it!"

Now at Seawall, he put his arms around me and kissed me on the cheek. I didn't like it, and I couldn't even understand it, not from Ferratino. "Yo, Vinny. It's nice seeing you and all, but what the fuck are they doing to you in here?"

He said, "Nothing, why?" and backed off.

I figured I'd pull the "old neighborhood trick," after he told me that he had been in the facility for almost three years. I was thinking about the shit clothes I was wearing, so I asked him, "Hey, can you do the right thing for me with some clothes? You know, being as you're here a while, you've got some status. You've gotta have some connections."

He laughed at me and said somewhat cynically, "We don't do that here. This is not the joint, Vinny." I looked at him dumfounded. "Hey. Come on, man, this is me, Marino, remember?'' He shook his head from side to side and went negative. ''Maybe you better stay away from me. We might get into trouble together, and I don't want any.''

At that point I changed my tactic because I knew he was no dummy, and I wanted some information. ''What about the place here. Does it work?'' He looked at me straight in the eyes, something a junkie never did. ''Vinny, look at me. I'm clean, I'm healthy, I feel good. If you stick around and follow the rules, the place can work for you. I've been clean for three solid years, and you knew me from the streets. You figure it out.'' The conversation with Ferratino had left me in a strange mood, which I carried with me into an encounter session that started less than fifteen minutes after I left him.

During the game some asshole was running a number that was such obvious crap that I couldn't help cutting in. I pulled him up hard. ''You know, you're fulla shit. You've never even broken a pimple. Some tough guy. All of a sudden now, because there's no violence in the room, you're gonna get like Little Abner? You were a piece of shit, no matter where you're from, and you still are a piece of shit, so grow the fuck up.''

When the encounter ended, the director called me into his office. I thought, ''Uh-oh, something must be up. Maybe he knows about Barbara, maybe Vinny gave me up, or maybe I said the wrong thing in the group.'' The director's name was Tappan. As I came in, we said hello and he offered me a seat on the other side of his desk. ''How much joint time have you done?'' he asked. I figured right there that he had my damn file, probably right on his desk, so I told him the truth. ''Oh, I don't know. Maybe five years, on and off.''

He looked at the file on his desk, then back up at me. ''You know, Vinny, we could use a guy like you on this project at the Nevada State Prison in Reno. We need someone from the East Coast and someone who can talk to cons.'' Right then I thought Animal had gotten me rotated out of there. I didn't particularly care since it felt too crowded, and I didn't want any more hassles. I just extended my hand for a shake. ''Sure, Reno. Whatever you say, I'll try it.'' Meanwhile, I'm thinking ''Where the hell is Reno, in the desert?''

''The van will be leaving tomorrow morning at ten. Be ready. Oh, nice to have you at Seawall, Vinny. You look like stand-up people, and I have a sense that you're going to make it. Give 'em hell in Reno.'' I gave Tappan a smile as I waved goodnight,

"Yes, sir. I give 'em hell wherever I go." I went out, quietly closing the door, when I was actually thinking about slamming the damn thing so hard the plate glass would shatter all over the floor of his Seawall facility. But those were visions from my earlier days and that was behind me. I was ready to be on my way—clean—up to Reno.

10 / Reno Clean

First light the next day, I got out of bed and packed my bag again, then went to the kitchen to see about some coffee. As soon as the caffeine took effect, I lit a cigarette and sat down to think about where I was heading. I wondered where Reno was and what it looked like. And then I considered what I would be doing—talking to cons from Nevada. What were the guys from Nevada like—Cowboy cons? With that I closed my mind on the subject and thought of saying goodbye to Vinny the Animal and Barbara.

Barbara was easy to locate, she was always standing in a group with two or three guys. She was street-wise, and I thought how it would be with her out hustling money for me as I approached to say my goodbyes. We hugged, and she whispered in my ear, "If you ever need anything, don't forget me." After that, I spend nearly an hour wandering around, sort of looking for Ferratino but with no luck. I gave up and got ready for the ten o'clock departure. As we pulled away from Synanon San Francisco, the driver made an announcement. "We will be stopping at the Tamales Bay facility in Marin County before we head out for Reno tomorrow. Some of you may be interested to know that our founder, Chuck Dederich, and his wife, Betty, are there now, so you will have the opportunity to meet them."

Right then we started to cross the Golden Gate Bridge, and the panoramic view hit my insides with a wide open feeling of wonder. Not long after that the driver turned off the freeway to swing by Muir Woods, beautiful old redwood trees standing tall. Throughout the ride, I said to myself, "Look at you, Marino.

Seeing the sights, having a good time, and no drugs.'' I couldn't believe it.

As we turned in the driveway to an unbelievable estate, the driver offered some history. ''The Tamales Bay facility was first built by the United States government for an Italian named Marconi who invented the wireless. They wanted to lure him to this country to complete his existing work and do research, and they must have spent a million dollars at the time because the estate covers a hell of a lot of acreage on the water. Well, the old man from Italy didn't like something about the deal, so he refused, and it's been lying empty ever since. Synanon picked it up dirt cheap since it was so badly run down from all that exposure to the salt air. We're just beginning to renovate the place now.''

We headed up a circular driveway to what looked like a grand old southern plantation house, except that it was painted powder-blue and was faded and peeling in most places. A hundred people or more were around, all at work on something—painting, construction, cement, or yardwork. Since I wasn't anxious to get into that kind of labor, I was thinking better of Reno all the time.

Asthe van stopped and we got off, I noticed maybe ten people gathered around someone off to my left. The driver walked by and said, ''That's Chuck Dederich.'' I decided, ''what the hell,'' and walked over to see the person who had put everything together for Synanon. I approached the outside edge of the circle, and I could see he was definitely a man with command presence. After we said hello and introduced ourselves, I said, ''You know, this is a very nice place, and I'm glad I came to Synanon for help.''

He stopped walking and pointed his finger at my face. ''We *know* it's nice, Vinny, but I'll tell you the trick to Synanon. The trick is to *stay* here. It'll be a hard life until you get the hang of it, but then it's heaven.'' Dedrich turned and walked away, toward the Pacific, with his wife on his arm. The Roman Catholics never told me God was married.

I stood there thinking about what he said for another thirty seconds and then let my gaze wander over the estate. It had incredible potential for improvement. I went to the point man at the entrance to the big house and asked about my bag since the driver had told us we'd be spending the night. He showed me to another person and said, ''He's a coordinator, and he'll give you a room assignment.'' I walked over to a guy who said his name was Danny, and he offered to take me upstairs and show me around. At that point the rooms were literally falling apart. Paint was peeling and some windows were cracked, then taped over. I got my room and I laid down for a nap before the evening meal.

Later I showered and changed clothes before going downstairs to meet some of the people and talk a bit before we ate. After the meal was a general meeting, followed by an encounter game, which I sat in but stayed out of. Then it was up the stairs and into bed by eleven o'clock.

Another beautiful morning brought the van around again at ten, and four of us boarded it, destined for Reno. After five or six hours on the road filled with incredible scenery, we came to Donner Pass and an hour down from the peak, we could see the city of Reno. As we drove in, the town seemed small. Another twenty minutes past the downtown area we drove up to my new home. The main house looked a lot like Synanon in Westport, with a smaller cottage-type building off to the right of the major facility. Maybe a couple of acres of grounds went with the buildings.

As we entered the front door, the driver was telling me, "Only sixteen people are in residence here in Reno. You should like it because it's private and peaceful." In the kitchen we ran into the directors, a married couple named Clapp. He shook my hand, saying, "I'm Dick. Welcome to Reno." When I turned to meet his wife, I thought I knew her. In another minute it all came back: "She's from the streets, but where?" I couldn't place her exactly at the time, but if she was the one I was thinking of, she was a real pig then, and she looked like she hadn't changed much by coming to Reno.

My guide suggested that we go see where I'd be living. That struck my fancy, so I picked up the suitcase and followed the guy out the main house and over to the smaller one, next door. It was almost new, made of raw wood, like a knotty pine. Inside it was broken up into six rooms, each about fifteen by eighteen with two comfortable single beds. Each room also had its own bathroom. The furniture was new or nearly new, and the rooms were decorated with taste, something I didn't see all that often back where I came from.

My guide, whose name was Marty, suggested I relax a bit before meeting everyone. When Marty had gone, I sat down and thought of the folks back home. I would write both momma and DiPrimio as soon as I got permission to tell them how far I had made it and thank them for the push into Synanon. DiPrimio had never charged me a dime for his services and actually gave me money from time to time. I owed them both a lot, and I hoped for the opportunity to repay them one day.

After a quick shower, I wanted to pick out a change of clothes, but looking over the rags Synanon had given me bent my mind, so I picked some clothes at random and put the rest away in the bureau. After dressing, I headed for the main building.

Inside the living room several people were sitting around, but most of them, I was told, "were out working." The thing that struck me about the people there was the length of their time at Synanon. A guy named Gary had been there for six years. Marty, the tour guide, had been in for five, and one woman had been around for three years, while the last guy arrived about eighteen months ago. The only thing I could think of after hearing their histories was "uh-oh, which job am I going to end up with after a thirty-two-day stay in Synanon?"

Soon another eight people poured into the room for introductions. All in all, they struck me as a fairly nice group, but it didn't seem like enough people to be ideal. I liked the idea of Westport more, with about fifty in residence. But I could have been assigned to join the crowds at Seawall or Tamales Bay, so I thanked my stars and kept my mouth shut for once.

In what seemed like no time, dinner was on the table, and I was immediately taken with the quality of the food. That first meal consisted of thick porterhouse steak, a baked potato, and fresh green salad, plus all the corn-on-the-cob I cared to eat. Later I discovered that the director, Clapp, had hustled the casinos in town for their "throwaways." The hotels and casinos threw almost everything away after a day or two if they hadn't used it. Clapp arranged for the Synanon truck to pick up their "trash" before it hit the can. From where I was sitting, it looked like one of the smartest moves a man ever made. Not only that, the casino donors got to write off the stuff as a loss on their corporate books. I thought of the slogan, Everybody wins, and I saw how it might apply to this case.

On my third morning in Reno, I was given a formal assignment to the kitchen crew, which I figured would be a good move, being next to all that good food. I took my new duties like Cinderella to her broom, as I swept and then mopped up the floor in the kitchen, set the tables for meals, happily bused the dishes and washed them up, took out the trash and performed the other peon jobs required from time to time.

Within thirty days at Reno, I was gaining weight evenly and looking good, even to myself in the mirror. My bad eye was looking much better, and it had been three months since I stopped wearing the black patch. But by then I was getting bored hanging out in the kitchen, so I figured to make a change. Over the next week, I looked around and checked the opportunities, concluding that the easiest way out was to step up and cook. Until then my experience with cooking was limited to what I had seen over mom's or grandma's shoulders. But I was determined and started to spend evenings after group meetings reading all the recipes in the cookbooks and watching in the kitchen.

One night I got a shot at some practice when the whole house returned from an outing. It was about ten-thirty, and everyone wanted a snack. I volunteered, "How about some egg sandwiches?" A chick named Shelly who usually cooked thought she was smart when she snickered, "Why don't you make them for us, Vinny?" I jumped out of my chair heading for the fridge. Now to make egg sandwiches takes no Harvard graduate, for sure, but what I did was add some spicy ingredients on the sly, and everyone was genuinely surprised with the taste. Several people commented, "I didn't know you knew how to cook."

With a sheepish grin, I said, "You never asked. Some people consider me a chef," and with that line I swallowed hard, smiled, and looked over at Shelley, the (ex) cook, just as her chin dropped right past her big tits and hit on her knees. I was delighted. Right after that I started making special gravies and then the pastas—macaroni, spaghetti, lasagna.

I played with variations in spices and finally became damn near a master, most notably at improvisation. I was enjoying myself, impressed that I could be there, have fun, feel good, and get high *without* drugs. Three months earlier, this scene would have seemed impossible to me.

After a couple of months in the kitchen, the routine there began to get boring, too, so I made up my mind that I wanted an assignment to the prison project, just to break up my day and get out of the house. I told Clapp that I was "definitely interested in getting into the prison project, anywhere you see fit." He was receptive and smiled. "As soon as I see an opening, I'll keep you in mind." And he did—Clapp kept his word. He started out by giving me a tour of all the prisons we were into:

the honor farm, the minimum security, and the place they called the Cave, for maxiumum security inmates.

I got a weird feeling the first time we went into the maximum security facility. Not all the inmates were involved with Synanon—most of them thought we were a bunch of stool pigeons or worse. In order to get to where we had to go, we walked through a long yard with a chain-link fence. The convicts behind it would catcall and chirp as we walked by and crowd up against the fence. I felt real fear, thinking, "if these guys catch me in the wrong place, there's no telling what they might do." From then on, I was deliberate with every move, especially when I went into the Cave. A lot of dangerous bastards were locked up in there.

By my fourth month at Reno, Clapp was making me his regular companion on prison trips, where I would attend the encounter sessions with the cons. He acted as "facilitator" and would put the "game" on each of them, then let the others get involved. A world of difference showed between the honor farm inmates and those in the Cave, and thinking about it, the gradations and separation between prisoners began to make sense to me.

Almost none of the cons in the Cave trusted me at all when they found out I had only been at Synanon four months. Most of them were old-timers, doing long bits for manslaughter or murder, assault, armed robbery—real heavy stuff—not the two-bit things I had been doing back in New York. They would say, "How can you sit there and tell me what to do, when I don't even know that you're gonna make it." I would answer them with, "I'm not here today for you to find out whether I'm going to make it. I'm only giving you the same information that Synanon has given me, and since it's nothing but common sense, it might just pay you to listen."

Before another month had passed, Clapp was impressed enough with my intentions and performance that he started to let me facilitate my own groups. At first, that only made the old-timers push me harder. But ultimately I would say to those hard cases, "Look, you can beat me up all day, I don't care. But when the day's over, I get up and leave here to go play miniature golf or see a show. Meanwhile, you go back to your cell. So, you're only fucking with yourself if you're looking to test me. The question is what's going to help you get the hell out of here and stay out of places like this?'' It wasn't long before I proved myself with most of them, and I enjoyed the prison work.

Of all three facilities, the honor farm drew most of my attention. That was natural because inmates got there from other prisons based on their good behavior. The farm had no locks, and they were pretty much free to move around as they pleased. The cons lived in a series of mobile homes that had been converted into dormitories, and they did some worthwhile things like farming vegetables, doing woodworking, metal work, construction, and learning other useful trades. Most of the guys there were already interested in helping themselves, so my job was a whole lot easier than at the other two joints.

Sometimes I would get into personal, one-on-one sessions with individuals, and we would go over our range of experiences as well as ''the way out.'' To my amazement, given my history, the honor-farm inmates were very pleasant to me. Since most of them were due to be released, they were trying to learn as much as they could to stay out.

No one understood that motive better than Marino from New York, but when I sensed that I wasn't coming across with them, I would call in Gary from the facility, who was from the Midwest and had been in Synanon three years. Back home, Gary was a ''hype''—which was what they called drug addicts in the Midwest. He had done some things and drawn time in various joints, so the Nevada cons tended to listen when he spoke, saying, ''Look, if I can make it, you can make it.''

Then as time went on, I started to see signs of boredom creeping in through the cracks of my act again. It started with the people at the facility. A couple of faces had changed because of rotation, and now almost all sixteen residents were from the Midwest. I had some real trouble relating to them, and I wasn't interested in any of the women, even though I wasn't yet eligible for a trap even if I wanted one.

I thought about putting in for a rotation to San Francisco, where at least I could talk to someone from the neighborhood like Ferratino. Thinking of the neighborhood and the folks back home brought to mind letters I was getting from everyone. Mamma wrote how proud she was. Frankie said he couldn't wait to see me, and Joey wrote, ''Come home, Vinny.'' Even pop sent me notes a couple of times. After these letters I would start to miss the streets and especially Hooks. I wondered how he was getting along, and whether he was still using or in the joint. I made a mental note to write him soon. One night a line from pop about a situation in Brooklyn had me outside for a walk on the grounds under a full moon, thinking, "What about my family? Am I ready to take this for a lifetime?"

To counter my boredom and the cons from the Cave who were giving me shit, I took up acting. I got so good I could get a charade described in half a minute. Then at the afternoon seminars, we started to play a game of mental gymnastics. You would be introduced to a subject as you stood up: "Okay, Marino, talk about equal rights." The person speaking would assume either a pro or a con position on the subject assigned for the first half hour. At that point, a bell would ring, and you would have to switch your viewpoint and argue the opposite side for another half hour.

The whole point was believability, and the audience would critique your "act," pointing out technicalities, such as, "Your eye contact was good, but watch what you do with your hands." The experience was constructive for me. I learned a lot about myself, especailly where I was stuck in some rigid thinking, like tunnel vision, which addicts were prone to. This was most evident when I changed from the positive to the negative point of view on a subject and tried to make people believe me on both sides of an argument.

I also found some things in my head that I didn't know where there. For one, I had thought of myself as dumb because I hadn't finished school. I developed real confidence in myself as I cleared some of these ideas out of the way. Finally, I realized how much I enjoyed standing in front of a group, holding their attention with what I was saying.

As I passed my six-month mark at Reno, I felt pretty good about myself, especially that I was learning and growing. But I was still wondering seriously about my future as a cowboy in those Nevada mountains in contrast to the streets of New York. To head off a collision between me and Synanon, I figured I needed a new challenge and I started to spend my late evening hours reading. The collection of books wasn't all that extensive, but it was deep. At first I had trouble because I didn't know enough about words. To correct that, I got myself a dictionary and looked up the meanings whenever I was stumped. Then I came across a book titled *Six Weeks to Words of Power*. I was determined to master it, and I did.

The first book I remember reading was *The Prince* by

Machiavelli, and his message struck home as soon as I figured it out: It's not important what you can do, it's what people *think* you are capable of doing that creates the doubt, the fear, or whatever effect you may want. I tucked that information away and went on to read Emerson, Thoreau, and Sartre. Then I got into self-help psychology books. Sometimes I would fall asleep with a book in my lap and wake up suddenly, wondering if I had overdosed. I would look down, see the book, and laugh to myself.

As my vocabulary became more extensive, I started to use it on the people in the facility, just for practice but sometimes to annoy them for the hell of it. Instead of calling a woman a bitch, I would say something like, ''Why do you consistently repudiate your femininity with arrogant and immature actions?'' I was just having some fun practicing my new lexicon, but most of the residents didn't like it at all. When I became persistent, they got indignant, and I would get the shit kicked out of me verbally by everyone in every encounter group we had.

It took one of the facility directors to crack me, though, and that was Ellie Clapp, the former hooker from New York. Three classes of prostitutes work on the streets of New York. From top to bottom, they are call girls, hookers, or hos. The call girls got a hundred dollars or more and kept themselves confined to the better hotels and the top businessmen. The hookers regularly walked the streets but did it with some class and kept themselves at least semisharp. Dead last came the hos, the real low-lifes, usually on junk, who just let themselves go. Hos would do anything for five bucks, and for ten, they'd do it three times. A woman on junk went down so fast you could see it. Their weight fell way off, their arms showed every mark and every miss, and some of them looked like Charles Laughton in pain. Hos were also notorious for stealing from johns, which caused trouble for everyone else on the street.

Ellie Clapp from Eighth Avenue in Manhattan had been a definite ho to the maxiumum, but her husband met her after she had cleaned up in a Synanon facility. They were together for about two years in a trap, then they got married. By the time I knew her she saw herself as some sort of royalty. As a facility director, she could have whatever she wanted, basically, and what she wanted at the time was to work over Marino. I started to hear things from her like, ''bring me breakfast in bed,'' or ''go get the vacuum and run it in our room.'' And she was using language she could never get away with on the street. I buttoned up and did what the queen said for quite some time, but then they had a baby and the shit hit the fan—figuratively speaking.

After the youngster had been around the house for a while, it became obvious that Ellie wasn't much interested in being a parent because she kept asking or telling various residents to baby-sit for her. One day she got to me, and I didn't feel like it. I looked down at Ricky, who was crawling at my feet, babbling da-da. Then I looked up at Ellie and thought about my duties at the prison that afternoon at two. "Ellie, I really don't want to watch the baby."

With that I saw a blue flame of rage light up her eyes, while her facial expression went totally nasty. She waved her right index finger close to my nose and flat dictated. "Listen, asshole. I'm a director of this facility, and you'll do what you're told." Shrugging my shoulders and turning back to the sink, I said, "Okay then, leave him here. I'll watch him. And if he heads off the deep end for an electric outlet, I'm going to watch him do that too." She registered shock, then scooped up her little Ricky. I never heard any more about baby-sitting, but I know she didn't forget the incident.

Later that evening I stepped out on the front porch for some serious thinking. I had been at Synanon for almost a year, and that made me feel a warm glow inside. I also felt good about the inmates who had responded to me and about everything I was learning. I felt the absolute best about being clean for that long. But then another thought shot in, "Yeah, you're clean, but there's got to be more to life than just being clean. Lots of people are clean. What is your *purpose?*" I couldn't answer my self-imposed question and that bothered me.

Then my mind wandered again to my family and New York, and I knew right then I wasn't a cowboy and didn't belong in those mountains. Then I thought about the economic picture. Was I ready to live on Synanon's maxiumum salary of fifty dollars a month, *when* I was finally eligible, for the rest of my life? Was I willing to put up with that lifestyle for all of my days? I couldn't come up with a concrete answer to anything that night.

After that night under the stars, I began to withdraw more and more from interacting with the people in the house. They were getting more boring, and I was getting more into books. Then I accidentally came across a book called *Rules for Radicals* by

Saul Alinsky. The message from him was that I could be doing the same shit I was doing here out on the streets but for positive, genuine purposes. What I needed was something ethical to get behind with all my might. I liked Alinsky's writing so much that I ordered a copy of his other book, *Revelle for a Radical*.

Meanwhile, I still had to attend all the regular house functions and follow all the rules. One night I went into another encounter game with no particular interest in participating, since I was only about halfway through Alinsky's second book. After about an hour of this boring session, someone started to rap about being "the victim" and "a martyr" for the rest of us, like he was the only one paddling to keep the boat away from the relief. I had had it with the idiot anyway, so something snapped, and I unloaded on that unfortunate bastard with the most cynical, abusive verbal blast I had never administered.

Right after the game was over, Ellie, the Queen Mother, stopped me and called me into Dick's office. Inside I saw her husband Dick and Gary, my coordinator at the prison. I figured it was time for me to take a verbal blast or two. Sure enough, all three of them landed on me to conduct a verbal "haircut," with the queen leading the way. "Marino, you're a dummy in deep shit around here. Your attitude simply sucks. You've managed to turn off every individual in the house with your dictionary words and fancy phrases. You've isolated yourself, and you don't do what you're told."

Then Dick cut in. "The only thing which seems to interest you is your work at the prison. In fact, we conclude that you excel at running groups there." I heard what he said, nodded my head, and held back a smile as Ellie snipped, "Because you like the prison project so much, we're taking it away from you. From tomorrow on, you're confined to the facility." My thoughts ran straight to the position she was putting me in and what to do about it, just as Gary screamed, "As of right now you're in the dishpan!"

I hung my head and damn near cried with that one, but again I said nothing, figuring I'd get more mileage out of it. I just kept my head low and shook it from side to side, waiting for the bullshit haircut to be finished. Ellie was the one who kissed me off when she said, "Why don't you go straight to your room now and do some positive thinking about how you're going to handle this one."

At seven o'clock the next morning, I was told to report to the director's office. Queen Ellie was standing next to the desk, barking out the definition, "Asshole, get this: The dishpan means that where there's water, there's Marino. It starts after breakfast when you add water to the dishes and wash them. Then you put clean water in a bucket and mop the floor in the kitchen. Next you go straight upstairs and clean every shitter. After that, you come back and knock on my door, and we'll figure out where you go from there." I smiled. "Sure, Ellie, whatever you say," and tickled little Ricky under the chin.

As I washed up, I wondered whether things could or should be patched up. They would probably hold me down from prison work for maybe two or three weeks, but if I was leaving, why wait? By the time I got to mopping floors, I thought, "Well, let's just sit on it for the time being and see what happens." I pressed through the rest of my duties in an hour, and reported back to the queen's chamber.

As soon as she opened the door I smelled trouble, and sure enough Ellie was the courier. "Marino, I was just on my way to see you. Something's wrong with the cesspool out back. I called Rotorooter, but they can't be here until four o'clock this afternoon. Take a shovel and a bucket and go out and fix the problem." I walked to the kitchen pantry and grabbed an old five-gallon white plastic bucket, figuring I would at least go out in the yard and size up the problem. As I closed the back door, I got wind of a foul smelling odor, but I held my nose and headed in the general direction of the source. When I actually looked at the mess, I knew in a flash that this was it. Synanon could consider me gone.

That night at the general meeting after dinner, I walked in with a smile on my face and sat down. Clapp opened on a serious subject and noticed that I was grinning. Naturally, he pulled me up for it. "Okay, Marino, what the fuck are you so happy about? You just lost your job, you're in the dishpan, and you're gonna stay as a spare part, cleaning up dog shit, cat shit and cesspools until you straighten out your act. Now what is so goddamned funny?"

I looked at Clapp and grinned again as I said, "Dick, I have finally made a decision." He looked somewhat flustered. "What the hell does that mean, you 'finally made a decision'?" I smiled again. "It means that I've made up my mind I know what I'm going to do." He put his hands on his waist and challenged me. "Does that mean you're going to leave?"

I smiled as I said, "Dick, I really don't think I want to go any further with this conversation," and with that I clammed up for the rest of the meeting, no matter what was said. I was thinking about packing in the morning. As I headed toward the small cottage for bed, I saw the moon and wondered if it was shining on my old neighborhood. My mind ran through pictures of every person in my family, and I smiled thinking of all the things I had been missing for over a year.

I was up by six-thirty, whistling as I shaved. I sang to myself in the shower and did a couple of calisthenics while drying off. I looked in the mirror and felt great as I ran a comb through my hair. Then I remembered the box of clothing my family had sent, which for some reason I had never reported to the directors. I took everything out and picked out a nifty shirt, a pair of beige gabardine slacks, and a three-hundred dollar black leather jacket I had stolen from Bonwit Teller's a long time ago.

I packed up the rest in my suitcase, left all the old stuff Synanon issued me in the bureau drawers, and got dressed. As I walked across the lawn toward the main house, I figured it would be a great day. I opened the front door, set my bag down in the foyer, and took a last look around. Inhaling deeply, I gathered myself before going to see Dick in his office. I knocked twice.

Inside I folded my hands in front of me and looked him straight in the eye. "Dick, I just want to tell you, because I think I owe you the courtesy, that Synanon is a nice organization, and the Reno facility is great too. I like it here, and the organization has helped a lot of people. I myself have learned a lot of things, but now I have to go."

Clapp looked like he already knew what was up, and he came back with their standard line. "You know, Vinny, you're gonna die out there on the streets." Since I was fairly certain of my ability to survive almost anywhere, I simply told him, "Dick, I have no bitter feelings, I'm not angry with anyone. I just think a year of my time is enough. I have the information now, and I have to go out and apply it, or life is just not going to work for me." He tried to change my mind, but eventually saw that there was no stopping me, so he resigned himself and dealt with the reality.

"We don't want you on the streets around here, Vinny. We're too visible already. So you can leave, but we will put you on a bus to San Francisco. Gary will drive you to the station and buy you a ticket."

"Thanks, Dick, and thanks for your help while I've been here. I appreciate it."

The residents were just beginning to roll in for breakfast as I went out the other way to the car in the driveway. Throwing my bag in back, I jumped in the passenger side, waiting for Gary who came out five minutes later with a look of shock on his face. "Vinny, do you know what you're doing?" I waved him in the car with my left hand. "Sure. Come on, let's go." He got behind the wheel, started the car, and pulled away. He and I had worked together for some time at the prison, so I knew the questioning wasn't over. "Where the hell will you go, Vinny?" I told him what he already knew. "San Francisco first. You're buying my ticket, right?"

I had never experienced the way Synanon worked a "departure" like that. The first step was to sit me down in a chair while he walked up to the window and bought the ticket. He came back with a long face and the ticket in his hand. "Come on, I'll take you to the bus," and he actually walked me on like you would your son and pointed me to a seat as he handed the ticket to the driver. "This is for him," he said as he nodded at me.

The driver looked at the ticket, and his face had this big question mark on it, like, "Why is this guy handing me the ticket when that guy's going for the ride?" He looked at Gary, then he looked at me, and finally he shrugged his shoulders and looked out the front window of the bus, waiting for the minutes to tick off so he could finish his run. At two minutes before departure time, Gary said his final farewell and added, "Good luck, Vinny." He got off the bus and waited, still looking back in the window at me. I waved. He stood his ground.

With only sixty seconds left, my thoughts wandered onto the Synanon stories I used to hear about "Loser's Corner," what happened to people when they left, like I was doing. Everyone had told me what to expect: "They give you one dollar and drive you to the nearest state line. At the border, they stop and tell you to get out, figuring that since you were creative enough to have gotten that far, you'll be creative enough to get where you want to go, or back to Synanon."

I had just beaten the Loser's Corner routine because there I was sitting on a bus to San Francisco with my ticket all paid for. But who said I wanted to go? As we started down the street full of casinos and flashing lights, I thought, "Hey, this might be something to see." So I went to the front and signaled the driver while we were stopped at the first traffic light.

When he looked up at me, I acted totally anxious. "Jesus, I just remembered I left my wallet at home on Dickerson Drive. Can I have my ticket back please? I'll have to catch a later bus." The driver looked at me with just as much dumbfounded surprise as he had earlier, but he didn't argue or say a word, he just handed it over and opened the door. I jumped off the bus before the light changed.

I went straight back to the ticket window at the station and got a refund after telling the girl, "I just realized that I lost my wallet, so I can't afford to go anywhere." I got the money and noticed that it was 8:35 in the morning, Reno time, so that would make it what, 10:35, 11:35 back in New York? Who would be home at that time? I immediately thought of my old rectory coworker and diamond exchange partner Angela. I pulled out my phone book, pumped a dime into the phone and dialed for the operator. I gave her the number and asked to call collect.

Angela answered and accepted immediately. "My God, Vinny, how are you? I've been trying to get in touch. I called your mom and she told me you were in Synanon on the West Coast." I laughed and said, "You're beautiful, Angie. I can't wait to see you. I'm leaving Reno in a couple of days, but in the meantime I need some money for the trip across the country. You got any spare change, honey?"

"I haven't got much, but I can always get some for you. How much do you want?" I thought a minute, and concluded, "Three hundred would be nice."

"I'll get it, Vinny, don't worry. Where do you want it sent?" Again I didn't have my bearings, so I had to think a minute before telling her, "Go to Western Union and have them wire it to their office in Reno made out to me." We talked a bit more, back and forth, then Angie concluded our conversation with, "I'll be wiring you this afternoon. Bye, Vinny."

I hung up and checked to see how far the cash would carry me—less than thirty dollars. I picked up my bag and stuffed it into a twenty-five cent locker at the bus station, figuring to look around town until Angie's wire arrived. It wasn't long until I was on the main street of town near Harrah's. Twenty minutes later, I concluded that the whole damn city was nothing but a front for the casino operations. In three or four blocks the place just seemed to peter out to nothing.

I decided to walk back to Harrah's, remembering the sign, Special Lucky Dollar Breakfast. I figured the price was right as I walked in through the casiono. Suddenly slot machine bells hit me from everywhere. I saw two women standing side by side, each with a cupful of silver dollars, working two bandits each. It struck me funny that these broads didn't seem to care about what happened to the wheel. They just dropped in a coin, jerked down the handle, and moved right on to the next machine.

I walked past some blackjack tables and stood behind a guy sitting in the last position at a twenty-five-dollar-minimum game, as I tried to recall the strategy. The dealer sent cards around the table, and it all started to come back: count the aces and the faces, double down on ten or eleven, and quit when you're ahead. There was more, but my stomach growled again for something to eat.

In the restaurant I ordered the dollar breafkast—two eggs, hash browns, bacon, toast and coffee. The food was excellent. When the check came for only one dollar I felt slightly embarrassed and left a buck for the waitress and dropped another single on cashier's counter as I walked out. Back in the casino, I drifted around the action for a couple of hours. It was strange, being there straight out of Synanon and not even gambling. I wanted to play blackjack but decided to show some restraint for once. Instead I changed my quarters into nickels and headed for the nickel slots off in the far corner of the casino. It took damn near two hours for me to lose five bucks in nickels.

I managed to kill a few more hours, then I headed towards the Western Union office. As I walked in, I thought about the identification I would need and reached into my pocket for my New York driver's license. Pulling it out, I said to the cashier, "Hi, my name is Vinny Marino. Is there a telegram here for me from New York?"

"Oh, yes, Mr. Marino. Here it is." She handed me the wire as I handed her my license and signed the receipt. At another window they cashed it for three hundred dollars, and I headed back to Harrah's. I swung by the bus depot and picked up my bag, then hustled over to the reception desk at Harrah's hotel, where I took a single room at seventeen dollars a night.

The first thought that came to my head after the bellman left with his tip was to shower and lie down for a minute to relax. I must have fallen asleep for a couple of hours because I woke with a start and noticed it was already dark. I got dressed and headed down to the casino for an hour or two of blackjack. As soon as the first three hands were dealth, I sensed it was my lucky night because I bet a dollar on the first hand and won, then let the two ride and caught a twenty-one. That gave me five. I left it again and drew a seven to a rough ten-four hand, making twenty-one, beating the dealer's pat twenty. Somewhat chicken, I pulled back to a three dollar bet, yet won the fourth hand. At the end of an hour and a half, I had two hundred more than I had started with, and the night was still young.

As I got up to cash in my chips, I felt good about everything. I got the money and looked around for the nearest bar. On my way to the dimly lit casino cafe, I remembered something the people at Synanon had told me over and over about the future if you left: "First you'll end up with a drink in your hand, and before you know it you'll be back on junk, and then you'll fall down dead, alone in the gutter, or wind up in the slammer for the rest of your life." With over a year of reminders on that single point—plus I had never liked whiskey much anyway—I slid onto a barstool and ordered a Coke.

I had a look around the room with my drink, and on the first swing, I spotted a cute little blond sitting alone at a table having a drink. With nothing to lose, I smiled and said, "Hello, how's your luck tonight?" She looked up from her drink. "I'm not much of a gambler." Taking my glass, I got up from the stool and walked to her table. "Well, then what do you do? Oh, by the way, my name is Vinny. What's yours?" I could tell we had more to explore as she smiled with her eyes. "Please sit down. I'm Terri." She looked to be about tewnty-five and had a beautiful mouth and stunning blue eyes. She talked in a drawl, but she was the first one to say, "Ya'll talk funny." I thought just the opposite, but we had a most interesting two and a half hour conversation about all kinds of things. When the waitress interrupted us for an order, I gestured to Terri who said, "A vodka and tonic please, with a twist of lemon." I told her, "Make it two, please," and turned back to Terri.

I learned she was from Sweetwater, Texas, and in Reno to get a quickie divorce from her fifty-two year old lawyer husband. Terri had money, I could tell right away, but that wasn't what I wanted to concentrate on. So this beautiful lady and I talked at length about each other. For my background, I came up with being a "counselor on a prison project." As time went on and we got to the verge of being drunk, I suggested the obvious: "Let's go to my room." Terri didn't offer the slightest hesitation.

When we got there and I opened the door, Terri rushed right in and fell on the bed, drunk and ready. She held out her arms and whispered, "Come here, Vinny." With that, I dropped everything unnecessary and went to the foot of the bed where I knelt and started to kiss "My little Terri," first on the ankles but heading higher all the time.

We hit it off better than I could've imagined and spent pretty much of the next four days in the hotel room, mostly naked and always ordering from room service—something to eat "and another bottle of Smirnoff vokda, some Schweppes tonic, ice and a plateful of lemon twists on the side." We had sex as often as either one of us thought about it, and we had fun sitting around getting drunk and then sobering up by sleeping in each other's arms.

After our first night together, Terri moved in and insisted on paying for nearly all the extras we were getting. She showed me a roll of hundred dollar bills, which I put at two thousand or more when I first saw it. Instead of taking her off, I just sat back and watched her spent it almost down to nothing. It was then that she said quietly one morning, "Vinny, ah have to go back to Texas today," as she kissed me on the chin. I didn't think to argue with her, since the all-day-in-bed routine was due for a small break for fresh air and a look outside the same four walls. We did roll around on the bed once again before she took off, though.

After Terri left town I got back into blackjack and sometimes played craps but mainly hung in with the drinking. I took advantage of all the free drinks while I was gambling. I won a little, maybe a hundred, and lost a little, about the same, until I woke up on the sixth morning in Reno with a hellish hangover, and I couldn't remember what had happened just before I went to sleep. After fifteen minutes, I dragged my ass out of the bed and looked in my pants for a cigarette and to make sure I hadn't lost all my money somewhere along the vodka trail. Incredibly, I had three hundred left.

With more than a little trouble, I located my toothbrush, the tube of paste, and brushed up before starting to shave. As I looked in the mirror, the thought hit me again: "Leave Synanon and you die. No one has ever left and been successful. First they hit the bottle, then they hit the junk, and last they hit the morgue or draw a telephone-number stretch in the joint.'' I looked hard at myself. ''Is that what I'm doing?''

Why did I have to get loaded in some way to feel good? What about the year I spent in Reno, clean all the way, feeling great about washing dishes, cooking, mopping floors, raking leaves, taking all the shit, and yet in some kind of way still happy. Then the reverse thought came down. ''Why not go back and spend another year or two with Synanon? By that time, you'll be on top of the world.''

I got into a lot of confusion about the future and what to do, when it occurred to me that I hadn't called momma since leaving Synanon. I knew that Synanon normally notified the families of ''splitees'' to tell them that they had flown the coop, so I picked up the phone to call. When mom answered, I said, ''Ma, it's me, Vinny. How are you ma?'' At first I couldn't hear anything but silence; then it was shock. ''Vinny, my God, where are you now? Are you alright? The people at Synanon called and said you had left.''

''Ma, don't worry. I'm in Reno still, but I'm leaving today to come home and see you.'' It caught me off guard to hear her say, ''No, Vinny, don't do that. You go back to Synanon and do what they tell you.'' I didn't like the idea of being rejected. ''Ma, look. I got all the information they had to offer, and it's time for me to apply it now. I'm not using drugs, ma, I promise. I just want to see you.''

What I didn't know at the time was that the Synanon people had in fact called my mom and told her that I was doing fine and making progress. They explained that one year is a crucial time, and this happens to a lot of people. ''Above all, if your son should happen to call you, urge him to return to Synanon, no matter what you do, send him no money or plane tickets.'' Mom was trying to think of what to say next to persuade me. ''Vinny, you listen to me. The Synanon people tell me you were 'doing real good' and I want you to go back and finish what you started with them.''

Suddenly it hit me, ''Mom's right, idiot, so tell her you agree.'' I followed my conscience and said, ''Momma, I'm going to do what you say. I'm going back to Synanon today.''

''Oh, Vinny, thank God. You promise?''

''Yeah, ma, I know you're right, and what I'm doing is stupid, so I'm going back, as soon as I pack up.'' She sighed in relief and made me promise to have Synanon call collect when I was back safely, and we said our goodbyes.

I looked at the bottle of Smirnoff, poured a short one and called my brother Frank. When he answered the phone, the response was the same. "Vinny, don't be stupid. Why throw away all that good time? Go back, Vinny, it's the best thing." So I hung up and had another drink to drown out the thought of calling Synanon with my hat in my hand. Halfway through the second ring, Dick picked up the phone with "Good afternoon, Synanon."

"Yo, Dick, Vinny Marino. I've had some time to think, and now I'm thinking I made a mistake by leaving. I shouldn't have done it, and I'd like to come back." Dick didn't hesitate. "Where are you now?"

"Downtown Reno."

"Good. Tell me where, and we'll pick you up in twenty minutes."

"Hurrah's Casino."

"Be outside the main casino in twenty minutes. Look for the car." And with that the phone went dead, so I looked around the room, then decided I had to pack to leave. I poured another drink, chugged nearly half, then sat it down, and started opening drawers. Just before leaving, I poured the rest of the vodka down the drain, brushed my teeth, picked up my bag, and headed for checkout. I paid my tab and took a last shot at the crap table and went broke except for three dollars. Then I went out the front door to wait for my pick up.

Within five minutes Gary pulled up front. I swung the door open on my side and chirped, as if nothing had happened, "Hey, Gary, how are things back at the ranch?" Gary said nothing and stared straight ahead all the way back to the house. Stepping inside, I saw Dick standing there, ready with some orders as he lifted my bag from me. "Vinny, go sit in that corner and face the wall. Say nothing to anyone for any reason."

I said, "Okay," and did what he said. The house went to dinner and I sat. Then they went through clean-up, and I sat. Finally, after nearly five hours, Dick called a general meeting and when everyone else was in the room, he came out and told me to come in. I followed him into the room and took one of the remaining seats, hoping to stay low profile for a while, but it was not meant to be. "Stand up, Vinny." I did and held my head humble with my eyes closed. Dick asked a question, "Okay, sucker, what do you want?"

I couldn't look at anyone as I said toward the ground, "Well, I'd like to come back and get another chance." Dick wasn't kind as he cut into me. "Why, Vinny? You tell me why we should take you? You're nothin' but a pain in the ass to everyone, ever since you came, so why should we think any different of you now?" Dick went on and on into the harassment, including such charges as "your an asshole . . . a spare parts piece of shit . . . a running scum bag."

I suddenly thought again to myself, "Why am I putting up with this verbal abuse? It's all bullshit, and it's coming from assholes I wouldn't even associate with back in New York. They could never make it my neighborhood, which is exactly where I belong."

Dick's wife and codirector, Queen Ellie, stood up next. "Vinny, we want your wig, and we're gonna put on some special wax when you're bald to make your head shine. And then you're gonna wear a sandwich sign everywhere you go that'll say, What an asshole I am."

At that point, the meeting turned into a free-for-all, when some long-timer said, "I want his jacket" and pointed to the fancy leather one I was wearing. Another shot in with, "I want that sweater," and one of them spoke out for my suitcase sitting in the middle of the floor. A thought shot through my brain, and I acted on it like an instinct, knowing I had made a bad move. Standing up, I said, "Look, forget it. I'm leaving." Dick tried to put me back down. "Sit down and shut the fuck up, Vinny, you're—"

"No! You shut the fuck up, Dick, and don't touch the suitcase. I changed my mind, and I'm leaving." Everyone was dumbfounded, but no one followed me as I picked up my bag and went out the door, figuring to walk to the freeway and hitchhike home from Reno. It never occurred to me to check directions as the first car I flagged came to a stop. Instead, I jumped in and only found out five miles down the road that the driver was "heading to 'Frisco." Rather than get out and turn around, I just sat back and ran down my options as we crossed over the Sierras, heading West. I had only two or three dollars left after paying my room tab and a last gambling shot at Harrah's.

In a little over five hours on the road, stopping only to fill up, we reached Oakland and Berkley, and then I saw the city by the bay. The driver let me out on the corner of Market and Union downtown, and my first thought was about starving, so I walked into a cafeteria counting my money. I came up with a total of $2.85. When I got to the end of the line with a burger, some fries and a Coke, the cashier rang up $1.98 on the register, and I handed over my last two singles.

I was munching on the burger and pondering my future when I remembered that a cousin of mine on my mom's side lived in Hayward. I finished up my meal in the wee hours and thought maybe I could borrow some money from Cousin Tony for a hotel room. Or, maybe he'd be kind enough to let me stay at his place until I could get money wired from home. Out on the street again, I found a pay phone and dialed Hayward information. Tony was listed, and the operator wanted thirty-five cents to complete the call, leaving me with four measly bits and a penny in my pocket. After the phone rang three times, a man answered. "Hello."

"Cousin Tony? Tony D'Onofrio? It's me, Vinny Marino, Gemma's son, from New York." Tony knew that I was a drug addict and supposedly getting "cured" at Synanon in Reno. Tony paused, then finally said, "Yeah. Oh yeah, Vinny Marino. What time is it?"

I thought, "What the hell kind of question is *that,* at this hour?" But I told Tony, "Early in the morning. Listen, Tony, I'm in San Francisco, on my way to New York, and I need some help. Can I come over and talk to you?" Tony waited again, not answering. When he did speak, he hemmed and hawed until I knew that he wanted no part of it. "Listen, Vinny, I'll tell you the turth. You know, this is a small neighborhood, and my wife . . ."

I understood right away, so I looked for another angle, anything to save my ass at that hour. "Sure, Tony, I understand. Say, do you think I could borrow enough for a one-way plane tick—" Cousin Tony hung up at his end, leaving me with a dial tone and not much else. Without cursing him, I resigned myself to surviving and picked up my suitcase, rattling the two remaining quarters in my pocket as I walked along with no particular purpose.

11 Smart Money on the Move

There I was, walking along Market Street in San Francisco, thinking to myself, "So much for your family connection. What now, smart money?" For no reason at all, I turned left and headed up a side street, where I soon saw a blue neon sign reading Greyhound. Inside the bus station, I checked my bag into a locker for my next-to-last quarter, put the key in my pocket, and headed back to the street for a quick check around. I figured I could always sleep on a bench in the terminal, though I didn't really like the idea.

Four blocks from the bus staion, I saw opportunity walking up the street. The thought of a "clean year" hit my insides as I weighed the likelihood of making a successful move on the drunk who was approaching—an older guy, maybe fifty-five, dressed in an cxpensive coat. He was about two feet away and singing to himself when the adrenalin shot through my body. I put a cigarette in my mouth and stopped him by saying, "Hey, buddy, got a light?"

He looked at me with a question mark, then said, "I think so" as he went fishing in his left trouser pocket. With no time to waste, I dropped the cigarette and grabbed him hard by the throat with my right hand, pushing him backwards to the wall of the building. I reached into his jacket pocket for his wallet, but he hit the wall and coughed hard. He was about to fall, so I let him go and looked in the wallet, seeing cash and credit cards. I just took the cash and dropped the wallet at his feet, then ran to beat hell away from the scene. Twelve blocks away I slowed down to consider my next move. I figure to wait an hour or so before returning to the Greyhound station to pick up my bag, then find a room at least for one night.

I slipped quietly into another greasy-spoon and over burnt coffee and a stale chocolate donut, I counted the cash under the table, making the total at $123. I paid and caught a cab back to the terminal, where I asked the cabbie to wait. When I returned with my suitcase, the cabbie asked, "Where to now?" The question caught me off guard, since I knew absolutely noting about the guts of San Francisco. I figured the cabbie might know and told him to take me to where "all the action is in town." As he pulled away from the curb, I noticed that he looked like a Latin and was in his twenties. He said, "What kind of action you looking for?"

I figured to give him a list and let him do his own shopping, so I said, "Oh, I dunno. I'm from New York. What about women, entertainment, getting high?" He thought for a second before he came back with, "Well, it's kinda late for things tonight, but you should consider the Tenderloin district. A lot is always going down in that area."

"Great. What about a room in that section? Any decent hotels?" He looked back over his shoulder and asked, "How much you want to spend?" I figured quickly from my limited-funds position and said, "Not much. I'm damn near broke."

He drove past several flophouses before I settled on one and told him to stop. I had him keep the meter running while I checked to see if space was available. A skinny old character at the desk told me rooms were six dollars, counting what was left of tonight. I was too tired to look around so I signed in and got my bag from the cab. Once that was taken care of, all I could think about was crawling into bed, which is exactly what I did.

It was after two in the afternoon when I got it together again and lifted out of the bed to have a look around. The room had nothing but trash furniture, so I touched as little as I could on my way to shave and shower. At least the towels were white and clean, but I knew that I had to get out of that place soon. I was dressed and out on the street just after three o'clock when I noticed a junkie couple walking down Polk. Their condition was immediately obvious to me, with the look in their eyes and the way they were handling themselves. He was short and Chinese. She was white, and must have been quite pretty, once.

I said, "Hi, I'm Vinny from New York, and new in this town. You guys know where to cop?" She stepped back and he stopped dead. I knew I had them both off guard, so I took advantage and pressed them further, "Look, I'm from the East Coast, you know? I just want to get my head cleared up before I go back home." She remained still, but he spoke, "They call me Ching and why don't you slow down, man?"

With that, he tried to step out of my way, but I wouldn't let him pass, pleading, "Listen, no shit, I'll get off in front of you. I'm not the heat. I just came out of Synanon." There must have been a ring of truth in what I said because he reluctantly agreed and then took the girl by the arm. Ching motioned for me to follow, and that's what I did, right up to his apartment, which was a fourth-floor walkup in a fairly decent building.

Inside Ching squinted his pupils and asked, "Do you have money? It's only five dollars a bag." I was immediately hesitant because I had confronted them on the street. I was clean and could only take one or maybe even half a bag at the most, so I told Ching, "Listen, the thing is that I'm clean, so how good is the stuff?"

He told me the truth. "I'd say for you, one bag's about it." I felt good about meeting them like this, with no trouble, so I volunteered, "Say Ching, why not I buy three? One for you, one for your lady, and one for me." He smiled at me all the way from the depths of his Far Eastern origins and as if by magic whipped out a cooker. I dipped into my pocket and handed him the money. He added the water to the bottle cap and barked out, "Mimi, bring us three bags."

As I tied up, Ching cooked, and Mimi watched the ritual in earnest, since she was going to get off too. Ching loaded the dropper and handed it to me with the spike. I got it ready and looked for a vein. It seemed that all of them were greedy after a year off junk. I punched a hole without any trouble and sent everything in.

The pit of my stomach instantly jumped around in shock. It twisted and almost retched but then relaxed under the sedative before panic could reign. With no sign of pain, my head lifted off, and I thought of the familiar heavens I had missed for so long. Drifting away from concern like a kite on a breeze, I thought about staying out here for a year. In less than a flash, everything I knew about Synanon was gone.

After maybe an hour and a half in our own private worlds, mainly nodding, we started to talk about histories and experiences. I only told them I was, "Vinny from New York. I was strung out and ended up in Synanon in Reno for a year.'' Ching said that his family was originally from Hong Kong, but he was born in Chinatown so he knew all the best connections. Mimi was from Minnesota somewhere. She had been the homecoming queen at the university there, once upon her prime, but she was mostly beat up now with the junk habit. I guess that Mimi was maybe twenty-three or twenty-four, but she looked a lot older.

We went on to talk about the scene in the Tenderloin, and I heard about the hookers and the faggots taking over center city and the swag scene. I thought to myself, ''This sounds like midtown Manhattan. I might end up staying a while.'' Then Mimi encouraged me when she said, ''Say, Vinny, I have a girlfriend who just got back into town from Las Vegas. How'd you like to meet her?'' I thought about my bankroll for a minute and said, ''What's she like?'' Mimi laughed and told me, ''She's a dancer. You'll really like her.'' I said, ''Sure, anytime. Just let me know.''

Events really flowed for me in San Francisco. Next day Mimi introduced me to Penny, a redheaded dancer with freckles on her pretty face and all over the tops of her incredible thirty-six inch bust. I went for her in a flash. We hit it off right away, and I learned that she was into pills, mainly valiums and quaaludes, while I went straight back to junk. Penny danced on tables at one of the topless joints in North Beach, near Carol Doda's. She also did some selling of herself on the side, when it came up, but had never associated with a pimp. At any rate, I moved in with Penny at her apartment on Polk Street after only two nights in the boardinghouse dive.

I had something in mind and told her about it. ''We're going to double up on some of your johns.'' For the caper I was planning I was going to need a gun, which I arranged through a connection of Ching's. It was a .25 caliber Baretta and very compact. I could almost conceal it in the palm of my hand. After I had the piece, I went cruising the hotels in the area, looking for one that might accept hookers for their one-hour stands. I watched enough girls go into one hotel that I figured, ''This would be a good place to operate. Class girls—Penny's type.'' I walked in and approached the night clerk on duty with a line about ''some girls who would be needing rooms.''

He said, ''How many girls?'' as his eyes lit up. ''A few,'' I said with a smile, ''They belong to the circus that's coming to town.'' ''When does this start and for how long?'' I shot straight back, "It starts tomorrow, and I want one room that's really safe." Then I asked him if he knew the vice cops in the neighborhood. He told me he'd been in business a long time and knew them all and that everything was cool.

So me and this guy on the desk named Al made a deal within ten minutes. If there was any trouble at all, Penny would buzz the desk, and Al would ring me in our apartment, just around the corner. For his trouble, Al was to get five bucks per trick, plus the rent for the room everyday, which the johns paid.

Penny started picking them up off the street, and then I would barge into the room as her irate husband or boyfriend, whatever it took to shake the john loose from an extra twenty-five or fifty. Sometimes I had to smack a guy around a couple of times before he got the message that I was serious about finding him in my marital bed, but most of the victims were businessmen who wanted no trouble.

Some of the suckers tried to get out of it saying, "Hey pal, I'm sorry. I didn't know she was your wife, and she approached me." In those cases Penny cut in with a pointed finger, "How can you say that? You approached me, you lying sonofabitch!" At that point, I would step in and give the guy a backhand slap saying, "Shut up. No matter what, how can I tolerate you here, fucking my wife? I feel like tearing your arm off and making you eat it. Now what? Do I rob you or do I beat the shit out of you?" So it went, fifty here, a hundred there, and junk all over. Soon two months had passed me by in San Francisco.

By that time, Penny and I had four hotels wired for buzzer protection, and only one of the johns ever complained, though we hit one every other day the whole time. After awhile, she was getting a kick out of it, and I was like a crazy man with the johns. Then we moved up a step with the invention of a phone code for Penny to use from the john's hotel room in case he insisted on going there. She would get inside the room and tell the guy, "I have to check in with my service, so why don't you get ready?" Then she would dial me, saying which hotel, the room number, and how long she expected to be there. Penny always managed to stay on top of the trick until I knocked on the door when she would jump up and open it before he could say or do anything. Sometimes I would waye the piece for effect, which usually got me tiwce as much money.

In the odd times away from the street scene, Penny and I would make love, if you could call it that, with me back on junk and her with a bellyful of idiot pills. It sure was a twisted experience. I was hardly thinking about what I was doing, until one day I was forced to.

Penny called in from the Mark Hopkins Hotel, telling me the room number and giving herself forty-five minutes to an hour. I sat back on a pile of pillows, still loaded but thinking through the fog, "Wow, the Mark Hopkins. That's up on Nob Hill. This john has some money, that's for sure."

Within five minutes I managed to get the gun in my belt, put on a shirt and a jacket, and get in a cab heading for his hotel room. I stumbled a little getting out of the cab but paid the driver off before any of the doormen noticed. Walking briskly inside, I went straight for the elevators along one wall of the huge lobby. I got a little leery when I realized they had elevator operators, and the one I was in was giving me peculiar looks. I got off the elevator at the twenty-first floor and skipped down the hall, looking for room 2110. I knocked loud and fast three times and pulled the piece from my waist just in case I might need it.

Penny snapped the door open and then jumped backwards about a foot, trying to cover that glorious body with only her bare hands. Sitting up in the bed was this balding tycoon with gray hair all slicked down and a pencil-thin moustache. I picked up on his fancy clothes draped over a chair, as I showed him the gun and demanded, "What in the hell are you doing here with my wife?"

He said, "What!? I didn't know she was your wife. I got her off the street at Union Square." I said, "You rotten sonofabitch, taking advantage of my wife like that!" and cracked him with the back of my right hand, scaring him shitless. He offered me some money, but I leaned on him until he gave me all the money in his wallet, his Jules Jurgeson gold watch, and his diamond ring.

Backing away from him naked on the bed and her naked against the wall, it struck me that this caper was certain to cause trouble because of the Mark Hopkins and the man in question. As I was closing the door on them, I was mentally opening mine, considering the fastest way out of town. Bolting down the hall, my first thought was to take the exit door, which led to a stairwell, so I started down as fast as I could go. On the twentieth floor, I went back out into the hallway and took the elevator, then got off on two and walked down to the lobby, looking carefully through the door before exiting to the street.

I took a cab to our apartment where I emptied my pockets of everything. Out poured $637, a gold wristwatch, a three-carat diamond ring in a platinum setting, the gun from my belt, the gloves from the job, an old white handkerchief, and a crumpled pack of Viceroys.

Because of the speedball I had done earlier that morning, my thinking was totally paranoid, and I figured Penny had probably been caught in the room, still naked, and I wasn't sure if she would give me up or not. I went into near panic, packing my bag as fast as I could. Then I remembered another stash I had hidden in the bedroom closet, and I counted out four hundred more to get me the hell out of town. I located the rest of a bundle of junk in a dresser drawer plus a set of works and threw them both in the bag wrapped in a hand towel. Five minutes after setting foot in the room, I was ready to leave for parts unknown.

On the street again, I caught a cab and could only think of getting out of the neighborhood. I ordered the cabbie to Fisherman's Wharf, but on the way stopped him short and got off in front of another cheap hotel in the Haight-Ashbury district. The rates were the same as the Tenderloin—six dollars a night—so I checked in, expecting the worst, and got it. The room was so dirty all I did in it was shoot up to forget where I was. In an instant I knew that I had done too much because I nodded for over two hours and felt perilously close to blacking out. Without even unpacking my bag, I crawled into bed and slept the night away.

With the first light of day, I shook my head back and forth several times, trying to clear the cobwebs. I reached for my cooker, figuring a shot would make things straighten up, as I tied up my arm with a belt, looking for a vein. Once I had pushed in the needle and everything started to feel better, it occurred to me that a check of the morning paper was in order to see if a guest of the Mark Hopkins was looking for someone fitting my description. Then I noticed that I was almost out of junk, so I would definitely have to cop somewhere during the day.

I went out and bought a paper, then went into a coffee shop to "read all about it." All of the booths were taken, so I slipped onto a stool at the counter. By the time my order came, I was through section one with no mention of yesterday's caper in the hotel. It took the next thirty minutes to read every column inch of the damn thing. Nothing there. I figured, "The cops must be planning something," and I was highly relived to remember that

Penny didn't know my last name or anything else about me. She only knew my name was Vinny, I was from New York and had been in Synanon somewhere.

I went back to the hotel, showered, shaved, and checked out. As I walked out the front door I looked for a cab. Within five minutes I had one, and I told him to head for the North Beach area. Once we arrived, I picked out another likely cheap-shot hotel, where the guy behind the counter informed me that the rate for a single was ten dollars. Thinking there might be some extras at that price, I took it for one night.

When he turned the register around for me to sign, I put Hooks' name down and wrote Miami for my home town. I wanted no part of any formal signatures anywhere in San Francisco. Key in hand, I ran back to the cab and paid him. Then with my bag I walked back to this new "home," hoping for the best but finding everything pretty much like you would expect for ten bucks a night in the topless bar section of town. The room had a single bed and a broken down bedstand with a lamp on it.

"Who cares," I was thinking as I cooked up the last of my junk, "this is all that counts anyway." When my head was up in the clouds where it belonged, I calmed down enough to consider scoring again. I was afraid to try for a new connection and was lucky enough to reach Mimi at home. I went up to pick up my bundle and left again right away, after giving Mimi a bag and some story about Penny and me being on the outs.

In the cab ride back to North Beach, all kinds of thoughts ran through my head, starting with some lessons from Synanon: "Why are you such a weak bastard that you can't function without junk? Where are you running to now, asshole?" I tried to ignore those reminders by changing the subject to figuring out how the hell to get out of town. I thought about flying first class, then "why not take a quiet bus ride and think about things along the way?"

I was still stuck in that quandry when the cabbie pulled up in front of my current address. After I paid, I slipped out of the cab and walked to the corner store for a bottle of something to relax me from all the anxiety I was experiencing. They had a big display of Smirnoff Vodka, so I bought a fifth, two bottles of Schweppes tonic, and a small bag of ice cubes.

With my refreshments in a brown paper bag and my junk wrapped up in tinfoil, I shuffled down the street and went straight to my room anticipating the true test. Everything worked as it was advertised, and I laid there against one of the four walls until I had shot up two of the bags and downed a little less than half of the booze. The rest I don't remember.

What I do recall was waking up to the smell of burning flesh and cloth. Then I felt pain in two places: my left hand and my prick. I looked down but couldn't move right away to correct what I saw. A cigarette was burning down between my fingers, plus there was smoke from my pants right next to the zipper. I slowly thought, "Hey, my cock's on fire!" as I started to beat out the smoldering with my good hand. After a couple of minutes it was still smoking, so I managed to get out of the pants and my underwear, and drop them in the sink. Still stuck in a fog, I looked at the burns on my fingers and felt totally disgusted with myself as I fell down to sleep it off for another seven hours.

When morning came, I looked around at the mess I had created. The ice had melted out of its plastic bag, making a puddle on the floor, and cigarette ashes were everywhere along with ten or twelve soggy butts. My cooker had been knocked over, dammit, and the bags of junk were loose on the floor along with the works. My expensive pants in the sink had a big hole, which rendered them useless. I held up my left hand and wished I had some salve to soothe the burns and make this pain get the hell out of my body. I went back to the bed, holding my head, wondering what possible direction I could take to save my sanity. I was sinking, and there was no way out that I could see.

When I woke up again, it dawned on me from nowhere, "You have to change your habits and take on a challenge or you'll go right down the tubes." And then the answer came: "Ditch the junk and knock off the booze, then hitchhike across country and go see your family." Way down deep the whole idea felt brilliant as it hit. I got out of bed, brushed my teeth, had a nice shave, took a hot shower, cleaned up the mess, packed my bag, and was ready to leave.

Before taking off, however, I figured to cop some dolophines and substitute them for heroin, so I called up a friend of Ching's who always seemed to have pills on hand, a guy named Wong. He said he had what I wanted and told me to come right over. When I got there I figured to trade the junk I didn't want for his pills. Without batting a slanted eyelash he agreed, and I got sixty dolophines for my fifteen five-dollar bags. Before I left, Wong offered me a fix of my own dope, which he was by then holding up. Incredibly, I mustered enough willpower to refuse.

As I hit the front stoop of his building, it occurred to me that I'd be much better off if I had a rough route figured out for the trip across the country. Luck was with me as I looked down the street and saw an orange Union 76 neon sign. They had a whole rack of free maps, and I took the Interstate Highway map and thanked the gas jockey as I crossed the street toward a luncheonette sign, thinking about one last meal before I skipped this damn town.

Over a fast tuna sandwich I looked over the map and saw the trail leading into Colorado, Kansas, Missouri. The truth hit me then. "This is going to be a long run." With that, I cleared the table and put the map away in my bag. While my hand was inside, I grabbed two Dolophines and swallowed them with the Coke. Ten minutes later I was ready to hit the road. My plan was to take a cab to the last freeway entrance for the Oakland Bay Bridge and hitch from there at the on-ramp.

As I was getting out of the cab, a car stopped behind us. The driver would have had to pull into the other lane to get around us, and he could see it would only take a minute for me to get out so he could move on. I waved my thumb at him and smiled, pointing up the ramp in the general direction of the East Coast. I knew in a flash I had him when I caught his eye, and he motioned me to come to the car as he reached over and unlocked the passenger side. I hustled up with my bag and set it down to open the door with a question, "Hi. Which way you heading?" He was a young guy with curly blonde hair and a full reddish beard. He was sliding things over on the front seat to make room for me, as he looked up and said, "All the way to Chicago."

"Great," I said as I threw my bag in the back seat and got in. Before I could close the door, he sped up the ramp and we were under way, heading east. When I settled down and looked over the left side, I could see the Navy's Treasure Island and beyond that the hilly skyline of Marin County. The driver broke into my thinking with a question, "Where you heading?"

I thought to lie for a moment, but then figured why bother and said, "Back home, to New York." He was right when he said, "That's one helluva distance from here. Probably take you at least five days. Oh, by the way, I'm Rick. I live in Evanston, outside of Chicago. Go to school there, at Northwestern University."

I thought to myself, "How 'bout this? A college brat whose old man no doubt gave him this LTD Ford." Instead of starting an argument over nothing, I came back with, "Oh, yeah, Northwestern. I used to be an instructor at the University of Nevada, in Reno." As the ride progressed through central California at seventy miles an hour, we went back and forth with made-up bullshit from my side and some likely facts from him. He seemed like a nice enough kid, although highly naive. I offered to dirve if he wanted, but he said, "Maybe later, when we hit that long stretch in Nevada." So I laid my head back to see if I couldn't catch a wink or two. I must have drifted off and what woke me was the distinct smell of sweet smoke—like marijuana. I looked over, and sure enough young Rick was toking on a joint. He offered me some, but I refused, saying, "Makes me too tired, that stuff, but thanks anyway."

He took another drag and held it all in saying, "Suit yourself, man. It sure makes for a mellow ride." I thought to myself as I looked out the window, "Yeah, kid, all drugs are mellow, as long as you have them running in your system. They only turn into monkeys when you try to get them off your back." But I said nothing and returned to the view with my thoughts.

The next interruption came just on the outskirts of Sacramento when Rick hit the brakes and drew my attention to another hitchhiker standing on the side of the road. We were two hundred yards past him by the time Rick ground to a halt and threw it in reverse to back up. By then this guy was running full tilt toward us, so I said, "Hold it. He's coming." Stoned now, Rick said, "Might as well pick up another guy. You don't mind, do you?" I didn't have an opinion—as long as he sat in the back—so I said, "No, hell no. Whatever you want to do. Here, there's plenty of room in the back." I shoved my bag over to the freeway side of the car and opened the rear door to admit our new crew member for this sail across the face of America. As soon as the newcomer stuck his head in the door, I knew we were in for a trip. He was a kid of maybe eighteen, with a crewcut—an obvious military maneuver—and he had that green duffle bag. He said, "Hey, you guys. Going to Denver?"

I figured it wasn't any of my business, just as Rick answered, "All the way. Hop in." He whooped, "All right!" and grinned, tossing the Army bag on top of my suitcase as he climbed in the rear door, slamming it hard. I wasn't up to talking to this young buck, so I eased two more dolophines from my shirt pocket and ate them after faking a cough while Rick talked on and on with our new rider. I sat there hoping that these guys would run out of things to talk about soon, but they were just warming up. As we crossed the border into Nevada, the guy whose name was Don leaned his elbows over the center of the seat, right in the middle of the conversation, and his eyes lit up like flashlights. "Hey. You guys want to get high?"

I looked over at him and thought, "On what kid. You got any smack?" but I shook my head no as Rick went for it, saying, "Hell, yeah, what have you got?" Don unsnapped the lock on the duffle and dipped into it as he said, "Some dynamite Nepalese hash. I picked it up for nothing in Bankok. We'll have to smoke it in a bong, though." Rick thought that was more of an opportunity than any kind of problem because he said, "That's all right, man. We'll stop at the first roadside diner we see, get high and a bite to eat, then hit the road again. What do you guys say?"

He looked at me with bright expectations, but I just nodded and said, "Sure. Whatever you want." Don got excited and pulled out his "works," which consisted of a chunk of black hasish, a switchblade to cut it into small pieces, and a glass pipe about a foot long. He loaded the bong with chips of the hash just as I spotted the First Casino in Nevada sign on the right side of the freeway.

Don lit up as we pulled into the far end of the parking lot. "Sure smells righteous to me, brother. Let's have a hit," Rick said. Don gave Rick the bong, as Marino went along with them, eating dolophines on the side. Within ten minutes, we were all tripping in one direction or another as we went through the door of the restaurant-gas station-casino. Inside, my first impression was that this might have been the first casino ever built in Nevada it was so broken down. The calendar on the wall behind the bar was two years old, unless I was losing track of time, but maybe the nude picture gave it staying power. The bartender was heavy on booze, judging from the bulbous red nose and blood-shot eyes. One lone traveler was playing blackjack, and three or four others were plugging the slots. We went into the dining room and ordered burgers and Cokes. The two of them were laughing and cursing out loud, almost enough to cause a disturbance, I thought, just as the peak of the dolophines hit me. With that, I joined them for a couple of laughs, and inside of thirty minutes we were ready to go.

The waitress brought only one check, so Rick tallied the individual totals. Some college kid. What he had to figure on paper, I had already totaled in my head long before him. As it was, each of us owed between two and three dollars, so I reached in my back pocket, where I kept the singles and fives, and came up with three. Rick pulled out three, too, and Don came out with this thick plastic wallet holding a bunch of twenty-dollar American Express traveler's checks. He said, beaming, "Why don't you guys just give me the cash, and I'll cover it with one of these."

I thought to myself, "You can cover a whole lot more with that fistful, my boy." We passed by the package store, and Don brought two six packs of Bud for the road. Back in the car, they bonged up again, there we all popped a beer, and Rick drove as we started up the freeway ramp. Before we got to Reno, I looked back at Don and offered the bait for a trap I had in mind, saying, "Hey Don, how would you like to make some quick money, guaranteed?" He stopped laughing long enough to look at me like I was crazy as he said, "Doing what, Vinny? You got one of those beat-the-casino books in your pocket?" I said, "Nah. None of that crap. This isn't gambling, it's a guaranteed winner. I've done it before." Without hesitating any further, he said, "Well, yeah, man, lay the trip on me." I leaned halfway over the rear seat and spoke slowly so I wouldn't lose the kid, "You know, those traveler's checks you have?"

He said, "Yeah, what about 'em?" I gave him a grin as I said, "Well, you can't lose them, did you know that?" He looked lost again as he asked, "What the hell do you mean, I can't lose them?" I told him, "They're insured by the company. So if you do happen to lose them, American Express will give you new ones to spend." He was still stuck in the maze I had created so I laid it on him slow. "Look, Don, here's the caper. You give me the traveler's checks with your ID card. I'll forge your signature, and we'll cash them between here and Colorado, buying small stuff like cigarettes and beer. We split all the cash that's left, and then when you get home, you call up the company, tell them you lost them on the way, and they give you all the money back. How's that for some fun between here and Denver?"

Don was a little puzzled at first, but he did know about the insurance since that's why he had bought traveler's checks in the first place. Within minutes he was convinced, and we were ready to swing into action. Rick said he wanted "no part of the money," but he had no objection to us pulling the caper as we went along. Don handed me the book of checks along with his Colorado drivers' license. I compared his written description with mine, and it wasn't that far off. We both had dark hair; he was five-ten and I was six feet. He was eighteen and I was twenty-five, which could have presented a problem but we'd see.

To make a long story short, we cashed all of his traveler's checks by the time we got to Utah. Two hundred of it went in Reno, then we did almost every little casino along the road until the total came to five hundred dollars. Usually I bought the beer, which turned out to be a mistake, because Rick and Don kept drinking and smoking hash until they were getting loud and boisterous, drawing unnecessary attention to us everywhere we went. As we came out of the last joint with no more checks to cash, I almost panicked with the idea of being picked up out there and ending up in the Nevada pen back in Reno—a cowboy con at last. What if this kid had stolen the traveler's checks? I said to myself, "At first the opportunity, you gotta get away from these guys."

My chance came not long after we crossed the stateline into Utah, when Rick suggested, "You guys want to get some sleep? We can split a cheap motel room." I was certain that he had seen the same sign I had, advertising the "Best rest you ever had, only $6.95, double occupancy." Rick exited the freeway at the indicated turnoff, and the motel was at the intersection, right there in the middle of nowhere except for a truck stop next door. It was nearly four in the morning, as I volunteered to do the room negotiations.

I woke the owner by ringing the doorbell, and when he opened the door, I said, "Sir, we are three servicemen going home on leave. How much for a room from now until noon?" He said, "Oh, I dunno. You guys servicemen? Okay, gimme ten bucks and be out before noon. You can have number 202. It's just upstairs." I paid him the ten, and he gave me the key as I went back to the car to tell "the guys." They were delighted when I held up the key and doubly so when I told them, "Aw, forget it. It wasn't that much. I covered it. Let's get to the rack."

Rick shut off the car, and we grabbed our bags and headed for the stairs to the second floor. I opened the door and saw one double bed and a couch. Before anyone had a chance, I said, "I'll take the couch." They didn't argue, since both were exhausted. They just fell into bed and were sleeping immediately.

"Well," I figured, "why not try that truck stop for a ride?" I ate two more dolophines and thought about taking off with Rick's car and everything they had but stopped myself short thinking, "you want to get away from them, not have them looking for you." Quietly, I picked up my bag and eased the motel room door open, then slid out and closed it again without making a sound. I did a brisk walk to the truck stop, where I could see only three people inside: the waitress and two enormous guys, both truckers. I breezed through the door, put my bag down next to the coat rack where I could see it, and went to the counter for a seat. In ten minutes, the two guys got up together and walked out the door talking, so there was no opportunity for me to pop my question about a ride. I was just about to give up and go back to the motel when I saw another set of truck lights coming down the freeway exit. I would give this guy a shot, and if he turned me down, I was going back to bed.

Luck was with me as the driver came into the diner with a cigarette hanging from his mouth, unlit. Since I came before the waitress in terms of who was near the door, he approached me and asked, "You got a match?" I reached in my pocket and said, "Sure. Here you go. Keep 'em." He smiled and said, "Thanks, pal," sitting down one stool away from me at the counter. After giving the wiatress his order, he turned to me and said, "Where you headin', buddy? I don't see any other cars out there in the lot."

He caught me off guard with the question since I was ready to ask him the same thing. I recovered and said, "I'm hitching home to New York. My mom's sick, but I didn't have the money to take a bus." He didn't fall over backwards, but he did say, "Well, I'm going as far as Chicago, if that'll help you." My eyes opened wide as I told him, "Sure. That would be great. Anytime you're ready."

Less than half an hour later I was hoisting myself at least six feet off the ground, climbing into the cab of this incredible Mack monster on wheels. When Joe, my new driver, turned that thing over, we could have moved mountains with the power behind that rig. We started steamrolling along when the small talk began, and we ran through the standard road travel exchange, with me faking it, while he was a "family man from South San Francisco. Two kids, a wife, and a mortgage. You know, Vinny, I don't normally pick up hitchhikers. Too risky these days."

It was back and forth with idle chatter mixed with stretches of alternating radio and total silence as we rumbled through the mountains of Utah and Colorado, then down to the prairies and wheat fields of Kansas. Joe broke out a snack about halfway through our trek and offered me some coffee and a Washington delicious apple. I took them gladly and thanked him directly.

As I was finishing the apple, I moved to wash down a couple more dolophines with what was left of the coffee when I saw three Highway Patrol cars on the berm of the road just ahead. They had pulled off a passenger car from California, and about six cops had it surrounded. We passed without incident, and once we were away Joe opened up with me, saying, ''Jeez, ya can't trust nobody these days. Never know who's out there on the road.'' I nodded and said, ''Yeah, Joe, you can't be too careful. These are dangerous times.''

Joe's face went grim, as he carried on with a story. ''I know, Vinny. Hell, I just got loaded up one day at the dock and not more than a block from the warehouse, two masked guys jumped on the running board of the rig I was in, and one of them pointed a gun at my head and told me to pull over. They tied me up and took the whole load of transistor radios, so from then on, I carry protection.''

I looked at him sideways and said, ''Really, Joe? That's heavy. What do you use for protection?'' He blurted out, ''A forty-five caliber automatic service revolver.'' I acted dumb and told him, ''Sounds like some weapon. I've never seen one of those. Can I look at it?'' He opened the glovebox and lifted some papers, revealing the handle of the piece. Then he reached in, pushed the clip eject button, and held it in his hand as he offered me the pistol for a cursory inspection. I was glad to know where it was, as I put it back, saying, ''You got a gun like that, Joe, there shouldn't be any more trouble.''

I kept that piece he was carrying clearly in my mind the rest of the time we were riding together. Not long after he showed it to me, a roadside diner came up on our right, so he made the obvious suggestion as the driver, ''Ready for a bite, Vinny?'' Being my paranoid self, I didn't want to tell him I had any more money, so I said, looking down, ''Sure, I'm ready to stop, Joe, but I can't eat. I'm broke. My last buck went for coffee at the diner.''

Joe from Frisco was true human being—not only did he buy all the meals from that point to Chicago, but as I climbed down from the cab, he pushed a folded twenty dollar bill across the seat, and said, ''Here, Vinny, take this. I hope you get home safe, and that your mom's okay.'' I thanked him as I was waving goodbye, standing on the side of the road all alone, holding my bag and wondering how soon I'd be on my way. About an hour later a new Pontiac station wagon pulled over, and I saw through the rear window a couple and a young kid in the back. They said they were heading for Pittsburgh and I climbed in and just slept until early morning. When they pulled off at the Monroeville exit, I asked them to leave me at the nearest restaurant.

Looking through the glass into one of Howard Johnson's places, I was happy to see it was open, given the hour, with at least ten or fifteen people inside. I dropped my bag in the entrance foyer and stood beside it with the thought of asking the first person for a ride. If I missed, then I'd get something to eat. I waited twenty minutes for the first people who were leaving, and they were only going to the next exit, so I ordered some breakfast, taking a seat at the counter.

That exit on the Pennsy Turnpike turned out to be a real bad-luck stop for me. It took three hours before a salesman offered me a ride to the Harrisburg area, and I had a helluva time getting a ride out of there. It had been almost another three hours since the salesman had dropped me, and it was nearly dark when a little sports car pulled up with a guy about my age at the wheel. He said, "Where you going?"

"New York City."

He said, "I'll take you about ten miles—that's two exists—if you want." I figured, "To hell with this place" and said, "Sure, that'll be great." I noticed something unusual about the driver within five minutes on the road. He started fumbling and fussing around with all kinds of things, from heater dials to the radio stations. Nothing seemed right to him, and he turned to me and said, "What do you want to hear?"

I thought, "Nothing from you, if that's a song," but instead I said, "I'm not from around here, so I don't know the stations. Whatever turns you on is fine." I wanted to take back my last sentence because he swung right into action. "That's fantastic. Let's listen to this," and he stopped screwing with the station dial, then got off at the first exit we came to. I figured, "This ain't right, he said two exist," and braced myself for possible trouble. At the stop sign, he turned right again and that was far enough for me, so I said, "Where the hell are you going?"

He shot up a dirt road, then stopped dead, saying, "I have to take a dump." He opened the door before I could react, and I grabbed the keys from the ignition and watched for him, carefully. When he came back to the car, he got in and was nervous as hell. I knew right then the guy was a fag. He said something about "Nice moon tonight," and I got pissed, so I went for an angle to see what he'd do with it. I said, looking him in the eye, "Hey man, they got laws about this kinda shit," and I grabbed his collar by the throat, finishing with "I'm still a minor." Then I let go and pushed him away, as I backed into my door to wait to see what he did. He got scared, and started pleading, "Don't hurt me. I didn't mean anything."

I wasn't about to let him off the hook, now that I had him, so I said, "Do you live with your family?" Too nervous to lie, he said yes and shut up again, as I went on. "Tell you what. Let me see your driver's license." He fumbled getting out his wallet and handed me the card from Pennsylvania. I stuck it in my shirt pocket and told him, "Drive me to your house. I'm going to tell your father and mother what you just tired to do to me." His eyes jumped with fright, and he cringed with the thought, saying, "No, please. I can't do that." There was no escape for him as I said, "Look, jerk. I gotta do what's right by the law, as a citizen. Your kind of perverted behavior has got to be stopped." The guy was damn near crying, as he pleaded with me, "No, no, please. Don't make me do that."

I gave him the only out he was going to see, saying, "How much money you got?" He reached for his wallet again, but I grabbed it from him as soon as he brought it into the open. Inside I counted only $12 in cash, but there was also a company check made out to him for $147. I took the check from the wallet, plus the cash, and told him, "Okay, cocksucker, if you want out of this shit, it's going to cost you sevent-five bucks more. Where do we cash the check?"

He slobbered and cried, saying, "No, no, I can't do that." I slapped him across the face once, hard, and gave an order, "Alright, then let's go home and see your old man, right now." He sobbed and started the car, saying, "No, no, I'll get it cashed." He turned around and drove to the main road, then went right, and it was about two miles before I spotted a shopping center ahead on the left.

He looked at me with fear, and said, "I can get it cashed in that center. There's a foodstore." I told him without any question, "Look, asshole. When you go in, I'm in your seat with the keys in the ignition. And if you come out with anyone else, I take your car and wreck it. That'll cost you more than seventy-five bucks, so go get the cash in a hurry. I'll be right by the front door watching you, and waiting. Here's your license."

He didn't do anything strange and, in fact, they gave him the cash faster than I used to get it when I pulled a stickup. As he turned to come back out, I went to get the keys again, and I had them as he approached. He had already counted out my seventy-five dollars and handed it over. I had him drive me to a busy corner, where I pulled out my bag and gave him a final warning. "Look, the thing for you to do is go home and forget about this. Think about women for a change."

I slammed the door with some fury, and he roared away burning rubber in every gear. I was thinking about forgetting with some dope but considered it too risky, so I asked the address of the bus station from a cashier in a nearby drugstore. It was only two blocks away, and you wouldn't believe the feeling of relief I felt when I learned that a Greyhound was leaving for New York in twenty-three minutes.

12 Back in the Tracks

After I bought my ticket to New York, I sat around the station for what secmed like forever. As soon as the driver opened the bus, I gave him my ticket and got on, looking all the way in the back for a seat. When I found one that suited my anxious mood, I settled in next to the window, leaning my head against the smoky glass. Suddenly I was hit with a rush of fear and pictured a state trooper hauling me off to the local lockup. I slid even farther down in the seat, trying to get more incognito into the picture and less Marino. I thought for a moment of actually getting under the seat to hide from my own worries about, "Damn! That faggot kid going to the cops."

The driver finally started up and got away exactly ninety-three seconds late. As the lights of the town disappeared, I felt relieved enough to breathe freely and let go of the raw terror. I couldn't believe that I had gotten away one more time, and with that realization I went to the john on the bus to relive myself of at least six more pounds of internal pressure. While I was there, I wished for one more shot of junk but settled for three more dolophines to last me the night. I went back to my seat and dozed until I saw the lights of the Lincoln Tunnel after four hours of nonstop driving.

Then I started thinking about where to from the Port Authority? It was somewhere around three-thirty in the morning, as I stretched after getting off the bus and noticed my breath in the crisp morning air. I felt good to be back in the city. I picked up my bag and headed in the direction of Broadway and Forty-third Street on the west side, only a couple of blocks away—an easy walk. I remembered a hotel that rented by the hour to hookers, so I figured to have about eight or ten hours all by myself.

The night clerk nodded when I asked him if he had a room, but he never got off his ass. He had a green accountant's visor pulled over his eyes, and his feet were resting on some overdue bills on the desk. When I asked him about the rates, he raised his right index finger and muttered, "On the card, Mac." I figured I'd need at least a week to get my bearings again, so I used the homosexual's hard cash to pay for the first seven days. After I made it to my room, I literally collapsed with the cumulative fatigue of thumbing rides across the entire country and kicking a slight habit of dolophines.

Twelve hours later I opened my eyes again, but it was more than fourteen until I could think about moving. The first clear thought to get through my muddy brain was about the family. I hadn't been in touch with any of them after that phone call I made from Harrah's back in Reno. Hell, that was twelve or thirteen weeks ago, so I had some major explaining to do. With that hanging over my head, it took a little longer to gather the motivation needed to get out of bed. In front of the bathroom mirror, I wondered about the wisdom of seeing anyone in this condition; maybe I ought to check in for a week to ten days of detox first. I changed my mind, ate two dolophines and started cleaning up as I planned to do "something productive" with the rest of the day.

As soon as I got dressed, I knew I had to let mom know I was okay. I couldn't get rid of the thought that she had been through enough and if someone else saw me in town before I called her, well, that would do it. It was time for me to face the music. When she answered the phone, I stammered, "Ahhh, hi, mom. It's me, Vinny." She was silent for a split second and even that weighed on my guilt feelings, then, "Vinny, Vinny, my God, Vinny. Are you all right? Where have you been? Where are you now? Why—"

I cut her off with, "Ma, it's okay, ma. I'm back home in the city." She was nearly hysterical, hearing my voice after enough time had gone by to conclude the worst. Between sobs for breath, she said, "Why in God's name didn't you call?" I couldn't do anything but lie, so I said, "I was working a job, ma—sixteen hours a day in San Francisco. Every night I just went to bed beat. I'm sorry, ma." She had been familiar with my bullshit for a long time, and I could tell she was suspicious when she said, "Vinny, you come over here right now." I tried to make a reasonable excuse, but she didn't give. "Vinny, I am very angry about this, and I want you home so I can see you."

"Okay, okay, mom. Tonight I'll be there, I promise." She said, "Vinny, you make it eight-thirty. Do you hear me, Vinny?" She made a last plea before we hung up, asking, "Vinny, are you using that stuff, drugs, right now?" I put on my best act and said proudly, "No, ma. I really feel good, and I've been clean for over a year."

"Well, thank God for that. We'll see you tonight. Goodbye, Vinny."

With that out of the way, I figured to make a few more calls while I was at it so no one could come down on me for being home and not calling. I rang up brother Frank, and at first he was as upset as mom, but then he got excited. "Over a year with no drugs? Congratulations, brother!" I felt a twinge of guilt about becoming a two-faced liar so fast again, but what was I going to say? "Oh, I'm only doing dolophines now where I was doing heroin, doridens, and dolophines before I went in, remember?"

I got the same reaction from pop, and we worked it out to see each other for dinner the next night. I promised to call him then at six-thirty. Next I thought to call Angie, who had wired three hundred dollars to me, but she was busy with someone and had to hang up. I hung up the receiver and thought of Hooks. When I dialed the last number I had on him, I got a recorded message, "We're sorry, the number you are calling is not in service . . ." I hung up before listening to the rest and figured to get a couple of things done before going over to mom's. First, I had to hit Harlem to check out what was happening and cop some dolophines and doridens so I could be fairly straight in front of the family. On my way over to mom's, I could stop at Hooks' parents' place to see if they had his current address.

Out on the street, everything felt basically the same, and I thought all I had to do in order to catch up was get used to the unique cadence and match my act with the existing pace. "That won't be hard," I was figuring to myself as the light turned green, and I shuffled through an intersection. It was the hour when the hookers come out on the sidewalks, and it was as if they appeared from nowhere. One minute there were none; the next minute you might see twenty. I strolled along, casually watching everything and then went down to take a subway to

Harlem. At the 96th Street station, I surfaced and began looking for a familiar face.

The first guy I recognized was standing on the corner of 101st and Second Avenue—old Haysoos, the Puerto Rican. We stood around shooting the shit about who was where and what was what until his face brightened, and he said, "Hey, Veeny, I bunt chew to meet a friend of mine. He leeves een Meedtown. You'll like heem."

I said, "Haysoos, why not. Can we cop there?" He looked at me and grinned, saying "Whatever there eees eeen town, Reek has thee best." So we carried on walking and talking until Haysoos stopped in front of one building and said, "You wait here, Veeny. I go see eef she's cool to come een."

As Haysoos disappeared up the steps I paid attention to the local action. It's hard to describe Harlem from a white man's point of view. One thing is you can never know anything about anything for sure, so you have to watch everything all the time. Once I was up there to cop with Hooks along for the ride and stoned out of his mind. We were walking around 105th and First and saw two guys arguing loudly. I nudged Hooks to be on the lookout as we moved closer to the buildings in order to pass them without any trouble. When we came within five feet, it was clear they were hassling over drug prices. One guy was selling doridens for forty cents a pill, undercutting the other guy by ten cents.

Just as we got next to them, one of them shoved the other and he got angry. He pulled a switchblade, flicked it open, and growled out a "muthafucker" as he nailed his opponent deep in the chest, overhand. It was so real and so sudden, I couldn't believe it—a man with the look of shock and near death on his face even before he realized what had happened. He tried to grab the blade and pull it out of his body but fell over backwards first, with blood coming out his mouth. Half-stoned, Hooks and I ran like jackrabbits to get away from any involvement. Next day the headlines read, "Harlem Stabbing Death. No Suspects."

I wasn't waiting long before Haysoos stumbled down the stairs, then started back up motioning me with, "Come on, man." We walked up to the third floor, which smelled halfway between urine and clorox, so strong it burnt my nostrils. I was relived to get out of the hall and into almost any room. Haysoos introduced this good-looking guy about twenty-eight or so, a sharp dresser. "Veeny, thees ess Reek, he ees good people."

We talked for five minutes before I asked him what he had and he came right back with, "What do you need?" I figured on some doriden and dolophines, but then I thought about coping a half load of junk "just for insurance" and to save a trip the next day. Once I had the drugs and Rick had the money, he asked if I wanted a fix. Thinking ahead to mom and Brooklyn, I said, "No, thanks. I'll just eat a few of these for now. I have some business I have to handle later today."

As I swallowed two of each, he could have cared less as he cooked up his own plus a little treat for Haysoos. As I was leaving, Rick said, "Hey, Vinny. Look me up if you want, in midtown. I'm usually around." I glanced back at him and thought how he might be a real player, dressed like he was and talking more or less plain English, an unusual thing in Spanish Harlem. I waved and said, "Yeah, Rick, I'll see you again, I'm sure."

I closed the door behind me and wasted no more time getting to mom's place. When I got to her door, I straightened out both me and my outfit and knocked three times, standing upright as best I could, since the chemicals were reaching their maximum effect. Mom opened the door and took me by the hand, leading me inside. Then she turned around and collapsed on my chest, crying as she threw her arms around me. "Vinny, oh Vinny, my son," was all she could get out. While we were still locked in that embrace, Frank and Joey came out of the kitchen and started slapping me on the shoulders, saying, "Hey, Vinny. Good to see you."

It wasn't long before everyone started to laugh, and we all sat down to hear my version of the last fifteen months. I got it together enough so they didn't suspect anything, but none of them was looking very closely, either. It amazes me to think of what I got away with then because nothing is more obvious to me now than someone who is stoned on drugs. At any rate, I told them about my responsibilities as a "facilitator" at the prison and what it was like living at Synanon.

When mom asked me directly about the lifetime commitment, I gave her a variation of the same line I had given Clapp in Reno, "I have all the information they had to offer, so now I have to go out in the real world and apply it." She looked a little skeptical, but her scrumptious dinner was nearly ready, which she didn't want to spoil with a hasty accusation. We all sat down to one of the best turkeys ever. As we had coffee, I flashed on the time I had spent without drugs, wondering what tomorrow would bring.

It was almost one o'clock by the time I got back to my room in midtown, and I was so tired from the ordeal of being straight for my family that I just crashed and slept without moving a muscle until ten-thirty the next morning. As soon as I could see well enough to orient myself, I thought of the half load I had copped last night, and I went looking for it and a set of works. After I had gotten off, I settled down to consider some action for the day. I had forgotten to stop at Hooks' folks to see what he was doing so I slowly went through the bathroom ritual and got dressed for the trip to Brooklyn.

As I walked up to his place, I felt something was up. My sixth sense was good enough to trust since it had saved my life more than once. With extreme caution I rang his parents' doorbell and stood back about three feet to wait. His pop appeared, and he didn't seem all that happy to see me, but he invited me in and told me Hooks was "away for a while." I knew it was some kind of trouble, but he wouldn't say. I pressed him a little harder, "Is he in any kind of trouble?" Hooks' old man glanced at me long enough to show his fear of the subject and then he looked away, saying, "Both you and him should have your asses kicked all over Brooklyn for using that stuff!"

Then he turned to me with vengeance in his eyes and pointed his finger directly at my face. He shook with anger as he said, "How could two young guys with brains be so fucking stupid?" He knew that Hooks and I had been using for ten years, give or take, and the heartache for him and his wife had been the same as the grief my family had to face.

He looked at me and said, "He tried to stick-up a cabbie right out front here, in broad daylight." I said, "Oh, no. Was he loaded at the time?" He looked at me like I was crazy and said, "Loaded? You mean using that stuff? When the hell wasn't he loaded? Of course he was all screwed up. He didn't even know where he was." I really didn't want to hear the end of the story, but I went on anyway. "Can you tell me what else happened?" He was getting madder all the time. "Yeah, Vinny, sure I'll tell you. So you can go out tomorrow and pull the same caper, eh? He stuck a knife to the cabbie's throat and said, 'gimmie all the money!' The cabbie watched for his opportunity and wrestled the knife away from him. So Hooks just scrambled out of the cab and came back up here as if nothing happened. In fact, he went to bed.''

I couldn't think of anything but, ''Oh, Christ,'' and I hung my head, thinking of the bit he must have drawn. ''Next thing, a whole squad of cops came barging in here from all directions, which scared the living shit out of his mother, and she hasn't been the same since.'' I put my hands in my pockets and looked at him in earnest, since I understood perfectly, saying, ''I can't believe it. I'm sorry.'' He didn't have much patience left for me, as he said, ''Yeah, yeah, he says he's sorry too. Meanwhile, his mother is still a wreck, and he's doing five years at Greenhaven.''

I knew it was time to go. His final line to me was, ''So now you're back, huh? I heard in the neighborhood you were doing real good in that program. Is that true, Vinny? Are you a new man?''

By the time he got that far, I was standing in the hallway, as I said, ''Well, not exactly new, but certainly better than I was. Goodbye.'' As I made my way back to the flophouse I was living in, I wondered about where all of this bullshit was leading me. Why had I left Synanon? For this? The next morning brought a shaft of sunlight into my room, but only for sixteen minutes. I was staying in a five-story walk-up and in order to see what the weather was like, I had to open the window and stick out my head to take a three-by-five look at the sky. But junkies are street people who typically look down. All they care about is staying alive and where the next fix is coming from—the sky doesn't matter.

Unable to make a coordinated move when I woke up, I started groping for a needle like I was blind. I struggled to sit upright in bed and think about where I hid the junk. I grabbed the works, then went through the whole ritual again until the spike was sticking in my vein and enough pain was going away that I could concentrate on what to do that day.

Checking things out on the streets, it wasn't long before I discovered that it was ''vogue'' for a player in midtown to have an old lady working for him—more than one if he was cool. The trip was like the one I was running in San Francisco. A working couple made an arrangement, and it was the guy's job to cop junk for both of them, and her job to screw people out of the money to pay for it. Smart hookers never carried much money with them, and after each trick they would drop off the cash with their old man, and I'm talking about all of it. If they kept even five for themselves, it was only after telling him. So in return for the money, the guy would arrange her hotel, plus have a direct line with the desk clerk to be sure she wasn't in any trouble, and, of course, go her bail if she happened to get busted.

That night at six-thirty sharp I swallowed a couple of dolophines before dialing pop's number. He had been napping and it took him a while for his memory to come around, but we finally agreed to meet at Christie's on Fifty-third for dinner. The meal with pop turned out to be pretty easy to get through, primarily because the food was excellent and I kept him busy talking about my Reno experience with Synanon. Then I told him about Terri from Texas at Harrah's. He never asked me about drugs because he was laughing so hard at my story about her. Pop assumed I was clean as a whistle, I'm sure, because I told him I never felt better and was looking forward to getting a job, right away.

Pop picked up his napkin and wiped the corners of his mouth with it, as he said, "You know, Vinny, in the end I'm kind of proud of you. Somehow I knew you could do it." He reached over and gave me a couple of encouraging slaps just as the waiter was bringing the check. I told him it was "my turn, pop," and I left a nice tip. We parted out front, planning to get together again, real soon. Pop turned and walked out of my sight, and I jumped in a cab and headed back to my room. Uppermost in my mind was whether I wanted to continue. Was this all there was? As I went up the steps of my flophouse hotel, my thinking was centered on some works and a fix: "Maybe that'll give me the answer."

Of course it didn't, but time dragged on anyway. After I had been home a little over a week, I noticed that Rick the Puerto Rican was in the area quite often and with four or five different broads in that short time. I figured he must be a hell of a player, so I started talking to him more, and we went to my place a couple of times to get off together. Rick told me he and his brother, Rod, used to work as a team. But Rod caught four rounds of a forty-five one night, which landed him in the graveyard. Now Rick was alone on the streets, heavy on junk, and having one hell of a time, primarily with different women.

One day we were loaded and horsing around in a Horn and Hardarts, a cafeteria where you put your money in the slot and open the door to retrieve the food. After Rick and I had picked up our food, he went over and started talking to a couple at another table. I was immediately fascinated with the lady and couldn't take my eyes off her. She was brunette, with hair to her shoulders, and she had a Latin look, but she was regal, with high cheekbones like an aristocratic women with a blue bloodline. I couldn't bring myself to believe a woman like that was a hooker, but it had to be true because I knew the guy beside her—his name was Frenchie and he was a junkie.

Rick and Frenchie were discussing some business, so I took the opportunity to play with her eyes and introduce myself, saying, "Hi, I'm Vinny. And now I can understand why I haven't seen Frenchie since I've been home. What's your name?" She smiled and looked down, then up again into my eyes, saying, "Nice to meet you, Vinny. I'm Patti. I feel like I've seen you somewhere before." Pointing out through the window, I said, "Maybe out there, dancing on the concrete?" She laughed, and Rick moved off toward the table we had spotted, so I smiled and said, "Later, Patti. Take care of this guy, won't you? He needs help." Frenchie smiled and waved, "Hey, Vinny. How you doin'?"

"Great, Frenchie. Looks like you are, too." I smiled at her first and at him dead last, then walked off to join Rick for our bite to eat. After we were finished eating, we started walking down the street, where Rick struck me as being more excited than usual. He had a big grin on his face, like something evil was blowing around in the wind. I asked him what its name was, and Rick came back with, "Heat, man, heat." I snapped my fingers to what I figured must be a new Puerto Rican tune and said, "Yeah, right. Heat, man, heat," as we bounced along on Forty-third Street. I didn't know where we were heading, but we sure as hell were having a good time on the way.

Then Rick did some fancy stepping up a set of tenement stairs and waltzed through the front door. I was high as hell at the time, playing the charade out for all it was worth. Sane people on the streets probably thought we were a couple of crazed addicts, in which case they were right. We stopped at one of the doors, and he knocked lightly. He spoke in Spanish to someone behind the closed door, which soon opened and we went inside. Right away, I saw what Rick was talking about when he said heat, because an arsenal of guns and ammunition sufficient to blow the average man's mind filled the bedroom.

Damn, there were shotguns and a couple of machine guns too. I thought for a minute, "these guys must be planning to take

New York back from the white man." But I stopped myself short with the joke because the guys in the room didn't look like they were in a mood for fun at all. Two other Puerto Ricans were there besides Rick, both nattily dressed, but their suit jackets were draped on the backs of two different chairs, which revealed the shoulder holsters under their right arms. I was careful not to make a false move because nobody was saying much, and I hadn't heard any introductions.

Rick went straight over to inspect all the pieces as the other two stood their ground and folded their arms to watch what he did. Rick checked out the action on quite a few pistols, then he cocked the hammers and pointed the guns around. After five minutes of this routine, he invited me to come over and play with the weaponry on the bed. So I tiptoed over and started doing the same, looking things over, wondering if this was a game. Before I had the answer, Rick asked, "See anything you like, Vinny?"

Although we seemed like two kids in a candy store, I corrected myself and considered the implications of the deadly metal all over the bed. Did I really want to carry this around? But a man hooked on heroin is not exactly strong on logic or common sense. You could almost say that the change of body chemistry induced by the drug results in totally impulsive behavior and rarely will a junkie think anything through before he does it. So I picked up an automatic .38 special and looked over at Rick with a smile, saying, "This will do fine."

I had guessed that he would buy me the gun because of a windfall a couple of days earlier when one of his hookers took off a john for roughly five thousand dollars. Rick waved his hand, "It's yours, Vinny. I'm going to take these," and he pointed to two semiautomatic Browning 9mm's on the bed. The other guy loosened up somewhat as Rick peeled off several hundred dollar bills, though I couldn't see exactly how much had changed hands. One of the arms dealers brought out a box of ammunition for each of the pistols, and we tucked everything away in our belts and pants pockets.

It's funny how conscious you become when you have a piece on your person. I couldn't take my mind off it, each and every time I was "packing." I wonder sometimes how beat cops feel, after days and weeks and months and years and careers of strapping on a gun and carrying the heat around everyday.

Back on the street inside the hour, we were still high and

patting our guns every block or so like we had added a new dimension to ourselves. It was all related to the power that came with feeling that you could do literally anything you wanted, when it got down to it, and always be able to back out by pointing the gun at someone and threatening instant death with a cock of a hammer. In the wrong hands, that kind of power is dangerous.

And I soon got dangerous, right there on the streets of midtown. I took off easy marks late at night by sticking them in the ribs with my piece saying, "Don't move, or I'll blow you away. Gimme your wallet and jewelry." After a hit like that I'd sit around and get stoned on speedballs, laughing out loud about the amazing looks that would appear on people's faces when they saw the business end of a gun aimed at their midsections. Most people froze in terror and watched the gun while I took whatever I wanted. Others would back up saying something like, "No, no!" Then some guys were incredibly cool, saying, "Please put that thing away, you can have what you want." Of course I never put it away but always took what I wanted. And I was getting away with it.

One day after about a month of this madness, I ran into Patti, the lady I had met with Rick and Frenchie in the cafeteria. She was standing alone and looking as lovely as I remembered her. She smiled openly from the minute our eyes met. "Hello, Patti. Are you willing to admit that you've never looked better than you do right now?" I stood back about a foot and admired everything I saw, from the top all the way down to her bottom. God, that broad must have really been something if she could look like this and be using junk.

She said, "Flattery will get you everywhere, Vinny." We moved out of the mainstream and off to the side of a shoe store as I asked her, "Say, Patti, what happened to Frenchie? Did you guys break up?" She smiled, picking up on the opportunity and said, "We had an argument about a television program, so we called it quits, and I moved out." It turned out she was staying a floor below in the same hotel I was. I could see that this situation was going to be cozy. After all, I was gaining notoriety on the streets each day because no one could ever figure out just what I might or might not do at any moment in time. You would definitely not cross me without knowing that you were also going to have to deal with me later.

Patti knew all this and also knew I was in a position to protect her while she operated. I was feeling brazen that day anyway, so I looked her in the eye as I said, "Patti, I feel like taking a day off from this rat-race and spending it with you. Do you feel like fooling around?" She smiled and stepped forward until we were touching, then said, "You lead the way." With that sweet invitation, I took her by the hand and led the way to my hotel room where we got undressed and into bed without delay, where she showed me a thing or two, very slowly.

That started it, and the next day brought step two as she abandoned her nest one floor down and flew upstairs to be with me. We spent most of those early days deeply intertwined, exploring new regions and then each other's minds, shooting junk between lovemaking. Of course, the time came when I had to make a move because of money, so I reluctantly dragged my frame from the bed. Those were some sessions with Patti in the beginning. She was so good for me physically that I decided to keep her off the streets, saying I'd take care of her.

It was like that for maybe two months, me taking off people when I saw a shot, plus dealing in swag, junk, and almost any other angle that came my way. One day I really got lucky when an expensively dressed little guy I robbed fell apart emotionally and begged me not to hurt him. I had already taken his money and jewelry. Then I said, "What else you got? This ain't enough. You have to die." He went totally paranoid, and said, "No, no, no. Look, come with me. I have money at home, I'll give it to you. Just don't hurt me. Please." I couldn't quite believe what he had offered me, but there was no way I was backing down, so I went along. We took a cab to his place on the east side, Sixty-eight Street, and nothing was said enroute. I had the gun in his ribs the whole time. When the cab driver stopped, I handed over a ten and said, "Keep it," ducking out the door before he could see my face clearly.

I pointed for my man to precede me up the stairs and then open the door, which he did. When we stepped into his place, I thought about throwing the asshole out and calling it home. He had a big color TV set, an incredible stereo system, one entire wall of vintage wines, and expensive knickknacks all over the living room. I pushed him forward, demanding, "Where's the rest of the money?" He was still begging me not to do anything, and he ran three steps over to a bureau, opened the bottom drawer, and came up with an 8½ × 11 inch manila envelope, which he handed to me saying, "Here, take it." Still pointing the gun in his direction, I saw a fistful of hundreds inside. I waved the gun at the guy for the last time, as I said, "Get in that closet and don't even think of coming out for the next fifteen minutes. You got that?"

He shook as he said, "Yes, yes," and grabbed the closet handle to open the door. I could hear a muffled "Thank you, thank you, God, thank you" through the closet door. Hustling away, then down the street as fast as I could, I caught a cab and went downtown near my hotel but not right in front. I shot up the stairs and got to the apartment fresh out of breath and full of adrenalin.

Patti was in a prone position on the couch, eating chocolate candy from the box while she watched a soap opera on a television set. I started to explain what happened as I dumped everything from my belt and pockets, trying to take a shower, get down with her, and than straight out with a fix, in that order. When the money hit the top of the bureau, Patti forgot all about the drama on TV and raced over to count it. "Holy hell, Vinny," she exclaimed, counting the bills, "there's over four thousand here. Where the fuck did you get this from?"

I laughed and hugged her once as she kissed me, than forgot about the shower and went straight for the bed, carrying her. Once we got there, I calmed down inside her, thinking about all kinds of things. After an hour or so of rolling around together, we were quietly nestled in each other's arms, saying nothing, when Patti got a brilliant idea. "Hey, Vinny, this is an incredible windfall. Let's go cop and do some speedballs. It's time for a party." Being in no mood to argue about anything, I agreed. So we showered together and got dressed for the trip to Harlem.. Before we left, I put $2,000 in a safe place—behind a light fixture on the ceiling—and took $2,200 with us. As soon as we hit the street, I figured to treat Patti to something special, and we went to Bloomingdales where I bought her whatever she wanted until the tally came to nearly $900.

I cut her off from the spree, saying, "Honey, there are bells ringing up in Harlem. Are you ready to fly?" She said, "Only if you're the pilot," and squeezed my hand. We loaded the Bloomingdale bags into a waiting cab out in front. I had the cab driver stop at our hotel and wait while I carried the packages upstairs. Then I jumped in the cab and gave him orders.

As we sailed along, Patti slid over on the seat to thank me with kisses and whisper about how much more there was to come. Of course I couldn't wait, so I touched her lightly in all the right places, just as the cabbie pulled over to the curb on Ninety-ninth and First Avenue. I said, "Honey, you wait here until I see what's available. Lock the door." She did what she was told, and I shot down the street to locate Chuck. In less than five minutes I scored six bundles of junk for $400 and a half-ounce of cocaine for $600 more. Chuck was all smiles as we completed the deal. "Vinny, you want a hit right now?"

I thought of Patti back in the cab and said, "Thanks, Chuck, maybe next time. My old lady's waiting." He waved me off and started to cook a fix for himself, saying, "Suit yourself. If she was one of mine, I'd let her wait."

On the way, we got off somewhere in the seventies on the upper east side and went through forty-five dollars worth of champagne and roast duck, plus side orders of greens and potatoes. When the meal was over, and I felt like a stuffed pig, Patti was the first to suggest the next logical step. "Honey, let's go back to the room and test what you scored."

Within minutes we were back home in our room, cooking up a little of each to try as a sample. It was some mighty stuff, I knew right away, and I thought to thank Chuck the next time I saw him before nodding out. Patti took a long time finding a vein, missing four or five times. Then she went to the bathroom mirror and finally found the mark in a vein on her neck after holding her breath. I was getting more stoned by the minute, and it hit me as weird, seeing her fish for a vein in the mirror. But after that nothing mattered anymore.

We ended up staying in the room for the next week, as the binge went into high gear. The only times I went out was to cop more coke from Chuck uptown or pick up food, juice, and sodas to bring back to the room. By the morning of the seventh day, we had only two hundred dollars left so I drew the inevitable conclusion: Time for the streets, and more grief. Another hour had gone by in bed before I managed to sit up on the edge and fifteen more gave me the energy to stand on my own two feet. I was thinking, "God, this is a miserable existence."

When I started to get dressed, Patti woke up and reached over for me. She was drosy, hungover, and strung out all at once, but she still managed to grab my pantsleg, trying to pull me down on the bed. I laughed a little and said, "Look, baby, I have to go out and see what I can do because this money's going down to nothing." Incredibly, without a word, she got up from the bed naked and stood by the door, blocking it. "Honey, you took care of me, and now I'm gong to take care of you." I wasn't particularly fascinated with the idea, given my oversized Mister Macho image at the time, so I said, "Bullshit," but she didn't budge. Instead she broke the whole proposal down for me, explaining, "Look, Vinny, if I go out and turn tricks, you know that I don't give a shit about the johns, it's just friction for money."

I reached for the gun on the bureau and told her, "I don't want to hear about it. You stay here. I'll take care of things." She ran straight from the doorway, saying, "Honey, please listen to me. If I get caught on the street, it's a half hour wait and a twenty-five dollar fine. Even if I robbed a john and they nabbed me, my record's clean in that department so what would I get? Probation? Thirty days? But if you get caught for a move like you made on that guy, you're talking ten years, maybe fifteen. Well, am I right or do you want to go to Sing-Sing?"

I almost cried as the audible truth hit me, just as Patti came running over in her bare flesh to relive me of the gun I had stuck in my belt. Then she put me to bed, where I belonged, but of course she neglected to tuck in my covers, and we played nasty by refusing to go to sleep for a good, long, warm while. From that day forward, I started to get fat, happy, and lazy. My "old lady" didn't start work on the turf until nine or so at night, so first thing in the morning we'd shoot up and eat chocolates until sometime after eleven. Then we'd shoot up again and watch some TV or nod around the room, maybe drink a half-dozen Cokes with eight fresh old-fashioned donuts, shoot up again by five o'clock. I'd lay on the bed or on her for a while, it didn't really matter, then cook up a helluva fix for both of us to hit just before the curtain would rise revealing the nighttime street scene.

Most of the hookers in that area worked out of hotels on Seventh, Eight, and Ninth, in the Forties. And most of the desk clerks knew what was going down, so I would go in with Patti and tell the guy, "Look, this is my old lady, I want you to watch out for her. If something happens in here it's your fault, I'm comin' to see you. I'll take care of you and give you what you want in terms of money, but keep your eye out for this woman. Got it?"

Of course they got it, and we never had any trouble in the hotels. On the street I would keep my eye on her to be sure no jackass john tried something stupid like threatening violence or pulling her into a car, things like that. When she got into a cab with a customer, I knew he had money because those guys would refuse to go to the sleazy hotels. Patti had the class and looks to score quite a few wealthy businessmen, so once again we created a code for her to use when she went to a place like the Plaza, the Park Lane, the Pierre—you know, the expensive joints. I would go back to our room and sit by the phone, probably shoot up again while waiting for her call. As soon as she got in the john's hotel room, she would say, "I have to call my service and let them know how long I'll be." Then she'd call me with all of the key information. When Patti sensed she had a real live one, she'd drop a verbal signal, and I'd take a cab over there to pull the "irate husband" routine.

After a while, Patti got so good at picking up guys with a wife and business career to consider, we could be virtually certain they had no intention of calling the cops. Some of the scenes were damn near comical. I would wave the gun—it rarely had a round in the chamber—first at her, "You pig bitch, get your clothes on!" She'd put on a panic and run for her clothes whimpering, "Please don't shoot, Billy, please don't."

I thought Billy was a great name for a Sicilian gangster, and I gave her a nickname too. "Sheila, shut your goddam mouth." Then I'd turn my attention to the john, shaking like a feather in the bed, point the gun at him and dictate, "You, asshole, pull the fucking sheet up over your head and pray like hell that I don't blow you away." While I emptied his wallet, his pockets, his dresser drawers, and his suitcases of all the money and valuables, Patti would grin at me while she was dressing. Hookers didn't normally bother wearing underpants, and she usually flashed me her ass as a signal she was ready to split.

We were banging in three and four hundred dollars a day in a short time, but the circle was vicious and I soon smelled rotten from my insides as well as up in my head. On the rare occasions I could see myself in the mirror, the questions would start: "Why do you need chemicals in your blood to feel good? How do you really feel about yourself? What the hell do you think is happening? Why did you run from Synanon? You're a quitter. If you had continued in Reno, where would you be now, if you had stayed clean? You damn well know what you're doing and you know why you're doing it. And you know that you're the idiot to blame for it." It all sounded Synanon familiar to me.

When the conscientious hard times came up, I would walk

away from the mirror in utter disgust with what I had seen, cook up a double load and send it in with God-awful vengeance, desperately trying to block out all the shitty thinking I had just done. Then I would do a turnaround and run my "tough guy" act, just as the peak of the high came on: "Those Synanon assholes actually had the balls to call me a baby. Well, you show me a baby who goes out every day on the streets, puts his life on the line, his balls on the line, his freedom on the line to earn money." With that I would either head out to the streets and do something outrageous or nod out in the room.

The team of Pat and Vinny shortly became notorious in midtown Manhattan, almost as if we were in show business. When Patti got all dressed up in that slinky silk she wore on the streets, I'd match her with cashmere coats, white-on-white shirts, and Countess Mara ties. You might have thought we owned something significant somewhere, when all we could do was "say" what we owned because there was no deed to the turf of the streets, not in New York City.

One night Frenchie was in the neighborhood about ten o'clock, paired up with another guy named Lorenzo, a Puerto Rican who was going to take him to a connection in Harlem. I wasn't there when Frenchie left, but I sure as hell was when he got back. His face was all broken up—the right eye black and swollen and the bottom lip was cracked open and bleeding. His shirt was torn, and he was totally insane, screaming for Lorenzo. As soon as I saw him I knew the trouble wasn't over yet. I calmed Frenchie down as much as I could and got at least some of the story.

It seemed Lorenzo had either set him up or had taken off from the scene, leaving him there with three jokers who proceeded to rob him, then beat the hell out of him, "Just for the exercise," they said before they did it. Frenchie paced around the alley we were in, saying, "That fucking creep Lorenzo, I'll kill him." I knew Frenchie was capable of anything, and we couldn't have been standing there ten minutes when he suddenly pointed his finger and bolted off like a jackrabbit. Frenchie was heading for Lorenzo, who he was walking in Duffy Park on the corner of Forty-seventh and Broadway.

Lorenzo didn't see Frenchie coming until it was too late, that is, until after Frenchie flicked out his K-5 knife and buried it deep in Lorenzo's gut. Then, using the blade as a lever, he lifted

Lorenzo off the damn ground nearly six inches. Lorenzo dropped to the deck with blood pouring from him like a stuck pig, while I hung my head over to puke with the sight.

After about six months into my scene with Patti, the cops had a chance to know all of the players because we had been out there for so long. Patti caught a couple of "one-hour specials," which cost her twenty-five bucks and about sixty minutes each time before she was out the door and back on the street again. But the point is that we were known to be into something, and they had definite suspicions that we were dope fiends, since both of us had a good start down the tubes at that point.

About a quarter to ten one night Patti went out loaded and made some dumb move with a narcotics detective on the street, and he had followed her home. Right after she came in, he knocked, and I hid the works and the junk on the ledge above the doorframe. Then I opened the door to admit the heat. This guy wasn't messing around because he came in and started tearing the place apart, "Looking for narcotics," he said. When he turned to face me he saw the damn tinfoil package up there on the door ledge above my head. I thought about playing it like a halo, but I knew it was time for deep shit instead.

Patti jumped in before the cop could stop her and said, "Look, it's mine. I'll take the weight. He didn't even know it was there. He doesn't use anymore, he cleaned up." The detective stuck the tinfoil of junk and the works in his coat pocket. After that, he looked at me and said, "You. Come here." I walked over with my head hung down like a schoolboy, and he told me to show him my hands and my arms, one at a time. He checked them over for needle tracks, but he was dumb and didn't see any. I was the "smart guy" who hid the tracks by shooting up in my wrist, then I wore a wide, expensive watchband to cover the holes so no one could see.

Well the cop bought the story, and Patti got busted on the spot and taken to the precinct for booking on a possession of narcotics and paraphernalia charge. I arranged for her bail by morning, but that night in the tank had strung her out badly. She looked battered to shit when she showed up in the courtroom, and I wondered if it was really her for a minute, but then I recognized the body and the clothing. Her face was strangely twisted from the grueling pain of the night she had taken.

After she was released, we cabbed it straight back to the

room, and she got straightened out with a fix, while we started plotting various angles to beat this bullshit possession rap. But as a result of the arrest we had to be extra careful with the junk in the future because if they busted either of us one more time, someone would be going to the joint for a good while. We got nervous as hell, and we tended to work farther uptown every night. During the day several times we had to go to court and postpone Patti's case. We had a good lawyer, so we pulled off all the stalls in the book and then some. After approximately nine weeks of this, she finally came up for sentencing, and the judge gave her sixty days at the Manhattan House of Detention for Women in Greenwich Village. Since we were already figuring she was going to do some time, I arranged for her to go to Dr. Grossman for a cure.

But that left me with no old lady and no more money and a helluva hunk habit to go with the first two problems. I also had no time to lose so I let it be known among the hookers on the street that I was "open for business." The business, of course, was protecting them on the streets, arranging for hotels and bail if need be, copping their junk, taking all of their money, and sleeping with them every once in a while, which wasn't often because my junk habit was costing more rotten money each passing day. Sometimes I felt like I was losing it completely—getting strung out staying up for three or four days at a time, shooting heroin and speedballs so that even I was getting paranoid about the cauldron of chemicals boiling inside my body. I felt like a witch stirring up an evil mixture over the flame and the heat. Something had to let go.

13 Setup and Knocked Down

I was caught dead in the middle between sickness and junk, with no real high left in the heroin anymore. Spending up to three hundred dollars a day just to stay part way straight and keep my act together, I knew that if I didn't slow down, I'd be off the deep end real soon. So I got out on the streets and checked around for the latest in the city's scheme of detox operations. I heard about the Morris Bernstein Institute from a professional jewel thief named Jimmy who was totally strung out too.

A madman no matter what he did, Jimmy was good at stealing or exchanging expensive rings, just like I used to do. He also had a zircon caper going. In a bar, Jimmy would point to an empty hole in a fancy ring and say to the stranger next to him, "Oh, shit. My goddam diamond fell out. It's worth three thousand dollars. I gotta find it." With that, he'd drop to the floor of the bar and within thirty seconds he had the victim down there looking too. Of course the "diamond" never turned up, and Jimmy would leave handing the guy a business card with a false address, telling him, "If you find that stone, I'll give you a three-hundred-dollar reward. Here's my card." After Jimmy left, his partner would stroll in, and naturally he would say, "Hey, look what I found!" while pulling out a loose zircon. I heard about one mark that ended up paying them five hundred bucks, thinking he had made a score.

Jimmy told me he was ready to detox again, so we went up to the institute on afternoon and arranged a stay within a couple of days. I planned to stow my stuff at pop's place while I was away for three weeks. No sense paying rent on an empty room, and everything I really needed to pack before leaving would fit in the palm of my hand, since it consisted of a needle, an eyedropper, a cooker, and some junk. Of course, when I told pop about storing stuff, he wondered why and demanded to see me before I checked in. I went over the day before I was due at the institute and dropped my bags. Then I decided to spend the night because I was sick and tired of the streets. If worse came to worse and I was forced to return, I could always find new girls to work, and Patti was still waiting for me, although in the joint, where I visited her.

I was sitting around over at pop's that night, when he started up with his treatment: "Vinny, sooner or later you gotta listen to me. You're no dumb kid, and you never have been. Who you kiddin? You could do anything you want, be a doctor, go to school, be a lawyer, anything. Why in the hell do you have to use drugs? What the hell is in those drugs? I swear, Vinny, sometimes I just don't understand you."

Pop poured himself another glass of his favorite drug, Miller beer, and looked over to me for an answer. But I didn't have any easy ones and was too damn tired to spend the creative energy necessary to come up with a new one. I just begged off, saying, "Pop, please. I know I've been crazy, and that's why I'm checking into the hospital tomorrow. This time it's for real. I have to give it up, and I know it. Let's get some sleep, okay?"

Pop went right on bitching, but under his breath. I spread out on the couch until pop got up off his favorite chair and went to his room, switching the light out on me as he left. I gave him ten minutes more, then slipped to the bathroom to cook up what I had left of my junk so I wouldn't be wrecked by the time they started me on methadone.

I managed a few hours sleep; then struggled up to make some coffee. Pop wouldn't leave me alone about the drugs and my future, and it was like that all the way downtown to the institute—pop badgering me about my bad habits and extolling the virtues of the straight and narrow path. He paid the cabbie, and we walked up the front steps to the Bernstein treatment center together.

Pop was still chirping at me to "get serious" when I noticed Jimmy there for his check-in, too, so I introduced them. Pop took one look at Jimmy and saw he had something going for him because, even though he was strung out, he had on a sharp mohair suit with a silk shirt, a pair of Stetson shoes, an Omega gold watch, and a brilliant diamond pinky ring. Pop whirled on Jimmy and tried to pick him apart, for his own good, plus to teach me a lesson. "Hey, the way you look, you're a sharp kid. You dress nice. What do you need to use that junk for?"

He wasn't at all interested in hearing what Jimmy had to offer, which was, "Aw, man, I like dope. I love heroin, and I love the high. I think the most of heroin and cocaine, mixed together. I go out and I make money, sometimes big scores, and I celebrate full speed until I get like I am now, all strung out. When I get too far over the edge, I come in to one of these joints for two or three weeks to reduce my habit and get my ribs out of hock. Then when I'm looking and feeling better, I jump on a plane to Miami for the weekend to pick up some color in the sun, maybe two, three broads, then fly on back to New York and get right into the scene again. What's wrong with that?" Pop put his right hand over his eyebrows and squeezed hard as he shook his head from side to side, turning away from Jimmy.

Jimmy and I stayed at the Morris Bernstein for fourteen or fifteen days filled with boredom and monotony. Looking back now, it's funny how quickly I could change my mind about drugs then. One day, deep in shit, I'd swear on my mother and God "never again!" But just as soon as the trouble was over, I'd go looking for my needle with never a second thought. One day Jimmy got up, shaved and showered, dressed, and announced that he was ready for Florida. We were then into the third week, and I felt as jumpy as he did, although I wasn't up for Miami. So we both just checked out after the morning dose of methadone was injected and grabbed a cab uptown, where I got off at my old hotel, and he went on to the airport. I looked up at the foyer and knew deep inside that this was not a good move, but I went in anyway since I was so used to doing the wrong thing then. I got my old room back at my old rate, $275 a month.

When I got to the room, it seemed like any other, with no sentimental residue at all. You'd think some of Patti's perfume would be lingering, but I couldn't smell any at all, and I was trying, believe me. I put my belongings away and sat down on the bed, thinking about the rest of my stuff over at pop's. But I couldn't go anywhere near there until the end of the week because he knew damn well that the institute program didn't end until Saturday. So I kicked off my shoes and fell asleep in the process of wondering what tomorrow would bring.

Later on that morning, I was still clean, and I thought about calling a neat lady. As I wandered through the little black book in my brain, Angela from Brooklyn came up. I had already repaid the three-hundred-dollar loan plus I gave her a bonus bag of junk every now and then when I was in her neighborhood. She cared about me in her own lonely way, and I still thought of her, but not all that often I must admit. I was too busy on the streets of midtown, and too many people in Brooklyn knew me for exactly what I was, which caused immediate trouble with the cops whenever I showed up. So I mainly avoided the old neighborhood, even though I sometimes missed all the regular "haunts."

Well, Angela wasn't home when I called, and it was too late to visit Patti at the Detention Center, so I thought to hit the streets and see what might be happening out there. Three blocks from my place, I ran across two girls who had just started working, and I walked up to them on the street. One I already knew, a young chick named Nickie, who was a fem little bitch and played with dykes when she wanted, but she also played with johns for money. I knew she always needed protection, and I explored the subject with her, asking, "Who's taking care of you now, Nicki?"

She stumbled, all strung out, and said, "No one now. My old man's in the can. Why, Vinny?" I took her by the arm and said, "Come with me and you'll see," as I turned her away from the bull bitch who showed me her teeth in anger because of what I had taken out of her mouth. Listen, those streets could get vicious at times, especially when you were dealing with dogs.

Anyway I took this little blonde bitch to my room, where we worked out on each other for over an hour, the first time. For the second round, we did a workout on the floor, with her up on top. Finally we get working on a deal for action on the streets. I said, "Why don't you plan on me protecting you?" She agreed, at least until her old man was released, and I said I'd cop for her. Opening her purse, she hurriedly pulled out every red cent she had and threw it at me on the floor, making a spray of bills. She was almost crying, as she said, "That's all I have. I swear."

I picked up over three hundred dollars in big bills before I stopped counting and thought to myself, "Damn, here we go again," as I scooped up the last bill off the floor. Nicki was standing there, a physical wreck, begging me to "save" her life and my own with some junk. It was a shitty thought, but what could I do. Like some brainless robot, I straightened up a little and went down to a cab on the corner. From there it was a beeline to Harlem, and after an hour or so of asking around, I found Rick, loaded to the gills as usual. It was also visible that his act was coming apart at the seams too.

He had loose money, dope and works all over this table out in the open. I could have been anyone, and he wouldn't have known or cared, sitting there just barely nodding his head, a cigarette burning his fingers. I shook out the butt and tried to shake his hand, but it was no use. He was close to an O.D. I checked on his breathing, got some coffee for him, and tried to prop him up to talk to me. He came around somewhat after an hour or so of this revival routine, and I wondered for a minute why the hell I was doing it. "Brotherly love, in return for some junk," was all I could think of, right then.

When Rick was okay, I asked him about scoring some of his dope, and he agreed. He gave me more than I deserved, and whipping out his cooker, Rick poured a load in and mixed it with water. Then he struck up a match and looked like a fiend as he bent over to boil the junk. I was sitting there getting anxious as hell. When it was ready, I sent it all in, and within seconds heaven was welcoming me home again, and Rick was flying in the same direction. We sat down and nodded for the better part of two hours. Once again, the web of rottenness was spinning all around me, and junk was the spider.

On my way back to reality after a couple of hours, I finally thought of Nickie waiting downtown, so I started off in her general direction. Flagging a cab on the street in a daze, I forgot my address at first, so I just told him to head downtown, but then I remembered, "Forty-third and Eighth." Nicki was furious when I walked into the room, and, hell, I hardly knew this bitch. Raging mad, she waved her hands and gripped her gut, saying, "Fuck, man. Where have you been? In Canada? Christ, I can't believe it. Hurry up!"

I said, reaching for my rusty old cooker, "Take it easy, Nickie, I got what you want. Be a good little girl, and I'll fix it up for you." She broke down, fell on her knees at my feet, and cried out, "I'll do anything, Vinny, please hurry." I thought of asking Nickie to get up off her knees and do the Mexican hat dance for me, just as I struck the match under the bottle cap, which made it hotter than hell in seconds. I handed her the dropper after filling it, and said, somewhat sadly, "Here's what you've been waiting for." Then I stood up and went to fall out on the bed. Nothing moved me for eight hours, and Nickie didn't go anywhere either.

Within two weeks, I was right back where I started, the only difference being one more hooker. Her name was Mousie, from her squeaky voice, because she had one helluva body. She had just arrived in Manhattan from Miami when I met her on the street coming out of a delicatessen. Nickie stayed in the room she had rented with her old man, and I preferred it that way. So I suggested as much to Mousie, saying, "Listen, honey, you'll be able to operate a lot better if you have your own room." Mousie moved in upstairs above me on five, and I protected her and Nickie on a nightly basis. I was running six different hotels in less than a month, making deals for my old ladies with the desk clerks, then watching what they got on the streets. I also watched them both go sliding down the tubes, their veins full of junk that I was buying for them in Harlem.

But there was incredible heat on the streets of Harlem then, so I was thinking of trying a new connection in Brooklyn that Mousie had mentioned to me the day before. Mousie turned her last trick at 3:15 one morning, then gave me the money, saying, "Hey, Vinny, let's get loaded again before we go score in Brooklyn." I thought of what I had left in my pad and went for all of it without hesitation, saying to Mousie, "Great idea. Let's go back to my room, right now." When we got there I mixed up damn near a lethal batch of heroin and speed, then sent it all in without thinking, and Mousie did the same. Before we left, I swallowed a couple of doridens just for good measure.

We were off in left field as we slid into a cab, ordering the driver to a certain address in Brooklyn to meet up with this new connection. I was thinking just clearly enough to take only sixty dollars in cash, since I wanted to see how smooth this was going to be before I started to lose any real money with the guy. When we got out of the cab and I paid the driver, Mousie looked at the paper in her hand and said, "Up this way." We walked to an alley and started down it in the dark. We saw this high fashion black cat coming toward us, decked out in a white suit, white bucks, and a white Panama hat with a pheasant feather band. He walked up and said, "Hey, man, I'm Leroy, and what do you need?"

Something was definitely not right, I sensed, by the feel of the situation. I should have known what it was, but my mind was bent under the crippling influence of the three different drugs.

Mousie was standing off to one side as I told him quietly, "We want to test out your shit, man. Gimmie four bags." As he reached for the tinfoil of junk, I turned to the side and drew out the money. I went to hand my brand new connection the bill, and he pressed the junk in my hand but suddenly backed up without taking the money.

At that instant, I heard a car door slam at the end of the alley, and I knew I'd been had. It was a setup! I ran in the opposite direction from the car and then tried to swallow all four bags of junk when I saw three guys running towards me in black suits with a black car parked on the street behind them. "Narcs!" I knew in a flash, as I spun on my heels and tried to take off. They grabbed me before I got very far at all. I knew one of the guys, McClean. He used to hassle my ass in the old neighborhood just for the hell of it.

I was fairly well stoned during all this, trying to get those bags down my gullet, and the cops had seen me. This guy McClean threw a choke hold on me from behind, telling me with unreal vengeance, "Spit up that shit, Marino," as he made the hold tighter all the time. He wasn't fucking around, and I still hadn't swallowed one of the bags. Desperately, I looked to hit him using an elbow to the stomach, but it barely phased him. He tightened his grip on my throat and choked me harder, so I wound up and elbowed him a second time. By then I was thinking, "Unless you get him now, he's going to kill you!"

I mustered everything I had with one last gulp of air and came back with my elbow to his midsection again. That shot finally got the bastard in the solar plexus, which made him cough and loosen the choke hold. As soon as he let go of my throat, the last bag dropped into my stomach, where the glassine wrapper began to rot from the effects of sitting in a stagnant pool of stomach acid. I felt sick when I looked up and saw this second cop coming toward me carrying a mean-ass look in his eye. He charged me, saying, "Fuckin' punk! Spit it up!" and he turned me around and headed me into a plate glass window, dead on with full force.

Somehow I managed to lead with my left hand and arm instead of my head, so my hand broke through the cheap, raw-edged plate glass. On my way I ripped a gash about three inches long and one inch deep, and the shard was still stuck in my wrist when I stopped moving forward. I was bleeding all over the place, and all that blood and broken glass shocked the cops too. Then McClean came at me again, this time grabbing my shirt and pushing me backwards, yelling out of control, "So you wanna fuck around with junk, Marino, and you wanna fuck with niggers, huh? Then you look to swallow the shit, fuckin' punk, then you look to hit me asshole." He reached into his pocket and came up with a bundle of junk, proclaiming, "See this bundle, fucker? It's yours. You had it on you. And when we load you in the back of the car, cocksucker, you wanna eat that, fine. Go ahead. Because when we get to the station, I'll bring more to you, on a goddamn plate by the pound, with a nice big spoon, and you can eat the shit until you fuckin' die. But you're under arrest, punk, so get up against the wall, hands first. Lean forward."

As I stumbled along the street towards their squad car holding my handkerchief over my cut, I had enough sense left to think about what had gone down, and I was pissed. There I was, not even trying to be a tough guy with him—I just wanted to get rid of the junk—and he tried to kill me. All I was doing was defending myself, and they knew it. Then I wondered who the stool pigeon was. I smeared and shook blood all over the back seat of their car and even got some on their suits. One of them, a Puerto Rican, slapped me in the face, and told me to sit still. I had had it with them, so I said, "Yeah, fuck it, kill me. What more can you do?" and I shook dripping blood at him again, from my knocked-down prone position on the seat.

First they took me to the hospital, where the emergency room crew got out the glass fairly quickly. After that, McClean and the other cops came for me, and this time I got handcuffed so I couldn't move and had to sit in my own blood on the back seat. It was just after six in the morning and things were beginning to get light as I stepped out of the car at the station. They informed me of my right to one phone call after checking in all my personal possessions. I couldn't think of anyone but pop at the moment. He was drowsy at first, but he finally caught on and agreed to come down as soon as he got dressed.

By the time pop got to the precinct forty minutes later, I was still in a cell next to the booking room with another guy. Just as pop walked into the station, a made-man all the cops knew came in to bail out my cell-mate. Pop knew the made-man, too, and said hello. Then he talked to me and I told him, "Pop, it's a total bum beef, I swear to God. They planted that shit on me and threw me through a plate glass window. It was a setup. One of them tried to choke me to death."

Pop saw that I wasn't lying, I could tell by his eyes, so he decided to see McClean, and he also saw the opportunity to play off the pressure of the made-man. Pop motioned McClean to the side and told him he "should tell the truth about what happened and do the right thing, and then I'll do the right thing." They had me booked on a 3305, possession of narcotics, carrying a potential sentence of a year, maybe up to three, if I ended up convicted of it.

About ten that morning, they called out our names and handcuffed us off in pairs, then pointed us toward their locked paddy wagons. We were loaded and locked in, then the driver popped the clutch to shake us all up, while they roared away laughing. Within minutes we were looking at the in door on the prisoner side of Brooklyn Court.

When my name was called, I told the baliff I'd take a public defender, and I got assigned one. The attorney, named Brant, came over and talked to me about what had gone down. I sensed he believed me, and I did tell him the truth, figuring what the hell. I admitted copping four bags but also that I had swallowed them before anyone saw what I had. I told him about McClean planting a bundle on me after pushing me through the window.

"Look, Mr. Brant. If I had attacked one of the cops, they would have charged me with assaulting a police officer, and if I didn't assault a police officer, how the hell do you explain the three-inch gash in my wrist?" Brant got the message and got ready to go to bat for me. When they called my name for arraignment, Brant requested an immediate hearing. We got it with a bang. After the session was called to order, the public defender called Detective McClean to the stand for testimony. Brant asked him straight off, "Detective McClean, what was the time this incident occurred?"

"Five or ten after five this morning."

"Good, thank you. So at that hour, was it totally dark or only partially dark, Detective McClean?"

McClean thought for a minute from his sandwiched position and said rather weakly, "Ahh, it was a little bit light." Brant didn't let up, as he said, "Oh, I see, so there was a little bit of light, and how far away from my client were you at the time?" McClean swallowed hard and said, "Oh, maybe forty or forty-five feet, when I first saw him."

"So from forty or forty-five feet away, in the semi-darkness at five o'clock in the morning, you say you saw what, Detective McClean?" McClean sat up straight in that witness chair and said, "I saw Marino there swallow some glassine bags of heroin."

Brant didn't need to be brilliant with his summary. "Your Honor, please. This testimony is absurd, and surely these actions constitute illegal harrassment of my client." McClean tried to cut back in and establish some credibility.

"Wait a minute, Mr. Brant. I've been on the Narcotics Squad for twelve years, and I deal with this type of case on a daily basis. I'm trained to look for that kind of thing."

"Mr. McClean, I don't think anyone can be trained to see something the size of a postage stamp from forty-five feet away at five o'clock in the morning—not in New York anyway," and Brant sat down with a look of confidence on his face.

Then came the clincher, and it could have gone either way because even Brant didn't know what he was asking when he said, "Detective McClean, prior to this morning at five o'clock, have you ever seen my client before?" Instead of recalling our history together, McClean said for the record, "No."

"Then, Mr. McClean, you obviously had no way of knowing that my client was a drug addict, is that right?" McClean nodded and said, "Yes."

"Then this man could have been anyone—an innocent man on his way to work or whatever. That's all the questions I have, Your Honor."

The judged asked all the parties to come up to his bench. He told the prosecutor, "This case is finished. I'm going to rule suppression under *Miranda*." The D.A. went pale and hung his head while the judge turned to my lawyer, "Mr. Brant, will you please make a motion to that effect?" Brant nodded his head in agreement, saying, "Yes, Your Honor." After Brant made the motion for dismissal, the judge adjusted his glasses, banged twice with his hammer, and shouted, "Motion granted! Case dismissed." They took me back to the bullpen to get my personal property, and then left.

I breathed a sigh of relief when I hit the streets except when I thought about facing pop and the rest of the day. I couldn't help dwelling on the raw terror I had felt when I knew that sonofabitch McClean was trying to choke me to death. What if my *head* had gone through the plate glass? And who was the rat-bastard that had set me up? Was it Mousie? She had been acting strange all day. All this was bothering me as pop broke in with a suggestion, "Say, Vinny, let's shoot across the street to that bar and get a beer, okay?"

Once again I couldn't think fast enough, and pop was already dragging me by the arm, so I went along. Once inside the place I started coming apart fast and had to bolt for the men's room where I got sick. I couldn't hold myself together so I just got up and told pop I had to go home and lay down. He was so totally flabbergasted by the move that his mouth was still open as I got into a waiting cab and grunted out my address bent over in pain.

I somehow got up to my room at the hotel, after telling the cabbie to wait. Inside I went straight for my stash, then back downstairs for the long ride to Harlem. By then I was nearly doubled up, and it had just started raining outside. Out of the cab, I gave less than a damn about anything except where I could cop as I splashed down hard in the middle of puddles, looking like a madman for Rick, Haysoos, Chuck—anyone with junk. No one was around and after fifteen minutes I was ready to go crazy on the corner of First Avenue and something street when I miraculously caught sight of Flocko, a Puerto Rican friend of Rick's.

He was standing under his umbrella across the street from me, but I was so desperate I just started towards him right through the heavy traffic. Thank God the cars were going slow as I patted front fenders, tripping for the other side. At first, Flocko thought it was funny; then he saw my condition and knew I was dead serious, or maybe I should say serious enough to be damn near dead. He was kind enough to get me off the streets that day, and he also saw to it that I spent all my money on heroin and cocaine, which we shared after he scored. Once I got mine, Flocko could have taken the rest and walked right out of the tenement we were in. I couldn't have chased him—not that day.

Not the next day either. As soon as my head cleared and I saw that I was still in Harlem, I struggled down six floors to the street and noticed that I had some junk and cocaine on me, but no works. Looking deeper in all my pockets, I soon found, "Dammit! No money." I had to find somebody soon to hit up for a ten or twenty, just enough to get back to my room. Wandering the streets aimlessly, I found a pool hall and went in. On my first look around I saw old Diego, my friend from "The Rock." He was quite happy to see me, and I knew I could borrow what I wanted, so I managed to relax somewhat and shoot the shit with Diego as he finished up his game.

When I finally got back to my room, I looked in the mirror and almost dropped over. Besides the god-awful tracks on my arms, I had a bandage on my wrist covered with dried blood, and my eyes were all shot from the junk, no sleep, and the beating I had taken. I fell on the bed, confused and down deep in despair, wondering if anything in life was worth living for.

Sometime after eight that night I woke up again, and it took ten minutes to gain my bearings and think about what to do next. I needed money; I was flat broke. The first thought was "fix up, get your head straight, then you'll be ready." So I went through the ritual again, stuck the needle in my arm, then put the dope and the works away. As things calmed down to where I could think, it hit me that I had to go out and check on Mousie and find out what the hell had happened last night. Had she sacrificed me to the cops as a "collar" for her freedom? If not, what was that black dude's name? I looked all over midtown for more than two hours that night and never did find her. At the hotel desk they told me she had checked out that morning. That answered my question about who the stool pigeon was, although I never saw Mousie again to confront her with it directly.

A week after the plate glass window incident, I saw my friend Nickie climb into a cab with a quite proper gentleman, and I was figuring to make $100 to $150 from the john, but that was the last I saw of her. I don't know what happened to her, and in my condition I didn't give a shit. I was sick, strung out, and tired of living.

My "working girls" were gone, I looked like a bum, and the heat from the narcs was coming down heavy all over town. Once again I was faced with the hard reality of getting enough money to stay alive. That's all I could think of one morning as I cooked up the last of the dope I had scored. After the load hit my stomach and I could relax, I sat down to think. The only caper I was really ready for was more cigarettes, since my cattle rustling coat was in storage at Hook's place, and I had long ago lost the finesse necessary for the diamond exchange.

I tried to make a move on an A&P, but the manager actually stopped me right in the store and held me there until the cops came. I was in a fog as they cuffed me and threw me in a car for the ride to the station. They booked me for attempted petty larceny, and I got my standard phone call. No answer at pop's;

same thing with Frank; my bondsman was "out of the office," so that left mom. When I reached her, she was nearly frantic. "Vinny, how can I take this?" I could tell she was holding back tears. As soon as we hung up, she apparently got right on the phone to Al DiPrimio again and got him to agree to come down for the arraignment and then to have a talk with me.

Thanks to Al, I was released on bail and right after that mom and DiPrimio hustled me into another restaurant booth, where Al threatened me directly, "Vinny, you are not going to make it doing what you are doing. We're going to commit you to an institution." I couldn't think of anything but my freedom for the day, so I said, "Maybe that's what I need. You tell me where, Al, and I'll go. I have to straighten out." They both seemed incredibly relieved, and so did I. Mom said, "Vinny, your friend Al is going to check on some openings tomorrow morning and I want you to be with him when he does it." Again I went along with it.

It was a little after ten the next morning when I made it to DiPrimio's office on the fifteenth floor of a new building on Park Avenue not far from my hotel. I had taken my good time to walk over there, thinking along the way, primarily about what to say. As it happened, I didn't have much of a chance since Al had our schedule all planned out. He called Synanon in Westport and brought Ted Brown up to current on my case. When he told Brown I wanted to return, Ted asked to speak to me. He got right to the point: "Vinny, is it true that you want to come back to Synanon?" I blinked without thinking and said, "Yeah, Ted, that's right. I'm not going to make it this way."

Ted said flatly, "Well now, if you're serious about this, we're going to have to interview you again, and there will also be a 'good faith'' donation to Synanon of fifteen hundred dollars. Are both of these conditions all right with you?" I was shaking my head toward DiPrimio with my right hand in the air, rubbing my thumb against the first two fingers signaling "no money." He waved me off and spoke to Brown, "We can arrange for the money. When can you see him for the interview?"

Brown saved my day, as he said, "Well, I have to go to California tomorrow, but I'll be back next Tuesday evening. What about Wednesday, a week from today?" I looked at Al with a shrug since he knew damn well that I didn't have a fixed schedule, and he told Brown, "Wednesday is good for us."

As we arranged a time and said our goodbyes I felt my heart

sinking because I had no real intention of going back to Synanon. It struck me as a step backwards in some way. I didn't have time to think before Al turned to me, "Vinny, I'm only a friend and not really in a position to tell you what to do. But your mother is also a friend of mine, and what you are putting her through is criminal. You've got no choice. You either commit yourself voluntarily, or your mom will do it, or the judge, but you're off the streets, pal. There's no way I can beat this one for you."

There was only one question in my mind at the time, so I asked it of Al, "Where will I get fifteen hundred for Synanon? I don't have it." He didn't hesitate at all. "Vinny, if you're serious and they accept you, I'll loan you the money, and you get it back to me when you can." I stood up slowly and reached for Al's hand as I said, "I don't know if I'd feel right taking it, Al, but I appreciate the offer and everything else you've done for me."

He shook my hand hard and said, "Hey, Vinny, there was a time back in school when I used to look up to you. Maybe this time you'll discover a way to let me admire you again." I looked away and said, almost under my breath, "Thanks, Al. I wish I could believe you." He stopped me by saying, "Come on, Vinny. You know the potential is there. By the way, where will you be, between now and Wednesday? I want to sit down and discuss the Lowe's suit, this cigarette case, and take some time to prepare for the Synanon interview."

I gave him the phone number at the hotel and told him the room I was in. Then, as I was walking over to the door, Al asked, "By the way, Vinny, what are you doing to make money right now?" I couldn't see any point in another lie, so I said, "Nothing legitimate." I saw panic rise in his eyes as he transformed himself into a good samaritan and went into his pocket, then handed me two hundred dollars with an admonition, "No, Vinny, take it. Just do me a favor and stay out of trouble until we can get you off the streets, okay?"

The next sequence of events illustrates the depths of illusion that can twist the mind of someone whose sole purpose is to escape reality using drugs, chemicals, or anything else to bring on "a high." No sooner had I hit the streets in front of DiPrimio's building when the two hundred he had given me was burning a hole in the pocket of my muddled brain. I could only think of Harlem, my second home—the place where dreams got started at the end of a dirty needle.

I flagged down a cab and gave him the same old directions. Not long after I got there, I copped two bundles for $150 and cabbed it back to the seclusion of my room in the hotel. I thought I was getting away with something as I cooked, tied up, and sent it all in. Within two minutes I knew what junk had done: It kept me from getting sick for the moment, but there was nothing high about what I was looking at—four walls of a broken down hotel in midtown New York and me at the end of a string ready to drop in the gutter.

Three days later I pulled off a heist in broad daylight at a delicatessen in the Fifties somewhere. Just after one o'clock I was checking out with a corned beef sandwich on rye when the cashier rung up the total. I saw the register full of bills, probably from the heavy lunch business, and since I didn't give a shit at the time and the exit door was two feet away, I just shoved the cashier backwards about three feet, took all the tens and twenties, and bolted through the door to the street. The take from that caper was over four hundred, but it didn't last long because I bought $350 worth of coke and junk the same night. Where the rest went I don't know, and three days after the deli I was flat broke and running out of dope all over again. By early evening I was absolutely desperate and had just shot the last of my stash. Down the street I could only come up with one idea: "Fuck it. Steal some cigarettes, that's always a quick buck."

By the time I hit the front door of the market with my haul, a security cop was already blocking it. The cops who responded to the call noticed right away that I was strung out, and they also noticed who I was. One of them remembered that I had been arrested for the same thing less than a week ago. "Hey, Marino you must be hooked on nicotine, too, huh?" He laughed and his partner broke up, too. I was thinking of how shitty my life was anyway, so I said nothing to add any fuel to the fire they were trying to stoke in my gut.

Another attempted petty larceny charge, another night sick in the tank with five or six other junkies. And then I was going to have to face Al DiPrimio once again. As I struggled to the sink the next morning for a splash of cold water on my face, it hit me: "Damn, today is scheduled for that Synanon interview in Westport. Well, there goes that opportunity, down the drain. Now what?"

Less than ten minutes later a hack called out my name along with several others, and we were led to the bullpen, handcuffed in pairs, and taken by van to the courtroom at the Tombs for arraignment. When the time came to meet with our lawyers, Al came in the door and I thought he was a walking miracle there to save me from ultimate destruction, but when he saw me everything seemed to sag visibly. His face went long and he shook his head from side to side, not believing he was there doing it again for Vinny Marino on the same charge. He broke the ice by speaking to me, but he did not offer to shake my hand. I hung my head, unable to look at his words as he said, "Vinny, am I dreaming? Are we driving to Westport, Connecticut, or are you here in the Tombs under arrest? And for what? Cigarettes? Now what do you want me to do, arrange for you to get out again? So I can get another call in the middle of the night to find out where you're being held and what the new charge is? Jesus Christ, man, what are you trying to do?"

I finally got the courage to look at him, and all I could muster up was, "Al, I don't know what to say. But I know that either I turn around now, or I'm a dead man."

"Well, I'll tell you this much. If this happens again, you are a dead man from my point of view, because I don't intend to defend you after this." Within an hour I was back on the front steps of the courthouse, looking at DiPrimio square in the eye. "Vinny, I couldn't even bring myself to tell your mother. Now what in hell do you intend to do about Synanon and the future?"

I tried to hedge a little by saying, "Don't worry, Al. I'll get in. If not Synanon, then something, I promise you." He didn't think twice before quipping, "Do me a favor, Vinny? Don't make me promises anymore. Just get into action, how's that?"

I smiled a little and said, "I always was a man of action anyway, Al. You watch me get into it this time. Nothing's gonna stop me." He gave me a smile and somewhat cynically said, "I haven't ever seen you get started, Vinny, but I know that you're capable of doing almost anything you shoot for. If you're serious, get your ass in gear, and then call me. Don't forget that your sentencing for the first cigarette rap is a week from tomorrow. So I'll hear from you long before that, right?" And he turned and walked away.

Standing there alone on the sidewalk, I had no idea which way to turn. It occurred to me to sit on the curb, but I decided not to stoop that low—at least not yet. I set myself in motion, trying to forget the gut pain and take some time to think about whether it was worth going on and if so, in what direction? I knew that if I kept using heroin, I'd be a dead man in no time. Either I'd fall under a wheel loaded or overdose fatally or some cop would connect with his club or a gun. Something had to happen, as stoned as I was.

And now two more cigarette busts—minor charges, except with my history. If I was lucky and drew a liberal judge, I might only get one year for each count. If they wanted to hit me hard though, I could get three. Damn, how could I make it through another three-year bit? I'd go crazy for sure. What about Synanon? Could I face them, could I do it again? What were the alternatives, if any?

The next day, running sacred, I checked into Metropolitan Hospital's detox ward. While I was there, I heard that a guy named Tommy LaCosta I had met in Synanon had left them and gone to a new organization located out on Staten Island called Daytop Village. So I looked up their number in the phone book, and dialed it. "Good morning, Daytop."

"Hello, I'm Vinny Marino. Can I speak to someone about getting into your program.?" She sang back to me, "Just a minute, Mr. Marino, I'll connect you." After a brief pause and another buzz, I heard, "This is Jack Karola, Daytop Coordinator. What can I do for you?"

"Hi, Jack. I'm Vinny Marino and I heard about your program. I need help badly and I want . . ." Jack cut me off sharply saying, "Look, Marino, I'm in a meeting right now. Can you call me back at ten-thirty?" I thought and said, "Sure." Then Karola concluded our conversation with, "Okay, do that," and hung up on me.

When I called back at ten-thirty on the dime, the receptionist said, "I'm sorry, Mr. Marino, but Mr. Karola says he's still in a meeting and asked if you would call back at noon." I distinctly remember being on time with the third call to Karola. It sounded like a different girl, and this one came back in a minute with, "I'm sorry, but it seems he's off the premises for lunch. Can you call back at one-thirty or two this afternoon?"

I was getting a trifle ticked off with all these dimes in the phones, like Ma Bell was becoming a one-armed bandit all of a sudden at my expense, so I said to the broad, "Listen, isn't there someone else who can handle my call? I just want some information about your program." She never hesitated. "If you want to talk about being accepted here, you have to speak to Mr. Karola."

I thought for a second about kissing it off but considered the issue. "Okay, whatever you say. Will you tell him, please, that I did call back at noon like he asked me to do and that I'll be calling again at one-thirty? The name is Vinny Marino."

To make a long story somewhat shorter, Karola refused to take my call at one-thirty and gave the receptionist a message to have me "call back at nine in the morning." I hung up the phone that last time and kicked the booth I was in twice and hard. I called Al the day before I was due in court and told him I was in Metropolitan Hospital and asked if he could get a continuation for another week. I figured by that time I would be in Daytop. He didn't sound too happy about Daytop because he had never heard of the program, and he told me it would be impossible to get a continuance. So I worked it out with the administration at the hospital to get a six-hour pass for the following morning, but it wasn't easy. I got up early the next morning, showered, shaved, dressed, and got a cab to the courthouse.

As I pushed through the door of our designated room on the third floor, Al was already seated at the defense table, tapping his fingers nervously on the top. I was anxious not to upset him any more than he was, so I hustled over to sit down beside him and whispered, "Sorry, Al. What are you planning?" He glanced at me negatively and then started to shuffle through a pile of papers as he said, "Don't worry about anything. I'll handle it." I knew I should have gone over to his office for a briefing the minute DiPrimio responded to the judge's question, "Are you ready for sentencing?"

"Your Honor, may it please the Court, I have a plea to enter on behalf of my client, Vincent Marino. This man is truly not a criminal, Your Honor, but he is sick and needs treatment. In all of the efforts he has made to detoxify and rehabilitate himself, the one that was most successful was Synanon. We have checked with people there and have every reason to believe that they will accept him into their program once again. Mr. Marino is eager to commit himself, and I can assure the court that this alternative is far superior than jailing him in New York, both in terms of expense and the liklihood of total rehabilitation."

I looked up at Al, thinking to myself, "What in the hell are you talking about? I'm not going to Synanon." At the same time, the judge was looking down at me as he said, "Mr. Marino, it is obvious from your running record that we cannot tolerate you on the streets of New York. So I am going to give you this one final opportunity to rectify what you've done and become a responsible citizen. I will sentence you to one year, suspended, assuming that you enter the Synanon program. Is that understood, Mr. Marino?'' I bowed my head. ''Yes, Your Honor.''

The judge ended my session for the day with a bang, right after he said, ''Very well then, you have one week to get yourself in. Report back to this court at 10:00 a.m. next Wednesday.''

When Al and I reached the steps of the courthouse outside, I was full of questions and I shot them at Al: ''Why the hell didn't you talk to me Al? I'm not going to Synanon. I want to go to Daytop, this new place out on Staten Island.'' Al looked at me rather deadpan: ''Well, Vinny, I definitely suggest you go someplace real soon because you heard the judge. And I'll tell you something else. You can go to hell if you think I'm chasing you down to discuss your problems.'' Al was pointing his finger at my chest and getting emotional as hell inside. ''Look, Al,'' I tugged lightly on his sleeve as he walked away, ''Please stop. Listen, I was working hard on getting into Daytop, that's why I didn't call. I'm sorry. And I'm going to do something about it.''

DiPrimio spun around on his heels so fast I thought he was in the military. He puffed up his chest and put his hands on his waist in a challenge, then bellowed, ''Goddamn it, Vinny, don't talk to me about anything you're 'going to do.' You want the truth? I can't trust you, so I don't want to hear any more about it. Just *do it* for once. You asshole, you're stuck in 'tomorrow, I'll do it!' You wanna know what I think, Vinny? I think that's what junk does. It takes you to the experience of tomorrow today. But that's a dream, and you're a great dreamer, and you ain't never going to collect on that dream because you can't get there from here. You can only trick your body into thinking it can get to tomorrow before it comes up naturally because in your soul you know, deep down, that you'll *kill* yourself by punching holes in your arms with those needles, and I hope to God, *if* he exists, that some higher court somewhere– if there is such a thing—finds you guilty as charged of murdering Vinny Marino, you evil, rotten sonofabitch! Vinny was a *friend* of mine! Now get the hell out of my sight! He turned and walked away.

14 A New Twist on Rehab

I caught a cab and headed back to the hospital. As soon as I got on the ward, I took my shot of methadone and went straight to the phone to call Daytop. "He's in a meeting . . . He's not on the facility . . . He went out to lunch . . . went out to dinner," and I was constantly told what time to call back. This went on through the week—Thursday, Friday, Saturday, Sunday, and Monday. Finally, late Monday afternoon, I actually got him on the phone, and he was about to give me another time to call back and hang up when I pleaded with him.

"Jack, I have to go to court for something on Wednesday. If I'm not in Daytop by Wednesday, I'm definitely going to prison. I've called you religiously for some time. I've never been late. What more do you want from me? I really need some help. I'm tired of running, I'm tired of using junk, and I'm tired of prison."

There was a short lull, and then he told me he was going to put me on hold. I waited until he came back on the line. "Be here tomorrow at eleven o'clock sharp. If you're late, don't bother showing up. And I want you to understand this is not a guarantee that you'll be accepted. It's only an appointment for an interview. If you fail the interview, then you'll fail getting into Daytop. Goodbye."

When I heard the word *fail* my heart skipped a beat because if that happened I was on my way to the joint, so I committed myself right then and there. "Dammit, I'm not going to die on the streets with my veins full of junk, no matter what else happens. I'm getting into Daytop."

I took a train, a ferry, and a bus, and by the time I reached the grounds it was only ten-thirty. Looking past the Daytop sign at the entrance gate, I noticed an estate covering several acres, complete with a baseball diamond and a small cottage located next to an immense old brown building that stood three stories high. I later learned that the place had been a Benedictine monastery.

Inside I identified myself and was directed to the prospect chair in a corner to sit and wait. The house was very big and very busy. Lots of people walked back and forth, but no one looked at me or acknowledged that I existed. I somehow got the feeling that I was really in a Synanon facility, and I couldn't see much difference from Westport. Only a few minutes before seven in the evening, Jack Karola came out of his office and walked down the stairs, offering his hand. We made our introductions, and he led me to his office where I was immediately startled by the presence of about fifteen people sitting around the room. Straight off I noticed a couple of familiar faces. A black guy there named Rudy used to cop from me in downtown Brooklyn. We called him a "hope fiend" because he would hang around hoping to get loaded by loaning his works. There was a hooker named Annie who once worked the streets around my hotel in midtown, and I had met Tommy LaCosta when he came to Reno from Seawall to pick up a cow from the ranch.

Everyone gave their names and titles, but I didn't remember any of them at the time except that of Art, the director, who began the questioning. "Okay, Vinny, why don't you tell us what you're doing here and what you want from us?"

Without hesitating I took the time to look briefly at each face, then I said, "I am sick and tired of both junk and the streets. I know that I'm a weak bastard, and I want the help that you people have to offer." With that, several of them asked me some standard questions, and I gave concise, truthful answers. What it got down to was that Art remained leery of accepting me just one day before I was due to be sentenced. If they did take me, it would mean that they would have to send a man to go to bat for me with the judge. The issues were, was I worth it and what were my intentions?

I told them in all candor, "Look, I have to be serious because if I stay out on the streets I know I'm a dead man, and if Daytop doesn't accept me, I'm going straight to prison." Rudy started yelling at me. "Look, asshole, we know you can run it! You've always been full of shit! You never really did anything in your life and you do know that you're a baby and that you're really afraid of going to prison! Come on, let's hear it sucker!"

"You're right. I am a baby. I am an asshole, and I'm scared of going to prison. I couldn't make it on the streets, and I need some help." Art was not yet totally convinced, which he said. "I frankly don't know how committed you are to the idea and principles of Daytop, plus the fact that you split from Brand X. In order to find out about you, we're going to play this game.

"Imagine that you are all alone in a tiny rowboat in the middle of the ocean. The boat springs a leak and starts to sink, and you have nothing to bail with but your hands and that isn't making it. Way off in the distance, you catch a glimpse of a luxury liner. The only possible way for you to save yourself is to scream from the bottom of your balls all the way across that stretch of ocean and get someone aboard that ship to hear you.

"So you had better call out for help, Vinny, because that's where you're sitting right now. You are drowning and you're going to die, and *we* are that ship. If you convince us we can save you. How long can you tread water, Vinny? One more day before they ship you back out to 'The Rock'? If you fail to convince us, right now, that we are the ship, you'll find that this program passes you by. Anytime you're ready, go ahead."

I took a deep breath and started screaming my ass off. I looked up at the ceiling and yelled to high heaven and then I looked at each of them, pleading for mercy. After five minutes of this, Art stopped me, looked around the room, and said, "Okay, Vinny, what do you want?" I said, "I want some help!"

"You got it. Welcome to Daytop." They then explained that the interview was deliberately set up to make it difficult for someone to get in unless they really wanted help. Next they read me the house rules, which were pretty much standard Synanon but with more rigid penalties and enforcements. For example, they appointed various people "expeditors," which meant that they would look for infractions and listen for out-of-bounds conversations, then bust people for violations.

Karola invited me to see where I'd be bunking, and I followed him into a dormitory area that held thirteen other guys on the third floor. He explained that as a man's seniority built up, he could expect to share a room with fewer and fewer people until he reached a position where he would have a single or double.

Karola mentioned there were about a hundred to a hundred and ten people in residence. After he assigned my bunk, he told me, "Get your shit together, then come down to the basement in ten minutes."

When I got there it was haircut time, although they didn't shave me totally bald, which was good because of my court appearance the next day. After my visit to the barber shop, I went to look up Tommy LaCosta. I spotted him in the kitchen next to the coffee urn, and he laughed when he saw me coming. "Hey, Vinny! How are you enjoying old home week?" I tipped my empty coffee cup toward him and quipped, "Better than Custer did at his last stand. How you doin', Tommy? Good to see you."

We filled our cups and went over to a table to sit down and shoot the bull. Tommy told me that in Daytop they referred to Synanon only as "Brand X." He had left Seawall and moved back to the city to be closer to his family; then he entered Daytop. I asked what it was like living at the facility and mentioned the trouble I had just trying to get Jack Karola on the phone.

"It's fairly rigid here, Vinny. And they deliberately do that with the phone calls from prospects; put you off for a week or so. They figure the candy-asses melt on the streets, and the serious people get in. I try not to pay much attention to the bullshit."

I nodded in agreement and then put one of the ultimate questions to him. "Can you see yourself staying here?" He thought about it for a few seconds and said, "Tough question, Vinny. You know they created a new twist with this program. You can *graduate* after two or three years, then either work for the organization or go back to the outside and take up your place as a cog in the wheel. I prefer to take it by the day."

Agreeing with him, I said, "Sounds like a plan to me. Sure beats the 'lifetime' bit they were preaching at Brand X." We went on to talk about the beef I was facing in court, my biggest worry was getting the judge to accept Daytop in place of Brand X. "You know, I could volunteer to go along with you and do a pitch to the judge on your behalf, if you think that would help." I slapped him on the shoulder. "Help? Hell, you might be able to save me from the joint. Can we go see Karola about it right now? I have to call my lawyer before the day's over anyway to see what he wants to do." Karola agreed and even suggested I call DiPrimio from his office in case he wanted some background information on Daytop.

Al's wife answered and put me through immediately when I gave her my name, so I knew that Al hadn't excommunicated me totally, at least not yet. "Vinny? Where are you?" Quickly I said, "Hello Al. Listen, I want to apologize for not getting back to you sooner than this, but I was all wrapped up in detoxification, appointments, and interviews. But here's the good news. I got accepted into the therapeutic community I told you about called Daytop. I'm already a resident." Al's voice dropped noticeably. "But Vinny, we told the judge Synanon, and that's what he agreed to."

"Al, this community was founded by a guy from Synanon, and the program is much more innovative. My chances for total rehabilitation are far greater here, believe me."

"Alright, Vinny. It's a positive step, and I'll make the best of it in the morning. Can you be in my office by 8:30? I want to discuss the details before we go in." I knew I needed permission so I looked over at Jack, and he cupped his mouthpiece before he nodded and told me, "Sure, as long as Tommy goes with you." I got back on with Al saying, "Eight-thirty is fine, Al. Oh, by the way, if it's okay with you, I'll be bringing another guy with me who knows all about Daytop community in case the judge asks, and he could also be a character witness for me since I knew him at Synanon." Al became more confident as he said, "Sure, bring him along. We need all the help we can get when it comes to keeping you out of the can."

With a burst of internal energy, I was awake the next morning before five o'clock, and I went downstairs to get some coffee. No one else was up, so I put a batch on to brew and sat down with the first light of morning to think about what was going to happen in the courtroom. By six-thirty Tommy and I had finished a bite of breakfast and were ready to go. We checked out with the person on the front desk and walked to the bus stop, took the bus to the ferry and arrived in the city, bound for midtown Manhattan. When we got to Al's office at twenty past eight, he wasn't in yet. Al finally walked in the door full of apologies at five minutes to nine, which left no time at all to discuss the case in his office. I introduced him to LaCosta, and all three of us jumped in a cab for the courthouse. My name was first on the docket, probably because it was a simple matter of whether or not I was in Synanon.

At ten o'clock sharp I knew something was wrong when I heard the words, "All rise please, the court is in session, Judge Baxter presiding." I looked over at Al in shock because Judge *Berman* had given me the chance to go back to Synanon, not Baxter. I wanted to bolt when the new judge sat down and read my case history. His face changed color, starting with a calm, neutral brown and becoming a fiery red. Before I could signal to Al, Baxter called the session to order and got right to the heart of the matter. "Mr. DiPrimio, is your client ready for sentencing?"

Al mentioned nothing about last week's Synanon verdict. Instead he attempted to paint the best verbal picture he could. "Your Honor, may it please the Court, my client, Vincent Marino, has had a long history of arrests, but each and every one of them has been due to a sickness: his addiction to heroin. He now knows absolutely that drastic action must be taken, and I am pleased to inform the Court that Mr. Marino has done just that. He took the initiative and voluntarily committed himself to a therapeutic community called Daytop on Staten Island. He is already in full-time residence there and wants to assure the Court that he intends to remain in the program and rehabilitate himself completely."

The judge didn't buy one word of it. Instead he looked down again at my record and blazed with both barrels. "Mr. DiPrimio, I heard everything you said, and if I didn't have this arrest record to look at, I might be inclined to believe you. But one glance tells me that I'm addressing a career criminal, a man with years of performance behind him. And you're going to tell me that now, one day before sentencing, he got into a therapeutic community to rid himself of the 'horror' of this dilemma? I'm sorry, Mr. DiPrimio, but this is the end of the line for your client as far as I'm concerned."

When Judge Baxter finished unloading his barrage, Al made an attempt to recover my character somewhat. "Your Honor, this time . . ." The judge banged his gavel. "Please, Mr. DiPrimio. Don't tell me 'this time' because there have been too many times in the past. If you want my opinion, your client, Vincent Marino, is nothing more than a communicable disease and as such should be locked *away* from society in order that he cannot possibly contaminate anyone else." I could only think, "Jesus, he's talking about me!" And my heart fell to my knees.

But Al hit a technicality and presented it along with the paper to back it up. "Your Honor, may I call your attention to the fact that Judge Berman presided on this case in the initial session, and he stated specifically in the minutes that he would be the sentencing judge.'' Baxter looked somewhat puzzled, but after checking Al's copy of the records, he said, ''Very well, you may proceed to the Court of Judge Berman for sentencing,'' and he told us which courtroom our man was ruling in that day.

Once we had it located, Al went in first to take the opportunity to get our case listed on the docket. When it was announced, Berman remembered his decision as soon as he opened the file. ''Mr. DiPrimio, what do you have to report?''

Al said, ''Your Honor,'' and then went on to tactfully break the ice with the switch of community names and locations. The judge was obviously reluctant to accept the change, so Al introduced Tommy as a ''former Synanon resident who has joined Daytop and can explain some of the differences and tell the Court what potential they see in Vincent Marino.''

Tommy took that cue and ran with it all until he made me and all of Daytop look like the saintliest community of ex-dope fiends you were likely to find anywhere. The sheet length of LaCosta's verbal tirade finally convinced the judge, who cut Tommy off after more than ten minutes. ''All right, Mr. LaCosta, you've made your point. You may sit down. Mr. Marino, I'm going to keep my word and suspend sentence. But you are to remain in this Daytop community until you are clinically released. Moreover, I want you to know that if you so much as sneeze in violation of this order, you are going to prison. Now, is what I said clear to you?''

I didn't look up as I nodded my head, ''Yes, Your Honor.'' He came down with a bang and concluded, ''Very well. Case dismissed.''

Before the decision was final, my stomach had been tied up in a snarl of knots similar to the pain of withdrawal. As we walked out, I relaxed and Tommy smiled broadly, basking in the limelight of his moving performance. Al shook my hand firmly. ''Well, Vinny, you just got yourself a brand new lease. I hope you'll pay your dues and do the right thing.''

''Al, this time I'm going to do something with my life, you watch. I'm going to take that lease and turn it into a 'down payment' in no time. Then I'm going to open my own business. Thanks for the push my friend. I'll never forget that you stood by when I needed someone.'' Al smiled and I could tell he had forgiven my past actions and was looking ahead to a brighter future for me.

When Tommy and I arrived back at the facility and stepped down into the living room, someone got on the house loudspeaker system and barked out the good news about my case. "We are pleased to report that Vinny Marino was placed on probation this morning and remanded into the custody of Daytop Village. Welcome aboard, Vinny." As soon as the walls of that old monastery took the sound from the speakers and echoed it back, thunderous live applause and loud cheering came booming out of every room.

I felt like the hero of a neighborhood stickball team, so I threw my arms up over my head and clasped my hands together, acting like a champ. I started dancing around in circles, and people clapped me on the back, screaming for more. I figured to play the act to the maxiumum, so I went on, using some royal terminology and reaching for my deepest baritone voice. "My loyal subjects, as your emperor, I hereby declare that this victory is true cause for celebration. Break out enough ice water, coffee and donuts to satisfy every man, woman, and child in the kingdom. Let's have a party!"

All the residents in the living room clenched their right fists and pumped their arms in the air, chanting, "Do-nuts. Do-nuts. Do-nuts." As the coffee was brought out from the kitchen, I sat down with a group of people on the floor. It was a great welcoming celebration for me, and I felt more at home right then than I ever had at Synanon.

After dinner that evening, I was given a job on the service crew and told about the routine of the house. It hit me as basically parallel to Synanon, except the structure was much more rigid and the penalties more ludicrous and lengthy. An example were the rules on shaving. Each individual was issued his or her own Wilkinson blade, at the rate of one a week. In order to get a new one, you had to turn in your old one. The catch was that you couldn't leave your blade lying around because if you didn't have one, you didn't get a new one, and then you had to wear a four-foot wooden model of a Wilkinson blade around your neck everywhere you went for maybe three, four, or five days.

I had a habit of leaving my blade perched on the sink after I shaved. Some expeditor would always be grabbing the damn thing, then would bust me for it over the loudspeaker. "Vincent

Marino, come to the coordinator's office.'' After a while, I wouldn't even bother trying to defend myself. I'd just say, ''Gimme the wooden blade. How long this time?'' That bothered me, especially since I was supposed to be a pretty aware guy. Why I kept leaving my razor blade around really confused me. It got so that seeing me without the sign would be a novelty.

It was one of the major things I really disliked about Daytop. They were very big on signs—sandwich signs that said 'I'm a dog' or 'Don't trust me.' They would use plastic baby bottles with strings attached to hang around your neck, and they also made people wear diapers during a general meeting. As a matter of fact, the only time people would not have to wear any of these signs was during the open house on Saturday evenings when community people came in to see what we were doing. These kinds of humiliating degradations really didn't seem to serve any purpose toward anything constructive.

Daytop was also very much into physical haircuts. If you did something they thought was not too cool, they would shave your head if you were a male, and females were given stocking caps. On a couple of occasions they shaved a guy's head but left a little piece in the front and tied a large bow on it. I don't know what was supposed to be accomplished by that except maybe some sick needs taken out by the people in power there.

One activity at the facility really caught my fancy, though, right off. Tommy LaCosta introduced it to me, and it started taking up a lot of my free time. Inside a separate building on the grounds two punching bags had been set up.

When I put on the gloves for the first time, I vented a thousand angry frustrations, slamming the hell out of the bag for more than an hour. Until that day when I stood in front of the bag and considered it my worst adversary, I never knew I had so much buried inside me waiting to come out with a vengeance. ''Bam!'' I would slam Brannigan for his bullshit. ''Whack!'' I would crack pop for his gambling and on down through the roster of tough guys and raw deals I felt life had handed me. Many times I would get so exhausted I could only hug the bag and hang on since I couldn't lift my arms to punch anymore.

Hitting that bag was better therapy than I had gotten from the legion of shrinks who had ''listened'' to my problems. With each hit, I would yell, ''YO!'' and let everything out. After I had been working out for a while, I would fantasize about being in boxing matches with various assholes that ran the facility, talking to the bag as if it were my victim. Those punching bag sessions were really beneficial for my mind and body. I discovered over time that I could tolerate the day-to-day routine much better, and I also noticed that I was slowly gaining weight in all the right places. It felt good to be involved with something physical, and I was amazed at the way I could free my mind from everything else and yet still think clearly.

Aside from the punching bag, the first week I was at Daytop, I found that the everyday routine got to me fast. Nothing was new or exciting about the inside of a toilet bowl, and I already knew every angle there was about slinging soapsuds in different directions, whistling while I worked. Within three or four days I started drawing designs on the bathroom floor with a wet mop, picturing myself as a fruitcake Picasso. When people would walk on my wet masterpiece, I bitched at them for "screwing up an artist's work" and sometimes chased the guilty party, shaking my mop. Of course it was all an act, but lots of people took my actions seriously. They would get angry and stay that way for days and weeks at a time. I couldn't be bothered thinking about their reactions; I was just trying to break up the grueling monotony any way I could.

At the end of my first week, Art, the director, announced what sounded like a new experience, at least on the surface. At a general meeting one night, he said, "One hour from now, beginning at 8:00 p.m., the house will be totally closed down for a week, and we will be going through a seven-day marathon. You've got one hour to clean up and put on something comfortable before we meet in the dining room." I had never encountered a session that long before. I remember thinking, "I can see myself getting bored at the end of day one. How in the hell am I going to get through *seven* days?" I felt somewhat relieved to hear at the beginning of the session that we were free to move from group to group or from room to room whenever we chose to. After hearing my initial room assignment, I dragged my feet for as long as I could in the dining room, drinking coffee and shooting the bull with a newcomer from Brooklyn. Finally a bell rang and a voice came over the loudspeaker. "The marathon is beginning. Go to your assigned rooms."

As everyone filed out of the dining room, I hustled up to Tommy LaCosta and elbowed his ribs as I started running in place beside him. "C'mon, Tommy, let's go. We're gonna win this marathon." Without batting an eyelash, LaCosta got with my pace in the line, kicking his knees high in the air, "We'll run circles around these idiots." Everyone else looked at us like we were all out of our minds.

Inside the room, everything struck me as strange. Fifteen or twenty candles were glowing in colored glass containers scattered around on the floor. Some heavy smoke filled the room, and I felt it sticking to my nostrils and tongue. Then I saw that the smoke was wafting from lit sticks of incense planted in tin cans all over the room.

I grabbed a seat to orient myself, and the public address system came alive, playing music that was a mixture of violins and crashing surf. The combined sound of twelve speakers throughout the house all playing at once with the sounds echoing off the walls everywhere was weird. I flashed on Boris Karloff hiding in the wings, all set to jump in with the ultimate scare tactic for getting junkies off their habits and onto the straight and narrow.

As soon as the game began, I knew I didn't want to play. I got bored with the same old stories we heard at the general meetings, which only lasted two or three hours. When the first spotlight hit me, I begged the question and took off for another room to hide in. In the second room, I figured it was close enough when the girl next to me got the "hot seat," so I left then. All in all, I managed to finagle my way through an entire day without ever answering a single question. I started to see myself as a fly on the wall. Sure, I was present, but from an upside-down position on the ceiling. All those people sure looked strange, and I wasn't about to get close enough to let them swat me in the ass.

Eventually the individual groups were all called together into the sunken living room. Art started the action there when he said to another guy, "Okay, Alex, the game is called 'emotion,' and here is how we play. Go around the room and one by one tell each person how lonely you are, how much you need a friend, and how you want that person to love you. The object is for you to convince each person to love you. Got it?"

As Alex moved around the room with his appeal for friendship and love, I found it humorous at first. But then it turned to boredom after he told maybe forty people the same story. By the time he got to me, I had decided not to play. After he made a dull plea about loving me, I looked him straight in the eye. "Alex, I'm sorry, but I don't even know you, so forget about 'love you.' What did you say your last name was? Now, as we get to know each other, we might become friends, but for right now if I were you, I'd pass on me.''

In a flash, the entire group sent boos and hisses at me, and I shot them a bird in response, smiling at the same time. A coordinator finally cut in. ''Come on, Vinny, why the hell are you stalling? You've been in Brand X; you know what this is all about.'' I thought, ''What the hell, nothing matters at these meetings anyway,'' so I told him the truth. ''Yeah, I might have spent a year at Brand X, but I'm brand *new* here. And on the one hand you keep preaching 'Don't do *anything* according to Brand X,' and then in the next breath you want me to switch to being a Brand X old-timer and give everybody a lesson. Well fuck it. From now on I don't know nothin' until I get it firsthand from you.''

The coordinator looked at me and barked, ''That's a selfish, shitty point of view. The object of the game is to share experiences, so that everyone can benefit.'' I got a cold and rotten, distant feeling. ''Look, I'm not here for anyone else's benefit. I'm here *only* for Vinny Marino. I couldn't give a shit about your benefit, her benefit, or the benefit of anyone else in this house.''

That did it. Cries of anguish came from all directions. The coordinator was first, and he banged in with, ''You ungrateful asshole, *we* kept you out of jail.'' I looked at him directly. ''Hold it. *You* didn't keep me out of jail, Tommy LaCosta did, with an act that you couldn't *think* about duplicating. So let's get off this 'we' shit, Lone Ranger.''

Obviously, no one liked that line either, because everyone chimed in with hoots and cat-calls, like a chorus of vultures hovering over a dying carcass. Imagine the look on their faces when the dead horse got up off his ass and walked with indifference out of the room. ''Who needs this?'' I thought as I cruised around the house, looking for the nearest place to turn into Mister Anonymous again.

After more than twenty hours of nonstop exercises, we got a four-hour sleep break, then back to the talk sessions. I purposely located a chair somewhat out of the way, pulled my knees up under my chin, hoping to hell I looked like a Chinese lotus in meditation so everyone would leave me alone. It took a radical black Muslim named Jabbo to shake me from a nice round of daydreams. He got up and started running his background on the group, making it sound like he was meaner than Bonnie and Clyde put together.

He said that he was king of a couple of blocks, and he would routinely cut white men's throats and watch them bleed. He went on with, nobody had ever given him shit, for any reason, because they knew they would die, and this all came down in that slick, jive-ass style of talk. After more than thirty minutes of this, I got tired of seeing everyone mesmerized by all the bullshit, so I figured to cut him off at the knees and see what he would do.

"Jabo, your jaws are working overtime, and you're nothing but a bullshit artist. You never cut up anything in your life besides rugs and paper. Why don't you just sit down and keep quiet?" Jabbo jumped nervously when he caught what I said and challenged me with some theory. "Marino, if we were on the streets right now, you'd be a dead man." I didn't even look up at him but said, "First of all, if you were a 'tough guy,' you'd be holding court on the streets right now, not sitting in here with candles, incense, and music."

"Fuck you, Marino. Who do you think you are?" I folded my arms across my chest and leaned back in the chair, lifing the two front legs about three inches off the ground, so I was looking at him directly. "Who *I* am doesn't matter, Jabbo. *You* were doing all the talking, intimidating these other assholes by running off at the mouth, but I know you're nothing but a piece of ordinary shit, and your jive-ass rhetoric ain't goin' down with me, so sit on it."

He pointed his finger at me again and took a step forward. "Marino, like I said, if we were on the streets, you'd pay for that." I never moved an inch as I said, "If we were on the streets, rubber gums, you'd never get your mouth back together right. You say 'Muslim' and 'karate' and 'street king' but I say 'nigger.' Why don't you go to the kitchen and grab yourself a whole watermelon, then shoot out to the back porch and cut it up with your switchblade. Oh, don't forget to spit out the seeds, and don't get any more than you have to on your shirt."

That's what it took for all hell to break loose. Jabbo headed for my chair, and I jumped up and slid into a crouched position, waiting. The group facilitator finally woke up and stopped Jabbo by giving him a bear hug, trapping both arms. Three other people came and surrounded me, so it was all over before it started. But that verbal exchange broke up the schedule. The director came on the mike calling for the entire house to meet in the sunken living room after a ten-minute break. When I got into the living room, no less than eight staff members confronted me, and the questions started. ''Vinny, how did the situation go down like it did?'' I looked at them and said quite matter of factly, ''That guy, Jabbo, sold me a ticket, so I walked into the arena.''

The director cut in at that point. ''You know the rules. No violence and no threats of violence.'' I said right back, ''I didn't do anything violent and didn't threaten any either. He gave me the theory, 'if we were on the streets' and I just played along like it was part of the game.'' One of the coordinators said, ''But you were in Brand X, you know not to involve yourself in that kind of petty shit.'' I put it directly to him, just as I had to the other one. ''Look, you people need to make up your minds. First you say to forget everything Brand X ever told me, then you pull me up for something, reminding me that I have a year under my belt at Brand X. It's like Catch 22, and I'm not going for it.'' The director called everything off by ordering me into a seat, since I was the newcomer, while Jabbo went to the basement and came back upstairs looking like a Mohawk Muslim.

After that, the marathon went on and on, while I got nothing more out of it. I figured that the whole object of the week-long game was to dissipate people to the point where they would say or admit to almost anything. Painful episodes poured out of personal memories in front of the whole group. People hugged each other, cried a lot, and exposed their inner feelings in myriad ways. I couldn't believe human life was so diverse in terms of experience—especially with females. I was amazed at the number of hookers who had come from homes where they were getting messed with by their fathers, and their mothers knew nothing about it. By the time they reached a place like Daytop, I would say that 90 percent of the women hated *all* men, and most of them with a vengeance.

One consistent element ran through the whole marathon, and it hit me like a flash. The pain. Most of the residents had been through some highly charged emotional situations involving physical or mental pain. It seemed, in order to pay it back, they had inflicted pain on themselves, with junk, and pain on their families, friends, or whomever, with their addicted condition and the subsequent lifestyle of crime, prostitution, and drugs. At least I could see that pattern clearly operating in my case, and it seemed to hold true for most of the other residents as well.

After we came out of the marathon, the whole place started to get childish as hell from my point of view. They dubbed me Noodlehead for the first thirty days, and people who made small mistakes had to wear four-foot-high dunce caps for a week. If you forgot to turn off a light, you got a five-foot fluorescent tube to carry around like a soldier. It might sound funny now, but it proved to be ultimately stupid because during the first month I was there, six or eight people couldn't handle it and split. One was a young kid of eighteen, a pretty girl named Sandy, who died ten days after she walked out the front door—overdosed in midtown. I thought it was a damned shame, but I kept my distance since I had to stay right where I was or face up to prison.

Before long, some of us "renegades" formed a new "tip," and we would sit around knocking all the petty bullshit. Tommy LaCosta was the main prankster besides me, and we teamed up to pull off a number of practical jokes, plus we worked out together on the punching bags. Most people thought we were weird, but it served a useful and positive purpose for us. We were cracking the shell of the nuthouse just to let some air in. And it was fun.

Basically, however, time was dragging for me and my insides were getting restless for a change of pace. I discovered to my dismay that there were no outside projects, and no one worked outside for a living. Daytop essentially begged for their money, and I didn't like the idea at all.

The only carrot they had to offer was a position on the staff, eventually, assuming the place grew in popularity with disgusted junkies from the streets. I didn't know if it would be worth my time to spend two to three years there only to become a staff member since I couldn't go for their "baby" routines, and there wasn't a single staff member I respected. I noticed the same thing at Daytop that I mentioned about Ellie Clapp in Reno. The low-lifes out on the streets would come into a community like this and look to become a god of some kind. With one inch of power, they would run all around the house abusing people with it.

After three or so more weeks had gone by, I was getting more and more upset with having to keep my mouth shut and do what I was told. The capper came down one day when I left my razor blade in the bathroom. My penance was I had to clean the caulking between every tile in a 30×50 foot john with comet on a toothbrush. As I sat there scrubbing my ass off, I decided I had to create an escape hatch soon so I put in a request to the director for what they called a "special." This was an emergency encounter session and you could pick your own participants. Usually a special was called when there was a beef between two or more people.

For my special, I listed everybody who was in any kind of status or staff position, plus a couple of the most obnoxious low-lifes. In all, I named eighteen or twenty people, including the director, two coordinators, the chief expeditor and his little indians, plus all the department heads. To top everything off, I asked for Tommy LaCosta, figuring he'd make one hell of an audience. My special was set for seven o'clock in the evening. As soon as I got inside the room, I could feel the tension and see it in everyone's eyes. They didn't like the idea of this at all, I could tell, so I took a deep breath and figured to give them a good reason for not liking it. The staff member who was facilitating the special session looked at me and said, "Okay, play."

Figuring the first thing to do was establish myself, I got on the edge of my chair and looked at each person individually without saying anything. After a minute or so of eye contact, I spoke slowly. "Look, I've been here almost two months now, and I want you people to know where I'm coming from. And where I'm coming from is not Brand X or wooden razor blades, dunce caps, fluorescent bulbs, or any of that shit which you clowns use.

"Where I'm coming from is a guy named Vinny Marino, and I'm asking for some common sense to apply to this house. You people have the power to control my future and my freedom, and I don't want it misused. I also don't want to be forced back to the streets or into prison just because I couldn't stand to wear a diaper for a week or sit still for ten hours with a dunce cap on my head. And so, if you guys make sense with your orders, I'll follow them. And if you try to fuck with my head using nonsense, you're going to hear about it. You see, I am just not like those little wimps running around downstairs, and I'm definitely not one of you guys. Now, let me run each one of you assholes down with some logic, and why not start at the top, with you, Art."

When I turned to face Art, I could tell he was terrified, so I took maximum advantage by assuming a vicious look and proceeded to lay out the truth about what I saw in him and his act, what I didn't like about him, what I didn't like about the way he handled his job, how his shit was coming out sideways and on which issues, and how I thought he was handling the power associated with his position. When I had finished after nearly forty minutes, Art didn't say a word, and neither did any of the others.

It took me almost five hours to get around the room, one by one. I finally sat back in my chair and wound up. "That's all I have to say. And now that I've said it, I need some help." It was astounding to see what happened in the room. The clarity of communication was most obvious because everyone spoke in plain English for once. Each one had something constructive to say about what I should do in order to make life easier all around, and none of them argued with my assessments. It took them nearly two more hours to finish with me, and we all felt better when the session came to an end.

Happily for everyone, I sensed a change in the general drift of things almost immediately. The rules lightened up a little, and the "eyes and ears" of the place—the expeditors—stopped acting like storm troopers. Then the weather outside turned warmer, and we started playing baseball in the diamond on the grounds, plus Art scheduled a picnic or an outing once a week that included everyone.

Inside the facility, I got the break I wanted after about four months when I was taking my one day a week off to play "seek and assume," which meant that you would look around for something you wanted to do and then just assume you had the position on your day off. I found the kitchen the most appealing place, and I started cooking breakfast. Within three weeks I made second lunch cook, then lunch cook. By the time my seventh month rolled around, I was the senior dinner cook for 108 people. I used to sit around with a paper and pencil, adding up potatoes, tomatoes, and how many pounds of meat. I spent a lot of time figuring quantities when I wasn't fooling around with some new recipe. I started fussing for hours with each batch of spaghetti sauce. Then I got a big white chef's hat, and I felt like old Tim Mixem Marino, but my six-gun was a two-barrel electric eggbeater.

Suddenly I had a whole bunch of new friends, since it always paid to know the cook. I started picking my own "tip" rather selectively, and some of the women were particularly jealous of my role as "the chef." When one of them approached me, I would just bow my big hat toward them, and say, "Look, I know you don't like me. I don't know why you don't like me because I don't think I ever did anything to you in my life, but that's okay. I just want you to know that I know you don't like me." With that, I would turn back to my stove. It drove women crazy, and I had a whole flock of chicks in the kitchen all trying to convince me that they did like me. But I couldn't get any of them into a trap for another five months, so I figured "why bother yourself?" and I would whip up some fresh cream and smear it all over some strawberries and shortcake, and get off on that dish by myself.

After a long day of slinging pots and pans, I couldn't do much more than read, so I started cracking books instead of the punching bag. My primary objective was to sharpen and expand my vocabulary, like an intellectual word game. Before long, I began to practice on the residents. Most people would listen to me, then start scratching their heads, wondering if I was losing it. Then they would come down on me like dive bombers when we got into an encounter session. They would point their fingers and shake, screaming. "Who the fuck do you think you are, with those fancy bits of wisdom? No one in this place can relate to you!"

By this time, the beginning of my eighth month at Daytop, I was in a position to assess the entire operation from the relative safety and perspective of being a chef in the kitchen. (When you're feeding people good, they don't bitch very loud or long. That's one I learned from my momma.) I wasn't being hassled much, but it was starting up all around me again. People with power used it sadistically to encorce their child's play and bullshit rules, and the director of the house ordered a dozen new diapers.

I watched with interest as the sands of wanderlust built up under my feet, and I could see myself working up enough traction to hit the trail. I looked long and hard at the people in power, and I knew that I didn't belong. And if that was the case, why would the existing power-mongers admit me into the circle? That would threaten them directly if I was on staff. It seemed like I was caught between layers of lasagna and that was as far as I was going to get.

But the simple fact was that I was on probation, with the strict condition that I "remain at Daytop until clinically released." I couldn't go anywhere even if I wanted to without violating my probation and ending up doing time in the joint. Even at Daytop I had to take one afternoon off each month and travel to the Tombs in Manhattan to see my probation officer, Ray Hamilton. I could say I was "clean," no kidding, I was a cook, and "yes, sir, I am learning, growing, and picking up everything I need to know in order to get a job real soon and go out and earn my own living." I felt especially great about looking people like him straight in the eye and not wondering which lie I was building up on. On the streets, trying to remember what I had said would almost drive me nuts sometimes.

After I marked my nine-month anniversary I decided to hop into the fire by requesting a job change before there was a crisis in terms of how-long-can-I-put-up-with-this-bullshit. So I cut off my negative thoughts and began to shop around for an opening in another department. I knew a guy named Sonny who worked in community services. He, I, and LaCosta became fairly good friends over time, so I went to visit Sonny bright and early one day to find out what he thought my chances were of getting into some public relations.

I got to the right place at the right time because the Daytop people were intending to branch out more into the community and start up an aggressive guest speaker program. Sonny was enthusiastic about me trying my hand with some public contact, and he put in the good word for me. I got the job change eight or nine days later. Sonny's boss liked my cooking much more than the idea of having me wise-assing around his operation all day, but Sonny and I both kept the pressure on. Finally I made the transfer and started getting on the phone to bankers and brokers, pitching them on us and inviting them over for lunch or open house to speak on their favorite subject, as long as it wasn't drugs.

In my new position I learned all about the places we were scoring our free goods and who the biggest donors were. I started to work on the parent and family meetings, which my mom and Frank attended regularly, and I assisted with the arrangements for special events, such as the yearly "clean" celebrations for residents, the open houses, and so forth.

The first sign of trouble came on a Saturday night almost six weeks after I had joined community services. An open house was scheduled, and our department head was away from the facility for some reason, which meant that his assistant was in charge. The assistant made straight for the throne as soon as the boss went out the door and started issuing orders to everyone who came in the office. He walked around the desks, dropping off big stacks of work and getting thoroughly into the role of acting dictator.

None of us could believe it when this assistant got on the PA system Saturday afternoon and called a meeting of all community service personnel. Our temporary boss arrived at the meeting dead last and immediately started talking. "Tonight at the open house, we will be hosting two very influential people from the community. These squares are in a position to help us directly with substantial contributions, but even more importantly, they have contacts all over the city and the state. What I want you to do tonight is sell the place and sell it hard. I want these people to leave here tonight thinking we're the seven dwarfs who can be trusted to keep Snow White in the attic without ever touching her. Each and every time I pass you guys, I want to hear you selling. Got that?" Sonny and I didn't think what he said merited a special meeting, so we talked about what an idiot he was as we came back down the stairs.

As things happened, I was particularly effective that night at the open house with one of the prominent men we had on our target list. He and I hit it off right away because he was a friend of someone I knew who knew someone else in Little Italy. Before the night was over, it was as if we came from the same family, and I could tell that when he got home he would be opening his checkbook. I was in a good mood afterwards but because of the psychic energy I had used during the evening, all I wanted was to get in bed. Just as I was about to turn in the speakers went on again with the assistant calling another "community services meeting, right now, in the annex."

Sonny and I looked at each other, and we both shrugged our shoulders. We dropped our coffee cups in the sink, and I ground out my cigarette in a Mason jar lid and headed for the stairwell. When we reached the room and took a seat, "the boss" stood up. "Each of you, go around the room and give me a status report on what you did at the open house. Okay, Vinny, how'd you do?"

I looked at him like he had just called a bullshit session, given the hour, and that the question was dumb. "Well, I sold both coffee urns, one refrigerator, took a down payment on the baseball diamond and I think we'll have an offer tomorrow for the couches in the living room. Now that's only from the first guy I met. Then there was . . ." "The boss" interrupted rudely. "Cut the shit, Vinny,'' just as everyone else in the room doubled up in laughter. The wind went out of his meeting sails faster than it leaves a balloon pricked with a pin, and he saw it was pointless to continue. ''We'll take this up on Monday,'' he said and walked out mumbling to himself about how nobody was taking anything seriously. After he left, I stayed for a round of congratulations from my coworkers for shutting down another dull session, so I patted myself on the back for a job well done by copping a bundle from the sandman and went straight to my bunk.

Two or three days later I got a shock one morning at breakfast when I heard Sonny had pulled out the night before, and he did it without saying a word to me. I thought that was strange since we were quite close by then. I left my coffee sitting on the kitchen table and went to find LaCosta, figuring he might know what had pushed Sonny out the door. Tommy knew nothing, and neither did anyone else. All that day I had trouble with my feelings, wondering what had motivated Sonny to bolt. Towards evening, I wandered out to the front porch and sat there looking at the sky and pondering my future. For a minute I thought about leaving myself, but I put it off and went in to do some reading instead.

Less than a week later, another idiotic incident started a chain reaction. Four of us were in the kitchen drinking coffee after breakfast when something momentous came on the news concerning the war in Vietnam and having to do with a massacre at My Lai. The attraction was the bodies of dead children. We left our coffee and hustled to the TV in the living room. Five minutes later, one of our expeditors walked into the kitchen and found the cups out of place. The sight caused something to crack inside the maniac's head, and he got on the loudspeaker and asked that the people last in the kitchen come to the annex immediately.

None of us knew what the hell it was for. When all four of us had taken a seat, this expeditor named Butch read us the riot act about the coffee cups, saying that we were ''worse than pigs.'' I couldn't believe how serious he was being over four lousy cups being on the kitchen table for less than ten minutes. ''Okay, for being such slobs, we're going to take off your mops. All of you down to the basement.''

Fool that he was, Butch went one step over the line in my head when he announced the penalty for being such bad boys and girls. Without thinking twice, I said, ''The hell with this,'' and got up heading for the door. Butch grabbed me by the sleeve and pulled on it. "What did you say, Marino?" I picked his hand off my shirt and shoved it hard into his pants pocket. "I said 'to hell with this,' and now I'm saying keep your fucking hands to yourself, asshole."

Butch was dumbfounded as I left the room, intending to pack up and leave. Back in my dorm, I threw a couple of essentials into a bag and ignored all the questions being put to me by Butch, who had followed me, still trying to pull a power number. "Marino, what the hell do you think you're doing? Get your ass to the basement with the rest of the troops."

I put the bag down on the floor for a minute and picked the little bastard up, then set him down in a corner. "Tell you what, Butch. You wait right here for ten minutes or I'll break you in half, then you come down to the basement and find me. Got it?" He shook and stayed where he was, while I picked up my bag to leave. As I got to the expeditor near the front door, he saw me coming. "Hey, Vinny, you taking a trip?" I breezed right on by him. "Yeah, Jack, a long one. Put my tag in the 'out' slot, will you? I'm hittin' it." His jaw dropped six inches as I slammed the door and thought about what to do next.

I'll never forget the flash in my mind that came up. "Get loaded first, then figure things out. That's why you bolted."

15 / Peddling Softcore and Swag

Nearly eleven months of clean time, and all I could think of was heroin. Knowing it was a sick idea but ignoring that thought, I figured to borrow some money from brother Frank. So after a bus ride and a boat trip across the water, I was in Brooklyn less than two hours later, making a beeline for Frank's apartment. As I got there I knew he was in because I heard a radio playing behind the closed door. When I knocked, Frank turned the radio down and came over to see who it was through the peephole. ''Vinny, goddam. What are you doing here? Daytop just hung up with me on the phone, and they said you left. What the hell are you trying to pull this time?''

He hadn't opened the door for me yet. ''Open the door, Frank, and I'll tell you all about it.'' He knew exactly what I wanted, since I was following a thirteen-year habitual pattern. ''No way, Vinny. Go back to Daytop where you belong.'' I thought as fast as I could and pleaded. ''Come on, Frank. I'm your brother. Open the door.''

''Vinny, I don't have anything for you. I got no money, and I got no junk. Go back to Daytop.'' I knocked again, four or five times, but all I could hear was the radio playing full blast. Standing there frustrated as hell, I flashed, ''who else in Brooklyn?'' and came up with Angela again. I turned to walk over to Angie's place, only a few blocks away.

Luckily or unluckily enough, she was home, and more than glad to see me. When I said who it was, she flung the door open and hugged me. We talked a bit and I borrowed fifty dollars and the name of her connection, who lived about a mile away. I took a cab and in less than ten minutes we reached the corner I wanted, and I spotted the buy, named Dink, standing out in front of a barber shop. I called out to him, but Dink wasn't thinking too straight by the look on his face. His eyes were half-closed and totally sunken, and drool was running from the corner of his mouth. He looked in my direction but had a lot of trouble focusing. "Hey, it's—Vinny. Vinny Marino. What? Am I dreamin'?"

I held onto his right arm to be sure he didn't fall down. "Yeah, this is a bad dream, Dink. You got any dope I can cop?" He was so out of it that even when we got to his apartment, he couldn't find the keys for four or five minutes, and I was anxious as hell. He dipped into his back pocket for the key, and I helped him zero in on the lock.

I opened the door and walked straight into an experience that nearly put me in shock. The filth of the place was appalling, and it smelled like a mixture of urine and burnt matches. More than a hundred paper plates from take-out places were scattered all over the room so you couldn't even see the furniture anymore. The cockroaches were as big as your finger and having a ball, and green mold was growing on all that dead food. I almost retched until I saw the tinfoil of junk. It stood out like a diamond, and I went for it blindly, picking up one bag for inspection.

I turned back to Dink. "Here's the money." I handed him a twenty for four bags. He stuck the bill in his shirt pocket as I asked, "Where's the cooker and your works?" Dink didn't answer; he just started throwing paper plates around and finally came up with everything we needed. I tied up my arm as I queried Dink further. "Hey, I've been clean for a year. How much of this will I need?" He shrugged at me. "I dunno, Vinny. Take one bag and see."

So I loaded the cooker and added some water, then lit a match to get it all going. "This is insane," I was thinking, just as the glow hit my stomach, causing the familiar nauseous feeling. I didn't even get the needle out of my vein before I heard myself saying, "Here you go, doing exactly what they said you would. Right back on the same lousy track, and you're still on probation. You left Daytop before they released you, dummy, and you're going to be violated for it." When I looked over at Dink and took in the filth of the room, a bolt of fear shot through every fiber in my body. It was the first time I could remember getting hyper on heroin when I shot it.

The thought of slipping back into the madness of the streets sent me out the door as fast as I could manage. Panic-stricken, my only thought was getting back to Daytop as fast as I could. I jumped in a cab and had the driver take me to the ferry where I boarded a boat for Staten Island. Inside an hour and a half I was standing at the front door of the house, and a wave of relief hit my body, as I thought, "I'm home."

I banged on the door and stood back to wait with a grin on my face, like I was expecting my mother to come let me in. Instead it was an ex-junkie named Jenny. I could tell she knew I was stoned to the gills, straightaway. Her face went totally white, and her mouth fell open. "Holy hell! It's Vinny!" She reached for my hand. "Hi, Jenny. How've you been?" I said—or something stupid like that. She had me sit in the prospect chair while she called Art to let him know who had just blown back in, high as a kite. Within three minutes Art came down the stairs with Jack Karola. I could tell by the looks on their faces that I was due for the dishpan, but suddenly the thought of slinging soapsuds was more than a little bit funny, and I was laughing out loud when Art got to me. "Alright, Vinny, what the hell did you do?"

I looked up at him and toned down the smile on my face. "Art, I took a walk, and I'm sorry. I want to come back." He told me flatly, "Give me your money and the cigarettes. Sit in that chair, and don't move off it without my permission. And don't talk to anyone. You got that?" I nodded in agreement and gave him what he asked for, then sat back to float with the heroin.

They left me in that damn prospect chair for over fifteen hours, and I nearly went nuts sitting there. First I was high, but then it turned to depression and paranoia. I felt as if I would have to stay inside an institution for the rest of my life because I couldn't be trusted out on the streets. Leave me alone for ten minutes out there, and I would find a needle like a magnet in a haystack. I was a weak and dangerous bastard, maybe even the "communicable disease" that the judge had accused me of earlier.

At six in the morning, Karola came down. "Go upstairs, shave, and take a shower, then hit the basement. You have fifteen minutes, and don't talk to anyone." I nodded, stood up to stretch, feeling the pain of being in one position for so long. A shaved head was coming, and I wondered why they wouldn't cut it first, then let me shower. But I did just what Karola told me to do and went down to the basement on time.

A black guy named Lenny was the "Mohawk" specialist, and that's exactly what Karola told him to give me. He cut it all off except for a triangular tuft in the front, making me look like a total idiot. Before I got out of the chair, Karola had grabbed a plastic container of baby powder and dumped about half of it on my head. I couldn't see for the dust, and I wondered if there was any point in taking the humiliation, but I stayed there and kept my mouth shut. Karola told me where it was at, saying "You're a baby, so we're going to treat you like one. Stay right here."

Next Karola got me a complete female wardrobe, which he brought in with a grin on his face. "Put these on, little girl," he said, handing me a skirt and a blouse. I gave him every bit of visual disgust I could muster without saying a word, then did what he said. The blouse wouldn't button, it was too small. I had to leave the zipper open on the skirt, so everything looked ridiculous. But, Karola wasn't finished.

"Okay, Vinny, come on upstairs. We're having some special signs made, just for you." When we got into the sunken living room, he showed me the sandwich boards. One said Sorrento as a reference to my singing as a cook, and the other said Eat at Momma's. He had me tie a rope between the two and hang them over my shoulder while he went to the broadcasting system and announced a general meeting right away.

Karola dragged the prospect chair into the middle of the living room and told me to sit in it, just as all the residents started to gather for my special session. I felt like crawling under the rug but stopped myself short. When everyone had gathered in the room, Art started off. "Okay, Vinny, would you mind telling everyone what the hell you're doing here?" I kept it low and humble. "I wasn't thinking when I left, and now I want to come back." Art hit me again. "Why did you leave?"

"I made a mistake." Art looked around at everyone in the room and said, "What do you people think of this baby? Should we take him back?" Well, that was like opening up Pandora's box because everyone I had ever stuck before with a play on words or a practical joke came at me with heavy things. "Why should we take you, asshole? You ain't worth a shit, yet you think yours doesn't stink, using all them big words. You want everyone to think you're an intellectual of some kind and then go out like a baby and stick a needle in your arm."

This harassment went on for nearly two hours before one of the coordinators stopped it. "Alright now, Vinny. What do you want from us?" I looked at him and made a plea with my eyes. "I need your help. I want to come back." Karola cut in. "Okay, tell you what. jenny, you go up to the attic and sit there. Vinny, you get down on your knees and scream at the top of your lungs 'I need help, please somebody help me!' until Jenny hears you. Jenny, don't come down until you hear him. Got that?"

She said yes and took off up the stairs, while I thought about making a mad dash for the door. Karola stopped me, saying, "Down on your knees, Vinny."

As I knelt down, I felt nauseous and said to myself, "Look at the position you got yourself in this time. Look at this childishness, the embarrassment. This is sick, and you're stuck in the middle." With that I screamed for nearly five minutes before Jenny came down with a grin on her face.

"Vinny, we're going to take you back, but only on a stiff contract. First of all, you are nothing but spare parts until we tell you otherwise. You are on duty twenty-four hours a day, whenever you're needed. You take your meals to the basement and eat them. You sleep on the couch alone in this room from midnight until six a.m. And you get one cigarette every two hours, but only after you ask Ellen for it. Other than that, you don't talk to anybody." (Ellen was one of the chicks I used to throw out of the kitchen in my days as a chef. She didn't like me at all.)

Getting up off my knees, I wondered about there being some reason for this sort of treatment. I couldn't think of any. I knew the contract would last at least thirty days, and I considered walking out the door but pulled myself up when I thought about the shaved head and violating probation. Without doing any more serious thinking, I went to the bathroom and started cleaning up.

It quickly became a matter of whether or not I was going to break under the pressure. I made up my mind to ride the thing out, grit my teeth, and go all the way. The first thing I did was cut way back on my smoking. I had been up to a pack or so a day, but I would only approach Ellen for a smoke two or three times a day. Next, I made up my mind to do all the work absolutely right so there would be no repercussions from the white-glove inspections. I cleaned the barbeque grill until the damn thing shined. Even the boss commented on how nice it was before he had me take a toothbrush and get up a ladder on the front porch to scrub the decorative trellis.

I thought of taking off many times, but it was a strict 'survival' thing that kept me going. I said nothing and did my work. The same thing was true of the games, general meetings, and seminars. I said the absolute minimum. Of course everyone came down hard on me for being quiet, but that didn't change my mind. I was learning a lot about conditioning myself as a discipline I didn't enjoy the conditions, but it seemed a good way to inject some self-restraint into my system. I felt okay about the way I was standing up under the workload and the humiliation.

About two weeks into the exercise, the boss, whose name was Eddie, was getting aggravated with my silence. He ordered me into the bed of a pickup truck we had. "Get in the back, Vinny. You, me, and Jabbo are going over to pick up the groceries for next week." I didn't say a word as I jumped in the back of the truck and sat down. Eddie said, "Ready?" and I banged on the cab with my hand, signaling thumbs up. He jerked the damn truck into gear and went whizzing down the street. We were doing at least sixty by the time we hit the first bump. It sent me straight up into the air about three feet, and I hit hard on my tailbone. I knew right away that I was hurt so I turned over on my side and banged on the cab again, signaling pull over to Eddie.

When we got to the curb he rolled down his window. "Yeah, what the hell is it?" I came back with a grimace, "Christ, man, you hit that bump and cracked the hell out of my ass. I think you broke a bone."

He gave me some bullshit about me manipulating him, but he finally drove me back to the house. I had to go have Xrays at the hospital. Nothing was broken, but I was badly bruised. The doc gave me Darvon for the pain and recommended "complete bed rest" for ten days. Technically, I was still "spare parts," but now they were bringing me Darvons three times a day, plus all my meals. LaCosta came up and we shot the shit, then usually played cards to pass some more time.

Naturally, I played out the bed rest period to the maximum. When I got up and around again, Art called me into his office. "Vinny, we're taking you off the contract, effective right now. I hope you learned something from it. You're being assigned to the service crew." "Thanks, Art," I said, "I did learn something." By the time I got back downstairs, Art had gone on the PA system to make the announcement about the end of my contract, and several people clapped.

So it was back to the same old routine, but I kept my act strictly in line and made a point of avoiding all confrontations. Within another month I had made "ramrod," Daytop slang for straw boss. One day I got an itch to get back into the kitchen, so I spoke to Karola who agreed to it with some restrictions—only on Sundays, and "Understand this. You give no directions, you take no directions. You're not involved in set up or clean up, just cooking." I looked at him with sincerity and said, "Thanks, Jack. I'll do exactly that, and I appreciate the break."

When the first Sunday came, it happened that all the staff had gone out for some reason. The only person on the staff left was Butch, the expeditor who had caused me to bolt the last time. I was in the kitchen after cooking breakfast, hanging up my towel and just about ready to leave, when Butch walked in and came up to me pointing his finger. "Vinny, take those two garbage cans out to the dumpster and empty them."

My back was somewhat better, but I was still not supposed to lift anything, especially not garbage cans that weighed thirty pounds apiece. "Look, Butch, Jack Karola gave me this job and he specifically told me to go in and cook, nothing else. I'm not supposed to give any directions or take any either. Besides, my back is still bothering me."

He got a mean look on his face. "Asshole, with everyone out, I'm issuing the orders in this place, right now. And I'm telling you to take out those cans. Do it." I put my hands on my waist and looked down at this character and told him flatly, "Butch, I have no intention of picking up any garbage cans."

He shook his finger at me again. "Are you saying that you're defying a direct order?" I pointed my finger in his face, "No, Butch, what I'm telling you is that if I do anything with those garbage cans, it would be to lift one up and bounce it right off your thick skull. Now get out of my way."

Later that day, when all the brass got back to the house, the loudspeaker went off within minutes, and I knew Butch had blown the whistle. "Vinny Marino, report to the Director's office." I started in the direction of Art's office, figuring I'd take a verbal haircut for threatening Butch but nothing more. When I got into Art's place eight or nine people were sitting in the room, all senior staff, and then there was Butch. Art spoke to me first. "Vinny, do you know why you're here?" I said, "I think so."

"Well, why are you here?" I thought for a moment. "There was an incident with Butch in the kitchen. He wanted me to carry out some garbage cans, but Jack had told me not to do anything but cook, and besides my back is still bothering me. I can't lift anything heavy like that." Butch broke in sideways, pointing his finger again, which irritated me. He whined, "That's not what happened, asshole. You threatened to bean me with a garbage can, that's what happened." Art asked me the next question. "Well, Vinny, did you threaten Butch with that?" I looked at each one of them personally, pleading for nothing but common sense. "Look, I did tell him that but only after . . ."

Butch sliced in, "Shut up. Look, Marino, you ain't runnin' this program the way you want it, you're gonna follow the rules. We've looked at your track record, and we have decided that you didn't learn anything from the first contract, so we're putting you back on a new contract, and we're gonna shave your head again. Get down to the basement."

That did it. I felt something snap in the back of my head. I walked straight over to Butch and stood not six inches from his chair. "My little man, you are not going to shave my head. If anything, you might get your jaw broken, but that's all. On the streets you were a piece of shit and a fucking weasel. Now in here you hide behind the rubber-bullet bullshit power they gave you. Well, I say fuck you, fuck every other asshole in this room, and fuck Daytop."

I mock saluted the crew, then did an about face, and walked like a Nazi out of the room, slamming the door as I left. Going down the hall, I remembered I had no clothes to speak of, so I dispensed with the idea of packing and headed straight for the front door and freedom. I looked at the woman at the desk and snapped, "I'm going to New York. Hang my tag under the 'permanent outs' will you?"

Outside the very first thing that occurred to me was money, the fact that I didn't have any and what to do about it. I headed in the direction of the bus stop, figuring to try an angle on the first person I met. I passed a corner drugstore, walked in, went straight to the cashier, and gave her a story. "Miss, you might not believe this, but I just lost my wallet or someone stole it from me, I don't know which. All my money and cards were in it, and could you lend me five dollars just to get home? I live in

Jersey, and I give you my word that I'll get it back to you, either in person or by mail. Can you help me out, please?''

She was young, maybe nineteen or twenty, and she went for it. She gave me five dollars and told me her name was Kathy Naylor. I got the store's address, promising to mail back the money that same night.

On the Staten Island Ferry, it dawned on me that Daytop would be making phone calls to everyone including my probation officer, telling them I had split the facility again. I called Hamilton as soon as we docked. When my probation officer got on the phone, his response let me know that Daytop hadn't called him yet. ''Oh, hello, Vinny. How's it going out there?''

''Well, Ray, that's what I wanted to talk to you about. You see, I've been at Daytop for a little over a year now. I've learned a lot and I'm cured of heroin, so I want to get back into the mainstream of life, go out and get a job, maybe even have a family. I want to leave the facility now, and I would like your permission to do it.'' Hamilton didn't think twice. ''Vinny, if you walk out the door, that very minute I'll violate you and have you locked up within the hour.''

''Look, Ray. Please listen to reason. Daytop is an institution, and nothing ever happens in the place. It's all dull routine. I've been in over a year . . .'' Hamilton didn't listen to reason—at least not mine—but he sure stood his ground. ''Marino, you listen to me because I'm not budging on this. You belong in Daytop and you're gonna stay in Daytop. That's all there is to it.''

I swallowed hard, and bit the bullet. ''Ray, I thought you were a human being. Instead, you motherless cocksucker, fuck you and your probation too. I'm hangin' up on your ass and if by chance we should meet, *then* we'll discuss how much time I owe or I don't owe.'' I sat on a bench and started to think about where to go and who to see. Frank and mom were definitely out of the question, because both the cops and Daytop knew where they lived, and there would be warrants out on me within two or three hours.

What about pop? He was living with another woman then, so I hadn't seen much of him at the facility. I figured I would give him a call. He might have a couple of job leads. Above all, I knew there was no way I could get into heroin and stay out of the joint. If I started up with the junk again, I'd have to start stealing, and sooner or later I'd get busted. I intended to keep my act clean and stay out of sight as much as humanly possible.

I called pop at work and asked for help finding a job—a new one from me. He told me to meet him in an hour at the limousine service where he worked as a chauffeur. Pop was genuinely elated as soon as he laid eyes on me. From more than ten feet away, I threw open my arms and yelled, "Hey, pop! How you doin', pop?" We got into our old bear-hug routine, jostling each other around, laughing, and doing some small talk. "You sure are lookin' good, son."

"Yeah, pop, I feel great too. No more drugs for me, you can believe it." We went to a bar where pop ordered a beer and I got a Coke.

"So, Vinny, did you finish the course?" "Yeah, pop, I graduated. Now it's time for bigger and better things. I need to get a quiet job so I can get back into things slowly. You know any chauffeur openings or doormen jobs?"

"Not off the top of my head, but why don't we go downtown to a couple of clubs and see who's around the old neighborhood? You know, around Hester and Elizabeth." Of course he was talking about Little Italy.

We drove in pop's car down to Little Italy and spent about two hours drifting around, talking to various people until pop spotted a guy called Little Jackie, an old school chum. Those two got together and talked about old times for a minute until pop introduced me. As soon as I saw the guy I liked something about him, and I could tell he liked me. Within five minutes pop was asking him, "Jackie, you look at this kid. He's honest, hard working, and he's got some brains. Any job openings for someone like that?" Jackie thought of a slot almost immediately. "There might be something I can do. Tell you what, Vinny. Meet me at ten tomorrow morning. Here's the address," and he wrote it down on a piece of paper, then handed it to me.

Pop had a few more beers, then we went to his apartment where I slept on the couch, dead to the world. In the morning pop had to be at work the same time I was due to meet Jackie, so he got me up. His girlfriend was already at work, he explained. "She has to be there by eight. You'll meet her later."

The only aspect of the upcoming deal with Jackie that bothered me was the location on Forty-second Street. It was perilously close to my old operating area on Forty-third, and I knew that proximity could spell trouble, but only if I let it. I kicked the nagging question out of my mind and headed into a spray of hot water. After the shower. I cooked up some egg omelettes for me and pop, which he said were excellent. As we went out his door together, pop gave me fifty bucks until I could get on my feet.

When I got to the number Jackie had written down, I peered in the window to see a combination pornographic bookstore and "marital aids" shop. A beady-eyed twerp was sitting behind the counter, and he hit me right off as a second-class thief from the streets. I went in and asked for Jackie, and he rang a buzzer next to the cash register. Within twenty seconds Jackie appeared from behind a door in the rear of the store. He motioned to me, and I followed him into a storeroom that was nearly empty except for a couple of dirty magazines and a desk with two chairs. Jackie ran down the operation for me, explaining that this and another store nearby were a front for his partner, a Jewish guy named Abe. Jackie said he was responsible for manning the place and for protection. Then he told me the problem. "I think the clerks are robbing us blind, Vinny, but I'm never here, so I can't prove it."

I looked him directly in the eye. "Nothing gets past me, Jackie. I'll find out what's going on in no time." Jackie was obviously pleased with my attitude and eagerness. "Vinny, I like the way you handle yourself, so I'm gonna give you a shot. You come in at eleven tomorrow, and I'll show you the inventory and the details of the operation. I'll start you off at two hundred cash a week, and then we'll see what happens to the profit picture. If it improves, then there'll be some bonus money for you. You're on from eleven to seven, six days a week. How's that?"

I wasn't looking at any better opportunities, so I extended my hand with enthusiasm. "Jackie, I'll take it. And you'll like the results. I'll see you at eleven tomorrow." He smiled as I got up to leave. "Okay, kid. Take it easy."

My only thought was to race over to pop's garage and let him know what had gone down. Hearing the news, he wanted to "take a break and have one beer." But I declined. "Pop, I'm going to start working tomorrow, so I gotta get settled someplace. I can't stay with you and your lady." Pop told me Grandma Rosa was in the hospital for a while, and I should approach her about staying there for a while. He had a key. It sounded like a plan, so I said I'd visit her and ask her myself.

But before I could go anywhere, I needed a change of clothing. I called Angela about retrieving the bag I had left at her place the first time I bolted from Daytop. She was home, and I shot over on a bus and got the suitcase and even remembered to pay her the forty-five dollars I had borrowed. Angie was high when I got there, so nothing seemed to matter to her. I thanked heaven for being off the junk myself, but I couldn't say anything to her about what she was doing to herself. All I told her was that my grandma was in the hospital so I had to get there in a hurry. She nodded and scratched her face, mumbling, "Okay, Vinny. See you later."

Repaying Angie tripped a signal in my head. "You still owe that girl in the Staten Island pharmacy five dollars." I stopped off in a post office, bought a pre-stamped envelope, and wrote a note to her. "Dear Kathy, Now I can tell you the truth. I am addicted to betting the horses, and yesterday you were kind enough to let me buy a winning ticket on number four in the eighth race. Enclosed is your share and thanks again. Vinny Marino." I stuck a ten dollar bill inside and sealed the envelope, then mailed it.

Grandma was not well when I got to the hospital, and it was obvious they were giving her drugs for the pain. Her eyes brightened somewhat when she saw me, but I could tell she was slow to react. I sat there on the edge of the bed for thirty minutes or so, holding her hand and offering what consolation I could. When I asked about her apartment, she patted my hand and said it was okay.

I went back and got the key from pop, then took a train downtown to Elizabeth Street. I was thinking about being alone in my grandmother's apartment with all those candles and statues of saints. I also thought about pornography and whether it was legal to sell the stuff. I decided it must be, otherwise the joint would have been raided and closed down. Once I hit the streets of Little Italy, everything seemed to come alive again, and I walked around for maybe two hours after dropping off my bag, checking out all the sights, but by ten o'clock I was stretched out on grandma's bed, totally exhausted.

The next morning I was back with Jackie on Forty-second Street learning all about the inventory downstairs. He told me that most of the stuff on the shelves was soft-core because the raw, hard-core material was illegal. Then he told me to memorize a certain phone number that was my connection for anything a customer might want in the hard-core category, Abe's business. After that, he introduced me to the clerks in both stores. When he was ready to leave, he closed by saying, "Just spend a couple of days getting a feel for the operation, and then we'll discuss it."

"Okay, Jackie, will do. I'll keep my eye on the clerks for you, too." For the first two or three days on the job, I just wandered around both stores, acting as if I was counting the merchandise and noticing how weird the content of the material was. The customers were equally weird. Some of them would try to sneak into the store, like nobody was supposed to see them.

During the first week I made two clerks who were stealing, and Jackie fired them both. Then during the second week I caught a third clerk in the act. He tried to act like a tough guy when I busted him for it, and he had the balls to try getting me in on it. Incredible as it may sound, I never stole from Jackie's operation the whole time I was there. Instead, I got fairly adept at stealing from the customers—indirectly. I was moving back and forth at random times between the two stores, tending the cash registers and watching carefully what the clerks were up to. I also noticed how funny a lot of the customers acted, especially the guys who headed for the gay magazine section or some other figazi stuff like "butch" or "dyke" books.

It was obvious that most of them wanted out of the store as fast as they could get out, so I took maximum advantage by stalling with their change. If a porno magazine cost two-fifty and a guy handed me a twenty, I'd immediately put the rag in a bag and give it to him with a smile. I'd take out the fifty cents in silver and put that in his hand but then I'd hesitate just a second before reaching for the seventeen dollars in paper. It was amazing how many of those weirdos would simply take off out the door, forgetting their change. After six weeks on the job, I was successfully hitting at least three, maybe four customers out of ten, and on the average, only one of them would come back to squawk about the loss, and then I always cooked up something to convince them they had made a mistake.

As I would up my second month on the job, nearly everything was looking good from my point of view. Jackie and Abe were thrilled with the extra money since the inside stealing was now almost nil. Jackie gave me a raise to $250 a week plus congratulations on a job well done. Then I was making an extra $25 or $50 a day using the stall at the register. The best part was that I didn't have to be there until eleven in the morning, so I had my evenings free and could still sleep late.

The only troublesome thing was a possible bust for selling hard-core material. As time went on, I got to know everything that was available—dogs, ponies, two ladies, whatever. And we were doing quite a business with that stuff, so there was a risk of getting arrested if the heat came in while I was on the cash register. I didn't give it much thought on a day-to-day basis, but it was in the back of my mind.

Word quickly spread among all my old addict friends in the area that I was back in town and running the porno stores. A lot of them would stop in to bullshit for a while or offer me swag, and I slowly started to move some of it for them in various clubs around Little Italy at night. By the end of the third month in porn, I had branched out into selling enough stolen merchandise that I had to store some of it in the back room. I figured I had better check with Jackie about operating from there before he found out from someone else. When I asked the question, he agreed without reservation because he knew the profit picture I had created for him. With Jackie's green light, I sent out the word to everyone: "Marino is open for business at the bookstore. He'll take any salable swag you got, and he's paying fair prices with no hassles."

My announcement spread like wildfire, and the back storeroom was damn near filled in no time flat. I was paying people 25 to 35 percent of what the retail tag said, or what I estimated, and then reselling the merchandise at 40 to 50 percent of retail. Within a month, I felt like a genuine manufacturer's representative. I was taking orders at night in the clubs around Little Italy and Brooklyn, and then I would put out my "shopping list" the next morning. I even started to complain when I wasn't getting the merchandise fast enough. After a while, I was feeding the fads of two neighborhoods because when one person in a place like Little Italy had something in vogue, everyone wanted it.

As the sixth month rolled around, I was pocketing at least one or two thousand dollars a week just from swag and riding around in a brand new Olds 98 convertible. I had moved from grandma's place to a swank apartment in Brooklyn, complete with stereo and color TV. My mom felt much better about me when she saw I was clean, even though she was nervous about the warrants hanging over my head. I saw pop on a fairly regular basis, usually for a "quick beer" because his lady was demanding and she usually got her way. In order to keep track of all the action accurately, I was working double shifts, from eleven in the morning until midnight or one the next morning.

Everything was together, going along smoothly, and I felt on top of the world. I had money, a new car, two or three girlfriends, and I had been off junk for over eighteen months, with the exception of that one occasion with Dink when I split Daytop.

16 / A Handshake Back to Hell

One night around closing time, I was counting some cash behind the register in store number two, when who should walk in but a legendary character from the neighborhood named Max. Max was the only sixty-two-year-old junkie I ever knew. He always had a smile on his face, though everything on his back was at least ten years old, and he looked like a tattered rag doll. But everybody liked him and the girls on the street would always give him money for something to eat. Then most of the restaurant owners would give him leftover food, so Max used the money to keep a little junk flowing in his veins.

Since it was only Max, I relaxed my guard and went back to counting the money after waving to him. He came forward, extending his right hand as if to shake mine, but instead of taking my hand, he just grinned and dropped two pills into my palm. I thought they were doridens, but I didn't even look closely. Instead, I just followed that old reflex and swallowed them right on the spot. Four or five seconds later I realized what I had done. ''Max, what the hell were those pills?'' He grinned sheepishly. ''Baby aspirin.'' I looked at him hard. ''Come on, Max. What were they?'' Max didn't feel like sticking around for any kind of pressure from me over his gift, so he started shuffling around on his feet while he said, ''See you later, Vinny,'' and out the door he went.

I was so tired I didn't think any more about the pills. I just returned to total the cash register. After locking the money in the safe, I switched the lights off and went to the door, when—*Bam!* —the top of my head blew off from the pills. They *were* doridens, and I was sailing away on that smooth mellow plane I had forgotten for damn near two years.

Ten minutes of walking around in a drug daze and I decided that instead of a drink, "why not just one more shot of junk?" It felt like an incredible magnet pulling me, and I couldn't muster anything from my reservoir of self-restraint. I turned up the street and went looking for the nearest hooker with two bags to sell, never far away in that part of town. At Forty-seventh Street near Duffy Square, where Frenchie stabbed Lorenzo, I found a hooker who used to sell me swag from time to time. She was surprised when I asked about copping because she knew I was clean, but she sold me two bags.

Without thinking clearly, I went back to my car and drove to Brooklyn, patting the bags in my left shirt pocket the whole way home, anticipating high heaven again. I rushed to my room and didn't even close the door before I remembered, "Dammit, no works." Without hesitation I flashed on this neighborhood kid who was a dope fiend and would always handle any swag I brought to him. His building was only two blocks from mine, so I took a chance and walked to the address, then knocked on the door, twice lightly. Harvey showed up and stepped outside, somewhat confused. "Yeah, what's up, Vinny?" I had no time to waste. "You got works, Harvey?"

"Yeah, sure, but why? I thought you were clean."

"Never mind that. Just bring your works and come over to my place. How soon can you be there?" He was probably thinking of a good buy on swag as well as a bag or two of junk. "Hell, right away, Vinny. Five minutes."

"Hurry up. I'll be waiting," and I headed back to my place, nervous as a cat. When Harvey knocked I let him in immediately, and as he dumped the works on the kitchen table, he asked again, "Say, Vinny, are you sure that you wanna do this?"

"That's a stupid question. Here, cook it up," and I threw the bags on the table.

"Vinny, what did you take tonight?"

"A couple of doridens, why?"

"You mean to say that this is your first shot, in how long?"

"Nineteen, twenty months."

"Vinny, you really shouldn't take too much of this, cause it might be dynamite. I'd say half a bag at first, then see." I put the contents of one bag in the cooker, added water and lit a match while I watched it bubble up. I tied up, while Harvey loaded roughly one-half of it into the dropper. Well, I got off into space the instant it hit me, but I couldn't get rid of the thought, "Here you go again, right down the tubes." My response was one of total rebellion, "No way. This was a treat for tonight only." With that I went into a frenzy of sorts and walked all over the room, finally telling Harvey, "Take the rest from the cooker and take the other bag with you." Harvey didn't understand, but he didn't argue either.

Once he was gone, I felt completely drained since I had put in a fourteen hour day, taken the doridens, and then the junk. When the light of the next day finally got to me, it was already quarter past ten, which meant that I was going to be late for work, and I cursed the stupidity of the night before one more time. As I looked in the mirror, I said to the reflection, "Well, what now? You gave in to it once, do you keep going or stop?" Over the next several weeks, I answered the question halfway when I took up what was known as "joy-popping." I might shoot up on Saturday night, then lay off until Wednesday, do it again on Friday, and so forth.

Then, as I stepped back into the street scene while operating out of the porno stores, the traffic in swag I was doing kept building. Someone turned me on to a sweat shop downtown, and I had seamstresses sew Yves St. Laurent labels into shirts I got for two dollars. I also had them put Countess Mara tie labels onto some beauties we bought for fifty cents apiece.

I must have had a working inventory in the back rooms worth at least fifteen thousand, plus we were grossing anywhere from one to two thousand every day. It wasn't long before the pace had me nearly crazy, with all the traffic, the dealing, and the drive downtown to get the orders in after-hours clubs, then making the deliveries and collecting the cash. At the end of the tenth month in the porno bookstores, my habit was back in the range of a hundred dollars a day, and things were getting crazier all the time.

Early one afternoon a young street kid came puffing into the store, obviously on the run. I knew his face but not the name, since I would normally pay him for whatever he brought in, and he would get the hell out in a hurry. "You wanna buy a piece of jewelry?"

"More than likely. What is it?" I couldn't believe my eyes when I saw what he dropped on the counter. It was a brilliant white star pendant about two inches across, with ten perfect diamonds set in platimun at all of the points and line intersections. Each of the diamonds was a full carat, and in my head I calculated that the piece was "worth at least ten thousand tonight in Little Italy." I looked it over carefully with my jeweler's magnifying glass as I asked the kid, "Well, I don't know. What do you want for it?" Without hesitating, he told me, "How 'bout two hundred?" I worked him down to one-seventy-five so he wouldn't see how excited I was. Then I pulled a few scams, selling the piece and reclaiming it, until I finally let it go for thirty-five hundred.

By June of 1967, the vicious circle was tightening into a hangman's noose, but, of course, I was going so fast I didn't see it. Fourth of July was a three-day holiday, and any holiday in New York turned out to be a feast for junkies because so many wealthy people left their apartments and brownstones for Long Island beach cottages or second homes in the country. Also the number of on-duty cops was significantly reduced on those days. That weekend swag traffic was so heavy I was forced to work double shifts all the way from Thursday to Sunday.

When I got to the store each day, a line of ten to fifteen people would be waiting to sell me something, and it never let up until well after midnight. It seemed that every thief and junkie in the city was hustling as hard as he or she could, and I got greedy, buying all of it. By Sunday afternoon, both of the storerooms were filled. I bought furs, leather coats, TV sets, stereos, radios, luggage, cameras, jewelry, dresses, blouses, shirts, ties, shoes, you name it. But I knew it had to be moved because the risk was too great. I figured it would take a rental truck to move it all at once unless I could get a couple of cars into the act besides mine. I rang up brother Frank and asked him and Joey to help. They both agreed to drive over and help me out at one o'clock Monday morning.

Ten-thirty that night, I was shocked when the front door of the store opened and Abe, Jackie's partner, walked in. "Dammit," I thought to myself as he came toward me, "the guy comes in twice a year, and he picks tonight for a visit." I said, "Hello, Abe," and then the only thing I could think of was keeping him the hell away from the back room. I talked about business, but he wandered around the store. Then he made the fatal turn toward the storeroom door. I panicked. "Abe! Did you see the way we redid the shelves in the other store?" He glanced over his shoulder as he opened the door to my warehouse. "No, I haven't. Not yet."

When he saw that room full of swag, Abe's jaw dropped so far his Havana cigar fell out and hit the floor. I put my hand to my forehead and squeezed, hoping I was seeing things or that Abe would suddenly go blind. Instead, he didn't even bother to retrieve his cigar before he looked at me. "What the fuck do you think we're runnin' here," he pointed to the storeroom with his hand, "a Sears and Roebuck? I mean, what is this, Bonwit Teller?"

I recovered as fast as I could. "Ah, it'll be gone by later tonight, Abe. Don't worry." He went wild. "Worry? You're gonna get me arested you dumb sonofabitch!" I tried to calm him down, telling him Jackie had given me the green light. Abe flew off the handle. "Look, I don't go for this at all, and I want this shit gone! Now!"

"Aw, fuck, Abe . . ."

"Don't 'aw, fuck' me, Vinny, or you're fired."

"Fired? Shit man, every cent these stores have made in the last year was due to my efforts, while you sat on your dead ass and collected. Fired! My ass!" Abe got red in the face and went for the door. "No, Vinny, you got it wrong. Your ass is fired as of right now!" and he slammed the front door as he left.

I locked up and got my brothers to come over right away. We loaded all the stuff into the cars and were heading downtown to begin deliveries by one-thirty in the morning. By seven-thirty, we managed to get rid of about half of it, and as the sun came up I figured to get in touch with Jackie to see if he couldn't calm Abe. When I reached Jackie on the phone, Abe had beat me to it. We decided to meet for breakfast and talk things over.

He was already sitting in the place by the time I arrived, and he didn't look all that happy to see me coming. When I was seated, he started. "Jesus, kid, what the hell happaned?"

"Well, I had a lot of swag because of the long weekend, and Abe flew off the handle when he saw it." He looked at me dubiously. "Look, Vinny, I told you it was okay to operate, but with a little shade and common sense, eh." He still had questions in his mind. "Why would you give Abe any shit? That I don't understand."

I shook my head, feeling sorry about what happened with Abe. "Jackie, I want to apologize to Abe. Can you handle it for me?" Jackie looked down at his coffee for a second and then up at me. "I can't do that, Vinny. You blew it. Abe is so pissed he called me last night to tell me he fired you for getting out of line. After all, he is my partner. Tell you what, though, I'll look around and let you know if there's another opening." I forced a smile. "Sure, Jackie. Thanks." He left the rest of his breakfast roll and stood up pressing five hundred-dollar bills into my hand as he whispered, "You did a good job, kid. I'm sorry it came out like this."

Ten minutes after he left I wasn't sorry anymore because I had retired to the men's room and shot up the rest of the junk I was carrying. As soon as I felt good enough to fly, I got into a cab, heading for Forty-third Street, figuring to myself, "Fuck it, let's go. Who needs their warehouse? I'll open my own." So I rented a room at a flophouse hotel where I wheeled and dealed just like before from the stores. I juggled some junk on the side to support my own habit, which was racing toward insanity.

Inevitably, my past caught up with me again. When I was clean and working the porno stores while living in Brooklyn near Frank and his fiancee—a pretty girl named Irene—they would come over to my apartment on a regular basis. I would invite a girlfriend who would cook dinner. But when I lost my job and took a room in the midtown hotel, I didn't call Frank or give up my Brooklyn apartment, so he was beginning to wonder where in hell I was and why he hadn't heard from me. Besides, he was due to be married in September, only two months away, and I was supposed to be his best man.

I had one more-or-less girlfriend in Brooklyn who was puzzled by my absence too. Her name was Tina, and she was a stand-up girl, nice looking Italian, the kind I could take home to meet mom and her boyfriend. Tina had a regular job, and she didn't use junk—she never had. I felt good about my times with her, listening to the stereo and not even thinking about being high on anything else. But that had been back then. When I lost my job I said, "Fuck it all, I'm a misfit, and I'll take what comes my way. Daytop was shit, Synanon was shit, and here I am drowning in junk just like they said I would. So fuck it."

Right after I got fired, I jammed so much junk in my arms, trying desperately to block out the thinking, that I blew my entire bankroll of more than twenty-five thousand cash in less than eight weeks. No sooner did I get really strung out then the heat started coming hard, both on junk and the swag it took to support my habit. The same narc who had busted my old lady Patti was the heat, only now he was raising holy hell on the streets, hitting every addict in sight with a 1533—loitering for the purpose of obtaining narcotics. It wasn't long before all the hard-core dope fiends like me were afraid to go out on the streets. When I was down to about three hundred dollars, I decided, "screw this," and took a cab back to my apartment in Brooklyn. I would pick up my car in midtown later when I could see straight enough to drive.

Returning to my old home turf didn't change anything except the cost of cab fare to my connection in Harlem. Within two weeks, I was standing on street corners selling to old friends and nodding out myself. I was juggling maybe two or three bundles a day, worth $300 to $500 on the streets, which meant that $150 to $200 of that was going into my arm. By then I had decided that there was no hope for me, and as far as I was concerned, there was no future either, only today and my habit.

Early one morning I was stoned out of my mind near an all-night frankfurter stand on the corner of Pacific and Fourth in Brooklyn, a place notorious for who's got junk, who wants to barter pills for junk, who's got swag, questions like that. I couldn't believe my eyes when Tommy LaCosta walked by me. I noticed him first even though I was totally loaded. "Yo, Tommy! That you?" Tommy looked, then smiled, and came right over to me. "Well, I'll be, Vinny," as he grabbed me around the shoulders. "How you doin', Vinny?" I could see through the blur that Tommy was still clean, and he was neatly dressed. "Oh, I'm doin' okay, Tommy, jugglin' maybe two, three bundles a day."

"You look like you're strung out all the way to Shea Stadium. If you want some help, Vinny, I'm with a new organization. Here's my card." I took the card and pretended to look at it, then stuffed it in my pocket. "Yeah, thanks, Tommy. I'll keep it in mind." As he turned to leave, LaCosta couldn't help grabbing my shoulders and shaking them twice. "Vinny, you know this lifestyle ain't making it. Who are you kiddin' this time? Come see me." I nodded and faked a smile. "Yeah, Tommy, I will. I got your card. Hey, good to see you."

The next memorable incident, a week later, was my brother's wedding. By that time Frank regretted having asked me to be his best man. Everyone in the family knew I had lost my job and was hanging around downtown, loaded on junk. Most of the family just threw up their hands in disgust and hoped to God that

I would somehow magically disappear or come up clean overnight. For the two church rehearsals Frank had to come find me, and I was stoned out of my mind. Then he pulled me out of an overdose in my apartment to go get the tuxedos fitted.

On the day of the wedding at the Greek Ukranian Orthodox Church, everyone was as concerned with what I might do as they were about the ceremony. But I had committed to being a nice guy that day, so I only ate three dolophines an hour before the bells rang. Of course, I took along six bags of junk and some works to celebrate all by myself at the reception. Standing next to Frank at the altar, I flashed on the fact that I was twenty-eight, and I had never even seriously thought about getting married.

There wasn't any trouble with Frank's ceremony until the priest asked me for the rings. I fumbled around in all my pockets so fast that some people in the pews of the church started to laugh. Just as I found the bands, the priest started to chant, "Frank, do you take Irene to be . . ." and his voice cracked me up. No one had told me that Orthodox priests actually chanted during the ceremony. I noticed my mother holding her head over in the corner. Later at the reception she told people she thought I must have had "one too many drinks."

Frank's wedding must have made more of an impact on me than I realized because right afterwards I started using dope like more of a madman than ever, sometimes doing as much as $300, $400, or $500 a day. One night about four or five days after their wedding, I was so loaded I couldn't see, but I somehow managed to climb behind the wheel of my car. I drove a short distance until I had to negotiate my way through an underpass, which I failed to do. I racked off the walls from side to side until the car skidded to a stop, blocking the middle of the road. It was two or three in the morning with no traffic, so I just took off the license plate and dumped it in a sewer, then I abandoned the car on the spot.

By this time the hawk had landed in the city, and winter was approaching. Everytime I looked up I got depressed, thinking about how warm Frankie must be on his honeymoon, while I was freezing my ass off in Brooklyn, married to a monkey and a needle. Frank was doing real good in those days with a solid job, while brother Vinny was busy sticking needles in his arm five times a day, looking for relief.

I couldn't help thinking about those two clean years with Synanon and Daytop, and I knew in a flash who was responsible, yet I couldn't answer the question of why I was still running. Then I remembered I had Tommy LaCosta's card from the new program he had joined. I fished it from my wallet and headed for a phone, looking forward to a conversation with Tommy—anything to get my mind off all those haunting questions.

As soon as I got him on the line, I said, "Tommy, I gotta talk to someone. Can I come down there?"

"Sure, Vinny, come right over. The address is on the card I gave you." I told him I'd be there in an hour after cleaning up. But I got hit with a double load of fear and embarrassment since I had left Daytop without saying anything to Tommy. I cursed myself and cooked up one helluva load—almost eight bags of junk—and sent it all in to prepare for my meeting.

Somehow I got through a shave and a shower, into another outfit and a cab ride to LaCosta's office in Redhook. When I got out of the cab it was pouring rain. I was pretty well soaked when I got inside Tommy's door, and of course, stoned senseless. Tommy didn't seem to mind as he came straight toward me with a smile. "Hey, Vinny, it's great to see you. What's new?" He could tell by looking that I didn't know from anything in my condition, but I guess he figured to give me a chance. I stumbled over to a desk and sat in a chair.

I noticed a short Puerto Rican kid who introduced himself as Louie, and he started to tell me in broken English about this new program called Phoenix House. In the beginning I was only picking up bits and pieces because I was concentrating on his classy outfit—an expensive three-piece suit, silk shirt, gold cufflinks. As crazy and loaded as I was, I thought, "If these guys can get to where they are, imagine how far I could go if I applied myself."

That proved to be the challenge I needed because I started doing my best to listen and remember what was being said until Tommy realized my retention level was slipping towards zero. "Yo, Vinny. This ain't gettin' anybody anywhere. If you're really serious about this, get your ass home right now and sleep it off, then come back in here tomorrow morning at nine *before* you get loaded. After we talk, then you can get loaded if you want. How's that?"

I gave Tommy the best positive nod I could and said, "Great, Tommy. See you here again at nine tomorrow." I left with one indelible impression on my mind: "There *is* still a chance." So I stayed off the drugs for the rest of the day, and in the morning I made a point not to disappoint Tommy by being late.

Tommy told me that when I had left Daytop it caused him to do some serious thinking about the pettiness of the place, and then he found out that six exdope fiends from the Morris Bernstein Institute had formed this new program called Phoenix House, which of course was the "ultimate," while Brand X and Brand Z were total shit. "But," he added, "they don't have it set nearly as rigid with the rules, and you can graduate in eighteen months. Besides, there are only thirty or forty people in the program at the moment, Vinny, so you can get aboard and help shape the policy. How's that sound as an alternative to a diaper?"

I looked at him sincerely, and I meant it when I said, "Anything's got to be better than this dead end street shit, Tommy. What do I have to do next?" He told me Phoenix House had a screening facility for prospective redidents called Samaritan House Day Center located in Queens. I would have to attend the center on a daily basis from 9 a.m. to 5 p.m. for about three or so weeks, and by then I should be accepted as a resident into the program. I told him I wanted to start the next day.

He looked me straight in the eye. "Vinny, I think this place will work *for* you and what you want, instead of against you while you're trying to get there. Welcome to Phoenix. We rose from the ashes, you know?" LaCosta laughed out loud as he flapped his arms like wings, and I laughed at the thought of a silly yardbird like me finally getting up off my ass and flying the straight and narrow for one more death-defying attempt to drop junk before it dropped me into the gutter.

As I headed back to my apartment in Brooklyn, I thought about packing up and moving to Queens in order to be closer to the Samaritan House facility. Both Frank and his bride and my mom had recently moved to Queens, and my first hunch was to approach Frank to see what he thought. He wasn't particularly thrilled with the idea, since he and his wife were just back from their honeymoon, but I told him about the Samaritan House program. Frank was still my brother and he still cared. "Vinny, if I thought you were serious I'd invite you for dinner to talk it over with me and Irene. What do you say?"

"What time did you say dinner is served?" Frank laughed. "Seven sharp, Vinny. Don't disappoint my wife because her cooking is out of this world."

Maybe because I was excited about making a commitment to something positive, I went ahead and packed an overnight bag, figuring to spend the night at Frank's or mom's. That way I would be certain to make the first day at Samaritan House on time, ready for the ordeal. My habit was up in the range of $200 per day, and I had made no plans to detox before starting the Phoenix program, so it was going to be cold turkey in a therapeutic community. With that terrifying thought in my mind, I ate the last of my dolophines and headed to Frank and Irene's for dinner.

As soon as I arrived, I knew that Frankie had gone overboard. Irene served some lasagna that was better than any I had ever eaten, and she had taken the time to make fresh lemonade, which hit the spot and kept me from thinking too much about the absence of junk. It was funny to see Frank cuddling and cooing with his new wife, acting as if every question had to be answered by both of them. That was especially true when it came to explaining my plans, and then discussing the possibility of my bunking on the couch until I could be admitted to the Phoenix facility. "Vinny, are you serious? Because I don't intend to put Irene through anything if you're not."

Irene had no idea of what Frank had been through over the years as she said, "Don't worry about me, honey. Whatever you say is fine with me." Frankie smiled and lifted his lemonade. "Then here's to your future, brother. You're welcome here as long as you keep your word." Not long after that, we exchanged good-nights, and Frank hit the lights as I hit the couch to double up and hold in the pain that was already starting to wrench my gut.

In the morning I reached the address Tommy had given me, and after they got my vital stats on the application form, a new group of us was invited to have a seat for a general discussion. I immediately thought of getting out the rear exit. My habit was crashing down around me, causing all sorts of strange and violent reactions in my body. If it got any worse, I swore I'd leave and do a week or two of detox somewhere first rather than face the ugly pain that was wracking my body that first morning. Even the facility coordinator could see that I wasn't fit for active work duty that day. He pulled me aside and said, "Look, Vinny, are you doing any stumblebuttons?"

"No, my problem is junk this time," I said, halfway hoping he'd order me into detox. Instead, he said flatly, "Well, then, if you're really motivated to help yourself, you'll go over to that couch and kick cold, like a man."

I rode out the pain of hell for the next ten days, and I did twenty days in total at the Queens location without being late once. I must have been ready for something drastic at the time because I went through the transit system routine beginning at seven in the morning, worked all day or played encounter games at the House. At five o'clock or a little after, I boarded the rush hour train again for the trip to Frank and Irene's.

As I started to clean up and look better, I would stop in at mom's place on the way home. Again she wanted desperately to believe that I meant what I said this time. She told me that she was quite happy with the man she had married, which was good to hear.

Well, it wasn't long until I was feeling really good about myself again. I got a distinct feeling of personal pride when I thought, looking back over the first three weeks of clean under the Phoenix wing, about how something could actually be done *if* I wanted to do it badly enough. I thought of what it took for me to show that kind of restraint, courage, and balls, when only days before I was so deep in junk I thought there was no way out. I was also exalting myself for the self-discipline I had shown—holding it together under the cold turkey without any added drama-for-effect and avoiding all those people I knew who would have been only too happy to turn me on to "just one bag."

After the first ten days at Samaritan House, when I started to feel better, I wanted a transfer to a permanent facility so I could get out from burdening Frank and his wife. They kept stalling and dragging their feet to see if I was serious, and I kept pushing. Three weeks later I was told I had a bed in the Hart Island facility.

"Wait a minute. I thought I was all set for the facility on West Eighty-fifth Street." LaCoasta was located there, and I didn't want to leave the city if I could avoid it. The coordinator in charge looked at me rather coldly. "I'm sorry, Vinny, it's either Hart Island or nothing. You're due to report in at that facility at ten tomorrow morning." I took the number of the guy I should contact and read it over. "What's this Hart Island place like?" He looked at me and puzzled for a moment, then replied, "That's an interesting question, Vinny. We just opened it recently, and I've never been there. It's in the East River, not far from

Riker's Island. Roughly half of the island is taken up by Potter's Field, the city's burial grounds for indigents. The other half, which Phoenix picked up, used to be a penitentiary where 'workhouse' bits were served out—you know, like thirty or sixty days, minor stuff. More than that, I don't know."

I felt immediately discouraged, especially about being anywhere near a prison again. "Isn't there any way to wait here at Samaritan until something opens in the West Side facility?" He turned and walked away, as he said, "Vinny, do you want to hustle me, or are you interested in helping yourself? Get your ass to Hart Island like you've been told."

17 / Phoenix House Restoration

Early the next morning, as I got aboard a car for the Pelham Bay station, I wondered about being in a prison atmosphere again and how I would adapt to the situation. When the train pulled in at Pelham Bay, I noticed six or seven guys hanging around in the area, and I knew immediately they were dope fiends, so I started asking questions and found out we were all headed for the Phoenix facility on Hart Island. Aboard the boat, the first thing that hit me was Riker's—the Rock. It sent a chill down my spine, and I suddenly felt a wave of relief about heading toward Hart Island instead.

As we debarked on Hart Island, I saw seven or eight prison buildings all in standard drab gray. A van pulled up and a well dressed guy got out, then announced to the crew, "Welcome to Hart Island. My name is Jimmy Selman, and I'm the director of this facility. Please load your gear in the back of this van and get aboard." During the ride the director gave us more information about what we were getting into. "The city abandoned this workhouse facility almost six months ago, and that's how we got it. Approximately thirty people are in residence at the present time, and we're tearing down the 'prison' part and making the place our home. There are no women here, by the way."

When we got out at the first building, I could see what he meant. There were three tiers of dorm-sized rooms, maybe 150 by 200 feet each, and about twenty people were taking off the bars and the gates and painting them almost any color other than gray. Selman invited us to take seats on the prospect bench near the front door of building number one for interviews. He approached me as he glanced at my file. "Vinny, I see that you've been in Brand X and Brand Z. Well, this is Phoenix House and we are completely different, so I want you to forget everything you ever learned elsewhere and concentrate on what we are saying, right here and now. Got that?" I had heard the same thing at Daytop two years ago, but I nodded at Selman and said, "Yeah, Jim, I got it." He looked at me sternly. "Well, I sure hope so, because you're a runner and you've been one for damn near fifteen years, so you don't know everything. Just do what the fuck you're told and don't cause me any problems." Again I nodded.

I ended up assigned to a dorm on the second floor with twelve other guys. After I unpacked and relaxed for an hour or so, I spent a couple of idle hours before dinner snooping around the grounds and the buildings. One of the guardhouses was still manned by Department of Corrections guards, so I asked one of them why and discovered they were only watching over the Potter's Field burial site, which was gruesome. What they did was stack up five or six pine boxes in a trench, cover them with two feet of dirt, and then crush everything with a bulldozer. That first day I found a human skull, which I took back to the dorm and used as an ashtray.

That night at dinner I learned what all the commotion was about on Hart Island as it related to Phoenix House. Governor Rockefeller had gotten a new law passed known as "Civil Commitment for Drug Addicts." It was a program for stool pigeons that worked like this: Say your brother was a drug addict and you knew it, so you dropped a dime on him and called the Narcotics Division and whispered, "My brother is using drugs and I want him committed. Here's where he lives." Of course, the narcs would never say who had sent them, but they would round up the suspected addict, and if they found any tracks or any trace of drugs in his urine, it meant an automatic three-year mandatory sentence. And it was hard time, too, on Riker's Island, like a common criminal, except that a junkie's pen number always started with 967. Phoenix House had been selected to run encounter groups on Riker's for these "committed" dope fiends, and after they had gone through a series running from C to A, an inmate would be eligible for parole to Phoenix House on Hart Island. So we were supposed to be getting ready to accept hundreds of these people over the next while.

After dinner that evening, I was assigned to the service crew, the old standard of cleaning the toilets. In the beginning it was dull, but I figured it was still better than unbolting cell doors and carrying them outside, so I resigned myself and began to take pride in shining porcelain bowls. I set my own schedule and ran right through it, and I was ready for a white-finger inspection any time.

After about two and a half weeks on the island I ran into trouble in the third floor bathroom, where most of the resident staff and status people were staying. I noticed a turd perched on the rim of a bowl one morning, and toothpaste smeared all over a mirror. I wondered for a moment if it wasn't a deliberate move but forgot about that and went ahead with my clean-up. The second day the same shit was in the same place, with toothpaste on the same mirror. I cleaned it up again. The third day in a row convinced me that someone had a jaded sense of humor, so I determined to bring up the subject at the next morning meeting.

"Look, whoever lives up on the third floor, I would appreciate it if you guys would clean up after yourselves a little better. I don't mind cleaning the shitters, but you guys are missing the target, so I have to clean up your shit, and I don't like it. How about a little consideration for the cleaning crew?" No one said anything audible, so I went back to the kitchen and drew my mop and bucket for the morning routine, starting on the third floor. Sure enough, the same turd and the toothpaste were already in place. I started fuming and couldn't wait until the next morning meeting where I laid it out for them louder and clearer, only to have the same mess greet me on my rounds.

Next I went down to the coordinator's office and requested a "special" encounter session, calling for everyone living on the third floor to attend. The black guy who took the information and told me he'd get back to me. Meanwhile, I ate lunch with Johnny Gray, a new friend, and told him what I had done. His face dropped almost into the plate of tuna fish. "Vinny, you're crazy, absolutely crazy to call a special with all that strength. They'll make mincemeat outa you."

I filled my fork and shrugged my shoulders. "I don't give a damn. Someone on that floor is deliberately fucking with my head, and when I'm finished he's gonna know I'm around, even if I don't get to the bottom of it. There's no way I'm putting up with it as part of my 'duty.' They can shove their duties if that's what it includes."

At that point, the expeditor came up to our table and told me my special was set for one o'clock in the coordinator's office. Suddenly I felt leery of encountering twenty-eight people all at once, but then it dawned on me that I had done this sort of thing before, making my presence known in a facility right away.

Now that I look back, I guess my action had something to do with knowing that the staff would inevitably make it harder on me as a result of my confrontation. I must have felt I needed that to stay in line because the higher the intensity, the more I would grow from the experience. As I walked into the coordinator's office, though, I was getting cold feet remembering that the person who called a special usually got his load off, but then the game would come down hard the other way—on him.

"Screw it," I thought, looking over at Selman, then down the ladder twenty-seven times, "I gotta do what I gotta do." Just before I was given the floor to unload my verbal barrage, who should walk into the room but Butch, the sadistic bastard from Daytop, now an expeditor at Phoenix House. I went on anyway. "Look, I don't care about 'position' and titles or anything else. What I care about is that I have to clean up after a bunch of pigs living on the third floor. You're nothing but filthy, inconsiderate assholes to leave shit all over the place, and then you expect others to respect your rubber bullet power plays here in this joint. A lot of guys in here are not like me—I can leave, but they got sentenced to Hart Island so if they leave because of your bullshit, it's back to the joint, and I don't buy it."

When I had finished with the tongue lashing, Selman shocked me when *he* started in on them again. "You know, Vinny's right. I've seen what he's been up against, and you guys are a bunch of slobs." Following Selman, the next three guys in the power line agreed with him, and they even gave me a few strokes for putting up with the same condition over a week's time. I felt good as I left the room.

Two or three days later the loudspeaker in the facility went off with a voice crackling, "General meeting in ten minutes." As I responded to the call, I had no idea that it would be related to my earlier special session, since I thought I had won that one because Selman had ordered the third floor to clean their own bathroom for a week, relieving me of duty up there. As soon as everyone was seated, Selman started with his dialog. "Regrettably, it is now apparent that we have a bunch of pure slobs living in our home here on Hart Island. And we have identified those individuals, so as your name is called, you will stand up and let the rest of the family look at you and know you're a fucking swine as far as your living habits are concerned."

I sat back in my chair with a sigh of relief thinking, "Well, it's about time they busted some of these filthy bastards, especially if I have to clean the shitters." No sooner had I finished the sentence in my head when I heard Vincent Marino, and my heart sank two degrees, beating like hell. "Me?" I thought wildly. "No shit. I always showered twice a day, changed shirts two or three times, and even kept my dungarees neatly pressed. What do they want with me as a slob?"

I had no choice. I stood up with the other fifteen or sixteen people, and then I saw it was a payback for my "special." They were planning to open a second building very soon to be called Phoenix Number Two, and they needed a pioneer crew to go in and start the work. Why not include Marino the troublemaker from the third floor shitter incident?

No way were they going to get away with it, and I said as much to my pal Johnny Gray at lunch. He had also been named to the new slob dorm. I recruited him to round up everyone who would be going there, and we met in the new building that afternoon. No one else took the initiative, so I stood up. "Alright, you guys, here's the plan. If these assholes think we're pigs and that this is 'Slobsville,' someone's going to have to prove otherwise, and I think we can do it. I say we make this dorm the most outstanding on the whole goddam island. What do you say?" Everyone cheered in unison, and we vowed to keep the project a secret until we were ready for the ribbon-cutting ceremony.

The ceilings in those dorms were about thirty or forty feet high, scary from a ladder. Denny Hussong, an artist in our group, went all the way to the top with his talented brush and gave us a life-size dragon breathing fire on the long wall, then a Chinese pagoda and a holy mountain on the side walls. Looking at it, I felt as if we were on the approach ramp to the Bridge on the River Kwai. The place looked great, and we all took pride in what we had accomplished.

As my second month on Hart Island came to a close, I got a job change to the paint crew. Prior to that, I had only watched Denny Hussong paint the mural, but suddenly I found myself twenty-five feet up on a ladder holding an eight-foot pole with a roller on the end, trying to paint the ceiling without getting any in my eyes. Luckily for us it was latex-based paint, so it washed right off when we were finished each day. By then, I was getting the hang of things in the place and meeting more and more people every day as new admissions came in. When it came to the encounter games, I perfected my skills in verbal abuse to the point where I could perform "surgery" and open up a person in no time flat. The staff began to call me in for any specials that looked like they might get heavy. I had already spent two-plus years working with the concepts, so I naturally stood out from the rest of the uninitiated residents.

Everything went smoothly for the next month or so as we unbolted cell doors, took them away, then painted the open dorms in pastel colors. We all worked well together, and it was okay on Hart Island until a change of regime took place at the highest levels. A group of ex-Synanon people had just been hired by Phoenix House with a plan for major expansion of the program. A doctor by the name of Mitch Rosenthal was at the head of the new push, and his two main henchmen were a guy named Natale from Brooklyn and a black guy named Candy.

Not more than a week after the new powers were installed, Candy showed up one day and called a general meeting. "This environment on Hart is totally homosexual. You guys aren't for real; it's fulla shit. This whole joint is so fulla shit that we're going to come in and straighten it out. The first thing we're cutting out is the weekend passes."

I looked down at the floor and thought, "Dammit." We really liked those weekend passes. After a month on the island we'd get them every Friday night, and it was good for a ferry ride roundtrip. Then we each got eight dollars and it was okay to drink "sociably" as long as you were back on the ferry by Sunday night. I used to go and see my family or girlfriends. I must admit, though, that telling a dope fiend to drink sociably was like giving us a license to get loaded on booze. That ferry on Sunday was full of drunks going back to reality on Hart Island.

As time progressed we found out the new chief, Rosenthal, meant business. In a matter of weeks, Phoenix had satellite offices in seven different locations in all of the five boroughs, with the main "mother" house located on Eighty-fifth Street on the west side of Manhattan. The pressure was hot and heavy on the Hart Island residents to get the dorms ready fast enough to accommodate a stream of newcomers. Then Rosenthal invented a new type of game, called the bypass encounter. The director of each facility would select two people with good potential to represent that facility in a game to be played at the mother house, with Rosenthal presiding. Selman picked me and Johnny Gray for the first session, and we were sitting in the room at the main facility when Candy started talking.

All I could think of at the time was how he had set morale back on Hart with his homosexual dialogue a couple of weeks earlier, and I resented the asshole coming on like a god. But I held myself in check and instead addressed the infamous Rosenthal: psychiatrist, doctor, and chairman. I told him how we needed more support from home base and about the pressures we were under to get ready for hundreds of newcomers. Rosenthal couldn't say anything in effective rebuttal because I was coming from raw truth, and he knew it. Nevertheless, Candy cut in trying to save face as he said, "Marino, respect for the chair is in order."

I flashed on him with a mean look and got into it with him about his silly ass power plays. It was obvious that most of the other representatives felt the same as I did about the situation, because once I had opened the door, every one of them came out swinging, either at Candy, Rosenthal, or some other power figure from Synanon.

By my seventh month on the island I was still in the painting crew. In that short time frame, the population had grown from less than 50 people to roughly 250, and new people were arriving at the rate of 40 to 50 per week. We were extremely busy, and everything was changing rapidly. Selman, the director, had become a friend, and I usually confided in him before saying anything to anyone else, and he usually did something about the situation before any real trouble started. About this time we were ready to open Phoenix Number Three, the next prison building to be renovated. Selman approached me right after morning meeting one day. "Vinny, as you know, things are moving fast here in Phoenix. Effective today, they made me area coordinator, which means I'm responsible for the whole island and all the facilities. Simultaneously, I am naming you chief expeditor for Hart Island, and in that capacity you will have fourteen expeditors on your staff to get the job done. Congratulations." I beamed a wide smile and thanked Jimmy. "I don't believe it, Jimmy, but I'll give it my best shot."

"Vimnny, you just make sure you pick up the pulse-beat of the place and get the info to the chief coordinator. Everything else will fall in place from there." So I went into the business of keeping things moving forward in both buildings, and no major problems came up for another month or so.

It was then that the mayor of the city—the Honorable John Lindsay—announced that he wanted to come over to the island and sit in on one of these "revolutionary encounter groups" that were turning so many addicts into stand-up people, and what's more he wanted the session filmed for the evening news. I was one of the people picked to sit in the mayor's group. The day he was due, we were called into Selman's office: "Look, this is the mayor and he backs us. So be careful what you say and whatever you do, don't let him have it with both barrels."

That was too much rope for us. As soon as the cameras and microphones were in place, we opened up on Lindsay and politicians in general with some vengeance until even the cameramen and the producer got involved. Lindsay didn't know what to think as he sat there, but I got a kick out of it and laughed to myself. I learned later that they couldn't use the film because of the language, but Lindsay liked the experience because of "the candor," he said, and proceeded to give Phoenix even more active support. After the encounter session, I had the opportunity to meet him and shake his hand. He seemed a fairly nice guy with a plastic smile, like a politician. What more could you say about someone like that?

The political tie-up that Rosenthal had arranged with the city went something like this: Lindsay had created his own operation for dealing with addicts, called ASA, Addiction Services Agency. Then our chairman, Rosenthal, came up with an idea. The people at Phoenix House would train the ASA people in our methods, and the city would refer addicts to us for treatment on Hart Island or else institute some of the practices used in our other facilities.

We soon learned about this plan to bring these ASA squares in, with their college degrees and making $17,000 to $25,000 per year, for "training in how to deal with the addicted personality." It burned us to the core because we had busted our asses to redo Hart Island for no salary, and every time we asked about a salaried position, the word came back that there was "nothing open." To top it all off, we were being asked to show these squares from ASA how everything worked so they could go out and get even fatter salaries from the city.

The next step for me was a surprise—another promotion. It was my ninth month on Hart, just before our first ASA training, when Selman called me into his office. "Vinny, we're going into a phase of extremely rapid expansion because Rosenthal has arranged for an additional four or five borough centers to 'feed' us. We have to open Phoenix Four right away, and new buildings after that at the rate of one a month, or six weeks at the outside. To handle this flow, I'm making you senior coordinator for the island, to include all facilities and reporting to me." I was stunned and sat down, catching my breath. "I expect you to keep this place in line and act as my primary troubleshooter, Vinny. What's the problem?"

"No problems, Jimmy. It's just that I'm overwhelmed with opportunity." He extended his hand. Within five minutes I was out the door and heading down the hall with my new title dancing in front of my eyes. Then I saw Rick, the hotshot Puerto Rican drug dealer from midtown and my days with Patti in the hotel. As it happened, Rick had attended a center in Harlem and had just arrived on the island that day. He couldn't believe it when I told him that I was senior coordinator for the entire facility.

Less than a week later I was called into Jimmy Selman's office again. "Vinny, we're going to be conducting a thirty-six-hour special marathon to orient the squares from ASA. I want you to sit in on it and make sure they all plug in." I didn't like the idea and asked Jimmy about my options, but he was unwilling to shift. "I want you in that ASA session in case there's a need for quick surgery or if the group isn't progressing. You're good at that." I agreed reluctantly and prepared myself for a dull thirty-six hours with Mayor Lindsay's star employees.

When the session actually got underway, I couldn't believe the stuff that was coming out of these 'bright' guys. Of the fifteen in attendance, we uncovered two homosexuals in the first three hours. Another guy who liked to beat up on kids came out of the woodwork around midnight. By five in the morning—twelve hours into the exercise—it was clear that none of them had their lives straightened out, and yet they were going to be in positions of authority over me and everyone else in Phoenix House. When we broke for a meal at the twenty-four-hour point, I was so thoroughly disgusted I was ready to pack up and leave Phoenix for good. I figured that if that was what I was working toward—becoming a square—I'd rather be a dope fiend.

I was on my way back to my bunk in Slobsville with my head full of uncertainty when I ran into one of my coordinators, Paul

D'Annello, who also happened to be a friend. "Hey, Vinny, what's wrong?"

"Aw, I don't know, Paul. I've had it. The whole system is crazy. How in hell are those ASA guys going to teach anybody anything when they're all dogs? And you know what, Paul? The only difference between us and them is that they have a degree pasted up on a wall, so that makes them saints, and on this side of the fence, everyone is a permanent piece of shit. I can't see it anymore, so fuck it." I started to pack and Paul left.

The next thing I saw was a group of maybe eight to ten guys coming towards me, with Jimmy Selman leading the way. Paul had gone to get him. Nobody said anything, so I was thinking they were going to start with the 'silent stare' routine, but no, they subdued me physically, and about six of them carried me bodily into the Jewish chapel, where Jimmy's group had been meeting before Paul interrupted them with the news of my intentions. They sat me on a chair in the middle, and I immediately put my emotions on ice. Jimmy tried an exercise to get me involved, but it didn't succeed, and I just sat there while the others plugged into the game and let their emotions flow freely. Finally, Jimmy stopped everything and looked at me. "Vinny, what's wrong?"

I hung my head and looked at the floor. "Nothing, Jimmy. Look, out of respect for you I'll sit here until the group is finished, but then I'm leaving." In a flash, my words registered throughout the room and everyone sat still, waiting. I could only think to myself, "Well, asshole, what do you really want out of life? Here you go again, back to the streets, and for what?" Then it dawned on me that what I wanted out of life was to be a part of it, to be accepted, needed, maybe even loved, for myself—not because I had balls or I could steal good but just for being me. It was as if another person inside me had come alive and was burning to get out in the open. I couldn't resist crying. I cried for the anguish of living twenty-nine years with nothing but a tough skin to show for it. I cried for what I had done to my mom and what my pop had done to me. I cried with every individual in the room for more than three hours. Until that moment, I never knew I had those feelings bottled up inside me.

When the session ended, I felt like a new person, and the thought of leaving disappeared. The experience changed my outlook on where I was, which way I wanted to go, and who I wanted to be. From that point on, I gave up fighting the system and started planning on becoming the ethical person I knew I could be. I got a surge of energy from the experience that kept me going for the next several weeks, and at the same time, my relationships with Jimmy Selman, Johnny Gray, Rick, and several others got closer.

As my time on Hart Island approached the one-year mark, I knew it wouldn't be long until I was ready for re-entry, and I could start working toward either a salaried job with Phoenix or a return to the outside to work. One morning before breakfast Jimmy called me into his office and said with a smile, "Well, Vinny, you're coming up on one year with Phoenix, and everyone at the top agrees that you're ready for the next step. If you're interested, Mitch Rosenthal wants to discuss a job for you on Riker's Island running groups for us. What do you think?"

"Jimmy, all I know is that I appreciate the recognition and I feel good about myself, so I'm willing to talk to anyone anytime about new opportunities. Sure I'll see Mitch. When?"

My meeting with Mitch was confirmed for a Thursday, so on Monday at dinner the whole house had a farewell party for me, knowing that I would be moving on. Two days later I said my goodbyes to old friends personally and everyone else with a wave as I boarded the ferry bound for New York and an interview with Doctor Rosenthal about a job directing encounter groups on Riker's Island. I was excited and put on my best act so the meeting came off without a hitch, and I took the job on the Rock. After the meeting I went with my bag to check in at the Eighty-fourth Street re-entry facility.

The next morning I had one of the weirdest feelings of my life when I stood at the receiving door of Riker's Island Penitentiary, thinking about my past and the last time I was there. The first hack I encountered inside was a black guy I knew named Osporne. He had been the hack in my dorm when I was doing time and a mean sonofabitch to boot. I remembered him coming through the dorm five minutes before lights out, shouting, "Okay, assholes, this is Osporne. That's O-S-P-O-R-N and don't forget the E. When I say 'lights out,' if you gotta piss, tie your cock in a knot and forget it. If you gotta shit, stick your finger up your ass and save it 'til morning, cause there ain't no muthafucka hittin' that floor after lights out. Got it?"

As I approached him now, he saw the pass with my name. It said, "Department of Corrections, State of New York." I pointed at it and said, "Official visit. The name's Marino. That's M-A-

R-I-N and don't forget the O.'' Osporne looked at me in shock. ''Wow, Marino! For a piece of shit you sure came a long way.''

I walked right by him, saying, ''Yeah, I may have come some distance, but you're still stuck in the same keyhole. I'm sure glad I'm on the other side of the fence from you, asshole.'' He cocked his hat and wrote something down on his pad, and I went on through five different encounter groups that day. Three days after that meeting with Osporne at the gate, I was called down for my words with Osporne by Natale, who was then the director of re-entry. But I promised I'd cool it, and I kept my word.

Within two weeks of starting work on Riker's my schedule was so hectic I had trouble making all of my appointments on time. Every morning at six four of us did karate lessons; then it was breakfast at seven, followed by a math class. At eight-thirty, we jumped on a train cramped like sardines on the way to Riker's. During the day I would facilitate five groups of fifteen to eighteen men each, then do the reverse ride on the bus and train, since the city had built a bridge to the island. Back at Phoenix, dinner was at five-thirty; and if you had a duty such as clean-up, you did it after the meal was finished. At seven-thirty we had to go one block to the Phoenix Institute on West Eighty-fifth Street to hear lectures from professionals in different fields such as ''What It's Like to Be a Stockbroker on Wall Street.'' After those I would go back to my bunk and read until I fell asleep.

Bottom line, though, I was enjoying myself and making quite a few new and old friends in the process, especially out on the Rock. Several guys were familiar to me as soon as I walked in, and word spread quickly that I was doing encounter groups leading to some easy time on Hart Island. Things were moving along nicely, as I applied many of the concepts I had learned when working at the prison project with Synanon in Reno. Inside of one month, all my groups were filled to capacity, and I had recommended eight or nine guys for Hart Island, figuring that if I could get someone out of Riker's and onto Hart, he'd be a lot better off to start with, and in time what happened to me could happen to him.

The first sign of trouble in Phoenix came from a racial problem, and I found myself caught in the middle. My aggressiveness and quick tongue made me stand out, plus I had become rather tight with Natale. Also everyone knew that my best friend was Jimmy Selman, the area director of Hart Island. Some black people in the main facility resented those connections to power, I guess, because three of them started coming over to where I lived at the re-entry house after the Institute hour, wanting to hassle me over petty stuff that wasn't being done in the house. I calmly explained, "Look, my schedule is packed from six in the morning until nine at night, so you'll forgive me, please," and walked away.

The harrassment went on for two more days, led by two black guys, one I called Fishmouth and the other Little Eddie. The last straw was when Fishmouth started with, "What a fucking mess you got around your bunk here, Marino. You need a lesson in clean-up. Go get a broom and a dustpan, right now." I stood up slowly and surely and said, "Fishmouth, why don't you go fuck yourself? This dorm suits me quite nicely, and besides, I'm not in treatment anymore. This is re-entry, so go shoot your rubber bullets at somebody else." Fishmouth started to fume, shouting, "Who th' fuck do you think you're talking to, asshole?" I got up off my bunk and pushed him out of the way. "Not to you anymore, that's for sure. I'm leaving."

He backed up and went out the door to spread the news at the main house, and without thinking I grabbed a bag in anger and packed it within five minutes. Not bothering to say a word to Natale, my boss, or anyone else, I walked out of Phoenix in a rage acting totally on impulse. Three blocks and five minutes away I got hit by my conscience. "*Now* what the hell are you doing? You know this is a bad move because you haven't finished what you started. You're going to regret this and sooner than you think."

Don't ask me why I didn't act on my instinct and go back to Phoenix immediately, but by then my thoughts jumped to where I'd have to go if I retraced my steps—first, a shaved head, then back to treatment on Hart Island, and starting all over again. It was too much for the moment, so I jumped in a cab and thought of going downtown to the clubs, just to see if there wasn't someone I knew who might have a job opportunity. I wandered around in Little Italy and had a couple of drinks with some old friends for three or four hours, but I didn't hear anything positive about jobs. Then I thought to call pop and see about the key to Grandma Rosa's place. He met me and gave me the key plus a hundred dollars, and I went to Rosa's and crashed without doing any more thinking about where I was or where I was going.

The next two or three days I spent drifting around aimlessly, walking the streets or having a few drinks in the clubs and sleeping a lot. About ten o'clock on a Thursday I went up to the bar in a club on Mulberry Street and caught the eye of an old Tombs cellmate, a guy named Pinto. It came up in conversation that he was running a game there at night and needed a dealer for five card stud. So I went to work for Pinto behind a poker table and did well for myself in monetary terms—four to five hundred dollars for two days' work, but I was bored as hell in no time. To counter the monotony, I started drinking more and dealing odd pieces of swag for extra money, but I wasn't into it and something didn't feel right. I knew the problem within a month: I had learned too much at Phoenix and before that, at Daytop and Synanon. There was just no going back for me, and I couldn't identify at all with the people around me or in the old neighborhood.

It was strange, and I didn't know exactly what to do. I didn't have any dope fiends as friends and didn't want any. It was as if I was lost between the peaks, down in a valley called nowhere. Everything inside my head said, "Go back to Phoenix," but my pride stood in the way.

When I had been out of Phoenix maybe two weeks, someone in the mother house heard where I was dealing on weekends, and four guys came to see me the next Friday night—Selman and Rick from Hart Island, plus two guys from the Eighty-fourth Street facility where I had been staying. I sat down with them and listened somewhat, but again my ego was in the way, and I couldn't admit to them or myself that I really wanted to join Phoenix again. They just shook their heads and reluctantly walked out of the place while I finished my shift. I felt so rotten inside that all I could think of was just one shot to clear up my thinking.

I went to a connection I heard about in the Bedford Stuyvesant section, and by four o'clock in the morning I had a needle in my arm and another dream uppermost in mind. The next morning I looked hard at myself in the mirror and knew that my only hope was to get back to Phoenix House, period. Then, in that twisted state, I said to my reflected image, "Okay, if you gotta go back, you might as well have a little fun before you do it because when you get there, it'll be a shaved head plus a contract in the dishpan."

With that, I got back into dealing drugs again, buying in Bedford Stuyvesant and selling mainly around Pacific Street and Fourth Avenue. I also worked a deal for dilaudid, just as the heat was putting a lot of pressure on the streets for narcotics. By the time the second month of dealing drugs came around, I had enough dilaudid and dolophine tablets to open my own retail operation.

One night late, about two o'clock, I got caught short of junk. I walked nonchalantly into a flophouse hotel at that hour, then stepped into an elevator with three black guys and no one else, and I knew all of them were addicts. They were supposedly going to trade me dilaudids for junk, but two of them pulled switchblades instead as soon as the car started up the shaft. I froze, terrified, and backed up against the wall as the first black said, "We're takin' you off, honky," and waved the blade at me menacingly. Even in my drugged condition I knew they had me so I reached toward my overcoat pocket to give them the pills, hoping they didn't press for money. As soon as my hand moved, the second guy must have thought I was going for a gun, because he lunged at me, and his blade slit two knuckles and a finger right to the bone, because I blocked his move toward my throat.

I wasn't watching the third guy, who didn't have a knife, as he came from the floor with a blindside right that caught my jaw and knocked my head against the elevator wall. I immediately knew something was broken. All I could think was to give them the pills and hope that would distract them. I pulled out the bottle and flipped it up in the air, saying, "Here, man, take it. That's everything I got." The cat who caught the dilaudids stopped long enough to look at the label just as the car stopped on the fourth floor and the door opened. I bolted for my life down the hall, through the exit door and down four flights of stairs without ever looking back to see if anyone was behind.

In the madness, all I could think of was to get home, so I yelled at a cab and it stopped with a screech. At grandma's place the mirror once-again reflected my stupid condition: my right hand cut to ribbons, my jaw obviously broken and beginning to swell, but all I could think of was another fix to calm down enough to figure out what to do. I nervously cooked up eight dilaudids and sent it all in to block out my vision. Soon I realized I had to take action on the cut and have a doctor look at my jaw. I thought of Metropolitan Hospital, and I knew they had a detox ward where I could get methadone.

I wanted to clean-up so I could check back into Phoenix House right away, so I packed a bag quickly and grabbed another cab at close to four-thirty in the morning, telling the driver, "Emergency room, Metropolitan Hospital. And hurry, please, I've been cut in a knife attack." The cabbie didn't like the word *attack* at all. He looked around at me with bulging eyes and rattled, "Yeah, mac, no trouble. You'll be there in no time."

Less than fifteen minutes later, I stumbled into the emergency room babbling, "I've been hurt, you gotta help me." They wheeled me into a room where the young interns went to work and stitched up my hand. X-rays of my jaw revealed a "hairline fracture, coupled with the need for an operation to relieve the pressure." I was taken up to the OR where they put me under anesthesia and did an incision just above my right temple. Then they admitted me to the hospital with a semiprivate room under the temporary name of Mister X as they hadn't gotten my name when I came in.

I woke up in a cloud sometime around two the next afternoon, and I knew right away they had me on methadone, so I relaxed about the threat of pain from withdrawal. I got a mild shock when the wife of a friend of mine from Phoenix House came in wearing a nurse's uniform and headed straight for my chart. When she noticed who I was, her face went as white as her uniform. "My God, Vinny Marino. What are you doing here?"

"Elaine, I don't know how I got here." She picked up my chart and had a quick look. "Vinny, you're lucky to be alive. Why don't you do the sensible thing and go back to Phoenix?" I didn't have the strength to back up another lie. "I should never have left in the first place, but my pride is involved now, and I don't know what to do."

"How about if I speak to Tony tonight and see what he has to say about it?" I nodded from my pillow. "Sure, Elaine, that would be great."

Elaine informed her old man, and he took up the issue with the Phoenix chiefs. They said it would be okay for me to come over for an interview as soon as I was out of the hospital with my wounds healed sufficiently to permit dishpan treatment. I stayed in Metropolitan for seventeen days before checking out to go to my mom's in Queens for a couple more days of total rest. While I was there recuperating, I took the time to call Tommy LaCosta at the mother facility about the general atmosphere and what to expect when I finally darkened the doorstep.

Tommy gave me the inside line. "Well, Vinny, the word is that there's only one place for you—the mother house. Sandy and some of the other people have needs for you, and they don't want anyone else to be put in a position where you might manipulate them. So I would guess that they'll put you on contract right here and keep an eye on your actions.'' I smiled. ''Thanks, Tommy, I knew I could count on you. I'll be there in a day or two. See you then.''

While I sat waiting for the interview on my third morning out, a lot of my friends came up and asked how I was, even though they weren't supposed to have anything to do with me according to the rules. Inside, one of the directors got straight to the point. ''Vinny, we're putting you on a strict contract here in the house, and we expect you to follow it to the letter. We're not going to take your mop because it wouldn't prove anything. You've had over three years of this conceptual training under your belt, so there isn't much you would learn from it. What you need is a lesson in how to *apply* the information, so don't think you're getting away with anything.''

I knew I was supposed to be humble, yet on the other hand I didn't want any favors hanging over me. ''If you want my hair, fuck it, take it. I don't give a shit.'' He heard me and slapped his hand down hard on the table. ''You got it,'' and they shaved my hair to the scalp.

The Phoenix House powers had me sit in the prospect chair for five more hours until the general meeting began. Then the male director of the facility took me into the room where over a hundred and twenty-five people were waiting. He pointed to me. ''You know who this is back with us, and he's on a strict contract. No one talks to him, and whatever you do, don't listen to anything he has to say because every word of it is counterfeit. This asshole is full of shit because he has no ability to apply information, he can only soak it up like a mop and spit it back at you verbally. His tongue is so glib that it's dangerous, so I want everyone to steer clear of him until we tell you otherwise. Has everyone got that?''

There was a resounding chorus from the room, and I knew they had me dead to rights, so I just looked at the floor, thinking, ''It's true. What the hell am I gonna do this time?'' Right then I knew this was my last shot—the final run—because if I didn't make it, I didn't want to live any longer. Life just wasn't worth it. Finally I got the courage up to look at the people in the room, and as I stared carefully at each of them, I knew I had what it would take to be running the facility in less than six months if I put my mind to it and didn't let anything get in my way.

Ninety percent of the time for the next thirty days I was at the dishpan. They had a guy named Jake standing over me, watching everything I did while he worked me like a dog, but it was good because I needed some bastard to hate with a passion as a challenge to keep the soap in perpetual motion and not walk out the door. I thought a lot but, of course, I would say nothing to his face, and nobody in the house said anything to me either.

In the evening encounter groups I said nothing, and nobody uttered a word to me, so I got deeply into my own head with some down and dirty thinking like, "Damn this dishpan and silence are driving me nuts! I gotta get outa here! Hold it, this is your *last* chance. Blow this one and you die." That inner drama played itself out on me so much I was tense as hell all of the time.

One day after twenty-four days of this, a "special seminar" was announced on "Opportunities for a Career in Corporate Accounting." It was dull and I didn't want to go. What I wanted was to get a head start on the lunch dishes. I asked Jake, but he didn't buy it, ordering me to, "Get your ass to the lecture and work on the dishes when it's over."

When I got back to the kitchen two hours later, every dish, pot, plate, glass, and utensil in a kitchen that could feed two hundred people simultaneously was dirty and stacked every which way all over the sink and fourteen feet of running sideboards. I couldn't stand the sight of it, so I tossed my dish towel onto the mountain of plates and muttered, "Fuck it, I can't take this shit anymore. What is this bullshit and what am I? Some kind of fool?"

Just before exploding out loud I stomped off to the bathroom next to the kitchen. Slamming the door behind me, I let myself go at the same time. I cried like a baby and felt sorry for myself, not knowing which way to turn. The only thing that saved me from going over the edge was the thought, "Hey, you let these sonsabitches run you out once before, why do it again?" So I made a resolution and went back to the kitchen to finish the dishes, determined to ride out my contract and do something positive with my life before it was over.

Finally a good turn on the wheel of fortune came my way in the form of the female coordinator at the facility, Pat Moran. It started when I noticed that she was protecting me every once in a while; then it got to be more regular. She tried to make sure that no one in a position of authority started taking out their sick needs on me, which I appreciated. Then one night in a game, two or three people with titles were getting all over me verbally, and Pat started screaming, "No shit, will you leave the man alone? Can't you see he's had enough?" As she sat down I caught her eye and knew immediately that our relationship had just stepped up one level. Pat and I got closer over the next two weeks, as we sat around in the living room after dinner, exchanging stories, acting out charades, or every once in a while playing cards.

When I had been back in the house exactly thirty-one days, the director called a thirty-six-hour marathon. The first twenty-four hours would be spent playing the game, and the next twelve would be the feedback. So at eight in the evening, we all appeared in the second floor lounge, each with a pillow and a blanket, ready to take off on a day-long session of verbal abuse and rebuttal.

The most memorable thing that happened after nineteen hours involved a black girl, a pretty ex-hooker named Cindy, who came down on me real hard for some prank I had pulled on her. She carried on a tirade for almost fifteen minutes before I switched channels to tune it out. Five minutes more and I closed my eyes, thinking that I must remind her of somebody for her to get so mad over one little trick like that. Before I knew it, I had fallen asleep, and she was still yelling.

Somebody was shaking my arm suddenly, saying, "Vinny, wake up," and I looked in disbelief at what I was hearing from the same girl—a plea about how she loved me and wanted to be my friend. She was openly crying as she said it. I shook my head and wiped my eyes as Pat said to me, "Vinny, she needs you. Cindy wants to be your friend."

I screwed my face up into a puzzled look and glanced at Pat, then at Cindy. "Are you fucking crazy? You vomited on me for over twenty minutes and now you want to wipe it off and pretend it never happened with 'be my friend'? Tell you what, Cindy, you make some other friends, and I'll be my own friend. How's that?" It was too much for the group to take, and they started coming down on me for being so rough.

I sighed a big one, then looked all around the room. "Look, I don't want to be this broad's friend because I don't trust her and I don't like what she said to me because there was no reason to say it. You want her for a friend, be my guest." With that, everybody in the session became a shrink with statements like, "Look where she's coming from, she's sincere," and "Why aren't you willing to acknowledge another human being?"

I threw my hands up in the air as if to signal surrender. "Look, if you all are so anxious to have her 'acknowledged,' why don't you do it so I can go back to sleep? I really don't give a shit where she's coming from because I can't trust the bitch, and I'm here to protect me, plus I'm telling you she's not a friend of mine."

Suddenly one of the facility directors named Mary stood up and put her hands on her waist and took a deep breath before barking at me. "Well, I want to be your friend, Vinny. I've got more balls than you and you're a man, supposedly. What do you say to that?" I leaned back in my chair and crossed my arms over my chest. "Mary, there ain't no sense in you getting up because I'm not standing for anybody." She looked at me. "Vinny, no way can you make it without friends, no matter what you think, and I'm willing to be your friend. Now what are you going to do?"

I looked at her for a cold minute before I realized she was right. I gave in and embraced Mary and even went over to Cindy with my arms open for a big hug. I felt like I had let go of some major barrier.

Just then Mary announced a four-hour break. "Get some sleep and set your alarm clock. It's four-thirty now and I want you back in this room by eight-thirty, ready for another twelve hours." As soon as she said *break,* I stood up and stretched before I turned to Pat. "Do you feel like some coffee before you go to sleep?" She slipped her hand into mine as she smiled warmly at me. "Sure, Vinny." I looked down into her eyes and said truthfully, "Pat, I feel really good about you, and this relationship is moving past the friendship stage, I think." She put her head on my shoulder as we walked along, then said, "I couldn't agree more. Would you like to discuss a trap?" "Great idea," I said as I was drawing the coffee. We went off to a far corner to sit down and talk.

We were exhausted, so when I said, "Time to get to bed," after about twenty-five minutes, she stood up immediately with the empty coffee cups and carried them to the sink while I took the sugar container back to the cupboard. We went out through the double doors and down the hall to her dorm, where I kissed her lightly on the cheek before shoving off to fall down in my own bunk, thinking about the future and my relationship with Pat.

18 Even When I'm Innocent

At sometime around eight in the morning, the expeditor woke me up with a reminder that the marathon was due to start again in thirty minutes. I got out of bed, shaved, showered, and was back in the session by eight-thirty.

Exactly two weeks after the marathon, I was mopping the steps one day when a resident named Louie Zinzarella stopped me on the stairs. He told me my brother Frank had called to say that the cops were looking for me. "What for, I wonder?" was my first thought, but I couldn't think of anything since I had already handled my warrants with the probation officer. "Did Frankie say what they wanted me for?" Louie shook his head. "No, they just wanted to know where you were."

Two days later one of the coordinators caught me in the kitchen doing the floor and said to report to Mitch Rosenthal's office, "on the double." When I got inside I saw Rosenthal, Natale, and two other directors all looking rather solemn. "Sit down, Vinny. We just had a meeting with three cops. It seems you're a suspect in an armed robbery that took place during the marathon."

I was shocked. "What?" Rosenthal told me that two of the victims had pointed out my mug shot down at the precinct, and the cops wanted me for "questioning." I looked at each of them, then said, "Is this bullshit or what?" Rosenthal told me he had refused to let them see me, that it was impossible for me to have committed the crime since I was definitely in the marathon, and a whole slew of residents could testify to the fact.

Then Mitch started smiling. "Don't worry about a thing,

Vinny. This could be good for us. It could put Phoenix on the map if the publicity is handled right." I told him flatly to fuck the publicity, I would rather avoid any involvement with the cops. Natale stood up and started motioning with his hands. "Look, Vinny. You're being accused of something you couldn't possibly have done, so we're all going to benefit by it." "Some benefit," I thought as I looked at him, but I said, "So what's the next step?"

"Well," Mitch said, "the cops said they were going to the DA, and then they would issue a warrant." I looked down and shook my head. Again Natale tried to cheer me up. "Vinny, we're behind you on this 100 percent. We're going to hire the best lawyers we can get. I know one of the senior partners over at Dewey, Palmer, Bushman and Wood, and I think they'll take the case."

"Thanks a lot," I said, and then I asked Mitch if I couldn't go out to the library and look up what I had supposedly done in the newspapers. He agreed, and I couldn't believe it when I read that the offenses were three counts of armed robbery and felonious assault with a deadly weapon. I later saw an Associated Press wire that had been sent out while I was still asleep during the marathon break.

> Dateline New York . . . 19 April 1969 . . . At approximately 6:30 p.m. this evening two armed gunmen confronted an elevator operator at an exclusive Fifth Avenue apartment building. Threatening his execution, the perpetrators ordered the man to take them to a specific apartment on the eighth floor. When the maid answered the door the robbers pushed it into her face, smashing her nose and knocking her unconscious. The lady of the house heard the noise and screamed when she saw the guns and the men, then ran into the master bedroom and locked the door. The man of the house was shaving at the time and upon hearing his wife in hysterics, entered the living room and tried to jump one of the gunmen. He was savagely pistol-whipped for his efforts, then handcuffed with the elevator operator to the leg of a couch. The two children, aged ten and twelve, were threatened with violence and forced to enter a closet which the criminals locked them in. Next the gunmen gained entry to the master bedroom by shooting off the lock, and they handcuffed the lady to the bed and told her she would

> be shot if she made any noise. The robbers ransacked the apartment and made off with an undertermined amount of cash and approximately $15,000 worth of jewelry. One of the culprits was reportedly disguised with a false rubber nose and dark glasses. Police are looking for clues and no suspects have been arrested . . .

The newspaper article in the library stated that one of the gunmen had dark wavy hair (no mention of scars), while my mop at that point was only about half an inch long and looked almost like a crewcut from the shaved head I had gotten when I came back to Phoenix off the streets. As I walked out of the library, I couldn't believe the whole thing was real.

Natale set up an appointment for me to meet with my new lawyer, and when I got to their office in midtown, I was surprised to see that one of the partners—Dewey—had been governor of the State of New York. "Maybe these guys have the connections to cut this thing short." I was invited in to say hello to Mr. William Whitsett Brandon, otherwise known as Cap. He made a point of establishing the fact that they were quite a reputable firm but had never before handled a criminal case and were only taking it on as a favor for Phoenix House—at no charge for their services. He asked me the standard questions about where I was when the crime took place, and I told him the only truth I had. Cap asked me whether I had any witnesses, and I asked, "How many do you want?" He didn't seem too concerned after hearing my side of the story and said he wouldn't be surprised if the cops just dropped the whole thing, but if they did come again to be sure and call him.

Two days later in the early afternoon Zinzarella yelled at me up a flight of stairs. "Yo, Vinny. There are three cops at the front door looking for you. Go hide in the bathroom on the fifth floor, and hurry." "Damn," I was thinking as I hustled up the stairs, "even when I'm innocent I'm running." As I got behind the door of the crapper and locked it, I remembered that three cops always meant they *knew* who they were after and were going to arrest him—they're not "investigating" or "questioning" anymore—someone is going downtown in handcuffs.

The bulls handed Mitch the warrant for my arrest, and he objected vehemently. "It's impossible for Vinny Marino to have committed this crime. We can account for every minute of his time for a thirty-six hour period, and we have over a hundred people who can testify to that fact.'' The biggest of the cops said, ''Look, Dr. Rosenthal, we're just doing our jobs and what this here warrant says is that he's wanted to be in a lineup at the precinct tomorrow. If I were you, I'd have him there.''

That night Rosenthal called me into his office again. He, Cap Brandon, and seven other people were on hand to help formulate my strategy in the case. The trouble with my alibi was that the crime had taken place at six-thirty, and we had started our break at four-thirty. When I left Pat at her dorm it was five-of-five or maybe even five. That meant I would have had to get a wig and a gun, sneak past the expeditor at the front door, join my partner (whoever he was), take a cab or drive somebody's car all the way downtown to Ninth Street and Fifth Avenue, bust the door down, pistol whip some people, get rid of the haul somewhere, shoot back to Phoenix House, and sneak back in undetected once again, shave, shower and reassume my role on time in the group with not even a nervous twitch to show for it.

''Some dude in the prosecutor's office sure has a vivid imagination,'' was all I could say to Cap, but we agreed that it would probably be best to show up at the lineup and be cleared of the charges. Cap suggested that Zinzarella might accompany me as a possible witness, and we could even throw him in the lineup if we wanted. Everyone got excited about holding a news conference the next day, after I was cleared at the lineup. They thought we'd make the evening news, and I felt like some weird kind of hero.

Zinzarella and I showed up with Cap Brandon as the clock on the cops' wall stood at ten-of-ten—ten minutes before we were due in the lineup. I checked in with the desk sergeant and let him know I was fulfilling my obligation under the terms of the warrant. He got what I said without too much effort and showed me and Louie into a room with bright lights, a one-way mirror, and an elevated platform. Five plainclothes cops were already standing on the stage, and one indicated toward us to come up. Numbers running from one to eight were painted in black on the wall behind each one of us, and I went to the end of the line and stood in front of number seven, just for luck. Through a loudspeaker a bull said, ''Number five, turn to your right,'' and then ''Number seven, turn to your left.'' A chill shook my heart as I did what he said. ''Back front, number five and number seven.''

What I didn't know was that on the other side of the mirror were the man and woman who had been robbed, the maid, the front and back elevator operators, the maintenance man, and another guy who had seen the bandits as they left the building to hit the street for their getaway. The man on the street "wasn't sure of anyone he saw." The maid and one of the elevator operators said it was one of the cops, and the maintenance man and the other elevator operator said it was "definitely no one in the lineup." And God Almighty, the primary victims—a man and his wife in their forties—both pointed their right index fingers at me, held a conference, then agreed as they said, "Number seven is one of the men who robbed us." I didn't hear what they said, of course, but the cop standing with them sure did. He broadcast a direct message for me. "Number seven, go through the door in the back of the room on the left."

I should have known there'd be a cell behind that rotten gray steel sonofabitch. I couldn't believe it when a cop met me as I opened the door. He told me he couldn't quite believe that they had identified me either, but he had to book me and then lock me up until I could be arraigned. I wanted an opportunity to talk to the victims because I was figuring, "Hell, if someone pistol-whipped him and threatened her up close, surely they would remember a face like mine with a scar on my mouth, one over my left eye, and another on my chin. Yet they never mentioned any scars to the cops at the scene of the crime, and he supposedly had only said 'dark wavy hair.' "

The cops must have sensed something about the case because for the first time in my life they didn't handcuff me while I waited for transportation. In fact, we sat around and shot the bull about the Yankees until it was time for me to go. When I stood before the judge, Cap made a special point about my residence in Phoenix House so bail was set at only five thousand dollars, extremely low for the crimes I was charged with.

I knew it would only take around $250 in cash to spring me, so I assumed that Mitch and Phoenix House would go for it. But no one was there to cover my bail, and all I knew was that I was heading for the Tombs one more time. As we rode toward Center Street, I wondered if I would still be classified as a dope fiend and sent to the cattle floor.

Dead right. My stomach turned over as soon as the elevator door opened, and I got hit with the acrid smell of urine and vomit. I was checked in just when everyone was locked out in the day room, and it was like old home week as I immediately recognized fifteen or twenty people from the streets. Since I looked good and healthy—unlike most of them—they were eager to know where I'd been for so long. Finally one guy asked, "Hey, Vinny, what are you in for this time?" I almost laughed as I heard him because in the joint no one ever admits to being guilty, but I answered anyway. "I got a real bum beef. Three counts of armed robbery and assault with a deadly weapon." Of course no one believed I was innocent.

After talking a while, I plopped my ass down on the nearest bench to do some serious thinking. My mind raced to the thought of surviving the circumstance, and all I could come up with was, "Well, at least I'm lucky to have been living in Phoenix House when this damn thing happened. If I had been loose on the streets no way would I ever remember where I was, much less what I was doing at a particular time. Plus I had witnesses—a bunch of them—who could testify as to where I was at the time of the crime. But then, what the hell was I doing in the Tombs, locked up like a junkie?"

When they had us go back to our cells, I ended up with a black addict who was kicking a mighty habit. He was all doubled up in pain and moaning like someone had stabbed him in the guts. As I sat on my steel bunk with a dirty wool blanket watching that character kick cold, it brought back a vivid picture of my earlier days, and I felt good about my condition, even though I was locked up. At about eight-thirty that night, a hack came by with an announcement for me: "Marino, pack it up. You got bail."

As I descended in the car, once again a free man, I thanked the clouds above for the fact that I wasn't using junk and hadn't committed the crime in question. Then the thoughts turned to thanking the guys from Phoenix who had undoubtedly gone my bail. When I walked out into the fresh springtime air on Center Street, I was shocked to see my brothers standing there waiting. I walked right over and gave them both hugs and a smile. "Hey you guys. What are you doin' here?"

"We just went your bail, brother," Frankie said. "What are *we* doing here, you ask." I looked at him rather puzzled. "You mean Phoenix wouldn't spring for it?" Frankie shook his head. "No, hell no. Mitch Rosenthal gave me some cockamamy line about them being a nonprofit organization, so they couldn't get involved." "No shit," I said and thought to myself that Mitch was probably afraid I might bolt on the bail, and he'd lose his five thousand because I had left the place just a couple of months before that. The question of whether I was trustworthy must have been foremost in his mind.

Anyway, I said to my brothers, "Look, I'm really starving. Let's get something to eat, whadda say?" We had a good meal together, and I went back to Phoenix House. No sooner had I set foot in the living room when someone announced I was out on bail. Lots of folks started yelling, and again they made me feel like a hero of sorts. Suddenly I didn't take the situation all that seriously. I was still counting on that old line, "Justice will prevail in this case," and I joined the crowd to celebrate over coffee.

The next night my attitude changed when Cap came over to "interview" me about the facts in the case. I asked him, "What are you interested in all those details for? They're not important. All you need to know is that I was asleep in the house at the time." Cap looked at me intently. "Vinny, you may not think it's important, but we must tear that day apart, backwards and forwards. The DA is looking for twenty-five to life for you, so I would suggest that it's time to get damned serious about this. Not only that, the victim and his wife are convinced it was you. They're being adamant about it." I held my misery-filled head in my hands. "Cap, how can those people be convinced it was me when I was here the whole time?"

"Yeah, I know, but that four-hour break came at the wrong time. It is *possible* for you to have done it, although it's not probable. I'd like to make the odds a little better in our favor, if we can." Over the course of the next ten days, Cap came to the house nightly around seven and spoke to each person who had been in the marathon, plus the night man and anyone else who might have seen me moving around for any reason between five and eight o'clock on the fateful night of the crime.

Time dragged on under a gray cloud until a month later when the grand jury held their hearing and indicted me based on the only evidence they had: a positive identification by the two victims. I was shocked and scared at the same time, and I started to take the whole thing real seriously because if that one went wrong, I would end up behind bars maybe for the rest of my life. I looked over at Cap when they handed down the indictment. When the judge asked me, "How do you plead?" I said loud and clear, "Not guilty, Your Honor," and for once in my life I really meant it.

The heavy emotional thing that day in court had to do with the man and his wife who were the only ones accusing me. They both took the witness stand, and it gave me chills when the prosecutor first asked her, "Now, Mrs. Robinson, is the person who committed this crime present in the courtroom?" Without the slightest hesitation, the woman pointed at me angrily. "Yes! That's the man, right there!" I couldn't believe what she was saying, and I wanted to plead with her about how she had to be mistaken, but I never got the chance to cross-examine. Then her husband sat in the hot seat and repeated the same goddamn lie, or was it truly a case of mistaken identity?

Either way I stood to get burned as a result of what they were saying. Cap even questioned the man about the fact that neither he nor his wife had mentioned any scars on the gunman's face, and yet, "Vincent Marino has three very distinct scars on his face, scars you would certainly remember if he were the guilty party." Robinson stood up in the box to answer Cap's question, pointing at me and shouting, "I don't care how many scars he does or doesn't have, that man right there threatened my life, beat me with a pistol, said he'd kill my wife and kids, broke the maid's nose and robbed our apartment!" With that he sat back down, and I felt like crying out with the anguish of total innocence, but there was nothing I could say, under "the law." Because the court calendar was crowded, the trial was set for January 12, 1970, six months away.

Back at Phoenix House the days passed into weeks, and then the months flew by until October when the leaves started to turn. All through the summer I kept my mouth shut and my nose flush to the grindstone so that nothing interfered with my progress and learning. I was mainly into self-discipline and lots of reading. When my thoughts did drift to the upcoming trial, I usually dismissed them with, "All we can do is call on the Phoenix people to tell the truth and hope for the best."

Because of my good attitude, Zinzarella had me come to his office one day from the service crew job and told me that I was being named chief expeditor of the Eighty-fifth Street facility, effective immediately. I would be under nine coordinators. I thought about my earlier prediction of running the place in six months and smiled.

A meeting with the nine coordinators was soon called, and they were all happy I had been given the position since they knew I had the same job on Hart Island—plus I could run meetings, play a good encounter game, and still maintain my sense of humor, which was the secret to everything. As they sat down in the lounge all around me at our first meeting, my primary interest was to get some motivation back into the house—the "hum," that "feeling." They were all eager to know exactly what I thought of the way things were going and what changes I intended to make.

I begged off for the moment, telling them I just started. They pressed on with, "Come on, Vinny, you've been living here. What's missing?" Again I withheld commentary. "It's too early for me to tell you anything meaningful." One girl in particular wouldn't let up, as she said, "This is the first time I have ever heard you at a loss for words, Vinny. Come on, you're fresh eyes. What do you think?" I looked at her seriously. "Do you really want the truth, from the top of my head?" They all nodded, so I let them have it. "Okay, there are nine of you coordinators, and that's eight too many. We only need one."

In a flash they all went crazy and started babbling incoherently, just like I knew they would. But inside of two weeks eight of them got job changes and were rotated to facilities where they could get something positive accomplished instead of tripping over each other looking for make-work projects. By the time a month had gone by, Louie rotated my last boss and congratulated me for getting things buzzing again. Then he promoted me to the highest position a resident could hold at the facility, senior coordinator.

I had just assumed my new position and title officially when someone in the higher echelon got the bright idea that Phoenix House should take advantage of its nonprofit status and begin to set up raffles, selling the tickets all over town. I was given the responsibility of the midtown turf, and of course as the mother house, we were expected to outsell all the other facilities. We borrowed a truck, tables, and chairs from the warehouse, and covered the theater district from Forty-third to Forty-eighth Streets between Broadway and Eighth Avenue. Every block had a table set up with five or six residents at each location, and each table had one person in charge who was responsible for the well-being of the crew. Then I sat down with them at length and explained: "This is a very bad area. There's lots of drugs, lots of hookers, and lots of action. I'm sure, like me, that some of our people may run into dope fiends they knew before coming into Phoenix House." I didn't like the whole concept of selling raffles. To me it was just another form of begging, but I was doing exactly what I was told to do.

So six nights a week we were loading up the truck with tables, foghorns, raffle tickets, literature, and ex-junkies, driving down to Broadway where we sold chances for a dollar apiece. Inside of two weeks we were getting nightly quotas assigned, like two or three thousand dollars for my eight tables. The quotas meant that we had to stay on the streets until early morning, and what bothered me most about the whole enterprise was that my prediction unfortunately came true. By the end of the first two months with the raffles, fourteen people had split and in all probability gone back to their prior lifestyle. Some incredible pressure came down on me out there. At least fifty different people stopped to offer me drugs. Of course they saw I was clean and looking good, but none of them wanted to forget the ''old Vinny,'' and they knew how crazy I could be in that condition. It took a tremendous amount of self-restraint to keep myself from slipping into another concealed stairwell for ''just one more shot,'' my famous line from the past.

Back on the legal front, Cap Brandon was busy taking the depositions of everyone involved with the case, and one day he said that the district attorney wanted me to take a lie detector test. We weren't sure if that would be in my favor or not so we decided to try a private one first. When that came out neutral, Cap and I figured to do one for the DA as it wouldn't hurt. The time for the test came and Cap accompanied me to the DA's office, where they hooked me up to a polygraph. A mean-looking detective had me sit in a chair and started with the questions: ''Okay, Marino. Did you leave Phoenix House and rob Robert Robinson on the night of April 19?''

I tried to think as clearly and unemotionally as I could and then told the truth with a simple no. He barked a second question from his standing position. ''Isn't it true that you forced an elevator operator to take you to Apartment 8-D at Nine Fifth Avenue the night of April 19 at approximately 6:30 p.m.?'' I looked at him calmly. ''No.'' In all, I said the same no to ten or twelve loaded questions like that before he took a break and left Cap and me sitting alone in the room.

Five minutes later the detective came back in the room. ''Why don't you tell me what you did, Marino, because the machine says you're lying.'' My lawyer objected immediately, and I was wondering what the hell the cop was trying to pull when Cap got me out of there without making a statement. I concluded it was bullshit because I never heard anything else mentioned by the DA's office about the results of that test—it was never brought up again. My instinct that you couldn't trust the rat bastards who supposedly represented law and order was just reinforced.

At the same time life was beginning to get very political at Phoenix, with six or seven directors from different parts of the city trying to force the incumbent regime to step down and out. I was caught in the middle as the senior coordinator of the mother house, and I didn't like the trapped feeling at all. The outsiders came by our place for various meetings and tried to pull me in with them, but I felt I had no real choice in the matter because Mitch and Natale had arranged for my lawyers. No way did I want to start all over again with a new attorney, aside from the fact that it would have been very costly, something like fifty grand. So I tried to stay clear of the issues by telling them that my loyalty was to Phoenix House, no matter who was running it.

Incredibly, the existing powers held on, and all of the active insurgents got fired within a week after the ballots were cast. I could relax on that score and concentrate again on my duties within the administration. Phoenix House was grateful for the way I had handled myself and rewarded me with "graduation," which meant I would be earning a salary of $5,200 per year as the house manager. The only unfortunate part was that my girlfriend, Pat Moran, also graduated and was rotated to a facility upstate, so that ended that. We said our goodbyes and thanked each other.

The internal political flap at Phoenix had stirred the pot quite a bit, and suddenly a lot of new faces showed up with all kinds of new titles. Before I knew it, I was reporting to a new area director, and a new regional director was installed named Jerry Brode. Naturally as soon as Brode found out who his secretary was, he told her to call a regional meeting for Monday.

What Brodie had on his mind—primarily—was to let us know about his support and enthusiasm for the raffle program. I couldn't believe it. And then he landed on me directly. "Marino, I want you to personally lead the midtown crew. It made the most money for us last time, and I want the pace stepped up. Put tables all over the place and involve all the residents." I looked at him plaintively. "Jerry, you're my boss and if you want me to go to midtown and sell raffle tickets, I'll do it. But I am not taking any residents with me because too many have split and gone back to the streets. Besides, if we're preaching self-help, we should start up some legitimate business and get out of the monkey business of begging people to buy a chance on something.''

He boiled over at the mere suggestion that the raffles weren't the best invention to come down the pike since pantyhose and told me to shove it and do as I was told. I folded my arms across my chest and let him have it as easy as I could. ''Jerry, taking residents out on the streets is dangerous and foolish, so I'm not doing it. I'll take certain selected staff members with me, but I'm not going to take any residents. I don't think it's fair to them.'' Brode stood up in anger and flat dictated to me. ''Marino, I'm telling you to do what you're told, or you're fired. I'm chairing this meeting, not you.'' I just excused myself and left to go see Frank Natale.

Frank agreed with me, but he couldn't change the raffle program, he said, because so many of the big guns were fascinated with the idea. What he could do was find me another job, but that meant a rotation. By then I had started up a relationship with another girl in the facility, a pretty blonde from Minnesota named June. We had been together maybe a couple of weeks, and I wasn't anxious to let her get away if I could avoid it, so I asked her how she felt about a rotation. ''Vinny, I don't care where I'm located, really.'' I patted her backside and waited for Natale's call.

At around four o'clock his secretary asked me to come over for a meeting, and when I got there Frank was all smiles. ''Vinny, sit down. I think you're going to like this. How about a rotation to Phalan Place House in the Bronx and a job in the financial office? It's in a different region than Brode's. How's that?'' I figured anything but more of Jerry Brode, so I said, ''Great, Frank, but what about my relationship with June? Is there any way she can rotate to the Bronx with me?'' Natale picked up his ballpoint pen and scribbled quickly on a pad as he said, ''Yeah, I might be able to arrange something for her, but you report in tomorrow morning. I'll make a call and tell them you'll be arriving.'' I stood up and offered my hand.

The next morning Natale had arranged for a car to drive me and my possessions to my new residence. When I was all squared away with a private room at Phalan Place, I went back downtown to the business office to meet my new boss. His name was Bernie, and he introduced me to my list of duties. Within ten minutes it was obvious that I was going to be nothing but a glorified messenger boy. But what the hell, at least it was something new for a change. He told me that I'd be making bank deposits and delivering invoices, things like that. With the pressure of the upcoming trial, I didn't care and just got behind the job and did what I was told.

But sometimes when I had nothing to do in the office, I used to peek at the various houses' financial statements, looking to expand my areas of responsibility. Having worked clinical before, I knew that any time a resident was put on the dishpan or some other disciplinary action was taken, they automatically had to give up either their WAM (walking around money) or, if they were in the re-entry phase, their stipend. That—coupled with the profits from the vending machines at each facility—amounted to real money, which was not being returned to the financial department as it should have been. Because of this money, most of the houses had extra slush funds, and it turned out that the facility directors were keeping the money—not for themselves but for letting the residents go out at night, special food treats, stuff like that. Their intentions were good, but then I figured the money to be an average of fifty dollars per facility per month, and much more during the warmer months. We were really talking about over ten thousand dollars a year—too much money was falling between the cracks. So I tightened up on it and saved quite a bit of hard cash.

One month on the job and I had upgraded it to a position with status simply because I was saving so much money, and everybody in power knew it. With my own car and a personal driver, I became the official troubleshooter for the financial department, and I no longer did the bullshit clerical work. Instead, I was driven weekly to each of the Phoenix Houses where I looked at their books. The directors really couldn't do anything about it, even though they resented my destroying their slush funds, because I represented Frank Natale, co-director at that time.

People would erect all kinds of barriers to keep me at arm's length or try to get me to forget what I saw in black and white, but my ultimate loyalty was with Phoenix as an organization, and I busted every wrong number I found regardless of who was left holding the bag. In no time I got the ultimate ambition and wanted to have a look at the foundation books, where the big money was found in public and private grants. That was really the bucks as the budget was $6 million in one fiscal year then.

As it happened, an outsider was in charge of those records, and the closer I got to an appointment, the more slippery he got with excuses. When I finally made an informal demand for an audit, I immediately got a job change to induction. But that was fine with me because I was more interested in spending Christmas with June. After all, I was about to turn thirty-one and face the biggest trauma of my life.

19 On Trial for Life

Court trials in real life are not as drama packed as Perry Mason's writer would have you believe. Instead, they are tedious and drawn-out, boring to the point where I felt like leaving my own trial on several occasions.

Two days before our first court appearance, I was in Cap Brandon's office talking about our strategy at the upcoming proceedings. Cap briefed me on the important issue of testifying myself. "Vinny, according to the law, if you elect to take the stand, the DA has the right to bring up anything from your prior record, and you can bet that he'll do his best to paint an ugly picture that shows this incident as a logical extension of your long history of crimes. But if you stay off the stand, the prosecution can only present the facts in this particular case. Therefore, we strongly recommend that you do not testify."

I looked him square in the eye. "How can I sit still and say nothing when I'm innocent?" Cap nodded in sympathy with my point. "I know how you must feel, Vinny, but what about when the DA starts playing your arrest record to the jury?" That convinced me, and I agreed to keep my mouth shut throughout. What I didn't know then was that the trial would take thirteen grueling days and that I would feel like the focal point of an incredibly long encounter group with no chance at rebuttal.

As the curtain went up on the trial, the judge struck me as a man who had been leafing through books most of his life. His face was gaunt and bony—an ashen color that reminded me of what it must be like cooped up in "chambers" all day. The judge's name was Tiernan, and he wore a set of wire-rimmed glasses that his grandfather probably gave him when he got his law degree, a half century ago. They were bent slightly out of shape and hung off balance from his nose. As soon as the assistant DA prosecuting my case started to talk, he spelled trouble in capital letters. His name was Barry Wiseman, a young Jewish guy who thought that the way to win the jury over was to keep on talking, no matter what he had to say. Wiseman also had a flair for asking loaded questions by bringing up facts with one distortion included to see if the person giving testimony would pick up on the little twist he had inserted.

The longest part of the whole ordeal came at the beginning when Brandon and Wiseman had to agree on a jury of twelve of my "peers." As soon as the judge said the word *peers,* I started to wonder where in hell anyone could locate *one* more person like me, let alone a dozen. It took three full days, from ten in the morning until four in the afternoon, for everyone to be satisfied with the panel.

On the fourth day of the trial, the judge announced it was time for the prosecutor to call his witnesses. I knew the victims would be first on the stand, and by that time we had one hell of a conflict going on with them, which centered around Phoenix House. Mr. Robinson owned a chain of clothing stores, and several people from Phoenix had approached him before the robbery for donations, which he gave. The trouble came when he found out that I was from Phoenix. He pushed hard to have me arrested in the first place, even though Mitch Rosenthal and the others were ready to testify that it was impossible for me to have done what the Robinsons said. He then tried to maneuver some people at city hall to have me jailed until the trial came up. He gave strict orders to his maid not to accept service of Cap's subpoena to take her deposition because the maid had picked one of the cops at the lineup, so Mr. Robinson obviously wanted to make sure she didn't say anything to Cap. Cap felt all these points should be known to the judge and the jury, but the judge turned him aside, telling Cap to go to the Commissioner of Investigations with his complaints.

With that matter closed for debate, the judge asked the prosecutor to call his first witness. Of course, it was none other than our man Robinson. Wiseman didn't help my case when he took Robinson back through the scene of the crime and had him re-enact all the fear and horror associated with being pistol-whipped, handcuffed, robbed, then seeing his wife and children threatened with violence. Wiseman went over each detail, placing heavy emphasis on the amount of blood all over the place. "Mr. Robinson, you were struck many times about the head with a pistol?"

"Yes, I was, maybe ten or twenty."

"That many?"

"Yes, that many."

"Was there a flow of blood?"

"A lot of blood."

"Profuse blood?"

"Yes, running everywhere."

"And was there blood on the carpets after the robbers left?"

"Yes, there was."

"And was there blood on your clothing?" Robinson answered yes one more time, and I started thinking that Wiseman should work in an acting school where he could easily teach people all about dramatically overplaying the courtroom scene. Even still he wasn't finished. "Did you make any attempt to stop the flow of blood while the robbers were still there?" Robinson replied with his first no, and the DA pressed on. "So the blood was falling in your face and down your neck?" Robinson waved his hands toward the jury and looked like he was pleading with them. "Blood was all over the place." Wiseman was nodding in preparation for his next "bloody" question when Cap interrupted. "Your Honor, I think we have established that the witness was bleeding profusely as a result of the attack on his person. Can we please move on with the questioning?"

Everyone in the room sighed with relief when the judge agreed and instructed Wiseman to make his next point. The DA proceeded through the stitches Robinson needed, the scars left by the cuts, and the headaches he suffered for six months after the robbery. Finally, they got to the part I was vitally interested in—the robber who pistol-whipped him. Of course the DA skipped direct questions about descriptions because there was a discrepancy between what Robinson had said ten minutes after the crime and what he said later at my hearing. His original description to the detectives included "long wavy hair" and then at the hearing came up with "combed back dark hair, a little bit wavy." Cap effectively pointed out that Robinson was changing his story and sat back down after the DA's objection was overruled on the point.

Wiseman was clearly distressed as he asked Robinson, "How well was your apartment lit up the night of the crime?"

"It was very well lit."

"And did you get a good look at who hit you with the pistol, then handcuffed and robbed you?"

"A very clear look."

"And is that man who attacked and beat you in the courtroom today?" Robinson looked at the prosecutor but avoided my eyes because I was already staring at him. "Yes, he's here."

"Yes, and who is that man? Can you point him out for the jury?" I folded my hands and tried to look as contained as I could because I knew what was coming. Robinson raised his head and pointed a finger in my direction. "That's him. That man right there." I wasn't sure whether to remain absolutely motionless or start shaking my head, no, you're mistaken. To make some kind of reasonable move I leaned over and started whispering in Cap's ear as if I wanted to speak, but obviously I couldn't say anything. What other possible move was there when I was sitting at the defendant's table, not guilty for the first time in my life, and a man who was severcly beaten and robbed was saying that I did it?

Cap started to cross-examine Mr. Robinson and got straight to the heart of the matter. "Now, Mr. Robinson, do you recall what your answer was when the investigating police officers at the scene of the crime asked for a facial description of the man who attacked you?" Robinson hedged. "No, not exactly." Cap was ready for that one, and he called for the police report, offering it as evidence.

Cap continued his questioning. "Now, Mr. Robinson, did you make any comment to the police the night of the crime about any special marks or scars on the face of the man who attacked you?" Since the line was left blank on the detective's report, it would have been perjury for Robinson to say anything but the truth. He murmured a weak no as Cap pushed on. "And isn't it true, Mr. Robinson, that the first time you 'remembered' the scar on Vincent Marino was at the lineup, three weeks after the crime had taken place?" Robinson looked at the DA for some reassurance, but none was forthcoming. "As soon as I saw Marino I remembered the scar."

Cap made me nervous as hell, but he played his cards beautifully as he said, "May I ask that the defendant rise and approach the jury box?" The judge nodded, and I stood up and walked over to the twelve people deciding my fate. Cap lifted his right hand toward my face and started talking while I folded my hands in front and locked my eyes on each juror directly. "Ladies and gentlemen of the jury, please look at this man carefully and assume you had never seen him before this moment. Do you notice any marks on his face? Is the scar on his mouth at all obvious to you? And what about these other three marks and scars?" Since I had no choice I kept looking at each one of them, knowing that I hadn't done anything and that the discrepancy in Robinson's testimony might be the turning point in the case. I saw several jurors nod their heads, and I felt a lot better as I walked back to my seat.

Next witness for the prosecution was Mrs. Robinson, and of course she told the same story as her husband, with the DA coming down hard and heavy on the bloodbath again. I knew the pointed finger was coming up once again so I wrote a note to Cap suggesting we ask for a recess. He agreed and got the judge to give us twenty minutes. As we walked out to the hallway, looking for a place to have a quiet meeting, my insides were exploding with the weight of what Wiseman was saying. Plus he was playing up the drama of the crime to get the jury to agree that *somebody* was viciously beaten in truth, so let's put *somebody* in jail for it. The trouble was that Robinson was really a somebody while I was a junkie nobody facing a lot of time in prison.

I was furious when Cap couldn't find an empty office. "Look, Cap, I gotta talk to you in private. I'm sick of hearing all this shit from Wiseman with the added drama-for-effect." Cap opened the door to the stairwell, and we stepped in there as I closed it behind us. I let go with a verbal barrage that must have lasted fifteen minutes. "Goddam it, Cap, you can't let Wiseman run it like that with the blood. He's trying to involve the jury in the fucking drama instead of who did it. And you need to object to him faster. No shit, the judge says 'strike that from the record,' but who says the jury's got to strike it from their *minds*? I'm going crazy, not being able to talk out there!"

Cap tried to calm me down by opening his briefcase and hauling out some transcripts as he said, "Take it easy, Vinny, I think we're looking alright. That's just Wiseman's style, and I don't think I have to bend mine to match it." I didn't have the luxury of free time to screw around with, so I looked him directly in the eye. "Cap, this is my life we're talking about, and I don't want you to *match* the asshole, I want you to *beat* him to the punch out there. I know you want to be the 'gentleman lawyer,' but this one is a street fight, and you're caught in it so you can't afford to lose.'' He saw my point and agreed to keep Wiseman down a little if he could.

As the judge banged his gavel to reconvene the testimony, Wiseman still had the floor, and he came on as hard as he could with Mrs. Robinson. ''Now, ma'am, we keep referring to this man who beat your husband with a pistol. Is that man in the courtroom today?'' As expected, she pointed the finger at me, and it was duly recorded.

When the time came for cross-examination, Cap spent twenty minutes or so having Mrs. Robinson review some specific details at the scene of the crime before he finally asked her the crucial question. ''Now, Mrs. Robinson, at the time the police talked to you, immediately after the crime, do you recall mentioning any special marks or scars on the face of either of the robbers?''

''I didn't recall anything at the time.''

''And yet, Mrs. Robinson, you did recall for the police the fact that the man without the rubber nose had 'long wavy dark hair, like a pompadour,' and you remembered what both of them were wearing, yet nothing about any scars.'' She folded her arms across her chest and breathed out visibly as she shook her head. ''No, not then. I didn't remember that until later, when I saw him at the station.'' Cap made the conclusion for her as he said, ''So it was more than three weeks later before you remembered anything about a scar, and only then when you saw the defendant at the lineup?'' She made an extra point of it, claiming loudly, ''Yes, it was at the lineup. But as soon as I saw that Marino, I knew he was the man who broke into my house to attack my husband, to take my husband's life!''

Cap tried to keep the lid on the proceedings as he begged the judge, ''Excuse me, Your Honor.'' The judge said to the whole courtroom, ''Please, just a minute. Mrs. Robinson, please confine your answers to the specific question and do not volunteer any statements. Ladies and gentlemen of the jury, you will disregard the last statement by the witness since this case does not embrace that statement. Strike it from your minds.''

The next witness for the prosecution turned out to be the only point of comic relief in the trial—the elevator operator, a man of sixty or so with a big beer belly. His name was John Kelley. When he took the stand it was obvious he was suffering from a cold. His testimony changed so many times while he was up there even I nearly broke out laughing in the courtroom. At the lineup he had said it was none of the seven guys there, but at some later point Wiseman had convinced him that he had come to the lineup intending "not to get involved," and thus he wasn't going to name anyone no matter who he might have seen.

Naturally the DA skipped any questions about the lineup and went directly to the point after a couple of warm up questions. "Now, Mr. Kelley, I want you to look around this courtroom and tell me if you can positively identify the man that you have described as the one who beat Mr. Robinson with the pistol." The old man was hard of hearing and had to have the question repeated. Then he said, "Yes, sir, I can." And he pointed to me. Then it was Cap's turn. "Mr. Kelley, when you came to the police station to look at the lineup, did you see the defendant among the men inside the room?"

Kelley looked puzzled for a moment. "No sir." Cap couldn't quite believe it, so he asked again. "You did not see the defendant in the room at the lineup?" Kelley coughed and tried again. "You mean the defendant now?" Cap held his forehead. "Yes, Mr. Kelley, I mean the defendant in this case, Vincent Marino." Kelley smiled slightly and looked at Brandon. "Oh, yeah, sure I saw him in the lineup." Cap clinched it, "But you did not identify the defendant at the time of the lineup. Is that correct?" "That's right."

Cap put both of his hands on the oak box surrounding Kelley as he said, "Mr. Kelley, is it not true that at the lineup and again at the preliminary hearing in this case, you specifically said that 'it was no one in the lineup'?" Kelley was either lost completely or off the track somehow, because he said, "No, sir." Cap was beginning to burn by then, and he threw up his hands. "Mr. Kelley, isn't it a fact that your testimony here this morning is completely inconsistent with everything that you told everyone in this case from the very *outset?* Is that right?" Kelley fidgeted in his seat before he said, "Yeah, I guess."

Then Cap swung around for emphasis and barked, "Mr. Kelley, do you have any idea of what the magnitude of your testimony is? We have a man's future in question here. Do you realize how important that is?" Kelley held his head low and muttered, "Yes, sir." Cap took maximum advantage and did a one-eighty on his heels as he looked directly at the jury. "No further questions, Your Honor."

Other than the detective who had investigated the scene of the crime, the people had no more witnesses to call, and it was almost time for Cap to start our defensive parade. By then we were six or seven days into the trial, and I was getting tired of just sitting there, hour after hour, looking the whole room over and trying to get a feel for which way things were going. The one aspect of the proceedings that bothered me was the excessive time it would take to get ready to start or to take a recess. Each time the judge would make the same pronouncement to the jury about not discussing the details of the case with anyone. Cap had said the same thing to all the residents at Phoenix House when he took their depositions before the trial because we all knew the DA would try his damndest to discredit our whole group as lifetime liars and career criminals.

Just before the next sessions began, Cap told me that he was calling Mitch Rosenthal to the stand first. I couldn't have come up with a better choice because Mitch had been straight all his life—a psychiatrist—plus he was the director of Phoenix House and a deputy commissioner in the Addiction Services Agency set up by Mayor Lindsay. If anyone could save me by using his reputation, Rosenthal was my man.

The first thing Cap established was that Mitch had known me approximately two years prior to the crime in question and that I had split the house but returned just one month prior to the robbery. Then Cap asked Mitch directly, "Dr. Rosenthal, when Vincent Marino returned voluntarily to Phoenix House on March 18, 1969, what happened to him?" Mitch was unemotional and straight faced as he replied. "The night of March 18 he was put on what we call a 'contract,' which included a shaved head and being placed in a general meeting in front of all the residents of the house."

"So Marino's head was shaved to the scalp on March 18, 1969?"

"Yes, that's correct."

Brandon then approached the bench with a photograph taken of me sometime between April 1st and April 8th, showing my hair a quarter-inch long. I was a long way from the Robinsons' initial description of a man with "long wavy dark hair, like a pompadour in front." Cap showed the photograph to the jury foreman, who passed it around the jury box. Brandon went on to question Mitch about the marathon, and he confirmed I was part of the session in question, but Mitch wasn't in the house at the time of the four-hour break, so he couldn't be any help to me there.

In cross-examination Wiseman first tried to discredit the photograph of me with short hair by asking Mitch, "Now, Dr. Rosenthal, you stated that the photograph marked Defense Exhibit C is approximately how the defendant looked on April 18 through April 20, is that right?"

"Yes, that's correct."

"Doctor, do you know exactly when that picture was taken and by whom?" Cap objected but the judge overruled, and Mitch gave the answer. "No, I don't." Wiseman was no fool, and he came on with some undermining questions about what an incurable asshole I was. "Now, Doctor, Mr. Marino left the program once and went back to drugs, is that correct?"

"Yes."

"Now, when he came back, Doctor, did you or Phoenix House solicit his re-entry, or did the defendant solicit yours?"

"He solicited readmission." The DA asked his next question very quickly. "Doctor, was there much internal discussion among the supervisory staff at Phoenix House over the readmission of Vincent Marino?" Cap broke in before Mitch could respond. "Objection, Your Honor. Of what relevance is that?"

"Sustained."

The DA knew right where he wanted to go, and he kept pressing the idea that some people didn't want to let me back in Phoenix House. Cap objected and Wiseman asked a final question. "So, Doctor, on the night of the crime, April 19, 1969, a Saturday, do you, of your own personal knowledge, know if Vincent Marino was inside the Phoenix House at 205 West Eighty-fifth Street between the hours of 4:30 p.m. until after 7:00 p.m.?"

"No."

"No further questions, Your Honor." The DA requested a recess, and Cap and I stood and left the courtroom, walking down the hall to what we referred to as "our office"—the stairwell at the end of the corridor. Once we had closed the door behind us, Cap told me Wiseman had just made a proposal. "Vinny, they're offering you four years if you cop to a guilty plea right now." I didn't even think about it as I said, "Tell that bastard to shove the four years up his ass. And tell him don't bother offering me another deal because I'm innocent. And if he does offer something tell him no." Cap tapped two fingers on his leather briefcase as he looked at me. "Well, I do agree that things are going our way, but if the DA makes an offer, I'm legally bound to tell you about it. Let's get back to the courtroom and see what develops."

The clerk said, "All rise" as the judge made his entrance, and Cap proceeded to call up my Phoenix pal, Louie Zinzarella, who had been in the marathon session with me and had also gone to the lineup. He was dressed up real sharp and carried himself with distinction towards the witness chair. Cap approached Zinzarella and opened with every conceivable question about Louie's past habits with drugs, including how long he had been using junk, when he first started, what he would spend everyday—all the angles in an attempt to cut Wiseman off at the pass and make the further questioning on the subject appear to the jury as if the prosecutor was just fishing for questions with no real evidence to produce.

Right after his opening series, Cap launched into some specific interrogation about the four-hour break period, and nothing new came up except that Louie had signed a statement which said that he saw me with Pat up in the kitchen "about five o'clock or a little after." That was going to make it extremely difficult to get me out of Phoenix and all the way downtown to number nine Fifth Avenue to prove that I had committed the robbery. But Wiseman was a cunning bastard, and he tried all kinds of weird questions in an attempt to throw everything out of sequence. "Now, sir, you say you distinctly recall seeing the defendant with his girlfriend at exactly five o'clock or maybe a little after on the night of April 19, 1969, in the kitchen of the Phoenix House on West Eighty-fifth Street?" Zinzarella beamed with his eyes as he said, "Yes, sir." But Wiseman didn't bat an eyelash. "Mr. Zinzarella, you have amazing recall. Could you tell me what happened on April Fool's Day of that year, April first?" Zinzarella innocently said, "No."

Cap let the line of questioning take its course, so the DA went on. "Well, what if I told you that you were out of Phoenix House from 5:45 p.m. until 7 p.m.? Would that refresh your recollections of April Fool's Day?" Zinzarella sat still for a minute, then shook his head. "Not really."

"But the particular day in question you do recall very clearly and distinctly, is that right, sir?"

The smartass DA had even lost the judge who cut in with, "Wait a minute, which particular day are you referring to?" Wiseman looked sad that his superior didn't get the point. "The day of the marathon, Your Honor.'' But the spell had been broken, and Zinzarella didn't even have to answer the question because the DA shot straight into his next rapid-fire line of questions. ''How many times have you discussed this case with defense counsel, Mr. Zinzarella?''

''Two or three times.''

''Did you ever go up to their offices to discuss it?''

''Yes, once.''

''Have you ever discussed this case with the defendant, Vincent Marino?''

''No.''

''Have you *seen* the defendant since the night of the marathon?''

''Yes.''

''How many times?''

''I don't know, a lot.''

''And you never discussed any aspect of this case with him?''

''No.''

''Did you ever discuss the case with Dr. Rosenthal?''

''No.''

''Did you ever talk about it with any of the other alibi witnesses?''

''No.''

''Were you instructed not to by defense counsel?''

''Yes.''

''By the way, Mr. Zinzarella, were you on parole at the time of your first admission to Phoenix House?''

''I think so. I don't remember.''

''Mr. Zinzarella, do you have anything to hide about the story that you're telling me now?''

''No.''

It was obvious to me that we had Wiseman and his case on the run, but I never stopped being amazed at the agility a crafty lawyer displayed under pressure. He shifted gears to head into another confusing issue, which almost turned into a direct confrontation. ''Mr. Zinzarella, have you ever seen this document before?'' He handed Louie a request to appear, which meant that any potential witness for the defense could come to the DA's office and make a statement before the trial *if they wanted to,* which was the key. Naturally, we had elected to have all our witnesses stay away from the DA beforehand and only let him find out what they had to say on the day each one was called to testify. Cap knew right away that the DA was going to try to make it look like everyone who had been cited at Phoenix had just ignored or refused to obey a subpoena, but the truth was that the word *subpoena* didn't appear anywhere on the document.

"Yes, I've seen it," Louie said as he handed the paper back to the DA. "Your Honor, I wish a subpoena to be marked 'People's 18' for identification." Cap objected immediately to the DA's caper. "Your Honor, I object. The document in question is not a subpoena under any statute in the world. It is only a request to appear." Wiseman snapped back in a flash pleading, "Your Honor, the document speaks for itself and is merely being marked for identification. It is not in evidence."

Cap took up the same line of questioning with Zinzarella after the DA had finished. "Now, Mr. Zinzarella, when you received that piece of paper from the district attorney's office, what did you do with it?"

"I took it to Mitch Rosenthal and asked him what to do about it." A further series of questions established the fact that Mitch told Louie he didn't have to go unless he wanted to.

"Yeah, of course. Why should I go see the DA when I don't have to?" A couple of people in the courtroom, including my pop, got an open chuckle out of that line. "No further questions, Your Honor," Cap said, and Wiseman went up to the bench to ask for an off the record conference with the judge and a recess.

Cap and I took ten minutes to confer in our office. When we got there, Cap told me the latest Wiseman was offering. "No time, Vinny. All they want is a guilty plea, and they'll send you back to Phoenix House for an indeterminate period." I got furious. "Dammit, Cap, I don't want to hear about a deal. All that rat bastard wants is another conviction so his career looks good when it's time for a judgeship. Well, fuck him and his record. It's a matter of principle now, and I'm not copping to any plea. Let's go with it."

Cap didn't hesitate in reaching for my hand, and he smiled as we shook. "Vinny, I don't know where we're going with this thing, and I don't know what's about to happen, but I must say you've got a lot of balls." I didn't feel like smiling because it wasn't over by a long shot. "Balls don't count in that room, the jury does. And I know where I'm going if this doesn't work out—Sing-sing or Attica. So just keep up the pressure on Wiseman and his sideways questions, will you?"

Of course, it was inevitable that Cap would have my ex-girlfriend, Pat Moran, take the stand, but I wasn't anxious for that to happen. We were running the risk that the DA would be able to make it look like she was testifying in my favor just because of our relationship. Cap handled it like an old master, however, when he first established the fact that we hadn't seen each other for more than three months. Then he methodically went through all the potentially embarrassing stuff that Wiseman could ask her, establishing that we liked each other a lot and had "had relations" once after setting up a "trap."

Wiseman got up and took a strange angle with Pat, as he started to dig deeply into her wayward background. "Miss Moran, how many children do you have?"

"Two."

"And are they staying with your in-laws or where?"

"My son is with my in-laws and my daughter is in a foster home. I see both of them at least once a week."

"Now, when you were convicted for narcotics possession back in 1966, were you placed on probation?"

"Yes."

"And was that a one to three year probation?"

"I think so, yes."

"And did you violate that probation, Miss Moran?"

"Yes, I did."

"And were you then given a choice of Phoenix House or jail?"

"Well, it was Phoenix House after I detoxed at Morris Bernstein Institute, but yes, it was either that or jail."

"And how long had you been using narcotics at that point?"

"I'd say ten years or so."

"And you were using mainly heroin, is that right?"

"Yes, mainly."

"And how did you support that habit, ma'am?"

"Different ways. Do you want me to tell you about all of them?"

"Yes."

"Well, I boosted . . ."

"What is boosting?"

"Shoplifting, stealing. You know, taking stuff." Cap finally interrupted. "Your Honor, I fail to see where this line is taking us." The judge urged Wiseman to speed it up, and with that he backed off and tried to twist Pat on exact times during the break in the marathon, but it didn't work at all so she was excused from the stand.

Over the course of the next three days, six additional people from Phoenix House testified as to my whereabouts during the night in question. The only significant piece of new information came from a guy named Izzy Carrasquillo, a Puerto Rican who had been in Phoenix House about two years. He testified that he had passed by my dorm at around 7:30 and had seen me sleeping. That put the DA in another real bind to come up with proof-positive I could have physically gotten downtown and done what they were accusing me of.

Sixteen days after the ordeal began, the judge came down with his hammer and made a declaration: "That completes the record in this case, insofar as the submission of evidence is concerned. The court will now entertain motions." Cap immediately stood and made the boldest statement possible available to us. "Your Honor, the defense moves for dismissal of the indictment." The judge said, "What?" so Cap told him, "I move for dismissal, and if Your Honor is inclined to hear a brief argument on the reasons why, I'll be happy to offer them." Cap had tried the same tactic before at the beginning of the trial, but the judge had obviously denied it, so this time he said, "Mr. Brandon, only if you have something in addition to your earlier argument." Cap nodded. "I have nothing to add except the additional proof that has been entered on the record by the defense." The judge adjusted his glasses and ruled, "The court denies your motion, Mr. Brandon."

It was time for each side to present their respective summations. Final statements by both prosecution and defense before the jury would be charged to decide my fate. So the judge announced, "Mr. Brandon, you may proceed," whereupon Cap stood up and walked over to station himself in front of the jury.

In his opening he gave the usual review of justice, how it would be in the jury's hands, and then he began establishing the serious nature of what they had to do. Cap then moved on to a new area. "Now, this kind of case is described in law books as one of 'eye-witness identification' or it can be thought of as a case of 'mistaken identification.' And that, ladies and gentlemen, is the thrust of our defense. The defendant is a victim of mistaken identity, since it has been established clearly that a crime did take place at the Robinson apartment on April 19, 1969, but you must understand that there is absolutely no hard proof in evidence other than that fact.

"There were no fingerprints found at the scene of the crime.

None of the stolen merchandise or money was ever recovered. No other suspect has ever been arrested, and other than the testimony of individuals, there is absolutely no evidence that the defendant has ever been at the scene of the crime at any time in his life. In fact, the evidence in this case is quite to the contrary. The evidence, ladies and gentlemen, tells us that Vincent Marino was *not* at the scene of the crime.''

Cap went on to discuss the fact that I had not taken the stand and to state that I was under no obligation to come forth with a single word. As Cap was speaking, I was carefully looking at each juror for some sign of agreement or dismay, but all of them were paying strict attention, and no particular signal came to me.

Brandon went on. ''Now let us consider the four basic points in this case, any one of which could give you the 'reasonable doubt' necessary to acquit the defendant, but the state may not confront them one at a time. The state must overcome them all, as a group. So keep this in your mind as you look for reasonable doubt. Here are the four points, in order, ladies and gentlemen.

''First, there is direct contradiction about the identity of the real criminal from the eyewitnesses at the scene. Mr. and Mrs. Robinson say it was the defendant, but they had to wait three weeks to remember that he had scars and shorter hair. John Kelley said it was no one in the lineup and repeated that story at the grand jury hearing, then suddenly changed his testimony when he came here to the courtroom. But John Kelley is also the elevator man who took the real criminals up to the Robinson's apartment. Might his job be at stake in this matter? Does he have any reason to change his story in favor of the Robinsons? This you must ask yourselves.

''Secondly, you must consider the circumstances that were in effect at the Phoenix House on the particular weekend that this crime was committed, when it would have been extremely difficult if not physically impossible for the defendant to leave the house unnoticed, be absent for an extended period of time, and get back into the house undetected. Third, even if we assume that the defendant and his accomplice or accomplices had prearranged the crime for that night, Vincent Marino had no way of knowing precisely when or even if he would be available because the break was not scheduled, and it was announced suddenly without prior warning to anyone. That hardly seems like the method of the real criminals who knew which apartment they wanted, knew that there was cash and jewelry in the apartment, and knew what equipment they would need to take care of the job.

"Finally, ladies and gentlemen, we have submitted direct testimony from witnesses that they were actually with the defendant at the time the crime was being committed, and for an almost continuous period of time after that until the afternoon of the following day. Now any one of these four points is sufficient for you to say that you have a reasonable doubt, and the judge will tell you that a reasonable doubt is one you have in the jury room for which you could give a logical reason."

The judge interrupted. "Mr. Brandon, please. The court will charge as to reasonable doubt at the appropriate time. Please stick to your summation." Cap played it beautifully. "Thank you, Your Honor. Now, ladies and gentlemen, this case rests on the contradiction that exists between the two sides, so let us briefly review each one before you must make your final decision. On the one side we have the unfortunate victims of the crime, Mr. and Mrs. Robinson. These people were confronted with the real criminals under violent and shocking conditions for an extended period of time, maybe ten or fifteen minutes, and Mr. Robinson was severely beaten in a fight with one of the robbers, leaving his face in a stream of blood. Ten minutes after the crime Mr. Robinson described the man as having long wavy hair, and his wife told the police he had long wavy dark hair, like a pompadour, but on that day the defendant Vincent Marino was regrowing a shaved head! His hair was maybe one-quarter inch to one-half inch long and it looked like a GI haircut, almost to the scalp.

"Finally, none of the eyewitnesses said the real criminal had any special marks or scars on his face, and yet you have seen for yourself what the defendant's face looks like. Would you have noticed a scar or any marks on the face of Vincent Marino if he had spent ten or fifteen minutes robbing you in your own apartment? And yet, ladies and gentlemen, we know that Vincent Marino in fact *resembles* the real criminal, or we would not be sitting in this room today. Every witness for the prosecution testified to that fact, and we concede it. There is a resemblance, but no 'similarity' is sufficient to find a man guilty because this must be proven conclusively. So let us look into the possible motivation of the witnesses, from the standpoint of those with an interest in the case and then from a disinterested viewpoint."

Cap pointed out that Robinson had contributed to Phoenix

House and how vindictive he became when he learned I was from Phoenix. He suggested that Robinson had, in fact, made up his mind it was me, and he wasn't going to change it no matter what facts came out. Cap stated that our defense witnesses could have cooked up an iron-clad alibi if they had been willing to lie in order to protect me and Phoenix House, but in fact each witness had just given their own small take on the situation during the marathon. "If the people from Phoenix House had been lying, you would have heard only one story, over and over again. In summary, ladies and gentlemen, if you study the evidence submitted, you will see that we have proven the defendant Vincent Marino is innocent of the charges, and the wrong man is sitting in this courtroom. It is therefore your duty to find the defendant not guilty." As Cap turned to walk back to his seat at our table, I felt like clapping. It would have been terrific if the jury could go straight to a vote from his speech, but they didn't.

We had to face the final statement of the people as represented by Wiseman first. "May it please the court. Ladies and gentlemen of the jury, now that you have heard all of the testimony in this case, the law gives me the privilege and opportunity of summing up to you the evidence on behalf of the People of New York versus the defendant Vincent Marino. Now when it is put very simply, there is only one issue in this case, and you must never lose sight of it. Did this defendant on April 19 assault and rob the Robinsons? The issue is not whether Phoenix House has helped drug addicts, and the issue is not what the defendant looked like on that day. The issue is only whether or not he committed the crime in question.

"And how do you answer the issue in this case? Very simple—in a two-stage process. Number one, you have to recollect the testimony, and number two, you have to analyze the testimony and determine how much credibility, if any, is due each and every witness. You must look at the character of the witnesses. You must look at their past histories. You must look at their overall capacity for accurate observation and accurate recall.

"Now the defense says that the people's witnesses are mistaken. In fact they got a little more blunt with the Robinsons and suggested they are 'out to get' the defendant. They harp on the score of the hair, the clothes, the scars. And besides any of this, the case doesn't amount to a hill of beans, does it? Because the defendant was continuously inside Phoenix House throughout the course of the crime. So it all doesn't mean anything. Well, let's see. Let's begin right there. We are going to look at the witnesses called by the defense.

"First, Mr. Zinzarella. Did he admit to you openly that he split from Phoenix House three different times, walked out the door and went back to heroin? Yet when it gets down to what counts in this case, Zinzarella suddenly recalls seeing the defendant at 'five o'clock or maybe five after' on the night of the crime. I tell you it borders on the absurd." Wiseman went on, painting a bleak picture of the reliability of our witnesses—they were ex-junkies who during the marathon were worn out and bleary-eyed. He reminded the jury that no one from Phoenix House had been willing to come to his office, suggesting that the witnesses felt Phoenix House was on trial, not Vincent Marino.

As Wiseman was running his number in front of the jury, I wondered whether anyone was bothering to listen as he cited page after page of quotes from the record to establish all the tangential points he was trying to make. I had no doubt that the DA would have something nasty to say about my former girlfriend, Pat Moran. Sure enough it soon came out.

"Let's move on to Patricia Moran, who is now a salaried employee of the city. She admitted, very honestly, that she used drugs for ten years, that she shoplifted and burglarized. Very honest woman. She testified that she was with Vinny in the kitchen sometime between 4:30 and 5:00 the night of the crime. On cross-examination it came out that she had also written something down about the case. That paper was produced by defense counsel and shown. Now, all of a sudden the time is not 'between' 4:30 and 5:00, oh no, now it is five o'clock *exactly*. Moreover, Miss Moran testified she did not remember *who* had asked her to write down the details, *when* they asked her to write them down, or *why*. In fact, when she wrote that statement she wasn't even aware—this is on Page 533 of the record—that the defendant had been arrested or was being sought for robbery. She also doesn't know the date or time of the crime. To this day the poor lady is wandering around not knowing what day she's talking about or what time she's talking about. Does this strike you as logical, or is there some kind of great conspiracy of silence present? Everybody walks around in a tight-knit group, and no one to this day has even told her the time of the crime or the date that crime was committed?"

Wiseman continued his barrage, trying to establish a conspiracy on the part of the Phoenix House people, I scanned the jury to see if they felt like I did—what was he talking about?—or were they paying attention and buying his act? The DA was oblivious to my concern, however, and he just kept on going.

"But of course we mustn't forget the appearance of Doctor Mitchell Rosenthal, the director of Phoenix House. Why was he on the stand? Certainly not to shed any light on the case because he admitted he wasn't in the house when the crime took place. Could it be that they brought him to impress you, to add weight to the case? You give me one legitimate reason for Dr. Rosenthal's being on that stand, wasting our time. Not to help you, the jury, in the search for truth. Oh no, to add weight to this case. More weight for the defense side. Make it heavier than the people's side with the number of witnesses you call. You'll confuse someone on the jury. That was their motive. Look at all the fancy people they paraded past us: the director, the assistant director, two coordinators, all hand-picked people. Where are all the little people in Phoenix House? That's a funny army they are running up there, all generals. Where are the privates from Phoenix? Has the defense been giving it to you straight? Are you people firmly convinced that the house was locked up and that this is the alibi they say it is? If you knock off Dr. Rosenthal and all the rest with fancy titles, what are you left with?

"I'll tell you what you're left with. A lot of lengthy testimony but nothing of substance. That's what. They have all tried to set up what is known in the business as a smokescreen, a well-planned, articulated, well laid out smokescreen. Well, don't be taken in, ladies and gentlemen, don't be conned. I am not asking you to believe or disbelieve these witnesses because they have records. I have never asked you to do that. Forget about their past records, as far as I'm concerned. You judge their stories based on an inability to recall and a sincere desire on their part to help the defendant, to help Phoenix House. Most of them have no future without Phoenix House, so why would they want to do anything to jeopardize that future or to damage Phoenix House?" Wiseman went on and on like this, and then he hit it.

"The truth is that the defendant was not in that house with those other eighty-odd residents. He was out committing a crime. It becomes painfully obvious. You heard the testimony yourself. Let's go back to the path of fact and not of fantasy. Let's look at some of the hard evidence and see how it relates to the central issue . . .

"Now, remember this job and how professional it was. Guns, right? They had guns. And handcuffs. A very professional job. Do you know where it became not so professional? The rush, ladies and gentlemen. Why the great haste? Why all the cursing and rushing and throwing stuff all over the apartment? They could have missed another thirty thousand dollars up in that apartment. Because somebody had to be back at a certain place before his absence was noticed. Take another look at People's number fourteen, fifteen, and sixteen, all in evidence. Look at the mess that apartment was in after the criminals left. These two fellows were in a rush and had to be back. Now where did they have to be back to? Phoenix House, but remember, they say there's a danger of someone seeing him sneak in. And I say that's malarkey because if someone sees him sneaking back in he simply turns around and hits the street, that's all. Any hint that someone has seen him, and he takes off forever. Mr. Brandon told you that Phoenix House is not a prison; there are no guards in the place. It might turn out to be the perfect alibi, but there is nothing to detain him if it backfires. If anything went wrong with the plan, the defendant would have just left with 'Sorry about that, Charlie. Give me my Saint Francis sweatshirt and I'll be on my way.' That's it and he's out, a free man. So don't give the defendant great credit for rushing back there. That was the thing to do."

At that point I wanted Cap to cut in and stop the harangue Wiseman was into, but nothing could be said because it was his final summation, so the DA rambled on, tearing apart the contradictory statements about the appearance of the thief and suggesting I had been wearing a wig. Finally he started to wind down. "You people have good common sense. You figure it out. You look at the weight of the evidence, ladies ad gentlemen. You come up with a theory, as long as it is based on evidence, as long as it is reasonable, as long as it doesn't fly in the face of logic.

"And that, ladies and gentlemen, in substance, is the testimony of both sides in this case. Again I call upon you to assess the quality of the testimony and not the quantity. And remember the positive identifications we had in this courtroom. Remember them well. Why shouldn't Mr. and Mrs. Robinson be positive? A face, you know, is not a mark on a cheek. That's not a face. A face is a total picture. I don't know how good some of you people are at describing various things, but the old saying goes,

'When I see it, I know it.' Mr. Robinson wasn't looking to identify the face of a salesman in a department store he bought a pair of socks from. Oh no, this was the face of a man who had absolutely terrorized him for a quarter of an hour.

"Do you think the Robinsons will ever forget what happened to them that night? Imagine the impact of this event on the victims. Even more significant, remember the results at the lineup, a lineup that was fair in all aspects. The defendant with short hair stood in that lineup, and the Robinsons, who had just finished telling everybody that the guy had longer hair and who weren't sure about any marks on his face, pointed out Vincent Marino with no hesitation. The lineup shows you that the defendant's face will never leave the memories of the Robinsons."

My gut was wrenching with the thought that Wiseman was getting away with all that rambling dialogue, inventing wigs and conspiracies, and then he throws away the fact that the victims didn't notice any scars. But still Wiseman wasn't finished with the jury, as he continued. "One last point, ladies and gentlemen. Don't let the defense sugar-coat anything to you about the Robinsons because they are not mistaken. They cannot be called mistaken because they can't get off the hook that easily. They are either telling the truth, or they are out-and-out perjurors. If a man or a woman takes that witness stand, points to another man and says, 'That is the man who committed the crime; there is no doubt in my mind,' and there is the slightest doubt in his or her heart or mind, then that person is a perjuror, a liar, that person is committing a worse crime than Vincent Marino committed—cold-blooded, calculated perjury to see a guiltless man go to prison.

"Now, did the Robinsons strike you as the type of people who would do that kind of thing? Would they compound a horrible event? No one was killed, fortunately. Why would they compound it? After all, the event was over, so why didn't the Robinsons just forget about it? Why put themselves through the ordeal of a trial like this unless they were 100 percent certain that Vincent Marino was the man?

"Your job is to recognize the facts and stick to the facts. Use your good common sense to decide the only issue in this case. Did the defendant Vincent Marino rob and assault the Robinsons on April 19, 1969? That's what I ask you to do, and I ask you in the name of the People of the State of New York to find this defendant guilty as charged."

Wiseman turned away from the jury and went back to his seat, just as the judge started up. "Mr. Foreman, ladies and gentlemen of the jury. It is now nearly a quarter of two, and this court has a calendar to hear the issue of the fifteen city blocks to be cleared for the new World Trade Center, so we are going to postpone this case until 10:15 in the morning. You've been very patient with the long summations, and I want to thank you. Court is adjourned."

That night, January 26, 1970, was not the best one of my life. My nerves were shot to hell, my back ached, my ass hurt, my feet were swollen, and my head was pounding with the twisted words of the prosecutor. The one thing that bothered me the most was that I had no opportunity to deliver a verbal karate chop to Wiseman's eardrums, and I wanted to so badly. The rest of my life still hung in the balance. What was the jury thinking? Had he won them over? What if they found me guilty, and I had to go through the whole thing all over again in the form of an appeal? My emotions were pulled to the limits, and no way could I sleep. I just sat on the edge of my bed at the facility trying desperately to conjure up a solution.

Nothing came to mind until the next morning when it occurred to me that the best moves were to brush my teeth, shave, take a long leisurely shower, and finally walk the gangplank to the courtroom and face the inevitable. Since potentially dead men were always granted one last meal, I figured to have a big breakfast in the kitchen just in case it turned out to be my farewell meal with the troops. I dressed in my Sunday best that mom had sent over, but my stomach was fluttering like the wings of a hummingbird and nothing could cover up my jittery feelings as I walked in the door to face eighty other people. Everyone in Phoenix was strongly—and blindly—behind the idea that "justice would prevail," but most of them were naive as hell, and none of them had been through twelve long days in a courtroom listening to other people argue and make claims about what I did or did not do.

I didn't know quite what to say when they kept on treating me like some sort of hero figure. Everyone wanted to shake my hand and reassure me about the upcoming verdict with things like "Hey, Vinny, don't sweat it. We're throwing a party tonight," or "Hey, man, you'll beat this. You're innocent." I could only think of the fear I would face if the jury convicted me of this robbery when I had committed so many other crimes that could have put me in the same position but hadn't.

I couldn't actually handle the thought of eating a full breakfast, so I had two pieces of rye toast with a cup of coffee instead. After finishing up and saying some so longs, my escort and I drove over to Cap's office, taking it easy because a light snow was falling and we had plenty of time. Still, I was relieved when I saw Cap standing on the street waiting for us. He opened the door to the back seat and climbed in as our driver pulled out into traffic and headed for the courthouse.

Cap seemed quite calm as he smiled and offered me some encouragement. "Vinny, I thought a lot about the case last night, and I think that we're in the best position because Wiseman went emotional and we stayed rational. The jury is not going to be able to piece together anything he said if they even bother to try. There's no way they will convict you." I couldn't put on a smile in return because it just wasn't in me, so I looked out the window at the moving blur of New York and said, "Cap, if that's the case, why don't you wait for the verdict and I'll meet you in Philadelphia tonight in case you're wrong."

Cap asked the obvious. "Why are you being so negative, Vinny?" Again I didn't feel like looking at him or anyone else. "I don't know, Cap. Maybe it has something to do with the randomness of it all. Look at these streets. They're my home. I used to live here on the concrete, and I know I can always go back. Why don't I just get out at the corner and stay where I belong? Who needs this? At least if I died out there I'd go down like a man. I can't even begin to think about twenty-five years behind bars, and yet I am looking at it, and today is the day."

As we parked the car in the garage and headed toward the courthouse, I could see my breath through the crystal flakes of snow. I flashed on blowing town along with the storm, but something made me match Cap's pace and keep my commitment to see the trial through. I was reassured when I saw my mom, brother Joey, Frank with his wife Irene, and pop—all standing huddled together in a circle on the sidewalk, talking away as usual. Everybody ran up to me and took turns with hugs and kisses, yet nobody broke the silence. It was as if we all knew that there was nothing to say that could express the feelings in the air. It was something like the obvious concern you impart to the bereaved by just visiting to pay your respects at a funeral home.

Once inside the enormous hallway, we discovered that the courtroom was still locked, probably due to some bureaucratic incompetence with scheduling. Whatever the reason, that situation turned out to be interesting. As we waited in the hall around the water fountain, smoking cigarettes and talking just slightly over a whisper, all the jurors came in one by one and stood there waiting with us for the door to open. I felt a weird sensation all of a sudden, like I wanted to introduce my mother to those people because I was very proud of her. I was proud of all the family, of course, but that particular feeling was focused on mom. I wanted to take her around to each of the jurors and say, "This is my mother, Gemma." I wanted them to smile and know we were human as well, and that I wasn't guilty.

Without moving, I felt myself drawn to look at each juror directly and let our eyes meet. Somehow it seemed like a perfect way to express whatever confidence and innocent aura I could muster at the moment, and I certainly didn't want to appear afraid or as if I was hiding anything. I was looking for some kind of reassuring visual sign that said, "It's alright, kid, I know you're innocent," and I distinctly saw two smiles plus three other very friendly faces, which made me feel a little more relaxed about my chances since the DA would need a unanimous decision to nail me.

A little after ten, a nondescript city employee with more keys on his chain than they had out on Riker's Island came up to the jury's side of the room and let them in first. Then he opened up the main door to admit all the relatives, friends, Phoenix people, curiosity seekers and street riffraff who filled the main viewing area up almost to capacity. I felt like the Roman on trial with my proper English lawyer at my side, just as Wiseman the Jewish prosecutor walked in and the Irish Judge Tiernan was adjusting his robes in front of the mirrors in his separate chambers. When the clock hit ten-twenty, a court clerk stood up and said once again, "All rise please," and with that the judge quite properly entered the room.

When the formalities had been settled, and everything looked just as it had for so many days in a row, the judge proceeded to "charge" the jury with their duties and responsibilities in the case. He spoke about the issue of reasonable doubt and the fact that it was the burden of the state to prove my guilt; that I was to be presumed innocent until and unless specific proof was found during their deliberations. Then he told them that their vote had to be unanimous before they could emerge from the room with a verdict. Finally he charged them to go to the jury room for the purpose of seriously deliberating the facts of the case as it would certainly determine the future of the defendant Vincent Marino.

Before the jury stood up to file out of the box and go back to their special room, I stared at them all over again and tried to send out a look of innocence. No reactions were visible, however, and my heart pounded with the thought of what it was they were going out for. I figured that the sooner they came out, the better it would be for me. If their session turned out to be a half hour or less, there was no doubt I'd be acquitted, once again a free man.

20 / What Goes Around, Comes Around

During *the first twenty minutes* of waiting, I glanced around the room to see active signs of encouragement so I knew my perceptions about the jury were not wrong, and I relaxed somewhat. At the half hour point I felt my nerves threatening to start up a twitching movement all over my body. At forty minutes I wondered what the hell could they be discussing for so long? Was I *in* Phoenix or was I *out* of Phoenix on the night of the crime? It was that simple.

The first full sixty minutes with the jury deliberating ticked by on the clock. They had to be fighting, but fighting over what? Suddenly a flash of emotion hit me in the gut and heart areas, where I felt an electric kind of tingle. It was a rush of sorts, but one I had never experienced before, even on drugs. In a split second the feeling reached to the tips of my fingers and toes, yet I was still sitting motionless, watching everything in total silence, like a hawk. The room appeared to be frozen for that one moment, and all the sounds were very distant, but I was still there, with everything in sharp focus as I had what was an enlightening experience for me.

They say as a man dies, his whole life flashes before his eyes. Well, I think that's bullshit because I supposedly died once from a heroin overdose, and my ''death'' was verified by a hospital. On at least twenty-five other occasions someone called a Catholic priest to give me Last Rites because I had repeated the same dumb act. In each of those overdose situations, I only saw a black wall coming up, and I never felt anything leave my body, nor did I see any lights or other signs of a life beyond.

All my life I have been pretty much what I consider a stand-up guy. By that I mean that I always tried to do the right thing—which means that if I am your friend, it will be to the end. On the streets I handled myself in the "right" way, or I would never have gotten away with what I did. When I bought drugs, I paid off my bills so I was known and could always get more when things got tight. That is "stand-up" on the streets. I always tried to help out my family and friends; money was secondary to that. A stand-up guy "shits in other neighborhoods," as Hooks would say.

When I thought enough of myself to get into that first therapeutic community, I took my stand-up image along, but as I was sitting in the courtroom waiting for the jury to come in, the thought that flashed through me in that strange silent moment was this: "You say you're a stand-up character, Marino, but what are you standing *for*?"

Without moving, I let my eyes wander over to mom and the rest of the family. Of course I stood for my family, but they had their own lives to lead, and I couldn't do that any better for them than they could for me. "What about starting a family and standing for that?" I felt I wasn't yet ready, even though I was thirty-one years old. "What about standing for a straight job and a career?" What kind of jobs are there for fourth-class former drug addict criminal citizens like me? "Well, why not stay with an outfit like Phoenix House and make a name for yourself?" The thought of hassling internal politics and peddling raffle tickets left me cold, although I felt good about a lot of the elements there.

Just then an old phrase jumped into my head. "What goes around, comes around—only sometimes in different forms." With that, I saw this trial as my perfect reward—a symbol for fifteen years of negative activity. But would I finally perceive the message from the symbol?

With a shiver that started in my lower spine and slowly went up to my scalp, I got what seemed like the ultimate answer when I saw what the first question was? "Where is the bottom of the barrel for you?" Because when you reach the bottom of the barrel, it gets transparently clear that all you have left is your life, and so you begin to question whether even that is worth it. If you ultimately think that it is *not* worth it, you will end it. Some people push their self-destruct button by using heroin, some drink themselves to death, others smoke or work themselves to death. Of course, a person also has the ugly option of jumping to death or of committing suicide in some other bizarre fashion.

What dawned on me just then was that as a stand-up character, I could no longer entertain the idea of standing up for anything to do with death. I had been so deeply involved at the perilous edge of that pit for so long, I could never go there again. I realized that what I needed more than anything else in my life I had suddenly found—something to stand for. All I had there at the bottom of the barrel was being alive, and I knew at that moment I could make a total commitment to a fundamental purpose for the first time in my life, and I did it right then and there. My purpose is to support life itself, wherever I find it and to support those who think enough of their individual lives to do something positive in the form of direct action. Finally, I could stand up for "what goes around, comes around," since I figure it works in this universe, no matter how you call it—cause and effect, "as you sow, so shall you reap," the law of Karma, whatever—it's all the same thing.

Human beings who wake up cold and alone in the gutter of a city street do have a choice to make, whether they realize it or not. The choice is between continuing on the trail that is destroying life or choosing a path that supports life and allows a person to grow. It seems to me those are the only two choices you've got; your life is either going up or it is going down.

As soon as I worked this all out in my head, my attention snapped back to the courtroom, and I was terrified with the thought of a verdict and what it would hold. It seemed like forever but was actually just over three hours when the jury slowly filed back into the courtroom and took up their seats. Where before there had been smiles, none were now visible as the judge said, "Has the jury reached a verdict?" The foreman spoke for the rest. "We have, Your Honor." The judge asked for the paper and dictated, "The defendant will rise." As I stood there with my hands frozen on the chair in front of me, a dream starting with the pursuit of life itself as the goal came just before the words; "We find the defendant not guilty, Your Honor, on all of the counts in the indictment."

My first response was a wave of tremendous relief when the foreman said, "Not guilty," but then the judge thanked both Cap and the prosecutor for "a very well presented trial," and somehow I couldn't believe he didn't say a word to me—something like, "sorry for this ordeal, Mister Marino," or even "sorry to take up nine and a half months of your life," would have been nice.

Everyone on my side was all smiles, with some tears, cheers, and open laughter, so I swallowed my pride quickly for once and bathed in the limelight. Mom came toward me, sobbing openly. I put my arms around her and knew right then that no matter what else might come in life, I could not put her through another ordeal; it would certainly kill her. I cried with her and swore silently to myself. "From here on in, my life is going to be positive!" Frank and Joey crowded around me jumping up and down with excitement, and at least a dozen people from Phoenix swarmed all around me, shouting their congratulations.

We drifted out of the courtroom as a group and got into a whole fleet of cabs and cars for the trip back to the facility. On the way, I laid my head back against the seat, wondering what my next step would be. I was finally a free man again but still caught up in the politics and realities of Phoenix House, which in all likelihood was not going to change. I realized then that I would have to leave Phoenix House for some better alternative, but nothing came to mind at the moment, so I put it aside.

As things turned out, about six weeks after the trial my first break came in the form of a doctor at Columbia Presbyterian Hospital in Manhattan. And from that time in my life to this, I realized you get what you ask for, so some caution is in order. Ironically, the doctor's name was the same as that of the prosecutor who tried to hang me—Wiseman—but this guy was an incredible human being. He had heard me lecture on the hazards of drug abuse once, and he must have been impressed because he called me in early March of 1970 and said he wanted to discuss a drug prevention program. He had convinced the hospital administration where he worked that they needed one, and he wanted to interview me for the position of director.

Right after I hung up the phone with Doctor Wiseman, I sat back in my chair and got hit with an incredible sensation of guilt about my past. I mentally ran through all the crimes I'd committed, the people I'd hurt, the racism and prejudices I'd harbored, the lives left behind me that were twisted beyond recognition, and the unbelievable number of people I knew who were dead or languishing in prison. Again I remembered my turning point and promised myself I'd make as many positive contributions as I had on the negative side.

At the interview with Doctor Wiseman, whose first name was Russell, we hit it off perfectly. He told me they wanted to start with a simple prevention program because the whole idea was still experimental. The salary would be ten thousand per year, but they had only secured funding for six months to see what kind of results could be expected. I thanked him for offering me the job and said I'd let him know my decision within a week. As soon as I got back to Phoenix I went over to see my friend Frank Natale to lay all the cards on the table and see what he thought.

Natale could tell something was up as soon as I walked in the room. I started by telling him how much I felt I owed Phoenix House, even though things had been changing in ways I didn't much like. Then I told him about the job offer from Columbia. Without blinking an eye he said, "If I were you, I'd take it. It looks like a step up, and I wouldn't bet on things changing all that much around here." I breathed a sigh of relief and extended my right hand to him. "Frank, you know that I love you for being who you are. We can't lose this friendship because I value it, so this is not a goodbye. I'll give you as much time as you need to find a replacement and I'll train him for you if you'd like." With that I turned and walked from his office, looking forward to the adventure of another new project.

Ten days later I was in position at Columbia, where I charged into the assignment like a bull hits the color red. Working eighteen hours a day, I scheduled and held drug seminars with all the hospital departments, set up and did speaking engagements at outside meetings, let the emergency room know that I would personally talk with any drug addict who might come in and ask for help, and when I wasn't busy, I painted my office. I got the idea that it would be extremely useful for squares to know exactly what to look for when a person starts using drugs. So I started talking to people about the telltale signs: a change in behavior, either an abrupt or a gradual subtle change in habits, a difference in a person's dress and hygenic habits, those kinds of things. Before long I was being asked to come to schools, civic groups, and various churches to speak on the problem that was increasing each day in New York. I always made a spcial point of emphasizing the ultimate importance of family communication and trust in stopping drug use before it starts or before it gets going full speed toward disaster.

After I had been at Columbia ten or eleven weeks, a surprise call came from an old friend, Jimmy Selman, who had been the director of the Hart Island Phoenix facility. "Yo, Vinny!" he sang into the phone. "It's Jimmy Selman and I've had one helluva time tracking you down."

"Hey, Jimmy, what's happening?"

"A new program called RAP, and it's in Washington, D.C." I was startled that he had left Phoenix but didn't want to press that button. "You sure do move fast. What's RAP?" He laughed. "It stands for Regional Addiction Prevention, and Ron Clark is with me. We're right on the ground floor and could use someone like you, now." I reviewed my short history at Columbia and said, "Well, I certainly owe it to you to at least check it out." We made plans for me to spend a weekend in Washington.

At that time I was dating an airline stewardess, so I asked her to go along, and we found Selman's new project without complications. He was genuinely elated to see me and enthusiastically described what they had bitten off. I liked the general setup and the ideas he wanted to implement, but he went on to explain that their funding was still uncertain. They'd only be able to pay me twenty-five dollars per week plus room, board, and expenses. I told him my situation at Columbia was also up in the air because of money and asked what he wanted me to do in the RAP organization. He smiled. "You'll have a free reign here. Start off by becoming the director of the treatment facility, and if we make it, the sky's the limit." I wound up telling him I needed some time to think it over.

On the way back to New York Sunday night, my thoughts were jumping all over the place. On the one hand I was already a director at Columbia, but the program really lacked teeth. We were basically referring people to other rehabilitation programs rather than doing anything ourselves. When I had asked if we couldn't open a detox ward, the hospital administration came back with a flat no. Yet, I owed Russ because he had strongly backed everything I wanted to do. I drew up a list of the pros and cons and took it with me to Russ's office the first thing Monday morning. He listened carefully to what I was considering and told me what he knew about the future. He finished by giving me the green light to go with his full backing. I called Selman and told him I'd take the RAP position.

As things happened, it took me nearly two weeks to finish my business in the city because I had to close my apartment and store all my belongings, resign and clear out my office, plus make the rounds of my family and friends. By the time I made the move to Washington, I hadn't spoken to Selman for almost a week, and when I got there, he was gone. Ron Clark was the executive director, and I found out fast that he wasn't at all like Jimmy Selman. Not only that, he had no idea where Jimmy was, or at least that's what he said. There I was, trapped in a way. My apartment in New York was gone, and I had just reassured the family about my intention to make the Washington project work for me. My only choice was to make the best of it.

I forced a positive attitude and a smile and went over to meet the people in the facility I would be directing. It turned out about fifty kids were in residency—a nice bunch. I got myself checked into a room and started working long hours to shut out any and all negative thinking. But it soon became apparent that Ron wanted the final say in things, and he and I were worlds apart when it came to basic philosophy and procedures.

The situation broke when I heard about a hospital in Alexandria, Virginia, that was interested in setting up a drug rehabilitation program. Without hesitating, I sent them a resume accompanied by a letter of introduction, and they called me for an interview less than a week later. I was again being considered for the position of director and was getting excited with the prospect of moving to Virginia, although they hadn't yet offered me the job.

Then one day—one of my days off, actually, when I usually stayed out of the facility to relax, unwind, and clear my head—I happened to wander in and pass the front desk. I overheard the girl on the phone ask the caller to please spell a name again so she could take a message. Then I heard her recite the name Zinzarella. I immediately flashed on Louie from Phoenix House and told the receptionist to transfer the call to my office. I shot up the stairs and eagerly lifted the receiver. "Hey, Louie! This is Vinny Marino! How the hell are you?"

The female at the other end was surprised to hear my voice,although she recognized me. "Vinny Marino? This isn't Louie. It's Imogene, his ex-wife. We're separated now."

"Oh, Ima, I'm sorry to hear that. What can I do for you?"

"Well, I'm trying to reach Ron Clark to talk to him about Jimmy Selman."

"Maybe I can help you, Ima. Jimmy was here until six weeks ago. Then he left and we haven't seen him since."

"I know," she said. "He's here in Hawaii." I was stunned. "Where did you say?" She repeated for my benefit. "You heard right, Vinny. In paradise—Hawaii.'' I thought, ''Well, I'll be,'' and said, ''How did you get there, Ima?''

''Well, I wanted to get as far away from the city as I could after Louie and I broke up, so I flew over here to the islands and started a new program called Communiversity.''

''Not bad,'' I thought to myself and told her as much. ''Congratulations, Ima. All the way to paradise, that's great. But what about Selman? What's he doing? I thought I was coming down here to work with him, but he just disappeared.''

''He's here working as my director of induction, but I'm getting more and more suspicious that he's back into drugs. His behavior is sporadic, like he disappears for days at a time. Vinny, I need someone heading up induction who is reliable, and I need that person now. This is a crucial time for me and the Communiversity program.''

I fantasized bare-breasted hula dancers, swaying palm trees, and living in paradise, then decided to ask her directly. ''Could you use a guy like me for the job? I'm looking to make a change anyway.'' She knew my capabilities from Phoenix House, and she bit. ''Of course I'd be interested in talking to you about it, if you're willing to relocate to the islands.'' I told her it was a move I would definitely consider and with that she laid out her basic operation, how she wanted it to work, and how she wanted it to be.

She explained that the salary would be a thousand a month plus a car and expenses. Everything sounded good except the question of what would happen if we had major differences about the program philosophy and/or day-to-day policy matters. She sold me on the idea of making the change when she replied. ''Look, Vinny. In the end, this is my baby. But if you don't like what's going on, this state is wide open. It's only been a state for eleven years, and they need programs like this.'' That was the line that did it for me, and my spirit of adventure caught fire. ''Ima, that's all I needed to hear. I'll take the job.'' I told her it would take me a couple of weeks to get everything finished up here. She wanted me sooner, but she agreed.

As soon as I hung up, I walked to the window and looked out, wondering what on earth I had just talked myself into. Hawaii? What would it be like? Did the natives have a drug problem? How would I fit as a mean-streets New Yorker? Turning away from a wintery November day in Washington, I opened an encyclopedia and looked up Hawaii, where I discovered the average temperature was 78 degrees all year round.

When I approached Clark to tell him, he seemed relieved. He saw that his intentions were taking him in one direction, while I was heading in another, but our parting was on good terms and he wished me well. I packed my belongings in less than an hour, said my goodbyes to the residents, and headed north to New York.

You should have seen the looks when I told everyone in the city what I had up my sleeve. Mom looked at me like I had lost my marbles. "My God, Vinny, you must be crazy. Hawaii isn't even civilized yet!" Frankie was just as shocked. "You can't be serious. Six thousand miles? We'll never see you again." Pop laughed. "You sure you're ready for those natives?"

Even Frank Natale had a negative comment. "Sounds like a great move, Vinny. I hope you can make it in the islands. I'll be happy to write you a letter of recommendation, but I would watch out for Imogene." That threw me a bit. "Why, Frank? What do you know that I don't?" He said what I already knew. "Well, there have been times when she's a little strange. Not consistent, you know." I nodded my head, "Yeah, I know, Frank," and I asked if he wouldn't dictate that letter of reference anyway. Then I went back to my brother Frank's place where I was staying.

Without knowing exactly why, I started to separate my things as soon as I got inside Frank's apartment, putting the winter stuff in one pile and the summer wear in another. I had decided to fly out that night, with no further delays because of all the negativity that everyone was throwing at me. My instinct was telling me to go, but each minute I stuck around brought up more questions, and I was starting to get scared about making it. I cut all my uncertainty by calling an airline and booking myself a one-way ticket for eleven o'clock that same night. Frank kept asking me if I knew what I was doing all the way to the airport. The last time was just before I got on the plane, and I finally said, "Frank, I don't really know if I know what I'm doing. In fact, I don't really know where I'm going. But I can tell you this much. Once I get there, they'll definitely know I've been there." As I left him at the gate and walked to the plane it was starting to snow.

As soon as we were airborne, I started having my own second thoughts about Hawaii. What was I doing? My God, the only person I knew in the islands was Imogene. I rented a headset and decided to watch the movie to eliminate the negative thinking. After that I dozed for a while until we landed in Los Angeles, then I fell asleep when we were airborne again for our final destination. When I opened my eyes the sun was coming up on the horizon, and the pilot got on the loudspeaker to announce, "Ladies and gentlemen, on the right side of the aircraft you can see the island of Oahu."

The visual impact of the island below us was so astounding that I pulled back and took a deep breath to be certain I wasn't high or dreaming. I leaned forward and looked again to make sure. I had never seen so many different shades of green, and I was overwhelmed by Diamond Head crater. At that point I said to myself, "Dummy, if you don't like this lifestyle, you *belong* in a Manhattan gutter."

Imogene and a resident were waiting for me, and I noticed that Ima looked a lot better now than the last time I had seen her. She had rosy cheeks, a nice tan, and had gained maybe ten pounds, all in the right places. Island living must be good for her. As soon as she caught sight of me, she ran over and put a sweet smelling lei around my neck, then kissed me on the cheek as she said, "Aloha, Vinny. Welcome to Hawaii." I felt like some kind of misplaced idiot in my winter clothing, but I couldn't resist the warm tropical greeting, so I said, "Hello, Imogene, it's nice to see you again." She introduced me to her companion, and we headed off to pick up my bags.

Ima and I sat in the back seat for the drive back to the facility, which was in the town of Ewa Beach on the leeward side of Oahu. On the way there, she offered me the opportunity to take a few days off to recover from the jet lag. I didn't argue. But twenty minutes later when we pulled up at the main facility, I met the fourteen residents and noticed they were quite excited to have me aboard. My legend had preceded me in that Ima had related some stories of my earlier escapades at Phoenix House. The local Hawaiian kids wanted to hear what was happening in New York, and as it turned out, I sat there with them in casual conversation for a few hours until I was so exhausted that I went to my room in the staff quarters and hit the sack. I got up once, had dinner, hung around for a while, then went back to sleep.

Early in the morning I met Ima for breakfast, and she ran down some general facts about the operation, including how long she had been in the business with Communiversity and what she wanted me to do as director of induction. She also assigned me an assistant who knew his way around the island—a big friendly Hawaiian kid by the name of Keone. After acclimating for a couple of days, I took to my job like a true workaholic, and within a week Keone had shown me the basics of the leeward side of Oahu, as well as Waikiki, the drug clinic there, the courthouses in Honolulu, the state hospital, and, of course, the prisons.

By New Year's Day of 1971, I had inducted a dozen new residents, and the whole of Communiversity was buzzing with activity. Of course I was often the focal point of attention since I was inducting everyone who came in, and Ima didn't like it at all. She started to slow down the whole operation at regular intervals, I guess just to let everyone know who was master. I shrugged it off at first, but then she would do rude things like interrupt me in the middle of a seminar to bark out an order or come into a group I was running. I tried to keep my cool, and I spoke to her in private about what it was she really wanted. "Ima, I want Communiversity to grow to its fullest potential, as fast as it can. Things are already heppening. Can't we work together on this?" She went cold with her eyes and backed off the question. "All you need to do is learn to follow orders and things will be fine."

I couldn't bring myself to respond, so instead I sat back and lit a cigarette as I thought to myself, "Dammit, here we go again with the power-play problems. Who needs it? And this time you're six thousand miles from home. Now what are you going to do?" Somehow I managed to let things ride for the next week, until Ima pressed me to the wall with her irrational orders and especially the way she approached the residents. But I was determined to avoid another confrontation, so I came up with the idea of approaching the chairman of the Communiversity board, primarily to see if there were any other openings for a guy like me in the state of Hawaii.

When he agreed to see me two days later, he knew right away there was a problem, even though I tried hard to avoid making any negative comments about Imogene and the way she was running things. His name was Neal Winn, and he worked at Kapiolani Hospital as an obstetrician and gynecologist. I liked him as soon as I met him, when he looked me directly in the eye as he asked, "Are you here because you want to change jobs, or is it that you have a problem working with Imogene?" I tried to avoid answering his question, but he closed me in again by asking, "Well, if it is Imogene, are you going to run, or are you willing to stick around and see if we can't work it out?" That last question brought the fighter to the surface. "Dr. Winn, there was a time when I was among the best runners in New York but no longer. If there is a way to work it out, I want to find it."

"All right then, I'll call a board meeting as soon as possible, and I'll invite you in so we can have some open dialogue."

When Imogene heard about my meeting with the chairman and what was coming up, she got so distant that I thought I had become an alien from another planet. She'd see me coming down the hall, for example, and would do a one-eighty on her heels without so much as a good morning. I could see the handwriting on the wall, so I decided to at least cover my ass, and I made a phone call to the hospital in Virginia to see if they had filled the slot I had been up for. They hadn't yet, and I succeeded in reopening the negotiations with them, just in case I got my walking papers at the Communiversity board meeting.

Monday night of the following week we all appeared before the board, but Imogene had brought along some additional people to support her. In short, what was supposed to be a meeting turned into a full-on encounter session. In the end, Neal cut the session short by saying, "All right, enough of this. It is obviously imperative that we rearrange the work relationships and responsibilities at Communiversity, and we will do that, one week from today. Is that acceptable to both of you?"

Well, I could see the look in Imogene's eyes when she consented, so I asked Neal and the rest of the board for some reassurance that Ima could not fire me between then and the next meeting.

Neal and the others agreed and so did Ima, reluctantly. But it was obviously not okay with her, and she proved it the next morning when she handed me a piece of paper and walked away without saying a word. I knew it wasn't a birthday card. The exact greeting was, "Effective this morning at 8:00 a.m. you are hereby suspended from Communiversity for one week." My anger flashed to the surface, but I held it in check as I thought, "This woman is not only power hungry, she's treacherous." Instead of retaliating and causing more strife, I concluded it was time to consider other alternatives, which I did.

The first thing was arrange my own transportation, so I had Keone drive me to a leasing company where I rented a car. Then I called a local girl I was dating and asked if she would be willing to let me stay with her until my future with the Communiversity was decided. She agreed, and I drove into Honolulu wondering how on earth I had managed to get myself into such a situation—less than six weeks in paradise, and it looked like the adventure was already over.

The night of the second board meeting, Imogene walked in flanked by two of her senior residents, and all three of them looked extremely cold, though everyone else was cordial. Before she uttered a word, Ima tossed a sheaf of papers at each one of the board members and me. The papers were a new set of bylaws: the board of directors had been fired, effective immediately, and Vinny Marino was fired, period. As Neal Winn read the words, his face went white. "This baffles me completely." I stood up, made with a bow, and said, "Well, I'm not at all baffled. I'm leaving. Good night folks."

While walking back to the staff house to pack up the rest of my belongings, I explained what was happening to my girlfriend who had met me there. Apparently during the week that I was suspended, Ima had wired up the residents by telling them that I was a vilc animal attempting to take advantage of a poor, defenseless woman for the sole purpose of taking over her program. As a result of the things she said, the residents were highly emotional and somewhat hostile towards me. In fact, Ima's boyfriend stood in my way at the door and said, "Don't go in the house. You're not welcome."

My first thought was to bounce him off the nearest wall, but instead I said, "Look, tough guy, my belongings are inside, and I intend to get them. So just stay where you are, and let's do this like gentlemen because my patience could run out." With that I took my girl, Pat, by the hand and went around him, heading straight for my room. Five minutes later, I was throwing things hurriedly in a bag, when I heard some fierce knocking at my door. One of the female residents was screaming incoherently out in the hall, so Pat turned to me with a what-to-do-next look. "Tell her I don't want to talk to anyone, please. I really don't want to get the residents involved, it's not fair to them."

Pat eased the door open and tried to calm the young girl, who was getting hysterical. Finally I agreed to let the resident in to sit on the edge of the bed where I got her to slow down her crying. Through sobs she kept muttering, "Vinny, don't leave me here. You can't leave me here. You brought me here. Wherever you're going I want to go along." Before I could tell her the truth, which was—How the hell can I take you with me when I don't know where I'm going?—another resident popped into the room making the same stand. Then another came on, and another until six residents were standing in the room, threatening that if I didn't take them with me, they were all leaving for the streets, saying, "It's not fair because you promised us that this was a good program, and we really believe in you, Vinny."

What could I say? I had in fact inducted each of them into Communiversity, but I had no place to go and no idea what to do with six more people, even for one night. Then two staff members, Bob and his wife Rosie, stopped me and asked if I would take them along too. I hit on a temporary solution—we would go back to the Waikiki Drug Clinic and speak to Neal Winn about the problem. If we were lucky, he'd still be there. That settled in my head, I said to the residents, "Okay, you can come along if you choose, but I don't know where we're going to end up." Thirty minutes later the caravan was ready, so we loaded both cars full of bodies and luggage, heading for Waikiki and a possible meeting with Neal and the rest of the board.

Less than two hours later I had managed to reach him and another board member, and they both agreed to meet us at a place called Hale Kipa, a residence for runaway girls. As soon as I had outlined the predicament, Neal came up with the best spur-of-the-moment solution he could think of. "We could rent hotel rooms on a temporary basis, one room for the girls, another for the guys and one for you, Vinny." I flashed on the reaction of a Waikiki hotelier when asked to let seven former drug addicts share three rooms, and I also remembered what had happened when Phoenix House residents got too close to the streets of New York with the raffles. "Neal, with all due respect, these kids should not be separated if it can be avoided. They're not in a position to understand, and I would predict they might do some crazy things."

At that moment the other board member present, a man named Mickey, chimed in with a suggestion. "Listen, I own a house that is empty right now in Kailua on the windward side. It's only got two and a half bedrooms, and one and a half baths, but you could stay there for a few days until we sort out this mess and determine what to do about Imogene." Without hesitating, I came back with, "Mickey, that would be perfect. Give me the directions on how to get there and let me get these kids settled in for the night." Mickey volunteered to show us the house personally, and Neal wanted to be sure everything came off without a hitch so we headed up the Pali Highway over the mountains that were covered in a solid sheet of rain.

No one said a word in my car because no one knew what to say about the situation or themselves. In a way, it looked like a funeral procession. Mickey was in the lead car; I had the next car; Pat was behind me, and Neal was pulling up the rear to make sure that we didn't get lost. When Mickey opened up the front door of the house, and we started to look around, the general reaction was, "Wow! Look at this!" It had a pool table, a swimming pool, and it looked like a very comfortable alternative to a hotel in Waikiki. After Neal and Mickey were satisfied and had said their goodbyes, I assigned the master bedroom to Bob and Rosie, and the other bedroom to the females. I instructed the males to sack out wherever they could find space, while I took the half bedroom. Not that it mattered much because the place had no furniture, and everyone slept on the floor.

In the ensuing week to ten days, Neal was calling board meetings every other day or so, where all they did was talk about how to fight Imogene. All I was into at the time was the kids over in that Kailua house. So while the board bickered over tactics with Ima, I was going out to the jails, the courts, and the state hospital, inducting more people. Also during that time, three or four other residents split from Imogene, and through the Waikiki Drug Clinic they had no trouble finding us. At the end of two weeks in Kailua, I had twenty-three people living in that little house including me. We were hustling up a bed here, a mattress there, some food, one vehicle that barely ran, things like that. I enlisted the help of the Windward Coalition of Ministers and the United Council of Churches, and both groups enthusiastically supported the project, even though no one quite knew what we did or how long it would be in existence.

One day Neal Winn and two other board members knocked at the front door to have a look for themselves. They were thunderstruck at what we had done to the place. It looked like a regular facility, with everything in order—although crowded like sardines—and signs up all over the place. Mickey, the owner of the house, threw his hands up in the air as he walked around. Then he said, "Vinny, you can't take one more person into this house. It's a potential fire hazard." I grinned to myself and said to him, "Mickey, how 'bout if we drain the pool and get some tents for the back yard? That wouldn't be a fire hazard."

He didn't say anything more as he made his way out, shaking his head as if to say, "This started out with nine people for two nights, and now look what I've got on my hands!" Since Mickey had not specifically denied my suggestion about tents in the backyard, I went ahead and got some. Neal and the board continued to hold meetings once a week, and I kept adding new residents.

This went on for another couple of weeks until they called an emergency board meeting, and it was during that session that Neal announced the board's intention to call us the "Windward Communiversity and name Vinny Marino and Bob Wahl as codirectors of the new facility in Kailua." When he said codirector, I sat back in my chair and knew that it wouldn't work, although I didn't say a word at the time. This was Bob's first employment since graduating from the program. He was a nice enough character, but he liked to get lofty and philosophical, often going way over the heads of the residents, especially the local kids who spoke mainly pidgin.

One day about three weeks after we had been named codirectors, I returned home from a day in court to find Bob running a seminar, reading from Erich Fromm's "The Art of Loving." I don't deny it's a good book, but the words had a lot of the local kids absolutely befuddled. They didn't understand one word in five, which was clear to me from the puzzled looks on their faces. After listening to Bob run the meeting for about ten minutes, I excused myself for interrupting and asked one of the Hawaiian residents, "Damien, can you explain what Bob just said?" The kid looked at me and said, "I dunno, brah. I tink he just talk story." Then I looked at another kid and asked him the same question, which evoked a second "I dunno." So I asked Bob, "Can we have a word in the office before you continue?"

As soon as we stepped inside, Bob assumed a negative attitude because I had interrupted him, so I said quite simply, "Look, Bob, you gotta get down to the level these kids are on. Reading that kind of material can only make them feel inferior because they can't comprehend it. Therefore, you're teaching them nothing." He took a deep breath and got huffy with me. "Hey, Vinny, you take care of the outside work—induction, the courts, prison—and I'll take care of the inner workings." His suggestion brought an immediate response, and I said a flat, "No way. In fact, let's call a special board meeting as soon as possible

because it is impossible to have two captains running one ship."
He agreed and two days later, I spoke before our board.

"My experience tells me that there can only be one chief of any facility. I want the job of executive director or I'm leaving. So you people must choose between us." Neal damn near panicked since he was facing another crisis from the top. Once again he tried to placate everybody. "All right, let's do it this way. Vinny, you have your concepts and philosophy about how a program should be run, and Bob has his. So we'll give you two a week to write a proposal covering what you would do as the executive director and then we'll make our decision." I chuckled to myself because none of the board members had ever been in a managerial position in a therapeutic community, but I agreed to it just to see what would happen.

Over the next seven days, I had very little time since I was out interviewing potential inductees all over town, so I took to jotting notes between trips, and every once in a while I'd stop at the beach for some emotional inspiration to help me sort out my proposal. As things turned out, I didn't need it because one night I came home from the drug clinic, and Bob had some news. "Me and Rosie are leaving. We have no more money left and to be honest with you, I don't think this program is ever really going to get on its feet." I made sure that I didn't show any outward signs of joy, but I was delighted. "It would only be fair to call a general meeting and announce your decision to all the residents. I think you owe them that much."

The residents seemed eagerly pleased, too, as they sang the traditional "Aloha 'Oe." To be sure their decision was final, I physically drove Bob and Rosie to the airport.

On the way back to Kailua, I went to the beach and sat on a rock. On one hand I felt a surge of relief that Bob and Rosie had decided to leave. On the other, my thoughts were in a heavy state of ambiguity, as I wondered if I could handle this. I'd had problems in every program I'd been in. Would I just succeed at making nothing more than a real ass of myself? At best, the most I had yet accomplished in this type of business was as a good facility director with someone else always there to make the decisions. Now, I'd be getting involved in public relations and policy-making decisions. And the position of executive director also meant automatic board membership. What did I really know about parliamentary procedure or Robert's Rules of Order? Did I really have what it would take to get this infant program on its feet?

As I left the beach, it dawned on me that if I was going to make something of the phenomenon I had going, I wasn't going to do it with the thinking of the present board of directors, and no way would I want to use the name Windward Communiversity. If it was to be my ship, I was going to name it and run it to the best of my ability. On the trip back over the mountains, I stopped at notorious Pali Lookout, where the winds were kicking at more than thirty miles per hour. I walked over to the edge and leaned out. For an instant I felt like I was flying high again, only naturally this time.

EPILOGUE

The question you have to ask yourself is this: If Vinny Marino turned around, quit dope and all his other antisocial behavior as a mainline addict from age fourteen to thirty, can anyone else do it? My answer is a definite yes. Anyone can kick dope and change antisocial behavior with a good program. What I started in 1970 with forty-four kids all crowded into a four-room house became such a program, a very successful one. We changed the name to Habilitat in May of 1971, which comes from *rehabilitation* and the French word *habitat,* meaning a place to live. And Habilitat has been going and growing ever since that rough beginning.

I took all the things that worked and that I liked from the programs I had been through and discarded the things I was against, the things that didn't make any sense to me. Then I inserted some ideas of my own that I thought should be in the program. Synanon seemed like a good thing when I joined. I liked the concepts and overall philosophy and especially the candor and honesty with which people spoke. Playing "the game," Synanon's brand of encounter session, taught me a lot about myself and how people perceived me, and also about how people operate.

But Synanon was a lifetime program. Chuck Dederich's idea was that the world was an ocean of insanity, and Synanon was an island where life was sane. According to him, once you stepped off that island, you became insane or you died. To me joining Synanon was like becoming a Trappist monk, except instead of serving God you served Synanon and its teachings. I couldn't swallow that for a lifetime bit.

Daytop had some good concepts like Synanon, too, those of self-help and self-reliance—the idea that the world doesn't owe you a living and there's no free lunch. The problem was with their rigidity and the stupid humiliations they practiced—making people march around carrying a long fluorescnt tube like a rifle when they forgot to turn off a light or dressing people up like babies in diapers or having them wear a large wooden blade when they left razors in the bathroom. The discipline was too petty and was carried too far. It became the sick ego games of power-hungry people. I'll never forget the general meeting when I came back after splitting. First I sat on the chair for six days and six nights, although I was allowed to sleep on the floor with a blanket between one and six in the morning. Then they dressed me up as a female, put a sandwich sign on me, and held a meeting that went on for two hours. The only thing that I learned in that kind of setting was that if ever I was in a position of authority, I would never permit that kind of sickness to prevail.

Phoenix House felt good, like home when I started there. They had the same philosophies and concepts as Synanon and Daytop, but it was also loose and caring. This changed when a whole lot of people came in from Synanon to fill the top-echelon posts. Then Phoenix House shifted away from a place that had a family feeling into a business that happened to run a therapeutic program on the side. Their raffle program was just another form of begging, and many many residents split when they couldn't deal with the embarrassment or say no to the offers they got out on the streets. They actually had people with bald heads going out into the community selling raffles for a dollar a piece. The split rate during that time was astronomical, but the raffles went on anyway because the money took precedence over everything else that Phoenix stood for. It played a major reason in why I resigned from Phoenix after I graduated.

Where they get their money is a major flaw in most "therapeutic communities"—which is really just a polite term for a drug abuse center. Although many programs preach self-help and self-reliance, they do little if anything to supplement their own incomes, which means they rely on a big government check or outright begging. This doesn't make sense to me. You can collect what the government is giving away, but sooner or later you start getting caught up in some of the bureaucratic strings that are attached to the money. These strings eventually tie up the delivery of the same services you're trying to provide. The program becomes just another arm of the government with little or no autonomy—or effectiveness. It doesn't work. Seed money from the government is okay because it does take a lot of bucks to begin any kind of residential program.

Ever since I stopped using drugs, I've been dealing in common sense, and common sense says to me that it's impossible to straighten out a person's life emotionally, educationally, and intellectually without teaching that person a viable skill. With some kind of skill a person can move back out into the mainstream of society, get a job, and become a productive, tax-paying citizen. But how can you teach what you don't practice—even if you preach it all day, every day?

What makes Habilitat different is our emphasis on training people for reentry into something like a normal life complete with a livelihood. You can call Habilitat a drug rehabilitation program, but I call it a survival school that teaches people how to use common sense, feel good about themselves, and learn a vocation and a trade. Let's be honest—not every drug addict can graduate from a program and become a staff member. A lot of junkies and people with character disorders who display antisocial behavior leave something to be desired in the areas of intelligence, personality, and charisma. But that doesn't mean they can't learn to take care of themselves, earn a living, pay taxes, and have a family. Everyone deserves a chance at these things.

Our business is motivating people to want to change, motivating the unmotivated. Habilitat is a twenty-four-hour environment because people with our kind of character disorders and addictive personalities are very manipulative. You can see that from my story—fooling doctors, shrinks, social workers, and parole officers, even my family, though they were very close to me.

Habilitat has many of the same features as other rehabilitation centers—a disciplined program, encounter groups, and seminars with some tough mental gymnastics to break down the rigidities characteristic of people who use drugs or display other types of antisocial behavior. But some things we don't do, "I feel that you think that you don't like me and I feel that you believe that I didn't like you when I said hello this morning, etc., etc., etc."

We don't do that. This is serious business, and we don't play silly useless games.

Residents who have a history of using drugs, including alcohol, have to be detoxed—clean—when they come in, and they come in from all over the United States. The 125 residents first take part in a structured nine-to-fifteen-month treatment program. Then they graduate into the re-entry phase, which also lasts from nine-to-fifteen months; this enables them to develop a sense of responsibility and a gut understanding of who they are. The average stay is 2-½ to 3 years. In addition to self-discipline and a vocation, people pick up the samc basic values anyone learns growing up in a good family—honesty, trust, loyalty, self-respect, ambition, friendship, love, and the importance of communication.

'Ohana is an old Hawaiian tradition that Habilitat embodies; it means "extended family." In the ancient island society, whenever people couldn't take care of their kids because of illness or death of a spouse, divorce, not enough food, or whatever, they farmed them out to families in a better position to raise them. That's part of what makes Habilitat unique. We have a closely knit family-type environment where people care about each other.

Another ancient Hawaiian tradition Habilitat has adopted as its own is the idea of the City of Refuge. The old story goes that whenever a person—a fallen warrior or anyone else—was disgraced for whatever reason, if they could make it to the City of Refuge, no one could raise a hand against them. We have become a City of Refuge by taking people from the courts. In lieu of going to prison or being under an early parole, they have the chance to come to Habilitat to straighten out their lives and work towards taking their place in the greater community.

But the crux of what makes Habilitat different—the best program in the United States according to many worldwide experts—is our vocational training. We can teach people landscaping, construction, pool maintenance, wood-working, painting, farming, and sales and marketing. We do this by on-the-job training in our own businesses that function just like any other business does. Our fund-raising department has held concerts, telethons, walkathons, youth fairs, trashathons; we've sold t-shirts, pressed and sold records, and printed celebrity cookbooks. In fact, we'll do anything legal that's creative and innovative under the free-enterprise system. Of our annual $3.4 million budget, only a small percentage comes from the government. And from the way things look, that's going to get smaller even faster than we had planned.

These realistic business enterprises do more than give residents a chance to learn viable skills and bring money into the program; they also give the people working in them an opportunity to put back in the pot what they took out. People who work know they're pulling their share, and it greatly reduces the amount of guilt that a lot of people have for the program that helped save their lives. Running businesses as a part of the program is a simple straightforward way to help the rehabilitation process.

Statistics taken from the latest survey by the National Institute on Drug Abuse point out that the national average of success for residential facilities is 17 per cent. Hawaii has a higher average of 34 per cent, probably due to Habilitat's success rate averaged at 53.6 per cent by the NIDA. Close to 1,000 graduates have gone through the entire program, and many people who left before they completed all phases of the program are still doing well as employed, tax-paying, productive citizens. We do not take credit for these people statistically, however.

That's Habilitat out in Hawaii. What about the rest of the country? In 1981 Richard Hamilton, director of the Maryland state Drug Abuse Administration, said that in one year they treated 15,000 people in their outpatient programs and another 175 in residential programs, which by the way are extremely costly. And Maryland is a small state. There are about 2-½ million known addicts nationwide. One hundred junkies loose on the streets supporting a modest $50-a-day habit have to come up with nearly $2 million a year any way they can. Most of that money will come from stolen goods, and everyone knows where they come from. We all pay the costs directly or through taxes for more police protection, court costs, prisons, and other forms of penal institutions, and government-funded drug abuse centers. Habilitat's cost per resident per month is $800, and for our level of success I'll match that with any other program in the country.

For many years now the public has assumed that drugs were used mainly by minority ghetto types looking for a way out of their miserable lives. True, but that isn't the whole picture. Over the last three decades drug abuse has moved straight towards the middle class and up. Cocaine use among people who can afford it—movie stars and sports heros—has been widely publicized, and thousands of young adults from middle-income backgrounds have recently started experimenting with cocaine and heroin, and the heroin is often easy to get and cheap compared to cocaine. Chippers—the name for weekend junkies—snort, skin-pop, or smoke the stuff, mistakenly thinking that they can't get hooked.

Also, the greatest worldwide killer of teenagers is suicide. Drug abuse is just a slower approach to the same end—it's self-destructive behavior. Because of mass media, kids today are more sophisticated. They know a lot more about the world-at-large than we did as kids, including the double and triple standards that go down and that most politicians are blatantly out for only number one. These kids on drugs who don't see any future for themselves in the world turn up in every town and neighborhood. It's no longer a problem over there, on the other side of the country or far away in the big city; it's a kid you know, maybe even one of your own.

The point is there's no reason why a program like Habilitat couldn't be set up anywhere. Not everyone can come to us, but the same principles should work wherever they're applied because they're universal, they're based on good common sense. The story of how we put Habilitat together and made it a success along with a lot of the mistakes we made is the sequel to this book. It's called *The Making of Habilitat,* and in it I talk about what it took to start the program, the intricacies and tricks, and how to do the same thing so that any community can set up its own qualitative program to help substance abusers and people who are emotionally immature and cannot manage their lives.

A good working program can be started without much government support except perhaps money to get started. It's not easy—that you should know, and I speak from an enormous amount of experience. But it is possible; it doesn't bleed the taxpayer, and it works.

Another thing you should know is that the medical community, especially psychiatrists and psychologists, don't want programs like Habilitat to open in their bailiwick. It costs them money in lost clients, especially when you figure that the average psychiatrist or psychologist gets somewhere between $65 and $100 an hour to work with the same people we can help get straightened out and back in the mainstream on their own for much less cost. The fees for their services are often paid from taxes. Many so-called professionals have put a lot of obstacles in the paths of reputable working programs through their massive lobbying both in Washington and on the state level. They've come up with new laws concerning licensing, staffing ratio, certification, accreditation, how many cubic inches of living space per bed space, how many bathrooms, and on and on. Even if a program can overcome the initial obstacles that these so-called professionals place on them, they then have to be monitored by the same professionals, which is ironic because good programs are being monitored by people who couldn't do the same jobs themselves because obviously if they could they would have opened their own programs.

Then there's always the problem of neighbors who, even though they might like what you do, don't want you to do it in *their* neighborhood. Lots of problems, there are always lots of problems. Every time you field one, another comes up. You learn a few shortcuts and you keep on going. For every obstacle that anyone on a city, state, federal, county or neighborhood level can come up with, you can find numerous ways to overcome them. We did and I'll tell you about each and every one of them.

If a person believes that the human potential is limitless, that "what the mind of man can conceive and believe, it can achieve," as I do, nothing can stop you. A few people with guts and vision, and maybe some bull-headed stubbornness, can set up a productive, successful program dealing with the antisocial character-disordered individual, addicted or not.

The story of my life as a junkie and a thief and a person who was in the gutter is meant as a message of hope to anyone close to someone involved with drugs. No matter how bad the situation looks, don't give up. A turnaround is a realistic possibility for any person with the right kind of help, most likely in a structured, monitored environment such as Habilitat. The right kind of a program can help a person straighten out. I changed my own painful, nonexistent life around, and someone else can do the same.

The one thing that the sequel will explain is that nobody ever comes to Habilitat for help. They come because of the pressure—pressure from the courts, the streets, the police, parents, a brother, a sister, a husband, a wife, a loved one, or a friend. It is really up to the program to motivate that person to want to do something with his or her life. And it's never too late.

Vinny Marino